Critical Acclaim

"Mr. Manchester passes quickly over the familiar, refurbishing it as he goes, adds much that is new, and has joined new and old into a generally well-proportioned narrative that affords an adequate outline of Mr. Mencken's career and portrays his charm, vigor, and humor with notable effect."

—*The Nation*

"Worthy of the man and of his influence on American letters."

—*New York Herald Tribune*

"Written with verve, intellectual sophistication, and a prickly wit worthy of its eminent subject . . . A first-class piece of literate entertainment."

—RICHARD H. ROVERE in *The New Yorker*

"A work of scope and importance . . . a remarkable book about a remarkable man."

—LOUIS UNTERMEYER

"May induce a generation in Britain, to which Mr. Mencken is perhaps only a name, to go exploring his works for themselves."

—London *Times Weekly Review*

WILLIAM MANCHESTER

H. L. MENCKEN:

OF THE

DISTURBER

PEACE

With an Introduction by

GERALD W. JOHNSON

COLLIER BOOKS

NEW YORK, N.Y.

H. L. Mencken; Disturber of the Peace originally appeared under the title *Disturber of the Peace: The Life of H. L. Mencken*

This Collier Books edition is published by arrangement with the author

Collier Books is a division of The Crowell-Collier Publishing Company

First Collier Books Edition 1962

Grateful acknowledgment is made to the following, for permission to reprint the material listed below:
MR. BERTON BRALEY for "Mencken, Nathan, and God."

The Evening Sun (Baltimore, Md.) for four dispatches by H. L. Mencken from Dayton, Tenn.
        Copyright, 1925, by *The Evening Sun.*
MR. R. P. HARRISS for the entry from his diary on March 24, 1938.
ALFRED A. KNOPF, INC. for selections from:
    Prejudices, Fourth Series by H. L. Mencken.
        Copyright, 1924, by Alfred A. Knopf, Inc.
    A Book of Prefaces by H. L. Mencken.
        Copyright, 1917, by Alfred A. Knopf, Inc.
        Copyright, 1945, by H. L. Mencken.
    The American Language by H. L. Mencken.
        Copyright, 1919, by Alfred A. Knopf, Inc.
        Copyright, 1947, by H. L. Mencken.
The Intimate Notebooks of George Jean Nathan by George Jean Nathan.
        Copyright, 1931, 1932, by George Jean Nathan.
    "Editorial," *The American Mercury,* October, 1925.
The Nation for "Beautifying American Literature" by Stuart P Sherman.

SHORE AND SHIPWRECK THAT for the contribution by Theodore Drieser to *The Man Who Saw* by Isaac Goldberg.

Copyright, 1923, by Simon and Schuster, Inc.

Mr. R. T. Wittnel for "H. T. Webster Writes a Poet to the West Side Y.M.C.A."

Copyright, 1936, by Stephen Parker Associates, Inc.

And to Mr. Harry C. Black, Mrs. Theodore Drieser, Mrs. Sinclair Lewis, Mr. H. L. Mencken, Mr. Eugene O'Neill, Mrs. J. Edwin Ellingby, Mr. Hamilton Owen, and Mr. Ellery Sedgwick, for letters included in this volume.

The liberation of the human mind has never been furthered by . . . dunderheads; it has been furthered by gay fellows who heaved dead cats into sanctuaries and then went roistering down the highways of the world, proving to all men that doubt, after all, was safe—that the god in the sanctuary was finite in his power, and hence a fraud. One horse-laugh is worth ten thousand syllogisms. It is not only more effective; it is also vastly more intelligent.

—Prejudices, Fourth Series

Any questioning of the moral ideas that prevail—the principal business, it must be plain, of the novelist, the serious dramatist, the professed inquirer into human motives and acts—is received with the utmost hostility. To attempt such an enterprise is to disturb the peace—and the disturber of the peace, in the national view, quickly passes over into the downright criminal.

—A Book of Prefaces

Order of Battle

Introduction

THE SIGNIFICANCE of H. L. Mencken in the second half of the twentieth century may well be greater, but it will be different from what it was in the first half. No doubt the kettle-drummer of the revolt of the twenties will continue to engage the interest of literary historians, and the creator of the Menckenian rhythm will continue to fascinate and baffle rhetors and prosodists; but it is already evident that the philologist is overshadowing all other manifestations of this versatile man, and it is conceivable that twenty-five years hence the fact that the author of *The American Language* was once a newspaper columnist will be as little known as the fact that the author of *The Decline and Fall of the Roman Empire* was once a lieutenant colonel.

Mr. Manchester's book comes, therefore, at a fortunate moment, when the metamorphosis of the Disturber of the Peace into the Savant is clearly in process but has not yet been accomplished. The book's timing has made it possible for the biographer to collect and preserve for the future an aspect of Mencken of which the future will have need.

This is not to be construed as a prediction that the particular kinds of false-faces, straw men, and pasteboard dragons that Mencken assailed will rise to trouble us again; but others will take their places as soon as the times once more grow lush and easy, for such things are bred of lush and easy times. It will be necessary for someone to attack them, and it will be a thankless task; so a record of how this man operated may serve as a beacon and encouragement to the free lance of the next generation. In that respect, indeed, it may be a more important contribution to civilization than the work of the scholar.

For Mencken's early career is a refutation of the heresy that "there is no arguing against a success." Mencken argued against nothing else. Many of them, indeed, proved to be false successes that eventually turned into lamentable failures; but at the moment of his assault they rode high. He attained power in a world whose statecraft had flowered in Calvin

11

Coolidge, its economics in Samuel Insull, its morality in Anthony Comstock, its theology in William J. Bryan, its philosophy in Orison Swett Marden, and its sociology in Prohibition. All these look dismal now, but at the moment when Mencken inveighed against them they were not merely successes, they were tremendous successes. But he attacked them, and if he thereby brought upon himself a storm of vituperation, he also provoked a storm of laughter and cheers.

This is a fact that should enhearten the next great crusader against nonsense. For the regimentation that is really to be feared in American life is not the regimentation imposed from without, by bayonets and policemen's clubs; it is the regimentation imposed from within, by adoration of "the bitch-goddess Success." Regimentation imposed from without is accepted sullenly and will be rejected at the first opportunity; but regimentation accomplished by a man's own decision to go along with the crowd is deterioration of character and likely to be permanent.

The pressure upon Americans to accept this form of regimentation was never greater than in the years when Mencken was editing *The Smart Set* and *The American Mercury*. The fact that under such pressure even one powerful intelligence resisted and rallied a strong minority under the banner of resistance is the best possible refutation of the cynicism that brands Americans as hopelessly unable to resist conformity when conformity represents wealth and prestige. Disgusted by the preposterous definitions given the word, Mencken has ever held "Americanism" in scorn; but in this respect he was himself an examplar of Americanism at its best.

The celluloid paladins and papier-mâché castles of his most glamorous years all went up with one cosmic *whoosh* when the torch was applied to them in 1929, leaving the crusader against nonsense pretty much out of a job. In such circumstances a small-souled man would have fallen into mere sour carping or, at best, into what Cleveland immortalized as "innocuous desuetude." The measure of Mencken's stature, not as an artist but as a man, is the fact that he turned instead to two works far larger than his polemics. One was the completion and perfection of his great dissertation on the language; the other was the writing of the *Days,* one of the very few autobiographies produced by a man who could repeat seriously what Margaret Fuller said hysterically, "I accept the universe."

In this country only Benjamin Franklin's account of his life is as free as Mencken's from any effort either to propagate the faith or to vindicate the writer. But Mencken's greatly excels Franklin's as a picture of a society that has almost disappeared. It is strictly genre painting, but it approaches perfection in its kind. If the portrayal of Baltimore at the end of the last century and the beginning of this is distinctly idealized, it is not falsified. Mencken sometimes leads his reader too far, but he invariably leads him in the direction of truth, and to overrun the truth is very different from missing it altogether.

One aspect of the man that is extremely difficult to define is yet one that can be overlooked by none who had dealings with him. It is his attitude toward other writers, particularly the young and obscure. To say that he was generous, even lavish, with sympathy and assistance for them is true enough, but not the whole truth; he also gave them the rarer gift of genuine admiration, and this to some who, as writers, did not deserve it.

He says somewhere, not as a boast but as a confession, that never did the spectacle of a man working hard fail to move him greatly. The quality of the work had less effect than the exertion put forth; and this repeatedly betrayed him into uttering loud cheers for some toiler who was, in sober truth, toiling idiotically.

The explanation undoubtedly is the fact that a man who is working hard is a man who is thoroughly alive, and vitality in any manifestation appealed irresistibly to a man who was himself more vividly alive than nine-tenths of his generation. "He denounces life and makes you want to live," said Walter Lippmann in perhaps the shrewdest estimate of the man ever compressed into a sentence. He gained the reputation of being unable to suffer fools gladly, but it was false; not only could he suffer them, but he could rejoice with exceeding great joy in fools, provided they were lively, agile, mercurial fools.

What he could least endure was not the fool, but the half-alive man, the Undead, the robot. Marcus Aurelius found the race to consist of spirits dragging corpses around with them; Mencken found it to consist largely of perfectly healthy bodies staggering under the weight of dead minds. This was his quarrel with the world; and that it was a shrewd arraignment few men of mature age will deny.

Thus although it seems likely that the coming generation will remember him as the Corregidor of Speech, and in that function sufficient and supreme, it will be well advised to remember also that in the beginning he operated in a different field. More—the coming generation might reasonably set itself to fasting and prayer if by such means it might hasten the coming of another so tremendously charged with the vital spark, so galvanic, so ruthlessly, joyously and utterly destructive of that which the psychologists call the Will to Death.

GERALD W. JOHNSON

Index

Chapter 1

Precede

THIS MUCH SEEMS CERTAIN: in the late fall of 1848, a lonely, proud Saxon youth named Burkhardt Ludwig Mencken landed in Baltimore with five hundred Thalers and a spanking new certificate bearing notice he had served apprenticeship to a cigar dealer. Burkhardt was just twenty. Behind him he had left a small estate, a host of family traditions, and a love of German institutions which was to affect his descendants for the next two generations.

Just why Burkhardt came to America is less certain. His eldest grandson later maintained he had come to view first hand the amusing spectacle of democracy. It may be so. The Menckens have an uncanny habit of handing down social attitudes. But a far more likely reason is suggested by the year of immigration, familiar to the haziest schoolboy as one of political and economic struggle in Europe. Earlier in the year Burkhardt had completed five years of indenture in Oschatz, Saxony, and nineteenth-century indenture, under the best of conditions, was a dreary business. Like many another discontented European, Burkhardt may have chosen 1848 as the year to shift allegiance in hope of a better life.

In Baltimore, a growing German colony offered hospitable welcome, or at least a background against which newcomers might cast their lives until they learned the language. Here Burkhardt settled, unpacked his bag, and, pocketing his roll, hunted a job. This he found easy; a flash of his proficiency certificate and he was soon seated at a tobacco bench, rolling cigars. Saving his pennies and keeping a shrewd eye open for opportunities, he struggled through his first year in a strange country. Then he quit his job and set up a general store, selling tobacco, groceries, and odds and ends to the *hausfraus*. The store prospered and, after a time, was itself sold to buy a wholesale tobacco firm. By the early 1850's, Burkhardt had come into an estate where he could afford the proper quality collars to set off his somewhat stiff neck.

Despite the heavily German character of his new home, Burkhardt Mencken remained an individual apart. He was no mixer, he did not make friends easily, and toward the average immigrant, romping in the ecstasies of a classless state, he was openly disdainful. For his fellow businessmen, happy in their beery prosperity, he did not give an aristocratic damn—an attitude which they must have found exasperating. For the proletariat—the laborers who had lately exchanged a Saxon hoe for a Baltimore wrench—he had little but contempt. He was, as has been noted, lonely and proud, and his loneliness was largely due to his pride. This was not unreasonable. Europe, in 1848, was sending over its peasants, its tramps, its malcontents. Except, perhaps, in an incidental way, Burkhardt was not one of these. Discontented he may have been, though scarcely with political turmoil, in which he took but passing interest. Tramp he was not. And he was certainly no peasant.

In later years, as head of a prosperous family, Burkhardt would take his grandchildren on his knee and tell them of the glories of generations of Menckens before. It is a tribute to the inspired manner with which an otherwise austere man must have told the tale that those children listened eagerly and, in time, themselves learned to love the traditions as he had. And if, in those later years, he used the term glorious, he did not exaggerate. The name Mencken, which meant tobacco in the Baltimore of the 1880's, had meant quite something else in the Saxony of a century before. Long before the Ph.D. degree succumbed to Gresham's Law it had been handed down from Mencken to Mencken with astonishing regularity—almost, indeed, as a sort of intellectual legacy. Lawyers, doctors, and philosophers, the Menckens had strode through the halls of the University of Leipzig with assurance and gusto, with a tread so solid its echoes are not forgotten there to this day.

In the latter half of the seventeenth century, one Otto Mencken had broken with a mercantile tradition and studied at Leipzig. In 1690, or thereabouts, he founded the *Acta Eruditorium,* the first learned review in German history, and its editorship passed, in turn, to his son and grandson. At Leipzig, in 1715, Johann Mencken, the first of these, published a deadly satire, *De Charlateneria Eruditorium*, breaking pedantic heads and bringing the wrath of the college politicians down on his ears. The tradition continued, with no appreciable break. Burkhardt's grandfather, son of a law professor at the University of Wittenberg, was himself a noted attorney and served with distinction in the wars against Napoleon. With splendor but two generations back, it is small wonder Burkhardt Mencken, in his tailed coat and high, old-fashioned collars, should scorn the mob and become, in an age of characters, a striking figure on the streets of nineteenth-century Baltimore.

Three years after his immigration, Burkhardt married. The sketchy transcript of Harriet McLelland which has come down to us is stark in its pathos. Born in Jamaica of Scotch-Irish parents, she was wed at sixteen, bore her husband five children, of whom the last, Louis, died, and died herself in 1862 of tuberculosis. More than that we do not know. Her death can hardly have left Burkhardt, saddled with four children and still struggling the inevitable struggle of the immigrant, more amiable. Shortly thereafter he married again. Caroline Gerhardt, herself a widow, bore him one child and served admirably as stepmother and housewife.

Burkhardt was made for the role of patriarch. With all the pomp and authority of a Hapsburg, he presided over family councils, making every family decision and pouncing on young rebels within the household at first murmur. Perhaps he found in his family an outlet for the suppressed sociability of his early years in America—or perhaps he was just remembering the Leipzig Menckens. At any rate, he was something of a domestic tyrant, with just enough kindness and justice thrown in to make that tyranny bearable. As a second generation appeared, he became a doting grandfather, but there is no record of a softening in his role as father. Indeed, as head of the American Menckens he insisted on choosing names for the new children, supervising their education, and even pinch-hitting for their barbers when it pleased him. To his daughters-in-law he may have seemed heavy-handed, but they never argued with him.

In but one respect did this first American Mencken split with his ancestors. Theologians all, they had, to a man, been loyal to the church. Not so Burkhardt. His agnosticism did not prevent the baptism of his sons nor, although his authority carried on through the next generation, his grandsons. His religion, or lack of it, was not especially militant, but it does appear to have been articulate. Though he often visited Catholic brothers at St. Mary's Industrial School, bringing tobacco to those who would teach their charges the trade, he seldom left the building without roundly denouncing the God of their fathers. The brothers were a stubborn lot, and they never gave up trying to convince him. But he never came around.

Burkhardt's first-born son, August, had come into the world amid the fumes of cigar smoke on June 16, 1854. He never quite escaped them. From his first staggering steps, he was fetched by the stogie's glow, and by the time he was fifteen, he was squarely planted at his father's bench, rolling round, firm, eminently puffable cigars. His childhood ambitions, like those of any other boy, wandered at times. A predilection for mathematics at Walker's, a private school, had momentarily fired his imagination: he wanted to be an engineer. But though he fancied himself something of a mathematical wizard all his life, his engineering dreams never progressed beyond the imagination. It may have been just as well; the record of his mechanical accomplishments which has survived is anything but impressive.

Two years at the bench, some time on the road as a drummer, and a smattering of managerial experience gave August ideas of independence. His brother Henry, three years his junior, had like ideas; accordingly, in 1875, the year of August's majority, they struck out for themselves with thirty-five dollars between them. The firm of "Aug. Mencken and Bro.," cigar makers, prospered from its inception; with August in charge of the new factory at 368 West Baltimore Street and Henry supervising sales management, they pushed its credit rating to one hundred thousand dollars in ten years. Then, according to the custom of the time, they relaxed for the rest of their lives. Baltimore, in the late nineteenth century, was still a comfortable, leisurely town. The mornings sufficed for the execution of business and the inspection of products. In the afternoons August, after a comfortable nap at home, would return downtown to work furiously on an obscure arithmetic system he had invented known as "averages" or, if the season were right, to attend the nearest baseball game.

Like his father, August was a pronounced agnostic, a hard-headed businessman, and a conservative to the point of reaction. Unlike Burkhardt, he was never lonely. Spared the painful transplanting which had been his father's lot, he was expansive and genial, a loyal Shriner who loved to cavort in the outrageous costumery of that order. A practical joker, a strikebreaker, and an opportunist not above equipping his cigar boxes with the family coat of arms, he was in many ways the prototype of the late nineteenth-century merchant. Heavily respectable—he asked no more of a man than that he pay his debts; tolerant of corruption—so long as that corruption be harmonious with his enlightened self-interest; he was, by standards then current, scrupulously honest and was, by any standards, an excellent provider.

In appearance he was a handsome, tall, well-built man who dressed nattily and sported a fashionable brush mustache. A love of good beer and good music—he himself played the violin wretchedly—and an absolute fanatic about baseball, August loved to hob-nob with the other young German-Americans in West Baltimore. It was, indeed, at a West Baltimore picnic in the late 1870's that he met his future wife.

Anna Margaret Abhau, a slight, blonde, blue-eyed, wistful beauty, was born in Baltimore of Carl Heinrich Abhau and Eva Gegner in 1858. Abhau, like Burkhardt, was an immigrant of the class of 1848; his home had been in Hesse-Cassel. Anna's mother was one of a host of Bavarian Gegners who had settled in Baltimore in disgust after the first German railroads had ruined a profitable coach business.

Whether it was Anna's fancy or her pity which was attracted by August at that picnic we do not know. In later years, she told her children he had struck her as a sort of comic character and she had laughed at him for some time afterwards. "I assume," her eldest son commented tartly, "that he attempted to entertain her with clowning, for which he had no talent." Whatever the initial cause of attraction,

August must have succeeded in keeping Anna amused; in November, 1879, they married and repaired to a rented house on the south side of Lexington Street, west of Fremont Avenue. Today the neighborhood, which still stands, is in the heart of Baltimore's Negro slums, where sewage spews lazily in back yards and razors flash and men live miserably and die brutally; but seventy years ago it was quiet, clean, and attractive, and August had no cause to apologize to his bride for their new home.

Ten months later, on Sunday, September 12, 1880, there was a great pother in the Mencken home, and presently August emerged in pursuit of one Dr. C. L. Buddenbohm, needed to attend Anna, in labor with her first-born. The doctor left an auspicious celebration of Defender's Day, a local holiday—auspicious because, years later, the child now yearning to be born would boast to out-of-town friends that the parading bands were in his honor—and hurried to Lexington Street. Burkhardt, alerted in his North Caroline Street home, charged furiously over the cobblestone streets in his buggy, coattails flying, to officiate and make the decisions he was certain were expected of him. Decision, however, was in the hands of Dr. Buddenbohm that Sunday; to Mr. and Mrs. August Mencken he delivered an infant son for the fee of ten dollars; August subsequently was billed and remitted. In his sovereign state, the new grandfather consulted the roster of family names and issued his pronouncement.

In a subsequent ceremony, Henry Louis Mencken was so baptized.

On an October morning three years later, her neighbors perceived that Anna Mencken was in a terrible state. It was moving day in Baltimore; the Mencken brothers had bought adjoining houses nearby, and Anna was going about the normally simple task of depositing stacks of family belongings on the sidewalk. In this she was pursued and harassed by a chubby infant who persisted in toddling after her and getting in the way. "Harry!" she cried again and again, "Go *somewhere else!*" But Harry, having concluded that the business at hand was very much his business, had decided that where he was was where he wanted to be, and accordingly declined to budge. Eventually August arrived and, after complaining bitterly of his wife's inability to throw away anything, from an incipient file of *Godey's Lady's Book* to her gingham apron and slat bonnet, was assigned to the supervision of his eldest son. Toward the middle of the afternoon, the excitement abated, the rococo Victorian furniture was piled on a wagon, and the Menckens—August, Anna, Harry, and little Charlie, twenty months his junior—climbed into the family buggy and trotted over to their new house at 1524 Hollins Street.

Like most eastern cities of the time, Baltimore was expanding in a checkerboard pattern, the streets lined with two- and three-story houses with common side walls. Young Harry's new home was one of these, three stories high, of red brick, with a white stone stoop in front and a long, narrow, walled yard in back. Across the street, in the autumn of 1883, the leaves were turning in quiet, gracious Union Square, a block-long park which had at one time been guarded by a high iron railing, now removed to permit free access on all sides. In the center stood a quiet fish pond, flanked by a squarekeeper's house and a large cast-iron Greek temple. The neighborhood was still dotted with vacant lots, and a few blocks to the west began Steuart's Hill, a rolling, open area which ended in the stockyards of Calverton. Hollins Street itself was nearly free of traffic, for transportation was still largely limited to the buggy, and travelers preferred the smooth paved space between horsecar rails to the harsh cobblestones of side streets. The neighborhood had been chosen for this, for its rapid approach to the business district, and for its proximity to Burkhardt, a few blocks away.

In this neighborhood, young Harry enjoyed a childhood normal almost beyond normality; it is not unlikely that the suspicion with which he was later to view change and the ridicule he was to heap on stories of personalities distorted in early years stemmed from the vigor and health of his own early life. As an infant, he was precocious; he talked at an early age, at fourteen months he was walking, and at three years he painfully traced, with his mother's help, his first signature. Now at Hollins Street, hard by the summer house in the back yard, he industriously fashioned miniature railroads in the dirt while his mother, nearby, planted petunias and dahlias, strawberries and vegetables, and fondly watched the progress of the ferns on the north side, the morning glories in the rear, and the sprouting cherry, plum, and pear trees in between. After the births of August, Jr., and Gertrude, when the other children were in bed, Anna would read to her son by the red and waning light of the winter sun, and as he grew older, he began to play in the street before the house, watching, with the pathetic yearning of small boys to be older, the passing of the proud Hollins Street gang.

At five, he began to attend a Methodist Sunday School at the suggestion of one of August's friends; at six he was ready for formal schooling itself. Friedrich Knapp's Institute was situated opposite the City Hall, beside the famous Voshell House, in the heart of downtown Baltimore. Knapp was a strict disciplinarian of Burkhardt's generation, well thought of by the leaders of Baltimore's German colony. Under the headmaster were a half dozen teachers, mostly his relatives, who ran their charges through the gauntlet of primary subjects, with the emphasis on German, and concentrated on keeping them in line. At the end of each year came a recital on the European plan, with preening parents present and, afterwards, a picnic in Darley Park for all.

Two days before his sixth birthday, Harry and his cousin Pauline were taken aside by Uncle Henry, briefed on the route of the Baltimore Street horsecar, and told when and where to get off. The fall semester began next morning at Knapp's, and Pauline, in a clean little frock and taut pigtails, and Harry, in knee-length short pants and button shoes, gravely set out to find horsecar and school. The first day they made it. The second day they didn't. Somehow they managed to take a wrong turn at Holliday Street and wind up among the noise and tumult of the Pratt Street waterfront. Terrified, the children were dissolving in tears when a Negro dockhand came to the rescue and delivered them into the anxious hands of Professor Knapp.

Harry proved a good student. His German was poor, but

he led in English and drawing, and though he yanked his share of pigtails and was paddled often enough, his deportment, in the report cards carefully examined by August, was described as excellent. His chief blind spot was rote memory, which may have explained his painful progress in German; because of it he was reduced, in the annual recitations, to the solving of mathematics problems at the blackboard—to the secret delight of August, who sat in the back of the room and worked it all out with his inscrutable "averages."

Two years after his entrance at Knapp's, Harry became a recruit in the Hollins Street gang, fiercely loyal to Fire Engine House No. 14 and a sturdy combatant in the wars with other gangs, loyal to other engine companies. The official duties of the gang consisted of following No. 14 wherever *its* duties took it and of throwing up election-night bonfires for the enlightenment of the neighborhood. Harry became all but indispensable to this last function. In man-to-man street fighting he was wanting in weight—though not, to be sure, in spirit. But when it came to pilfering ash barrels, garbage boxes, and other incendiaries for the election-night festivities, he was the best sprinter in the gang and could easily outrun any grocery man within five miles. While not engaged in serious business, the gang retired to Steuart's Hill to scheme, hung around livery stables to watch the shoeing of horses, or sat at the feet of old Negro men and women who spun fantastic yarns of life in the South before the war.

Charlie followed his brother into the gang, but however much the boys might join in the formal and informal activities of the neighborhood's younger set, their chief diversion came from within the family. August saw to that. With that fine sense of integrity he had inherited from Burkhardt, he planned and directed endless adventures for the entire household. He was particularly concerned with his sons. Harry he took on his weekly business excursions to Washington, there to perch on a brass rail and sip sarsaparilla while his father chatted with sporting figures, and when the boy became interested in photography, he helped him set up a developing room on the third floor. For all the children he bought a Shetland pony, housing it in a small stable in the back of the yard. To escape the unbelievable summer heat of Baltimore, he and his brother rented a large double house near Ellicott City, a quaint, somewhat vertical town lying west and north of the city. There, while their father commuted on an ancient arm of the Baltimore and Ohio Railroad, the boys roamed the countryside along Sucker Branch, a small stream running through the property, during the summers of 1888 and 1889. Two years later, August bought a summer home on Belvedere Avenue, a wooded section half a mile from Baltimore's Roland Park.

Certain differences naturally cropped up between father and son. August had become part owner of a baseball club, and in the hope that Harry would take to the game, he bought a set of uniforms for the boys in the neighborhood of his summer home. But try as he might, Harry merely passed as a weak sandlot shortstop, and eventually he gave up the game as a bad thing. And, more propitiously, he began to balk at Sunday School. At eight, he had been switched from the Methodists to the Lutherans. At first the raucous singing had entertained him, but before long he was squirming and asking for freedom. August would have none of it. He liked his Sunday-morning naps.

These, of course, were not serious. The seeds for a real dispute between father and son were sprouting, however, and though neither August nor Harry could have been expected to have recognized them, various signs and portents were at hand. Briefly, the question was Harry's career. It seems absurd to speak of the approaching career of a boy still in short pants, and if the matter had been broached, doubtless they would have thought it absurd too. If either reflected on it they assumed, quite naturally, that the eldest son would follow his father into the tobacco business. Unlike most little boys, Harry wasted no time dreaming of soldiering, or tycooning, or even of joining Engine Company No. 14. Because the gang often spent idle afternoons baiting the neighborhood cop, copping was also out. At one time he did think of becoming an electrical lineman because dangling aloft seemed a pleasant way to spend one's lifetime, but when he pattered into the parlor with this news, August was much amused, and the urge quickly passed. Nevertheless, it was in these years that the groundwork was laid for the boy's ambition and resultant family strife.

The literary education of Henry Louis Mencken, insurgent critic of the twentieth century, began in his eighth year with a book-length story of four sixteen-year-old boys lost in the wilds of Maine. "The Moose Hunters" appeared in the 1887 issue of *Chatterbox*, an English miscellany brought out each year for the entertainment of children. Grandmother Mencken presented Harry with the pasteboard-bound book at Christmas, and he went after it with an alacrity which surprised his parents. Perched on the marble stoop, he struggled through successive installments until Anna, alarmed, warned him against reading in the hazy, late afternoon light. The print was fine; the words, for a seven-year-old, discouraging; the story, hard to follow. But Harry, hunched over on the front steps or sprawled across his bed, persevered through the spring of 1888 with increasing ease, learning to read as he went along. By early summer, he was finished.

A few weeks later, he performed his first act of literary criticism: the shelving of an inadequate translation of *Grimm's Fairy Tales* presented by Professor Knapp for excellent recitation. The stories were fanciful; they couldn't have happened; they annoyed him. But "The Moose Hunters" had whetted an appetite not easily satisfied. After setting aside the fairy tales in disgust, he began a systematic search of his home for printed matter. Supremely available, of course, were the daily copies of the *Sun* and the *Evening News;* from them he turned to his mother's files of *Godey's Lady's Book* and the *Ladies Home Journal.* The *Journal* particularly fascinated him. Thirty-five years later he was introduced to its perennial editor, Edward Bok. "Mr. Mencken, I've been reading you with admiration for years," said Bok. "Mr. Bok," he replied, "I was brought up on *you.*"

Early the following year, having worked his way through every available periodical in the house, he came upon his father's high, old-fashioned secretary in the living room and there made a remarkable discovery. Most of the books were stifling—weighty histories of the Civil War, tracts on Freemasonry, Federal officers' memoirs—but off in one corner

were a number of books by an author August had admired
for years: Mark Twain. Harry picked the handiest of these
—*Huckleberry Finn*—and retired to his bedroom. It was his
first contact with living literature, and the force of it cannot
be overestimated. Deeper and deeper he dug into the adventures of Huck and Jim and, straightway he finished, rushed
back to the secretary for more. The other Twains followed,
together with a varied assortment of encyclopedic articles,
Baedekers, and boys' books. One of these last, *Boys' Useful
Pastimes,* brought him the unhappy discovery that he would
never be quick with his hands, that he could not, in all truth,
hammer a nail without lacerating a thumb.

Two other influences, coming at about the same time, conspired with Harry's discovery of language to shape his future.
The first arrived at 1524 Hollins Street in the form of a
kindly German with enormous whiskers who came to instruct
him in the use of the Menckens' new piano. The boy's playing was more loud than delicate—to the delight of August,
who brought him into the sitting-room to pound away in-
nocently whenever an unwelcome visitor called. Nevertheless the lessons somehow inspired a love of good music
which survived despite the pedestrian quality of the instruc-
tion. In music as in literature, it may be noted, he showed a
curious early aversion to romance; he adored Mozart and
scorned Chopin.

The other determining instrument was nothing more than
an exposure to the mechanics of publishing. One lazy Thursday during the second of the Menckens' two summers at
Ellicott City, he undertook to explore the tortuous geography
of the town. Wandering about aimlessly, he came upon the
open pressroom of the *Ellicott City Times,* a weekly journal
run off on a hand press. Thursday was press day, and while
Harry gaped, two men huffed and puffed their way through
the one and only edition. Back he came the following Thursday, again the week later, and again and yet again, until he
became a familiar figure at the door—a shy, thin little boy
in button shoes and short pants, with a small, heart-shaped
face and intent blue eyes, solemnly watching their every
move, hoping for a recognition which never came.

That fall he demanded a printing press of his own. August

was equal to the order; on Christmas morning, in the manner of fathers, he undertook to explain the workings of the handsome self-inker and the font of type which came with it. It was an unfortunate gesture. Before he was done, he and his son were covered with ink and Anna's living room rug was a welter of smashed type. Harry was no handier than his father, but he was more persevering. The day after Christmas he went to work on the press, and what with scrubbing and studying learned to master it by the new year. He raided the hell box of a nearby printing establishment, turned out a batch of calling cards complete with Shriner's insignia for his father, and even assayed to publish a little neighborhood newspaper which went nameless because the thin fonts did not permit enough type for the flagstaff. The most profound effect of August's Christmas-morning capering, however, appeared in the little business card Harry printed for himself. Until then, he had always written his name "Henry L." or simply "Harry," but when he came to set type, he discovered his father had smashed all his lower case "r's." The legend therefore read simply, "H. L. Mencken." He liked it so well he decided to keep it.

Eleven years old, tall and gangling, Harry made his first considerable trip beyond the city limits of Baltimore. Anna's father planned to visit relatives in Ohio, and he decided to take the boy along. Hollins Street seethed with activity; Anna fretted over piles of winter clothing; August slipped his son bill after bill; Charlie sulked because he could not go; and Harry, in a perfect frenzy of excitement, did virtually no work at Knapp's. The month's trip was memorable but uneventful, save for its ending, which found the front door of the Mencken house adorned with a great black wreath. Burkhardt Mencken, sixty-two, had passed away in their absence. Boylike, Harry's only reflection climbing the stoop was that there would be no school for him the following day.

That June he was graduated from Knapp's and, to the horror of the old professor, who considered public education little better than the reformatory system, was entered in the Polytechnic Institute, a Baltimore high school, the following fall. There he excelled in chemistry, physiology, and the arts and continued his struggle with German. For a time he did very badly in algebra, but after a brief tutoring session, he mastered it and was, as a result, promoted an entire year. Meanwhile, his parents observed, he began to exhibit certain signs of puberty. Specifically, he was entranced by the lusty blonde daughter of a neighbor. He began parting his hair in the middle, after the fashion of Victorian dandies, and took to spending long hours at the piano, composing sonatas, Strauss waltzes, and, when the lady demurred, wild Sousa marches. He went so far as to write a comic opera which gained favor among the other boys at Poly and was publicly presented. The composer played in the pit. The pedal, as always, was *forte*.

By now, the simmering ingredients of his early reading had begun to give off steam. His first essay, encouraged by two English teachers at Poly, was on photography. This was followed by a specimen of abortive reporting—on one of the baseball games to which his father was forever taking him— and by painful, awkward strainings at the story, essay, and play forms. The piece on photography dealt with "A New Platinum Toning Bath, for Silver Prints." It began:

> Ever since the introduction of platinum paper, various toning baths have been described in the photographic magazines for giving silver prints the color of the platinotype. The basis of all these has been potassic chloroplatinite —a salt, by the way, which is difficult to prepare—combined with sodic chloride and a weak acid. . . .

Meantime, he was reading furiously. In a neighborhood branch of the Enoch Pratt Free Library, he pored over the French poetry forms in vogue during the Nineties, discovered Kipling—and wrote an imitative poem a day for several weeks—and then turned to prose. An entire winter was spent reading the collected works of Thackeray; turning backward, he read Addison, Steele, Pope, Johnson; backward still farther to Herrick, Shakespeare, and Ben Jonson. Addison and Steele and Pope he admired tremendously. Spenser and Milton he simply could not read.

All this study naturally tended to stoop his shoulders, and

August, taking note of the fact, decided the boy needed more exercise. He promptly enrolled him in a new Y.M.C.A. at nearby Baltimore and Carey Streets, and there, with some misgivings, Harry went. These doubts were rapidly translated into horror when he found himself cooped up in the fragrant gymnasium with a rosy-cheeked young fellow who shouted, "Follow me, *fel-lows!*" and then proceeded to leap and whoop his way across an obstacle course of horizontal bars and trapezes. Harry fled the Y. He protested to his father, but August was firm. Exercise, he insisted, was what his son needed. So back went Harry, to run along a quadrangular inside track—and skin his shins on its sides; to wallop a punching bag—and get walloped back by the bag on the bounce. Finally, when a boy falling from a trapeze side-swiped him and gave him a bloody nose, he retired indignantly to the Y library to study a Bible which, he later recalled, "was full of gaudy and horrible illustrations, some of which impressed me with a sense of sin I have never quite got rid of." In the library, to his final despair, he was cornered by a practicing idiot who insisted on reading aloud, in bell-shaped tones, from a book of platitudes. Even August found this too much. "You had better quit," he said, "before you hit him with a spittoon." The following Palm Sunday Harry was confirmed in his first pair of long pants. It was his farewell to organized Christianity.

His graduation from the Polytechnic Institute was preceded by a series of examinations which threw the school faculty into a tumult and the household at 1524 Hollins Street into an uproar. The first two days Harry passed as head of his class; August, parental pride swelling, offered a purse of one hundred dollars if he should stay in first place. Cramming day and night, he managed to do just that, winning, along the way, the gold medal which went to the best electricity student. The dumbfounded faculty conferred and decided that the medal should go to another boy; that examinations, after all, were no real test of electrical knowledge. August was disconsolate, but Harry, satisfied with his one hundred dollars, delivered the school valedictory on June 23, 1896. He was three months short of his sixteenth birthday.

Throughout his high school days, Harry had schemed with

another boy, whose brother was a reporter on the Baltimore *Morning Herald,* to lay siege to the city editor of that paper on graduation. But August had other plans. With each passing year, the firm of Aug. Mencken and Bro. had grown more affluent. Even the panic of 1893 and the destruction of the company's Paca Street warehouse by fire that year had not affected its prosperity appreciably; it was in 1893 that August hired a Spanish teacher for Harry, to prepare him for dealings with the Cuban market. So, when Harry came to him with the *Herald* plan, August would not hear of it. Halfheartedly, he suggested law or study at the Johns Hopkins University—and Harry would not hear of them. Adopting compromise as the only way out, the boy decided to stick with the tobacco business until the chance to break away came. It was an elusive chance. He waited for it for two and a half frustrated years.

The greater part of his first year, after a short term on the bench, was spent selling, a job for which he had scarcely any talent and less enthusiasm. Shy, sensitive, he was utterly wretched approaching a tavern owner or a general manager with a sample box of cigars. He simply could not bring himself to shine up to doubting customers or to argue with them. Consequently, he was transferred to the business office and from bad to worse. It seemed the son of the senior partner could do nothing right. He could not make out bills correctly; salesmen's accounts became confused; more and more often Daniel T. Orem, the firm's bookkeeper, had to follow him to the bank to straighten out errors. Trying to make letter copies from a screw press, he broke one of the castings. The valedictorian of his class was rapidly degenerating into a farcical character. Once, in the summer of 1898, he stormed into his father's office, determined to escape somehow, but August became so upset at the prospect of his leaving he hastily dropped the idea. He still could not defy his father.

For consolation, he turned to the branch library, reading Byron, Shelley, Keats, Howells, Stockton, Richard Harding Davis, Stephen Crane, and James Huneker. Returning from work each evening on the Baltimore Street horsecar, he would stop at the library and load up with books, retiring to his third-floor bedroom after supper. He was writing regularly now, and with increasing ease. With part of his small salary, he enrolled in a correspondence school founded by John Brisben Walker, the editor of *Cosmopolitan;* for the school he wrote descriptions of the Saturday-night alley brawls in the Union Square neighborhood. By the end of 1898, he was receiving little notes from the readers, telling him his work was among the best received. Often, in these unhappy years, when it seemed he would never be able to withdraw from the tobacco business, he would take his troubles to his mother. Anna said little; as a Victorian wife and mother, she was limited to an unspoken sympathy. But she understood.

Early in 1899 his life was suddenly and drastically changed. It had been a bitter winter. Harry, returning home from the library, had been taken with flu just after Christmas and was consigned to his bedroom. Everyone at the office had some sort of cold—everyone but August, who appeared to be escaping unscathed. On New Year's Eve Anna was talking to her husband in the sitting room when he gasped, stiffened, and slumped in his chair unconscious. There was no telephone and Harry was the only other person in the house. Anna ran to the third floor and told him he must fetch Dr. Z. K. Wiley, who lived nearby. On arrival, the doctor pronounced August to be suffering from an acute kidney infection. In the two weeks which followed, the patient sank lower and lower. The infection spread rapidly; August lost twenty pounds and sank into a coma. Toward the end, which approached painfully, Harry could scarcely recognize his father.

On January 13, 1899, while his grief-stricken wife and four children stood helplessly by, August Mencken, forty-four, died. Broken by fatigue and the ravages of his own illness, Harry fell into bed a few minutes after his father's death. He awoke the head of a family.

Two days later, on a Sunday, August was buried. The firm of Aug. Mencken and Bro. had been founded on a verbal partnership, which provided that on the death of either of the two general partners, the other might buy out his heirs by paying them half the book value of the current assets, with no allowance for good will. August had died intestate, and at eighteen, Harry could not give Uncle Henry a legal release, but his mother, who became legal administratrix of the estate, did so on his advice.

The boy was then free, at last, to call on the offices of the *Herald*.

Chapter 2

Copy!

(1899–1908)

A LIGHT RAIN was falling in downtown Baltimore on the evening of January 16, 1899, as Max Ways, city editor of the Baltimore *Morning Herald,* plodded up Fayette Street, crossed at St. Paul and made his way to the paper's swanky new fifth-floor offices. Max was in an expansive mood. A good meal, a brace of beers, and the assurance of at least two good top heads for his local page combined to produce in him a genial outlook on life. Crossing the city room, he turned story possibilities over in his mind. The penitentiary warden had broken his wrist a few days before under interesting circumstances; the pilfering of dog-license money promised a minor scandal in the City Hall. So preoccupied was Max it took him some time to discover he was being waited upon.

Indeed, he might have passed over his visitor altogether had not his eye been caught by an astonishingly high choker collar which glistened eerily in the bright copy desk light. An incredibly neat young man, his hair parted precisely in the middle and slicked down on either side, awaited an audience with Max. His name, it developed, was Henry Mencken, and Henry Mencken wanted a job. The conversation which transpired followed a timeworn pattern with city editors. The young man was asked if he had any newspaper experience. Lamentably, he had none. Education followed. The young man was a graduate of Baltimore Polytechnic Institute. He was asked why in blazes he wanted to be a reporter. He replied he felt the urge to write. He had, he hastily added, already written quite a bit. What? Practically everything. Anything published? Unfortunately not.

Max turned wearily to his desk; there was nothing new here. Macon—as he elected to call his young visitor—was told there was no vacancy on the staff. The applicant might leave his name in the unforeseeable circumstance that a vacancy should occur. Macon's face sank, and Max, turning, perhaps, for a final glance at the preposterous collar, saw it. He was, as noted, in a kindly mood; moreover, like most city editors, he was far from the blood-and-thunder myth which has somehow penetrated to the public. Macon was asked for more information, and on learning that he worked in the office of a tobacco firm headed by his uncle, Max ruminated and finally came up with the suggestion that he stay at his present berth, dropping around to the *Herald* office occasionally on the off chance that something might turn up. Possibly, he might pick up an assignment or two, as a sort of entrance examination. With luck and ability, he might some day have a shot at a staff job on the *Herald*.

The following evening, Macon was back at the office as quickly as his legs and his mother's supper admonitions would allow. Max was busy. The second night he shook his head, and so on the third and fourth. On successive nights, while the *Herald* hammered out its single edition, the boy was left to observe from a far corner the wonderful activity of reporters and telegraph editors and to reflect, as they all once had, on the heartbreaking difficulty of joining the newspaper business. As city editor of a metropolitan daily, Max had little time for any but the most pressing business, but once he did stop to chat with the dogged young man who appeared, on fair nights and foul, to await his pleasure. He asked, of an evening, what Macon thought of the *Herald*. Amused, apparently, by the boy's calculated enthusiasm, he invited him to return to his vigil.

Finally, on the bitter, snowy night of Friday, February 23, 1899, the lordly Max raised his head, glanced at the pinched, anxious figure, and said, "Go out to Govanstown and see if anything is happening out there. We're supposed to have a Govanstown correspondent, but he hasn't been heard from for six days." To Govanstown—a small community of winking lights five miles northeast of Baltimore—the boy went, zealously to badger volunteer firemen, undertakers, and other local celebrities. Notes in hand, he returned to the *Herald* building, conferred with Max, and was instructed to write up the successful exploit of a horse thief. Rushing to a vacant corner desk, he jammed the typewriter keys, unjammed them, sweated over a single paragraph, tore it from the machine, started again, and finally, with great hesitation, dropped the product into Max's copy basket. Before he could leave the office, he was called back to rewrite a neighborhood handout.

Early the following morning, as dawn broke over frosty Union Square, a newsboy working the 1500 block of Hollins Street was greeted by an impatient young scarecrow who grabbed a copy of the *Herald,* turned to the local pages, and found the following, printed as written:

A horse, a buggy, and several sets of harness, valued in all at about $250, were stolen last night from the stable of Howard Quinlan, near Kingsville. The county police are at work on the case, but so far no trace of either thieves or booty has been found.

At Otterbein Memorial U. B. Church, Roland and Fifth avenues, Hampden, Charles H. Stanley and J. Albert Loose entertained a large audience last night with an exhibition of war scenes by the cineograph.

In the days that followed, Macon (as he was introduced to the staff) was sent to the outlying principalities of Baltimore to dig up such instructive bits as the above. Before long, Max, encouraged, was sending him out on trivial city assignments, high school commencements, and the like, all, of course, on his own time and at his own expense. Between assignments, he read newspaper fiction, explored such meager journalism textbooks as then existed, and became acquainted with the city room. The *Herald* had been founded in 1875 and was in competition with the hoary Baltimore *American* and the mighty *Sun.* Under Ways it was a briskly written journal, patterned, as were many papers of the time, after Dana's New York *Sun.* Its quarters at Fayette and St. Paul Streets were, as noted, new and comfortable. Typewriters and telephones were making their debuts in city rooms; reporters came to work after lunch and worked the clock around, arriving in the office to write the next morning's copy at about 11 P.M. Newsgathering had not yet reached the frantic, machinelike stage; there were no rewrite men, no photographers, no real morgues. It was a day of long, leisurely assignments, with ample time for cockroach-racing and spittoon-pinging in between.

During the whole of this apprenticeship, Henry continued his dismal duties at Aug. Mencken and Bro., punctuated by conferences over the disposition of his father's estate. Max had told him he awaited only a staff opening to go on the payroll and finally, that summer, he was taken aside, provided with a trolley-car passbook, and told his first beat would be Southern Police District. His salary was seven dollars a week. Southern, as it was generally known, was quartered in a fancy stone building on the corner of Patapsco and Ostend Streets, in the center of the waterfront district. The duties of the police reporter stationed there were to investigate such knifings, flim-flams, and fires as occupied the police in the sprawling, seedy jungle that bordered six miles of shoreline. Southern was thickly populated with warring Negroes and partying seamen; between the Pratt Street wharves and the yards of Locust Point there was more than enough of the sublegal to engage the reporter until he returned to the *Herald* building to write his crop of stories. With a reasonable amount of help from the cops, Henry turned in a highly acceptable stint and was, before long, shifted to other districts—Western and Northwestern and, occasionally, Northern, a news desert so sterile even policemen raised their eyebrows when an occasional disorderly conduct charge found its vagrant way to the docket. On Saturday nights, when razors slithered and holdup artists lurked in dingy alleys, he saw heavy duty.

And he gloried in it. He became a young man on the town after midnight, a savorer of Planter's Punch, a connoisseur of "soft crabs . . . fried in the altogether, with maybe a small jockstrap of bacon added." When the last edition had been salted away, he would drop in at Frank Junker's saloon opposite the City Hall, to join the haughty stevedores, a reportorial fraternity, in the unloading of beer schooners. With Frank Kent, a young *Sun* reporter, he learned to humor the vagaries of the odd company with which morning newspaper reporters are thrown; before Kent had caught his late train to Walbrook and Henry his trolley to Hollins Street, they drank and exchanged confidences with broken-down actors, newspaper artists, and garish madams. At an age when others were attending lectures, studying counting room mysteries, and peeping surreptitiously at drawings of Gibson Girls' ankles, they had balcony seats at every considerable burlesque house in Baltimore—balcony seats and long, mean cigars.

After a few months in the outlying police stations, he was elevated to Middle District, by all odds the most news-productive bailiwick in Baltimore copdom, and scarcely had he begun to feel comfortable there when he was transferred to the City Hall. This was a signal honor, though he did not immediately recognize it as such. Politicians, with their eternal scheming and lying, were a poor substitute for colorful magistrates and the combination "dissecting room and brewery" odor of station houses. The *Sun* had moved Kent over to the same beat, however, and his ebullient enthusiasm for politics was contagious. Moreover, Henry found that the chicanery of the City Hall, properly exploited, was superb grist for his mill. Baltimore's chief political war then was between two Confederate veterans, the mayor and an attorney who dominated both branches of the City Council. The attorney's confidences were given to a small band of bosslets who met from time to time to consider strategy. Reporters were not privileged to meet with these councils or even to know of their decisions. More for his own amusement than for the edification of his readers, Henry wrote a fictitious account of one such meeting and Ways printed it in the Sunday paper. Mail flooded the *Herald* office and he repeated the performance. After several pieces one of the bosslets approached him, promising a true account of the meetings provided he be treated kindly. The attorney, indignant, did everything in his power to break up the plot, but he was unsuccessful, and the series went on from Sunday to Sunday, its Judas undiscovered, as long as Mencken covered the City Hall.

As early as the end of his first summer on the paper, Henry had written the election story, generally reserved for older men. By the end of the next year he was marked as the *Herald's* star reporter; the importance of a given event could be determined by Max's readiness to pull him away from the City Hall to cover it. He worked so hard, indeed, that his health began to falter. Since boyhood he had been troubled by hay fever;

other disorders of the upper respiratory tract began to crop up, and by early 1900 he was losing weight at an alarming rate. Dr. Wiley saw, or thought he saw, symptoms of tuberculosis, and advised a rest. Ways obligingly arranged a month's vacation, and within a few days Henry was outward bound from Pratt Street's Bowley's wharf, headed for Jamaica on a small British tramp for his first view of the tropics, with "the palm-trees suddenly bulging out of the darkness at dawn, the tremendous stillness, the sweetly acid smell, the immeasurable strangeness." In Kingston he roamed the streets, smoking black, spicy cigars and admiring the swagger of the British soldiers. In Spanish Town he searched musty documents for traces of Harriet McLelland and there found the will of a great-great uncle. And in Port Antonio he loitered on the veranda of the old Tichfield Hotel, chatted with plantation overseers, and caught a Norwegian tramp home.

By the beginning of his third year, he had known every form of flattery a city editor can bestow on a young reporter save one, and that was soon forthcoming. On May 2, 1901, a great fire swept Jacksonville, Florida, leaving much of the population homeless. The *Herald,* together with various other civic organizations, stocked a relief train with horseblankets and Maryland rye, and Henry was dispatched to the scene to relay reports of the city's gratitude. The trip was a nightmare. Arrested as a looter, badgered by the excited Florida militia, brushed aside by Jacksonville's mayor, he finally found the train—with its contents worthless in the crisis—filed a story, and returned to Baltimore, convinced that the doctrine of service "is mainly only blah."

His active days as a reporter rapidly drew to a close. With the beginning of that fall's theater season, he became the *Herald's* drama critic, and in October he became Sunday editor as well. For the next two years his duties were split between these and irregular stints of editorial writing. He revised the Sunday typography, threw out a full page of lodge news—which had taken up valuable space for as long as anyone could remember on the theory that joiners would buy the paper to see their names in print—and introduced a series of travel articles. Most of his editorial page work consisted of writing columns or, as they were then known, "colyums." The first of these, begun late in 1900 under the heading "Rhyme and Reason," leaned heavily on his schoolboy verse. "Knocks and Jollies," "Terse and Terrible Texts," and "Untold Tales" followed. "Untold Tales" were laid in Rome. The characters were American politicians, one of whom was hanged at the end of each article.

In drama, the main burden fell on Robert I. Carter, the paper's managing editor and himself a former critic with service dating back to the days of *Our American Cousin.* Carter preferred to see the heavier productions himself, and Henry was thus chiefly concerned with musicals and lighter plays. This suited him perfectly. The truth was that he didn't much care for the active theater. Printed plays fascinated him —he discovered Ibsen and Shaw in these years and boosted the first Baltimore presentation of *Ghosts*—but the actors, he decided, usually managed to maul the playwright's purpose. Several years later, as drama critic for the *Sun,* he wrote twenty-three unfavorable notices in a row. On receiving the inevitable reaction from playhouse managers, he withdrew and never wrote another line of theater criticism. Because of this feeling, he mastered the urge to become a playwright himself, and in 1903 he and Stuffy Davis of the New York *Globe* founded the Society of Dramatic Critics Who Have Never Written Plays, with themselves as its only members. The theater reviews were excellent experience, however, and it was from Carter that he learned the guiding principle of his own criticism. Profundity, Carter believed, was unimportant.

"The main idea," he said, "is to be interesting, to write a good story. Of course, I am not against accuracy, fairness, information, learning. But unless you can make people read your criticism, you may as well shut up your shop."

The household on Hollins Street was going through an inevitable period of transition. Charlie Mencken had become an engineer and was on the road; young August was preparing to follow him, and little Gertrude was sprouting and helping her mother with the housework. Save on Sundays, they saw little of Henry. Each morning at 3 the patrolman in quiet Union Square observed his slight, stooped, bowlegged figure scrambling up the north side of the park and entering the doorway two thirds of the way down the block. Inside he read while the house slept; in the morning he wrote before riding down to work. Journalism at the turn of the century paid poorly, and those who could wrote on the side, not from pleasure, but from the sheer necessity of supplementing their incomes. Henry's salary was soon boosted well beyond the initial seven dollars a week, but it never went so far that he could not use a little extra change on Saturday nights.

In the manner of a good German shopkeeper, he bought a little notebook, ruled off columns, and began to record the incomings and outgoings of manuscrips. Poetry accounted for his first sales. While still in police districts, he sent *Bookman* an anonymous poem. It was printed and he, acknowledging authorship, received in the return mail a check for ten dollars. The following winter he sold *Life, Leslie's Weekly, National Magazine,* and the *New England Magazine.* He began peddling news stories and Sunday features to out-of-town papers; the Philadelphia *Inquirer* and the New York *Telegraph* and *Sun* responded quickly, and before long this work was bringing him about eight dollars a week. In Baltimore he handled an assortment of hack jobs: jokes for Dockstader's minstrels, parodies for political meetings, He-She jokes for syndicates dealing in low comedy, and advertising layouts for a piano manufacturer, a milk dealer, and the United Fruit Company. When the magnificent new courthouse opened in Baltimore, in January, 1900, he wrote the text of a souvenir booklet for twenty-five dollars. Perhaps the most charming of these chores was done at the request of Loudon Park Cemetery, on the lookout for bodies to fill its lots. "Loudon Park's natural attractions and its unusual accessibility," wrote Henry Mencken, the advertising copywriter,

have long recommended it to those seeking a beautiful and convenient spot for the burial of their dead . . . an extensive waterworks system allows the proper care of plants and flowers. . . . Detailed information regarding the purchase of lots will be found on page 16 and all inquiries will be cheerfully answered at the office of the company.

His main earnings, however, came from the short story. Sweating in his third-floor bedroom, hunting and pecking at his second-hand typewriter, he learned to master the lachrymose fiction formula of the time. In August, 1900, *Short Stories* printed "The Cook's Delight," and soon he was appearing in *Munsey's, Ainslee's, Youth's Companion, Everybody's, Hearst's,* and *Frank Leslie's Popular Monthly.* Ellery Sedgwick, later to take over the *Atlantic Monthly,* was then editor of *Leslie's.* He became the steadiest of Henry's customers; a variety of odd jobs for him under the pseudonym "John F. Brownell" led eventually to the offer of an assistant editorship, which was spurned. All told, Henry sold about twenty-five short stories in these days. His poetry market was less satisfactory. One magazine, *The Smart Set,* alone returned about forty pieces of verse.

The stories were pat and polished. Under such titles as "The Last Cavalry Charge," and "The King and Tommy Cripps," they dealt with high adventure in far places, none of which, of course, had been seen by the author. One example serves to characterize them all. It comes from "The Cook's Victory, by Henry L. Mencken," which appeared in *Short Stories* for August, 1900. Thus the opening:

CAPTAIN HIRAM JOHNSON, of the oyster pungy Sally Jones, thought that buckwheat cakes reached the maximum of deliciousness when they were light, unbroken brown. Consequently, when Windmill, the colored cook of the Sally, placed before him a dozen which ranged in hue from a dirty, speckled russet to a lustrous black, he was very angry indeed.

Pushing his chair back from the swinging table, he leaned against the solitary berth in the Sally's cabin and swore earnestly and loudly.

"What do you mean, you black rascal," he said. "What do you mean, suh, by offerin' me such garbage? Huh?"

"Deed it warn't my fault, Cap'n," answered his dusky

servitor, meekly. "Dat dar la'd—"

"Don't you go blamin' it on that la'd!" roared the captain. "Don't you dare do it!"

"I was on'y a-goin' to say," began Windmill.

The success of his fiction set Henry to dreaming. He would, he decided, write a novel. The custom of the time—and he was still very much a slave to custom—was to choose a romantic historical character and dramatize his life. Henry picked Shakespeare. Early in 1900, his battered typewriter groaned under:

Chapter I

In the seventh year of the reign of the glorious Queen Elizabeth, when men were dying by the thousands in the Low countries and the princes of men were quaking in their shoes—that is to say, in the year of our blessed Lord one thousand, five hundred and sixty-five, and on the last day of April, being the day before Mayday, a son was born to Christopher Wailes, gentleman, and Mary, his wife, on the banks of the fair river Avon, not far beyond the limits of the town of Stratford.

He wrote seven chapters before the cold light broke. He was, he discovered, working under a tremendous handicap: he knew little about Shakespeare and less about the Elizabethan era. The manuscript was immediately abandoned; he showed it to no one. It was a product of his Dumas reading, replete with ladies who spent their time combing long golden tresses and men who fought incessantly. At one point the protagonist—presumably Mencken: the story was told in the first person—exchanged blows with Will Shakespeare himself. Shakespeare was husky and quick with his fists, and in the early stages of the fight he blackened both of Mencken's eyes. But Mencken, with tremendous staying power, managed to lay hold of Shakespeare's arm and give it a quick twist. "Enough!" cried the bard, and the fight was over.

Henry's first book was published through chance during his fourth year on the *Herald*. Two eager young Baltimore printers, looking for raw material on which to try their arts, came to him for suggestions. He produced his shy poems and they were printed, in an edition of one hundred copies, under the title *Ventures into Verse*. Half the press run went to the author, who distributed most of the copies to friends and reviewers. The reviews, on the whole, were excellent. The *Nation* and the Boston *Transcript* were unkind, but the loyal *Der Deutsche Amerikanes* wrote feverishly of "this Maryland genius whose star illuminates the Heaven of poetry and genius," and the New York *Sun,* noting the inspiration, observed that many of the verses "might have been written by the author of *Barrack Room Ballads.*" And so they might have. The tone of the book was gay enough. It led off with the "Preliminary Rebuke":

> *Don't Shoot the pianist; he's doing his best.*
> Gesundheit! Knockers! Have your fling!
> Unto an Anvilfest you're bid;
> It took a lot of Hammering
> To build Old Cheops' Pyramid!

The verses which followed were earnest but undistinguished. Most auspicious, perhaps, was the war song:

> For 'tis ever the weak must help the strong,
> Though they have no part in the triumph song
> And their glory is brief as their work is long—
> (Sing ho! for the saints of war!)

By 1903, when *Ventures into Verse* came out, Henry's writing activities had begun to slacken, and for the next two years he was chiefly concerned with the immediate problem of getting out a newspaper. Earlier in the year the *Herald's* editorial rooms had experienced one of those periodic upheavals which strike news offices from time to time, and when the smoke had drifted away Henry, still in his early twenties, was city editor. No one was more astonished than he was. It happened this way: Carter had resigned the previous autumn; his successor was Lynn R. Meekins, a former managing editor for the *Saturday Evening Post* lately come from the Baltimore *American*. Meekins, appraising the staff, decided the paper had slipped badly since Max Ways' departure into politics. He fired some of the worst hacks; still, the standards remained dismally low. Eventually he began to look for a new staff taskmaster, and Mencken, steaming along on the Sunday *Herald*, seemed likely. So the nod went to him, and after a brief consultation with his mother he took it, fired half the reporters, and undertook to restore the local pages to their former state. At first the depleted staff was a great handicap, and much of his time was spent rewriting the copy of those who were left. In time, however, he established something resembling order and appeared to be settling down as a bright young executive. He joined a new musical organization—they called it the Saturday Night Club—in its scrapings over a Saratoga Street violin shop, and it seemed pleasant and even rewarding to hammer away blissfully at an upright piano while the *Herald* presses rolled out "a new and unexcelled Sunday paper, with artistic supplements in full color" at the end of each week. Then, just as newspaper work had begun to bear promise, Henry, the *Herald*, and all Baltimore were blown sky-high by a really extraordinary disaster.

At midnight on the evening of February 6, 1904, the young city editor put his paper to bed, lit a fresh cigar, and adjourned to Junker's saloon with the staff. A bitter cold spell had given way to milder temperatures, with rain predicted for the next day, but shortly after midnight high winds and a plunging thermometer kept bar patrons in their seats, and it was after 3 o'clock when Henry excused himself and caught a trolley home. Shortly before noon he was awakened by a startling telephone call from the *Herald*. As he bounded back up the stairs after pants and a shirt, gray-haired Julian K. Schaefer, one of the *Herald's* older reporters, swung down Hollins Street behind a panting horse. A few minutes later Henry left with him. The great Baltimore fire of 1904 was then a little over an hour old.

Downtown Baltimore, on that faraway February morning, was a maze of narrow streets, dead-end alleys, and odd-shaped patios, lined with frame warehouses and buildings with cast-iron facings—ripe, in short, for a catastrophe, as Chicago's Conley's Patch had been ripe in 1871. The city had grown up next to the waterfront—its main intersection was four blocks from the Pratt Street wharves—and the dingy hovels of transient seamen blended curiously with banking houses and office buildings on a ragged fringe which ran just south of the great east-west artery of Baltimore Street. The firm of John E. Hurst and Company, wholesale drygoods merchants, was an outpost on that fringe. There it was, while Mencken still slept, the fire had begun. At 10:30 A.M. automatic alarm box 845 sounded in the firm's basement. It was followed, at intervals of two minutes, by thermostat-governed signals on successive floors as the fire spread through the elevator shaft. As firemen sauntered over to squirt out what seemed a routine blaze, another alarm sounded from an annex to the Hurst Building. Scarcely had two engines arrived and begun to unwind hose when an explosion knocked down the front wall of the Hurst Building, shattering the front windows of the National Exchange Bank across the street. The fire was on its way.

When Henry reached the *Herald* office a half dozen blocks away, smoke was already billowing out over the downtown area, and before he had assigned half his staff to strategic points, Meekins was at his elbow, ordering one extra and a 9 o'clock first-edition copy deadline. The number of alarms reached twenty-one, a multitude of firemen were carted off to the hospital, and engines from Washington, Wilmington, Philadelphia, and even New York began to arrive. Shortly after noon, those directing the fire-fighting had predicted an early end to the blaze, but a wind shift at 3 o'clock changed all that. At 3, one hundred and fifty barrels of whisky stored on the upper floors of a Hanover Street building exploded, and a rising westerly wind carried the brands far to the eastward, starting a number of smaller fires. The winds rose, firemen began to blast, and Mencken, running occasionally to the window to watch the fire's swath, planned his page-one ribbon.

By 8:30 P.M. the composing room stones were jammed with type. Just as the front page was being made up, two policemen rushed into the building. Dynamiting operations were about to begin across the street: the *Herald* would have to move elsewhere. Confident they would return, the men, led by Meekins and Mencken, trooped to the lobby of a hotel several blocks away to await the blasting. Henry called home and assured himself all was well there. He returned to find Meekins in a state. The dynamiters had had plenty of time, yet no explosions had been heard. Would Henry mind walking back to see what the matter might be?

Henry walked back, but he didn't stay long. The *Herald* building had been transformed into a wall of flame, brands were crashing through the windows of the city room, and across the street, a sixteen-story office building was roaring. The paper for Monday morning's edition was serving as kindling, and efforts to run a hose line through Circuit Court No. 2, in the adjoining courthouse, had proved unsuccessful; the force of the water could not break the *Herald's* basement windows. As Henry zigzagged back to the hotel, dodging the flying debris, a court clerk produced a pistol and shot the windows out, but he was too late: the building was doomed. Indeed, a four-foot fire wall which had been built with the *Herald* was all that saved the three-million-dollar courthouse.

Meekins, meanwhile, had abandoned hope of Baltimore publication. Scott C. Bone, managing editor of the Washington *Post*, had agreed by telephone to lease his facilities to the *Herald*, and the group headed wearily for Camden Station and Washington. On the way, word reached them that the *Sun* building at Baltimore and South Streets had been abandoned twenty minutes before edition time. Its staff was also en route to Washington and the rooms of the *Evening Star;* Frank Kent was writing the lead on the *Sun's* fire story in the bar of the old Lexington Hotel. The *American*, the third morning paper, had lasted fifteen minutes longer than the *Sun*.

In Washington, with the red glow on the horizon as a background, Meekins and Mencken got out thirty thousand four-page *Heralds* and dispatched them on a 6:30 A.M. milk train for Baltimore. The story began in column one and swung across eight columns, wrapped around three line drawings showing scenes of devastation. Standing by a make-up table in the *Post's* composing room, Mencken wrote the four-deck banner:

HEART OF BALTIMORE WRECKED BY GREATEST FIRE IN CITY'S HISTORY

A THOUSAND BUILDINGS BURNED; LOSS OVER $75,000,000

DYNAMITE USED TO COMBAT FLAMES IN VAIN —ALL OF CHIEF SKYSCRAPERS DESTROYED

EXTRA ENGINES BROUGHT HERE FROM ALL THE NEIGHBORING CITIES

ENTIRE DISTRICT BETWEEN HOWARD AND GAY, FAYETTE AND PRATT STREETS IN RUIN

Scarcely was the *Herald* on the news-hungry Baltimore streets before Bone informed Meekins that the *Post* had an emergency arrangement with the Baltimore *Evening News*, whose plant had also been gutted, and that his guests would have to find quarters elsewhere. The story was building up: fires raged uncontrolled throughout the downtown district, burned-out engines stood grimly in the ruins, and the loss was approaching $100,000,000. Desperately the staff returned to Baltimore to get out a job-shop nightmare in the rooms of the tiny Baltimore *World*, itself only a four-paged paper in the best of times. On the third night Mencken wheedled four pages from the hospitable Bone while Meekins, as a last resort, made arrangements with the *Evening Telegraph* in Philadelphia, one hundred miles away. There, for five homesick weeks, the staff operated, with field headquarters in Baltimore's Eutaw House, on the fringes of the burned-out area. Officially, the fire was out at 5 o'clock Monday afternoon. Actually, it raged for a week. When it was stopped at last by Jones Falls, a stream running through Baltimore, the whole of the downtown section—a little over a square mile—was in ruins. The firm of John E. Hurst alone lost $1,500,000.

For Mencken the fire was an immense personal experience.

Apart from the more profound effects the destruction must have had on one who had learned to love the city deeply, his physical performance alone was extraordinary. In the first paroxysm of activity, he went without sleep for sixty-four and a half hours, relieved, Wednesday night, by six restless hours in the spared Rennert Hotel. It was a week before he could get back to Hollins Street for a change of linen, and then he had to rush back to Philadelphia to carry his share of the burden there. "When I came out of it at last," he said later, "I was a settled and indeed almost a middle-aged man, spavined by responsibility and aching in every sinew. . . . I went into it a boy, and it was the hot gas of youth that kept me going."

After five weeks in an alien town, the *Herald's* men returned to Baltimore. They were not impressed by what they found. The paper had told its tenants the building was still sound and would be completely rebuilt within sixty days, but the city planners decided to widen St. Paul Street, and the editorial offices were set up in an old car barn on South Charles Street, by the waterfront. Mencken revisited the charred, grisly skeleton of the building, climbed perilously to the fifth floor, and found only a mound of white dust where his desk had stood. With it had perished most of his early clippings, a collection of hangmen's ropes, and a file of personal records. All that had survived was a battered old copy book and the frame of a gooseneck lamp.

Under Meekins and Mencken the *Herald* staggered on to an undeserved end. It was scarcely their fault; the paper was still briskly written and edited, but it suffered from too much brass and too little advertising. The owner and the business manager considered themselves—as men in their positions often do—born newspapermen, and were forever ordering *must* copy that crowded news into corners or out of the paper altogether. The advertising trend was away from morning papers, and eventually the management decided to run *both* morning and evening papers—with no extra staff! It was August, 1904, and Mencken, just back from covering the Republican National Convention in Chicago, spent twenty-four hours a day in the sweltering car barn, sleeping on a couch, with changes of clothes sent from Hollins Street. After a week the morning edition was abandoned, but the Sunday paper continued, with the city editor's work day on Saturdays running to nineteen hours straight.

Events moved rapidly the following year. Meekins was boosted to the office of editor-in-chief and Mencken, at the tender age of twenty-four, became managing editor. Disaster loomed heavily, and Meekins and Mencken spent their dinner hours arguing over the paper's chances. They were slim, and growing slimmer. On January 20, 1906, Frank F. Peard resigned as president of the publishing company, Meekins took his place, and Mencken was appointed secretary and editor. The larger advertisers tried to keep the *Evening Herald* going as a bulwark against Grasty's *Evening News,* and through that spring it floundered pathetically, rattling off at last on June 17 and leaving Mencken jobless.

He immediately joined Grasty as news editor, but after five weeks the *Sun* offered him forty dollars a week and the supervision of its expanding Sunday edition. He took it, beginning his duties on July 30, 1906. The stodgy *Sun* was shockingly different from the flexible *Herald;* the very circulation figures were unavailable to the Sunday editor. "The first duty of a good *Sun* man," he commented tartly, "was to assume as a cardinal article of faith that the circulation touched the extreme limits of the desirable and that there was not a single literate white person in all Maryland who did not read it." But the men around the office were agreeable enough, and it was pleasant to work on a newspaper which knew no financial crises. He even undertook, one day that August, to write an editorial on the side, picturing old Colonel Henry Watterson, the fiery editor of the Louisville *Courier-Journal,* as "astride his galloping cayuse, with a baleful glitter in his eye." Watterson, delighted and astounded to find a light touch in the *Sun,* answered editorially, "Think of it! The staid old Baltimore *Sun* has got itself a Whangdoodle. Nor is it one of those bogus Whangdoodles which we sometimes encounter in the sideshow business—merely a double-cross between a Gin-Rickey and a Gyascutis—but a genuine, guaranteed, imported direct from the mountains of Hepsidam."

Not only had the *Sun* found a Whangdoodle; the Whangdoodle had found himself. *Ventures into Verse* saw the last of Mencken's poetry, and his short-story writing petered out when he became city editor of the *Herald*. What spare time he had in those hectic days was devoted to the reading of Ibsen, Conrad, and Huxley, and just before the fire Will A. Page of the Washington *Post* introduced him to the plays of Bernard Shaw. During that fetid summer in the South Charles Street car barn he worked on a critical analysis of the playwright. The little book that resulted—it ran to but 107 pages—was rejected by Brentano, Shaw's American publisher, but John W. Luce of Boston agreed to take it after a few changes, and on April 11, 1905, Mencken made the last significant entry in the little ruled notebook: "Shaw manuscript to Luce." The study was spawned of admiration for Shaw's own *Quintessence of Ibsenism* and generally followed the pattern of that book. It sold badly and brought the author no profit, but because it was the first book on the playwright it brought a crop of notices, most of them favorable. The Boston *Herald* called it "comprehensive and brilliant"; the Boston *Transcript* found it "sensitive and sound." Only the *Nation* was affronted by the "horrid" style.

It was this style which marked the book. *George Bernard Shaw: His Plays* was hardly a critical triumph, but there, in the introduction, was the first defiant flickering of real critical genius; there notice was served, for those who wished to read it, that a genuine, guaranteed, full-blown Whangdoodle was ranging loose on the countryside, gathering speed, gathering power, winding up and flexing his biceps, preparing to sink his well-muscled fist into the soft solar plexus of American rectitude.

Darwin is dead now, and the public that reads the newspapers remembers him only as the person who first publicly noted the fact that men look a good deal like monkeys. But his soul goes marching on. Thomas Huxley and Herbert Spencer, like a new Ham and a new Shem, spent their lives seeing to that. From him, through Huxley, we have appendicitis, the seedless orange, and our affable indifference to hell. Through Spencer, in like manner, we have

Nietzsche, Sudermann, Hauptmann, Ibsen, our annual carnivals of catechetical revision, the stampede for church union, and the aforesaid George Bernard Shaw. . . . Before Darwin gave the world "The Origin of Species," the fight against orthodoxy, custom, and authority was necessarily a losing one. On the side of the defense were ignorance, antiquity, piety, organization and respectability—twelve-inch, wire-wound, rapid-fire guns, all of them. In the hands of the scattered, half-hearted, unorganized, attacking parties there were but two weapons—the blow-pipe of impious doubt and the bludgeon of sacrilege. Neither, unsupported, was very effective. Voltaire, who tried both, scared the defenders a bit, and for a while there was a great pother and scurrying about, but when the smoke cleared away, the walls were just as strong as before and the drawbridge was still up. One had to believe or be damned. There was no compromise and no middle ground.

And so, when Darwin bobbed up, armed with a new-fangled dynamite gun, that hurled shells charged with a new shrapnel—facts—the defenders laughed at the novel weapon and looked forward to slaying its bearer. . . . And then of a sudden there was a deafening roar and a blinding flash—and down went the walls. Ramparts of authority that had resisted doubts fell like hedge-rows before facts, and there began an intellectual reign of terror that swept like a whirlwind through Europe, America, Asia, Africa and Oceania. For six thousand years it had been necessary, in defending a doctrine, to show only that it was respectable or sacred. Since 1859, it has been needful to prove its truth.

If his readers were not stimulated, Mencken was. Immediately the Shaw book was done, he began work on a critique of the philosophy of Friedrich Wilhelm Nietzsche; Luce published it in 1908. He was surer of himself now, surer of his subject, ready to pass the sweeping judgments which henceforth were to characterize all his writing. As in everything with him, the Nietzschean influence was three-fourths precedent. The deep German roots of his family, the Spartan philosophy of his father, the character of his reading, and the brutal realism of the police districts had framed the target for the dart. Now he presented the outline of his case. The boy who had scorned high school pedagogues lumped all teachers into "the most ignorant and stupid class of men in the whole group of mental workers." The militant bachelor applauded "Man's happiness is 'I will.' Woman's happiness is 'He will'." The victim of the Baltimore Y.M.C.A. attacked the "destructive morality" of Christianity. The veteran political reporter gleefully relayed each Nietzschean blast at democracy.

The subject of *The Philosophy of Friedrich Nietzsche*, it is well to remember, was Mencken's Nietzsche, not Nietzsche's Nietzsche. There is a difference. To the Dionysian philosophy he expounded, Mencken gave Apollonian consent: *Ja!* answered *Ja!* with reservation. Where Nietzsche screamed, Mencken laughed. In Mencken the peroration turned inevitably into a preposterous exaggeration which left the attackee, not the attacker, ridiculous. Nietzsche participated. Mencken observed. Nietzsche was often mocked. Mencken was always the mocker. And he mocked, at twenty-seven, precisely the same values he had mocked as a child and was to mock forty years later. It is amazing how little the man had changed since boyhood—amazing, and revealing. For it was this very inelasticity which gave him a sense of rightness denied other men. It gave his opinions that lack of resiliency, that brass-bolted rigidity which confounded his enemies and served to fortify less determined men in whom he believed. It was always his greatest strength. It was also his greatest weakness.

That spring one of the last of Mencken's potboiling ventures brought him a friendship which was ultimately to shake to its foundations the national literature. He had agreed to ghost a series of scientific articles for a Baltimore physician. The doctor broached the matter to Theodore Dreiser, then editor of the Butterick publications, and Dreiser said he would wait to look at the manuscript before deciding. When the first piece arrived, "it bristled with gay phraseology and a largely suppressed though still peeping mirth," Dreiser later recalled, and he bought it on the spot. A few weeks later the ghoster himself called to discuss the rest of the series.

Dreiser recalled his visitor as

. . . a taut, ruddy, snub-nosed youth of twenty-eight or nine
whose brisk gait and ingratiating smile proved to be at once
enormously intriguing and amusing. I had, for some reason
not connected with his basic mentality you may be sure,
the sense of a small town roisterer or a college sophomore
of the crudest yet most disturbing charm and impishness
who, for some reason, had strayed into the field of letters.
More than anything else, he reminded me of a spoiled and
petted and possibly over-financed brewer's or wholesale
grocer's son who was out for a lark. With the sangfroid
of a Caesar or a Napoleon, he made himself comfortable
in a large and impressive chair which was designed primarily to reduce the over-confidence of the average be-
ginner. And from that particular and unintended vantage
point he beamed on me with the confidence of a smirking
fox about to devour a chicken. So I was the editor of the
Butterick publications. He had been told about me. However, in spite of *Sister Carrie,* I doubt if he had ever heard
of me before this. After studying him in that arch-episcopal
setting which the chair provided, I began to laugh. "Well,
well," I said. "If it isn't Anheuser's own brightest boy out
to see the town."

With what Dreiser called "that unfailing readiness for
nonsensical flight which has always characterized him,"
Mencken insisted that he *was* the son of Baltimore's richest
brewer. Didn't his yellow shoes and bright tie prove it? What
did Dreiser expect from a brewer's son? They immediately
arranged to meet again often, though neither then realized
how often their meetings would be, nor how significant for
both of them this first one had been. For Mencken, its ramifications came quickly. A few weeks afterwards, seething
within *The Smart Set* magazine led to the choice of a new
editor—Fred Splint, late a managing editor under Dreiser.
Splint's assistant was to be Norman Boyer, a former Baltimore reporter. Splint and Boyer put their heads together and
sent Mencken a letter, outlining the plan for a monthly

Smart Set article on books and offering him the job. He was to have, Mencken later recalled, "the rank and pay of a sergeant of artillery." He would not have to leave Baltimore. He wrote back, agreeing to the terms, and a meeting was arranged to discuss details on his next visit to New York.

Chapter 3

The Free Lance

(1908–1914)

AT PRECISELY 4 O'CLOCK on the bright afternoon of May 8, 1908, Mencken strode into *The Smart Set* offices at Fifth Avenue and Fortieth Street and was ushered into the domain of Norman Boyer. He was less than enthusiastic. For one thing, he knew Boyer as a bore. For another, the office was rather too lavishly furnished for his Spartan taste. His displeasure over the furnishings—editorial rooms should look like workshops, he felt, not Viennese bordellos—was somewhat heightened by the discovery that this interview was not for him alone. Seated by Boyer's desk, carelessly studying his nails, sat a meticulously dressed and incredibly handsome young man, the prototype of the New York dilettante. Channing Pollock, Boyer explained, had resigned as dramatic critic, and this man would take his place. His name, he murmured in introduction, was George Jean Nathan.

For the next half hour Boyer droned on, reciting the brief history of *The Smart Set,* the details of the book and theater departments, and the rather unique character of the magazine. Mencken fidgeted in his rumpled blue suit. Nathan yawned. At length, the game was called, and the two young men descended to the street below. Mencken was about to leave for the station when Nathan suggested a drink. He knew, he said, an excellent bar a block away, where the best Tavern cocktails in New York were to be had. Mencken hesitated. Absinthe was to his taste, the fellow seemed agreeable. . . .

"Boyer," he exploded, "is a horse's ass." Nathan grinned.

"An utter and complete horse's ass," he agreed. "Let's have a drink."

The ice broken, they set out for the Beaux Arts bar, each studying the other out of the corner of his eye. Nathan—who had not been half so uninterested in his new acquaintance as he had seemed—noted the peculiar manner in which

Mencken's left foot turned in, his careless posture, and the rather alarming determination with which he ground a freshly lit cigar between his teeth. And Mencken, in turn, marveled that so young a man as Nathan could wear his clothes so well and step so jauntily down the streets of a city which, as everyone in Baltimore knew, was populated with bandits, pugs, and infected young women.

Seated comfortably, with two cocktails between them, they explored their mutual background in the manner of young men first met, beginning with an interesting coincidence—in Fort Wayne, Indiana, Nathan's father had been part owner of the baseball team—and virtually ending there. Superficially, they had nothing in common. Nathan, before his graduation from Cornell and the University of Bologna, had studied abroad for years and included among his campus achievements an editorship of the Cornell *Widow*, a fencing championship, and membership in Kappa Sigma, the Quill and Dagger, the Savage Club, and the Masque. Mencken had been to no college and had never seen Europe. His clubs were limited to the informal musical group in Baltimore. Nathan had begun as a fifteen dollar-a-week reporter on the New York *Herald*, thought newspaper work "about as exciting as a stomach ache," and had once refused to cover police stations on the ground that his talents were above it. Mencken thought reporting, and particularly police reporting, the most magnificent career imaginable. Nathan (who had gone ahead quickly after his astonishing city room rebellion) had considerable experience as drama critic for the *Bohemian, Harper's Monthly*, and the *Bookman*. Mencken had written two or three book reviews for the *Sun* and his free-lance fiction; nothing more.

And yet, the two men quickly discovered, they were admirably suited. In virtually everything that mattered, they were agreed. Both had decided politicians, clergymen, and civic leaders were, without exception, numskulls of the lowest order. Democracy was fantastically corrupt and mismanaged; America was led by idiots and represented, in both literature and the drama, the cultural nadir of the world. Germany— home of the *Ueberbrett'l* movement which had produced Thoma, Wedekind, and such—was far better off. Censors, schoolmarms, and worshipers of the English had ganged up on the arts in the United States; only a few men—Dreiser, Bierce, Twain—had escaped the dead hand of Puritanism, and they were regarded as smutty fellows by the high command of American letters. Europe, which was producing Hauptmann, Conrad, and Ibsen, was free to produce enduring drama and literature. A vigorous critical lashing was needed to open the shutters which had kept dark the American literary scene, and to this end, as they reeled from the Beaux Arts after a staggering number of cocktails, Mencken and Nathan dedicated themselves. They exchanged addresses, vowed to meet again, and departed enthusiastically, Nathan for his Forty-fourth Street apartment at the Royalton and sleep; Mencken for the long ride home.

The Smart Set, the medium through which Mencken and Nathan planned to wage their ambitious campaign, had had a curious history, not so curious, to be sure, as was its future, but none the less unusual in that day of prim publications and primmer editors. It had been founded in 1900 by one Colonel William D'Alton Mann, a shadowy and somewhat unsavory figure whose fortune was built on New York scandalmongering. With profits from *Town Topics,* a weekly sheet reprinting the most preposterous gossip about the city's wealthy, he established *The Smart Set* as a monthly to be written by fashionable women with a literary bent. The idea flopped, perhaps because Fifth Avenue was too busy reading *Town Topics* to write itself, and the colonel lost interest in it. As a result, a succession of young editors, led by Arthur Grissom, had been given a free hand and had competed with *Ainslee's* for manuscripts from writers unable to satisfy the stuffy Howellses and Hamilton Wright Mabies controlling the more famous publications. *The Smart Set* had made a name for itself among the small and as yet little-known band of realistic writers in America, publishing stories by Ludwig Lewisohn, Damon Runyon, Jack London, John Erskine, James Branch Cabell, and Theodore Dreiser; poetry by Ezra Pound, Deems Taylor, Louis Untermeyer, and William Rose Benét; and, in what may have been the greatest publishing coup of the time, spreading before a national audience a young writer who signed his stories O. Henry.

Lately, however, *The Smart Set* had fallen on evil days. Colonel Mann, dissatisfied with his scheme and anxious to get rid of a $100,000 bond issue, had unloaded the magazine on John Adams Thayer, a get-rich-quick publishing marvel with a yearning to crash New York society. Thayer had bought *Everybody's* on notes for $75,000 with a partner and built it up into a $3,000,000 business. With his fortune, he had acquired literary aspirations. He looked to *The Smart Set*, for some unknown reason, to pave the way for him. Under Colonel Mann it had acquired some of the odor that flavored *Town Topics,* and Thayer's scheme was doomed from the start. Again, its publisher lost interest in *The Smart Set* and gave his editors a free hand: thus Splint's decision to establish a book section and Mencken's entrance through the back door.

To understand the really subversive nature of that first conversation between Mencken and Nathan one must remember that in 1908 the reform era which had been ushered in by the Populist Revolt of the Nineties was at its height. It was a day characterized by social consciousness, led by La-Follette and Bryan, and distinguished by a sublime belief in the therapeutic nature of legislation. Laws, it was universally believed, were the solution to the nation's ills, and of ills, it was conceded, there were many. Scarcely a month passed that someone did not write eloquently of *The Shame of the Cities,* the *Daughters of the Poor,* or *The Greatest Trust in the World*. The immediate answer to these was the crusade for legislation. Under the reformers—the "Uplifters" and "Forward-lookers," Mencken called them—war was waged against intemperance, child labor, the spoils system, limited suffrage, and the trusts. The white slavery crusade was fairly typical, both in its ignorance of the facts and the enthusiasm of its leadership. In 1908 scarcely a literate person in the United States did not believe that the slavers were everywhere—in theaters, hotel lobbies, and railroad stations—waiting with hypodermic needles, chloroform masks, and closed carriages to snare their prey.

For all the noise, there was little action. The moral indignation, like the shame which inspired it, was mainly bogus. When the fussing was over, the railroads still avoided rate regulation, the trusts remained powerful, and the slums were uncleared. Theodore Roosevelt, who was the greatest leader of the time, was also its greatest symbol. For all his prating about Manchester liberalism and the horrors of Mulberry Bend, Roosevelt remained a solid opponent of any real move toward reform. The end product of all the crusades was the channeling of movements which led to Wilson idealism and the inevitable reaction of the Twenties.

In literature, as Mencken and Nathan had noted, America had touched bottom. In the publishing houses and magazine offices of New York, no serious novel, no vigorous play, no verse with the stamp of individualism had a chance. Writers who tried to tell of life as they saw it, and there were a few, wrote for *The Smart Set* or, more often, filed their work away in attic trunks. The public wanted no part of anyone who denied the rewards of virtue or the sacred principle that literature should be the propagandizing of the prevailing manners, morals, and economic *status quo*. Gene Stratton Porter, John Fox, Jr., Kate Douglas Wiggin, and Harold Bell Wright were the great writers; *Freckles, The Trail of the Lonesome Pine, Rebecca of Sunnybrook Farm,* and *The Shepherd of the Hills* were their masterpieces. In the critical columns, their genius was praised by Hamilton Wright Mabie and Clayton Hamilton. Men who pined for the literary game followed a stereotyped pattern—Professor Baker's course at Harvard to a New York newspaper to eunuchdom—or they didn't play. In every book, magazine, or drama to reach the public the sexless and flappy figure of an archetypical Pollyanna, her maidenhead unsullied and unchallenged, lay sterile and pure.

These were the years when Robert Frost grew potatoes and wrote poetry slyly on the side; when Edgar Lee Masters practiced law, Sherwood Anderson manufactured paint, Edwin Arlington Robinson worked in a customshouse, and Vachel Lindsay roamed the country as a tramp. Dreiser edited at *Butterick's,* Willa Cather worked at *McClure's,* and in Richmond, James Branch Cabell quietly developed an intricate style no public, he was certain, would ever read. On the rare occasion when one of these found a publisher, his manuscript reached print emasculated, mutilated; this was the heyday of

Anthony Comstock, the great Comstock who convicted enough "lewd" writers to fill sixty-one passenger coaches, whose clawlike hand reached out beyond the grave to kill a chapter in Norris's posthumously published *Vandover and the Brute*.

The revolt against this insipience in our national culture may fairly date from November, 1908, when Mencken's first critical article, "The Good, the Bad, and the Best Sellers" appeared in the back of *The Smart Set*. Against all that was small and mean, against every corrupting influence, against everything vestigial in the minds of civilized men, he set himself squarely. His survey of the literary scene had convinced him that all prevailing forms of criticism were inadequate to deal with the enemy. Discrimination and poise were futile; gusto, energy, and a stallion prose were needed. These were Mencken's. Like Goethe, like the Beethoven he adored, the right man at the right time aimed for the first time at a national audience, threw his first shell into the breech, and fired. "Our American manufacturers of best sellers," he wrote acidly,

> having the souls of fudge-besotted high school girls, behold the human comedy as a mixture of a fashionable wedding and a three alarm fire, with the music by Frederic François Chopin; the pornographic lady novelists of England, having the outlook of elderly and immoral virgins, see it as a Paris peep show.

There was, as he later noted, "a great stirring beneath the college elms, as if a naked fancy woman had run across the campus"; for the first time, someone had spoken out against the regime. It was heresy but, perhaps, best ignored. Yet Mencken had decided it would *not* be ignored, and sweating every night in his third-floor workroom, he fired away at every accepted literary standard and a few that were not literary at all.

The prevailing criticism, he thundered, "smells of the pulpit, the chautauqua, the school room. Think of William Winter, Clayton Hamilton, Paul Elmer More, the old-maidishness of William Dean Howells, the elephantine tread of the *Dial* and the *Bookman!*" Was Howells the dean of criticism and Henry James the artful practitioner of English writing at its best? Then Howell's prose was "simpering, coquettish, over-corseted" and James, reminded him of the façades of Polish churches in mining towns. Were Eden Phillpots' novels selling well? They gave Mencken "unbearable agony"; he tossed them, unread, into his trash barrel, where they were hauled away in the night, "unwept, unhonored, and unsung, along with my archaic lingerie and my vacant beer bottles." Was William Allen White an up-and-coming novelist? Mencken roared with laughter. Imagine first-rate writing coming from the plains of "sunbaked, unwashed Kansas"! And were his comments unseemly? He admitted it.

I am by nature a vulgar fellow. I prefer "Tom Jones" to "The Rosary," Rabelais to the Elsie books, the Old Testament to the New, the expurgated parts of "Gulliver's Travels" to those that are left. I delight in beer stews, limericks, burlesque shows, New York City, and the music of Haydn, that beery, delightful old rascal! I swear in the presence of ladies and archdeacons. When the mercury is above ninety-five, I dine in my shirt sleeves and write poetry naked.

Well! said the old ladies on Beacon Street. Well! said the old men on the *Dial*. And on the storm rolled, month after month, until the months grew into years and the naked fancy women, like elves in the wood, flitted across the college campuses with increasing boldness and regularity.

His never-forgotten first principle, learned from Carter, was to make his reviews interesting, and *The Smart Set's* book department was artfully designed toward that effect. Each month the article led off with a dramatic essay, calculated to lead the reader into the opening review. "Call off the dogs and let in the poets!" he began one month.

Some of them have been waiting in my antechamber since way last Spring—all through the long sticky days of last Summer, sitting in their short sleeves, tickling their dulcimers, chasing flies, all through the scowling days of this last unearthly Winter, damning the weather, chattering prosody, scraping the sad, sad violin. It has cost me forty dollars a week for their victualing and medical attendance, and they have drunk three hundred carboys of my malt liquor and smoked two tons of my tobacco. Twice they have fought with harps, fiddlebows, and chair legs. Thrice has some ancient among them gasped his last dactyl and ceased to trouble, again to my cost and inconvenience. Four times I have had to send in a preacher to unite some bachelor bard to a blushing poetess, and my waiter to pass around the chicken and harlequin blocks. . . . Time flies. I am no trained nurse, no pediatrician, no connoisseur of colic. I open the door and have done with them before it is too late. . . .

Readers of *The Smart Set* were likely to find the quaintest tidbits tucked in between long pieces on Ibsen, Conrad, or Dreiser, or summaries of Dr. Levy's latest Nietzsche translations. A short review of a German book might appear entirely in German; Mencken might review a book of his own, praising it enormously; or he might, in the middle of a sober discussion, parenthetically greet an old friend—("How are you, La Monte, old top? What has become of you?"). He reviewed all types of books—on antiques, menus, magicians, baby care—to build up readership. Book publishers were constantly criticized, praised, or answered tartly for letters written him; on one occasion he brought forward an elaborate suggestion that they perfume their novels, with the odor of new-mown hay for Gene Stratton Porter, frankincense for Hall Caine, and carnation for Richard Harding Davis.

Thus he bubbled along through page after page of double-columned fine print, with the supreme happiness of a man who loves to write and is fascinated with his subject. He turned the fine spray of his prose—that curious combination of American vulgate and rakish English—on every conceivable subject, but he was at his uproarious best with the books he loved best and hated most. The average little concerned him; Mary Roberts Rinehart's detective stores, then two of faint praise for their craftsmanship. Dreiser was hymned constantly; *Sister Carrie,* then in the underground of suppression, was brought up at every conceivable opportunity as "one of the most thoughtful and impressive books of our latter day literature"; Nietzsche, Twain, Conrad, Shaw, Ibsen, Andreyev, Arnold Bennett, Max Beerbohm, Ezra Pound, Huneker, Kipling, Lewisohn, Frank Norris, and the writers of the Irish Renaissance were praised; Hamlin Garland, Upton Sinclair, and Jack London were chastised for the prostitution of their gifts.

His major targets were Anthony Comstock—"the great smeller," as he called him—and Harold Bell Wright. By no stretch or buckling of the imagination may his reviews of Wright's books be called fair, but it must be remembered that throughout Mencken's work was the implicit assumption that the reader had placed the decision in the hands of the critic. Mencken never tried to convince his readers, really. He was first convinced himself, and then he told them about it entertainingly. In the case of Wright, he sighted on the weakest point in a given novel and blasted away. He was delighted, for example, when Wright's publishers chose to preface *The Calling of Dan Matthews* with a biography and a photograph of the author. The photograph, which showed Wright astride a horse, starting across the desert to forward his manuscript to his publishers, fascinated Mencken. "As a work of art," he noted, "the picture has its merits, but as a likeness it is a failure, for the camera was set up astern of the author, and so we see only the back of his neck and the hindquarters of the mustang."

Comstock's power over authors was intolerable to him. "When Anthony sniffs and smacks his lips," he snorted, "they fall on their knees and strike foreheads to the dust. When he looses a yell, they reach for the bichloride tablets and send for the embalmer." He gave his full measure of pity to those who had "sprained their souls trying to live according to the preposterous and impossible rules that moralists, lawmakers, prophets, theologians and other such donkeys lay down."

Mencken was at his funniest and least discriminating in the field of poetry. Distrust of the emotions without which poetry cannot live killed his own poetical urge even before *Ventures into Verse* was published, and his concept of verse—that it should sing a song pleasantly and never attempt an idea—was downright medieval. Save for his praise of Ezra Pound, Louis Untermeyer, and Lizette Woodworth Reese, he found little worth supporting in contemporary poetry. Poets were treated as children and their poems subjected to the sharpest gibes. Free verse was scorned. On one occasion, he reviewed a little book which began with the strophe

San Francesco
San Francesco
San Francesco
D'Assisi
D'Assisi
D'Assisi

"I get no joy," he remarked tartly, "out of this college yell type of poetry."

The monthly battleground on which he waged his relentless and lonesome little war was situated in the last eight pages of *The Smart Set,* immediately after Nathan's theater review. It was, by current standards, quite long—some five to six thousand words in each issue—and it reviewed an incredible number of books. There were months when he read and considered as many as fifty, and he seldom dropped below twenty-five. In the six years which followed his first article, he reviewed close to two thousand books, and there were many others which he read and simply could not fit into his space. On those months when a new Dreiser or a new Conrad was published, half his department was devoted to it; the rest of the current output was jammed into the back of the section. At the very end of the article he would run a number of one-paragraph reviews under the heading, "Among the New Books" and, when books showed obvious plagiarism, parallel passages from plagiarist and plagiaree— precursors, in their way, of *The New Yorker's* "Briefly Noted" and "Funny Coincidence" departments.

It was in these years that Mencken built his reputation as a great literary critic. Eventually the corporal's guard of realists in America found they had a leader, a critic of power and imagination willing to fight their battle and defend their cause. They rallied around him—to Dreiser and Untermeyer he became a father confessor—and in time a definite movement took shape. In 1910 Harriet Monroe began soliciting fifty dollars a year from Chicago friends for the support of her forthcoming *Poetry: A Magazine of Verse*. In 1911 *The Masses* was founded, and in 1914 came *The New Republic*, "A journal of opinion which seeks to meet the challenge of a new time." A new feeling crept into the literary pages of the Chicago newspapers, Burton Rascoe began his championship of Dreiser and Cabell, and the "Little Renaissance" was born. At Columbia Professor J. E. Spingarn declared "We have done with all the old rules . . . with all moral judgment of art . . . ," and in Baltimore Mencken read furiously and shipped off his monthly article to New York, aware that he had at last found his milieu.

He worked on the third-floor rear at Hollins Street, in a room which had come to resemble a combination country newspaper office and department-store book section. After supper with his mother and sister Gertrude—Charlie and August, now engineers, were on the road—he excused himself and climbed two flights of winding stairs to his study for the evening's work. By the window a gaslight of obsolete type burned audibly, casting a rather uncertain light on a portable typewriter which, under merciless nightly pounding, already bore a thousand scars of abuse. Adjacent to his flat-topped desk a bookrack, five feet high and set on a pivot, was stocked with the month's literary output, sent him from New York; on the lower shelf were piled *Smart Set* issues and a hundred-odd pamphlets and church handouts. In a far corner, dancing in the flaring light, lay the cot on which he read.

He read at an incredible pace and always lying down. In an hour he had swept through a two-hundred-page book, scanning the pages almost as quickly as he could flip them. Then he turned to a serious book—a treatise on religion, perhaps, or Aristotle's *Poetics*. His appetite for prose was enormous, and purposefully without discrimination. *The Congressional Record*, the *Journal* of the American Medical

Association, Mary Baker Eddy's *Science and Health,* evangelical newspapers, bond prospectuses—all were read, digested, and filed away for future reference. He enjoyed them all because, he said, everything written represented an attempt at expression by some human being. The evening's reading done, he pounced up and strode over to a padded swivel chair whose springs, badly in need of oil, shrieked in protest as he settled down before his Corona typewriter, rolled in copy paper filched from the *Sun* office, and began to write. The project at hand might be an article for Dreiser's *Bohemian,* his monthly book article, or the piece on Socialism he was writing with a reporter on the *Evening News.* Chewing angrily on the unvarnished corncob pipe he now affected, he rapped off his title and byline; then, for several minutes, only the flickering of the gaslight could be heard as he planned the paragraph to come. Out it came, with a spasm; another long pause, an oath softly muttered, then with a grunt he was off on another paragraph, viciously punching the keys and squirming in the suffering and articulate swivel chair. Periodically he sprang to his feet and paddled into the bathroom, to indulge in a curious but very necessary writing habit: a complete and vigorous washing of the hands.

At 10 o'clock he was through for the evening and ready for the small amusement his Spartan life permitted. Turning off the gas jet, he descended to the second floor, cranked the walnut wall telephone, and called a friend—Theodor Hemberger, perhaps, or Max Broedel, both Saturday Night Club members. If it were winter, they might meet at the Rennert Hotel's semicircular bar and drink beer; if summer, the friend would come to sip with Mencken the gin, ginger beer, and lime drink of which he had become so fond. Summer weather meant a happier and more congenial Mencken, for when the heat settled down over Baltimore like a soggy old inner tube and his compatriots suffered, he did his best work. "I'm like the hippopotamus," he would tell his sweating visitor. "An essentially tropical animal."

Shortly after midnight he retired to his tiny third-floor hall bedroom. At 8 o'clock he rose, shaved, and ate his only small meal of the day—a breakfast of fruit, toast, and coffee.

Then, by street car, he traveled the twenty-odd blocks to Baltimore and Charles Street and a day of editorial writing at the *Sun*. Life at the *Sun* was pleasant and never demanding; under Walter Abell, now publisher, it was run in the comfortable and leisurely manner of a good club. Nearly everyone above the rank of copy boy was mistered by his fellows, and despite the revolution the linotype had created in journalism and the rise of Charles H. Grasty's *Evening News*—a competitor who grew more formidable every day—the *Sun* continued to prosper indifferently on the faith of some 75,000 subscribers who, Mencken vowed, "held as a cardinal article of faith that the *Sun* of 1887 could never be surpassed on this or any other earth, and that any attempt to change it was a sin against the Holy Ghost."

As editor of the smallish Sunday edition, he had tried changes once or twice. Each time he received Abell's gratifying but rather lonely support. There was a terrific protest when he introduced large pictures into the Sunday paper, and on that day when he ran an illustration the full width of the page, dropping down to half its length, "there was a moan that reverberated throughout the *Sun* building, and the next morning the president's office was jammed with complainants and objurgators." As editorial writer he was done with all that, however, and even the theatrical reviews had passed on to other hands. Thus he was free to devote his simmering energies to other projects, carrying on newspaper work as a sort of left-handed interest during business hours.

Mencken was, it must be remembered, essentially German bourgeois in his thought processes. Now in his late twenties, he gravitated toward settled habits; his evening work, his late evening recreation, his very lunch hour were spent in the same manner every day. He wore the same blue suit, smoked the same cigars—fragrant specimens known to Baltimoreans as "Uncle Willies"—and met the same friends each evening after work. It was this establishment of a definite pattern which permitted complete freedom in the abstract. He never had to make the minor choices of life—where to eat, what to wear, how to spend his Saturday evenings, and with whom—and thus he was free to devote his energies to the major decisions—the merit of a given novel, the soundness of a given philosophy, the turn of phrase best suited to a given idea. He began, shortly after joining the *Sun,* to lunch daily in the downstairs café of the Rennert, a large structure at the top of Liberty Hill with a stiff Victorian interior and the best seafood in Maryland. Each noon he left the editorial offices of the paper, strolled up Liberty Street to the side entrance of the hotel, ducked in, and ordered. He might meet a friend there—Al Hildebrand, the violin dealer, or H. E. Buchholz, or Ed Moffett, the grocer—or, again, he might eat alone. The Rennert suited him perfectly; he took to spending Christmas around its bar, bawling carols in maudlin tones and swilling down copious draughts of beer.

Saturday evenings were always spent with the club, over Hildebrand's violin shop on Fayette Street, where he banged out two-handed piano parts with Max Broedel amid a shambles of cigar butts, ashes, and music scores. The meetings began at 8 o'clock: at 8 sharp Mencken, always the first arrival, sat at the piano and demanded, "What are we going to play?" A terrific argument inevitably followed, with Hildebrand, perhaps, suggesting a Brahms sextet; Broedel, Beethoven; and Buchholz, Mozart. The arguments often grew heated, but they were part of the club; without them the members would have missed part of their Saturday nights. Once a new member, thinking to clear up an obstacle to harmony, suggested the program be settled each week in advance. There was a shocked silence; later he learned there was dark talk of heaving him out for heresy. In the end, Mencken always settled matters through compromise. They would play a *new* symphony, he informed them, made up of the first movement of the Eroica, the second movement of the Haydn Surprise, etc. At the stroke of 10, all playing stopped and they headed for the Rennert, there to drink beer and eat sandwiches until midnight, when they broke up, the infectious strains of the music still singing through their heads. So well did these sessions sit with Mencken he joined in the establishing of a Sunday Night Club with Hildebrand, Hemberger, Moffett, and Fred H. Gottlieb. The Sunday club met somewhat more irregularly at the homes of individual members—often at the Catonsville home of Willie Woollcott, glue-manufacturing brother of Alexander—but the motif was the same: music and beer.

Through the club, music became one of the two major private interests in his life. The other was his own body. Working fourteen or fifteen hours a day he needed, he insisted, complete co-operation from all his organs. He complained constantly of this ache or that pain, and his friends concluded he was a hypochondriac, an impression they never lost. In the strict sense of the word, he was not that: he did not imagine illnesses. He was simply acutely aware of the slightest malfunction in his body; when one developed, and he found himself unable to work, he rushed off to a doctor to demand he fix it. ("Yes, fix it, damn it! Fix it or put it out of its misery!") He studied medical journals, read up on diseases of the bronchial tubes, gall bladder, etc., and became something of a pest at the Rennert with his ill-timed announcements that sweet-breads were taken from the pancreases of horned cattle, the smaller intestines of swine, and the vermiform appendix of the cow.

He became fascinated with his body and decided, after contemplation, that it was badly put together. "Imagine," he wrote a friend,

> hanging the stones of a man *outside,* where they are forever getting themselves knocked, pinched and bruised. Any decent mechanic would have put them in the exact center of the body, protected by a body envelope twice as thick as even a Presbyterian's skull. Moreover, consider certain parts of the female—always too large or too small. The elemental notion of standardization seems to have never presented itself to the celestial Edison.

Nathan's first impression of his new associate, through letters from Baltimore, was that he must be far more sickly than he had at first seemed. Not a screed came without some physical complaint. "I have a sore mouth, can't smoke, my hooves hurt, it is 85 degrees, and at least twenty pests are in town," or "As for me, I am enjoying my usual decrepitude. A new disease has developed, hitherto unknown to the faculty: a dermatitis caused by the plates I wear for my arches. No one knows how to cure it. I shall thus go limping to the crematory." When he grew really depressed and was completely unable to work, he amused himself by listing every separate illness plaguing him, thus:

My ailments this morning come to the following:
a. A burn on the tongue (healing)
b. A pimple inside the jaw
c. A sour stomach
d. Pain in the prostate
e. Burning in the gospel pipe (always a preliminary of the hay fever season)
f. A cut finger
g. A small pimple inside the nose (going away)
h. A razor cut, smarting
i. Tired eyes

Nathan, deciding this was really too much, sent him a set of false teeth, a toupé, one cork leg, six bottles of liniment, and a copy of *What Every Boy Should Know*. In the return mail he received a complaint, asking why a bottle of asthma medicine was omitted. "I am hacking and wheezing like Polonius."

He scoffed constantly at "quacks," denounced them as enemies of humanity—and ended trying every cure they offered. A fever remedy could not reach the market without Mencken first to try it. He watched the results anxiously: "My carcass is a battleground, and I am somewhat rocky. Hay fever pollen is pouring into my nose by the quart, but in my arteries it encounters the violent opposition of hay fever vaccine, and as a result there is a considerable boiling and bubbling." If he weathered the fever well next autumn, all praise went to the cure. If he entertained it overmuch, he howled and proposed the manufacturers be hunted out and publicly hanged. When, in 1910, the fresh-air advocates came into vogue, he sneered at them publicly—and privately had a sleeping porch, complete with canvas curtains, built behind his third-floor study. There, winter and summer, he slept for the next twenty years, while winds blew over him and the rain seeped in. In the end, he wound up with chronic sinusitis and a violent hatred for all who proposed fresh air as a treatment for any illness whatsoever.

He became the most considerate visitor of the sick on record. Friends who, in health, would not see him for weeks or months, found him at their hospital doors each evening, so long as they remained bedridden, with stacks of fiction under his arm and evangelical quotes on his tongue. He always stayed just fifteen minutes, managed to find out the exact nature of the friend's illness, and then was gone until the next evening. He became a tradition at Johns Hopkins Hospital, an unfailing visitor of the ill, and this custom, which was in some curious way related to the fascination all physical frailty held for him, remained all his years.

In all but his writing habits he was solid and unchanging, and there he was utterly a creature of moods. Try as he might to confine his creative work to the same hours each day, he found it governed by a coquettish and damnable muse. There were evenings when he would produce two thousand words, and others when he could not finish a single page. After such a session he would storm down the stairs, snorting, "Why I waste my time in such idiotic nonsense I do *not* know! All authors are insane!" Mencken's friends could always tell when such a mood was upon him: envelopes postmarked Baltimore came bearing church pamphlets, quack-remedy broadsides, and advertisements for indoor chemical water closets. The letters accompanying these would be filled with advice from his two spiritual advisers, "Father Balderdash" and "Pastor Blanknagle." "I hear that the Presbyterian Holy Ghost has a naughty disease," he would confide, or "Did I tell you the rumor current down here that the Kingdom of God is at hand? It seems improbable, but I only tell you what I hear." Then, if the mood persisted, bulletins would arrive announcing the approaching end of the world and advising correspondents to reform their ways and prepare for eternity. He had, he said, private information, from authentic sources, that the date was fixed at the following Tuesday. Religious material, distributed by a Baltimore sect, would be enclosed. When Tuesday came, and the world went on dismally, a revised doomsday schedule would go out in the afternoon mail with the explanation that his advisers had erred in their calculations, had corrected the errors with the aid of the Apocalypse, and had now determined the true date of the world's passing as the *coming* Tuesday. This might go on for weeks, until the old typewriter began to hum once more and his muse was with him.

For all his bourgeois background he seemed little interested in what his labors brought in. When Dreiser accepted *The Artist* and asked him to name a price, Mencken was dismayed. "God knows," he wrote back. "I have never sold a play. Playwrights, I hear, get a lot of money. Therefore, about $1,000 would seem natural. If the rules forbid, give me whatever would be due for a short story of the same length." In the *Sun* payline, he seldom counted his money; once the envelope was in his hands, he jammed it in his pocket and forgot about it until it was needed. One day, while waiting for Frank Kent, he did open it. He peered inside, carelessly at first, then intently. At once he was back at the window, calling to Eddie Fry, the paymaster, "Eddie! You've given me too much!" "No, Mr. Mencken," came the answer. "That's your salary now. It was raised seven weeks ago."

"I am getting along toward thirty," he wrote Dreiser, "and it is time for me to be planning toward the future." His planning, such as it was, was haphazard; he simply worked at the idea before him and, once it was completed, looked for a market. His free-lance projects were legion and had this in common: they all failed. Indeed, he seemed a sort of Wandering Jew, who carried his collaborators down with him. His most ambitious enterprise in these years concerned a new translation of Ibsen's plays, done with Holger A. Koppel, then Danish consul to Baltimore. Mencken had begun to collect Ibseniana, shortly after the great fire. In the course of time he collected almost everything Ibsen ever wrote, including many first editions and hundreds of translations, commentaries, portraits, pamphlets, and autographs.[1] As a dramatic critic, he had found that most of the actors playing Ibsen thought the William Archer translations stiff and diffi-

---

[1] In 1928, he turned these over to the University of Leipzig.

cult, and this inspired the translation project. He discussed it with Harrison Hale Schraff, of Luce. Schraff suggested single volumes with elaborate introductions and notes, and Mencken and Koppel set to work evenings. Koppel would call off a rough, literal translation, and Mencken would compare it with two or three good German translations, turning it into idiomatic English later. Two plays—*A Doll's House* and *Little Eyolf*—were brought out in 1909. They failed utterly, and *Hedda Gabler*, which they had also translated, remained in manuscript.

From Ibsen he turned to Socialism. To Mencken, with his vast admiration for Nietzsche, Socialism was "nothing more than the theory that the slave is always more virtuous than his master." He said so, both in *The Smart Set* and the editorial columns of the *Sun*. His pieces caught the eye of one Robert Rives La Monte, a reporter on the *Evening News* who served also as editorialist for the *International Socialist Review*. La Monte began a controversial correspondence with Mencken; it prospered, and ultimately they decided to publish it. Henry Holt agreed to bring out the book. To Mencken's grim amusement the details were settled at La Monte's father's lavish estate at Bound Brook, New Jersey. Mencken—the defender of capitalism—arrived by day coach and was greeted at the station by La Monte—the champion of the common man—in an upholstered carriage driven by a liveried coachman. It was all the amusement he was to get out of the book; when published in 1910, it sold less than two hundred copies the first month. Most of the reviews were indifferent, though the New York *Times* was dismayed that "Gentlemen with foreign names should instruct Americans regarding their institutions."

His nightly labors, he pointed out to sympathizers, were therapeutic, not industrial; he wrote to relieve an inner tension, "as a cow relieves tension when she gives milk." Still, no one likes to fail, and the bust of the Ibsen scheme, followed by *Men Vs. the Man*, rather discouraged him. He decided to set aside book writing for a few years and string along with magazines. But even here, it seemed, he was something of an evil talisman. Since their first meeting, he and Dreiser had corresponded regularly, and Dreiser, grateful for the hymning *Sister Carrie* was receiving in *The Smart Set,* solicited manuscripts for the *Bohemian* and the man's page of the *Delineator.* For the *Bohemian,* Mencken wrote editorials on "The Gastronomic Value of the Knife," "In Defense of Profanity," and "The Psychology of Kissing." Finally, in December, 1909, the magazine printed his pleasant little farce, *The Artist.*

That month the *Bohemian* failed.

The *Sun* office was in a terrific uproar. The impossible had happened: the Abells had sold the paper. What was worse, the buyer was Charles H. Grasty, the hated Grasty of the *Evening News.* Something very like paralysis gripped the editorial rooms. Grasty, it was well known, had built up a first-rate staff on the *News* and was certain to bring most of it over with him. Men who had worked for the *Sun* for thirty years expected to be thrown out in the street. None was more certain to get the bounce than Mencken. Just four years before, he had walked out on Grasty after six weeks as news editor, and Grasty, as everyone knew, did not cotton to that sort of thing.

Miraculously, nothing happened to the old employees; even more miraculously, Mencken prospered under the new regime. Just as he was preparing to clean out his desk and head for home, Grasty sent word he had no intention of canning him; he was, indeed, planning new enterprises at the *Sun,* and he needed Mencken's help. Specifically, he wanted to enlarge the Sunday edition and establish an evening paper. As one of the few men in the organization with experience in the afternoon newspaper field, Mencken would be invaluable.

The *Evening Sun* came out on April 18, 1910, with John Haslup Adams as editor and Mencken as chief workhorse. Officially, his title was associate editor. He preferred to be known as "minister without portfolio." Haslup was ailing—which meant there were *two* men in the editorial rooms with bitter physical complaints—and the bulk of the work fell on his assistant. Each morning Mencken arrived at 8 o'clock and plunged into the writing of two editorials, which had to be finished by 11 o'clock. Between writing chores, he edited letters to The Forum, interviewed the odd fish who always plague newspaper offices, and, if Adams were ill or tied up, made up the editorial page at 11:30.

After lunch at the Rennert, he spent the afternoon on a long piece for the next day's editorial page. He wrote, on the average, from two to three thousand words a day, and when Adams was out, the wordage went far beyond that. One day, when sitting at a typewriter suddenly became unbearable, he turned to pen and ink for relief. Adams, suspecting the reason, let his assistant off some of the editorial writing for a while, but before long he was ill again and Mencken was turning in a double stint. Except for the massive amount of work, he enjoyed the paper and even learned to like Adams, despite their disagreement over everything basic save the Bill of Rights, which they favored, and the advance of the machine, which they did not. Once, toward the end of a long afternoon, Adams called Mencken in and asked him to find out what he could about airplanes. "It looks to me," he said, "as if they were coming in, and we ought to have somebody in the place who knows something about them. You're a graduate of the Polytechnic and should be able to find out how they work." Mencken agreed, somewhat doubtfully, to find out what he could. His doubt trebled when he looked into the matter. What *did* keep them up? Damned if he knew, he told Adams. According to his calculations—and he had mountains of figured paper to prove he had calculated—they could never get off the ground, and once up, they certainly should fall out of the sky. For the next few months, his *Smart Set* reviews were rife with grumbling about "new-fangled airships," and year after year, for the rest of his life, he rushed out of his house whenever a plane passed over Baltimore, in the vain hope of seeing it fall out of the sky.

He grew immensely fond of the new paper and talked it up among the doubtful in the office. When a young man named Paul Patterson, brought over from Washington to take the chair of managing editor, found himself without assigned duties and thought to leave, Mencken persuaded him to stay. But he never learned to like Grasty, who was on his way to becoming the chief journalistic supporter of

Woodrow Wilson. "Yesterday I spent an hour listening to Grasty's creed," he wrote Willard Huntington Wright, then a *Smart Set* assistant. "I think he stated it honestly. I know that it almost made me sick. It is staggering to think that an intelligent man should believe in such puerile bosh. And yet, as rightthinkers go, he belongs to the aristocracy. He lets me cavort as I please, of course within reasonable limits, and he shows little of the Puritan blood lust. But a country fed on such ideas!"

Yet it was the very flavor of impudence Grasty gave the *Evening Sun* which made possible the first projection of Mencken's personality on a heterogeneous public. Early in 1911 Harry C. Black, scion of a family owning large blocks of *Sun* stock, returned from a year's study in England. In London he had been impressed by Horatio Bottomley, the columnist; the tone of the new Baltimore paper, he felt, called for the same sort of thing at home. He even had the man to do it, a fellow who wrote with astonishing knowledge of the London theater in initialed editorial-page pieces. When Grasty, taking to the idea at once, called for suggestions, Black answered, "Whoever H. L. M. is—he can do it."

Thus was Mencken ushered into Grasty's office one May day in 1911 and instructed to begin a new and eye-catching column for the editorial page. It might deal with any subject whatever, so long as it remain irresponsible and readable. It was a significant order. It marked Mencken's final departure from the world of anonymous opinion. However much more he might write for newspapers and magazines—and he continued, all his years, one of the most prolific journalists of his time—he rarely again ever wrote without a byline. He had left, and for good, the army of unidentified writers who present a newspaper's daily information and commentary and had become a public personality, free to exploit his own name. The tone of the new column—irresponsible and hence readable—had been set by Grasty, but it could not have been more to Mencken's taste. *The Smart Set* had provided a channel for his literary opinions; now he was free to comment on the whole range of human idiocies and particularly on those in Baltimore. For had not Grasty, in his lordly manner, said, "Write anything you please—anything at all"?

Grasty had—but he soon was wishing fervently that he had not. From the very first number, on May 8, 1911, it became quite clear that Mencken was following his instructions to the letter—indeed, so irresponsible and readable did he become that by mid-summer he was the Antichrist of Baltimore culture, a local character of alarming proportions. From Jones' Falls to Steuart's Hill, from Guilford to the harbor, *Evening Sun* subscribers—and a surprising number of non-subscribers—seized their daily copy of the paper, turned to the editorial page, and swore their way through an unprecedented column of rude, outspoken, and rollicking criticism of their home town.

Superficially, there was nothing revolutionary about "The Free Lance"; in form, subject matter, and light treatment it paralleled the columns of Bert Leston Taylor, Franklin P. Adams, Don Marquis, and Christopher Morley, all irresponsible fellows and all local artists in the day before columns became syndicated and hence vapid. It was his outrageous attitude which distinguished Mencken. He opposed everything respectable, mocked everything sacred, inveighed against everything popular opinion supported. He defended prostitution, vivisection, Sunday sports, alcohol and war. He attacked democracy, Christian Science, osteopathy, the direct primary, the single tax, and every civic improvement boosted by the city fathers. He openly advocated armed resistance against the prohibitionists, the supporters of blue laws, and the tax exactions put upon Baltimore by Maryland's rural counties. The taxes and laws he did support were unquestionably the most bizarre ever advanced in the columns of a Baltimore newspaper. A dollar-a-day levy on bachelors was suggested on the ground that it was worth that to be free. To the conventional system of choosing husbands and wives he proposed matchmaking by the common hangman because, he said, the present method had proved itself unsatisfactory. He drew up and urged the passage of a law legalizing the assassination of public officials. On the lonesome occasion when he did support a popular movement—female suffrage—he did so on the ground that it would quickly reduce democracy to an absurdity.

His aim was "to combat, chiefly by ridicule, American piety, stupidity, tin-pot morality, cheap chauvinism in all their forms"; his chief target was the civic leader or, as he preferred to call him, the Honorary Pallbearer. Baltimore's prominent citizens, he announced, were first among the city's seven deadly curses; the others were a death rate higher than the Panamas, the blue laws, the City Council, the cobblestone, the Boomers, and Universal Manhood Suffrage. The Honorary Pallbearers were organized into a baseball team and their achievements recorded in box-score form, with hits scored for support of the Anti-Saloon League, Lord's Day Alliance, Society to Protect Children, Board of United Railways, Reform League, Drip-Coffee Chautauqua, S.P.C.A., Goucher College Board, Penitentiary Board, and Society for the Suppression of Vice. Each player's batting average was listed daily, with Mencken rooting for this or that Honorary Pallbearer and Baltimore, to its confusion, rooting with him. He organized a Society for the Suppression of Prominent Baltimoreans, wrote a statute requiring the licensing of Uplifters, and offered prizes for the worst public platitude of the week. The prizes were characteristic: a hair from the whiskers of Lyman Abbott, a can of vaseline, and, after the war had begun in Europe, a map of the areas in Germany conquered by England. He printed charts of the Uplift, ran a heavy black box containing "A Daily Thought" —usually a quotation from *Also Sprach Zarathustra* defending war or condemning Christianity—and drew up a spurious coat of arms for the Pallbearers, in which silk hats, a skull and crossbones, and gartered net chorus girls' stockings were neatly woven together.

These lethal and highly subversive ideas were couched in a language designed to inflame the greatest possible number of readers. "An Anti-vivisectionist," he wrote, "is one who strains at a guineapig but swallows a baby." When a posse of outraged old ladies stormed the Sun Building, he sarcastically noted that the headline POLICE KILL MAD DOG should have read MURDER since, "as the Anti-Vivisectionist Society has amply proven, every dog has a soul." For the

Uplifters, he designed Mencken's Law: "Whenever *A* annoys or injures *B* on the pretense of saving or improving *X*, *A* is a scoundrel." For the pedagogues he prayed, "From persons who know the difference between 'will' and 'shall' but don't know the difference between a Manhattan and a Martini—kind fates, deliver us!" When Maryland's General Assembly adjourned after what was generally considered a successful session, he commented acidly, "Let this be said for the Legislature just hauled to the dump: It might have been worse. And that, perhaps, is the highest praise that can ever be given to a General Assembly of Maryland. It is also the highest praise that can ever be given to a dead cat."

The Free Lance bristled with expletives, italics, and exclamation points. "Boil your drinking water!" he warned one day. "Look out for automobiles! Send your money to the boomers! Keep away from the harbor! Root for old Baltimore! Glue an eye on the City Hall!" and, on the next, "Boil your City Councilman! Watch your drinking water! Dodge your taxes!" The column fairly sang with that strange combination of tolerant misanthropy and *joi de vivre* which had become its author's salient characteristic. Its success— it had not been in the paper a month before the deluge of protests began—bore out a cherished theory: that people love to read abuse. The protestants were given their space in The Forum, which he still edited, on that same theory, and the editorial page soon became a battleground of vituperation, with "The Free Lance" pitted against the best brains in Baltimore. Before long the column, the letters, and the stream of visitors to his office were taking up all his time, and Adams had to relieve him of all other chores. "What are you doing, Harry?" his mother asked. "I'm stirring up the animals," he gleefully replied.

If the animals were stirred up, so was Grasty. Mencken he had known only as an experienced newspaperman with a gift for polemical writing; this full-scale assault upon Baltimore's proprieties he had neither expected nor allowed for. When the floodtide of indignation reached him, he was first dismayed, then undecided. Timidly, he issued cautionary orders; then, as the invective rolled on unabated, he took positive action. "The Free Lance's" most telling paragraphs were killed, sometimes in the form, and, the office gossip went, Mencken was to be called in on the carpet. This was not strictly true. Mencken was certainly called in, but it was Grasty who was on the carpet, not him. "The Free Lance" had followed orders exactly; it was eminently readable, and certainly it was the most irresponsible department in the paper—or, in all probability, in any other paper then publishing. Thus committed, Grasty had to weasel. Finally he compromised: "The Free Lance" would go on as before, provided Mencken continue to keep sacred the one institution not yet attacked—the Christian Church. Mencken agreed, and left the office with the mental reservation to acquaint himself with Grasty's prejudices and learn to play his likes against his dislikes.

This he did so well that Grasty was never again heard from on the subject of "Free Lance" censorship throughout the column's four-year history. As it happened, even the ban on religion was shortlived. With chief vestrymen denouncing Mencken from every street corner, with the town merchants hinting darkly of a conspiracy to ruin Baltimore—with the very mayor taking the stump against "The Free Lance"— they of the cloth could not resist temptation. Having been taken to the top of a high mountain and shown the Antichrist victorious on the plain below, the preachers leapt to the assault—and, in so doing, exposed a vulnerable flank. For Grasty, whatever else he may have been, was basically a newspaperman, and when the assembled clergy of Baltimore, cassocks to the wind, attacked "The Free Lance" from every Sunday's pulpit, Grasty released Mencken from his pledge. Mencken was ready. For weeks, with the aid of a clipping service, he had been collecting news stories of ministers accused of various crimes throughout the country. These he printed, with ripe insinuation, as the hubbub grew. At length, as the storm surged toward a climax, he scored an astonishing victory with the help of his old friends at police headquarters. A Methodist clergyman, head of the local vice crusade and an attacker of "The Free Lance," was seized at the local Y.M.C.A., closeted with a naked Boy Scout. While the town stood aghast, Mencken hurried over to headquarters, secured the clergyman's release, and shot him out of town on the next northbound train.

The Christian Scientists required somewhat different handling, since they believed themselves to be on a different level from the frocked clergy and hence unaffected by the illegal recreation of a Methodist preacher. In the end, it was their very anxiety to smite "The Free Lance" which proved their undoing. When Mencken persistently ranked them among the more unsavory Uplifters, they formed a sort of public relations committee to deal with him. The committee drew up a refined protest and sent it in to The Forum. Its argument was that Mencken had "defiled the memory of an elderly New England lady who has brought comfort to thousands." Mencken replied in the next day's "Free Lance" that he did not understand: Did they mean Mary Baker Eddy or Lydia E. Pinkham? Whereupon the Committee on Publications, in stovepipe hats and frock coats, marched into his office and primly announced that all they asked from "The Free Lance" was fairness. "Just a minute," interrupted Mencken, throwing up a chunky hand. "The *last* thing you'll get from me is fairness!" The committeemen blinked at one another, folded their frock coats, and solemnly filed out of the Sun Building without another word.

Oddly enough, he got on very well with most of the men he attacked personally—he never chose "muckers" for his enemies, he said—perhaps because they saw, and respected, how neatly he penetrated the hypocrisies of public life. William H. Anderson, head of the local Anti-Saloon League—later he went on to greater glory as chief of the New York league—was a frequent and always affable visitor to "The Free Lance" office, and politicians, however much they might be attacked themselves, flocked to Mencken with choice bits of scandal about their fellows. To Grasty's delight, and purposely so, Mencken's chief political war was with James H. Preston, the stuffy and ambitious mayor of Baltimore. The *Evening Sun* editorial writers, with the heavy hand of their craft, had fought Preston almost since the first issue of the paper, but it was not until Mencken pitched in that the battle became unrespectable and hence effective. Preston was a machine man, with his eye on the Vice-Presidency, but his attitudinizing in party councils had alienated most of his underlings, and scarcely a day passed one of them did not seek out Mencken with some piece of scandal about the mayor. The Baltimore *American* supported Preston for the municipal advertising it got; its solemn pronouncements on behalf of Preston's open yearning for national office were quoted just as solemnly in "The Free Lance"—and then followed, in boldface, by the vulgar comment, "HAR! HAR! HAR!" In the end, Mencken got his man. The Democratic National Convention of 1912 was held in Baltimore. Preston had gambled on Champ Clark of Missouri, another machine man who went down in the Wilson triumph. On a dreadful night of sultry heat and free booze, Preston was crushed in a fiasco so incredible, historians, unbelieving, have passed it by. In victory, it may be noted, Mencken was not generous. The ballot ink was scarcely dry before a numb and broken Preston was reading "Free Lance" advice to "put his tallow-pots and brass bands and hired sluggers behind him."

Among those Baltimoreans who remember it, "The Free Lance" is popularly supposed to have supported no worthwhile civic project. This is untrue. One of its most persistent campaigns was to reduce typhoid and intestinal diseases in Baltimore through an improved water filtration system. It was waged against terrific opposition, for in Baltimore an idea need but be new to be subject to the common wrath of industry, the clergy, and the politicoes. Naturally enough, he chose the most offensive possible avenue along which to battle: he openly assaulted the good name of the city. Two leagues were formed, the National and the American, with standings determined by the number of typhoid cases in a given city. Baltimore led its league all season, copped the World Series, and then, in an International World Series, swamped Constantinople. The assembled manufacturers of the city were up in arms by this time, but eventually the plumbing was cleaned up and thus "The Free Lance" was not, as Mencken once wrote a friend, "defeated in all campaigns." Through this work, he became something of a popular hero with the medical faculty of Baltimore. His absorbing interest in medicine—particularly in the frailties of his own body—had brought him in contact, more and more, with the leaders of Johns Hopkins Medical School, and in his "Free Lance" days he made two of his rare public appearances, before the Huxley Society at Hopkins and the Medical and Chirurgical Faculty of Maryland. Both addresses were made with grave misgiving and after much working and reworking of manuscript. Each time he mounted the rostrum in terror, and, after each, was seized anew with an onslaught of pimples, aches, razor cuts, arch pains, and asthma.

Long before "The Free Lance" was rung off at last, it had developed Mencken as one of the foremost polemical writers of his day and had taught him the intricacies of the libel laws, so useful in later years. It had, however, done far more than that. In its columns of fine body type lay the blueprint of all his future books. The *Prejudices* and the *Smart Set* and *American Mercury* editorials from which they were drawn; the "defense" of women; the diatribes against democracy, religion, and current morality; the very nostalgia of his later autobiographical works were all rooted deep in "The Free Lance." When he sat down, years later, to write his immortal "Sahara of the Bozart," he led off with a quotation discovered and first printed in his "Free Lance" days, and even the scholarship of his most enduring work as a lexicographer was but a sharp echo of enthusiasms expressed in these years. In his very first column he discussed the flexibility of English as spoken in this country. Forthwith he listed some sixty-four vulgar synonyms for beard, ranging from "alfalfa" to "zoroasters"; in a subsequent piece he itemized a score of American words meaning drunk, beginning with "awash" and ending with "zipped." Day by day, in his relentless attacks on the respectable, he made his own contributions to the language; words like osseocaput, baltimoralist, smuthound, boozehound, and snoutery fell into common use locally and, in some instances, found their way to the dictionaries. He began in these years to put quotations on cards for his own use and looked forward to a dictionary recording them. "What is needed," he wrote early in 1911, "is a new book of quotations—a book made up of quotations never heard before. Has any gentleman in the house a contribution for this book? If so, send it to me, and I'll print it. A serial book of quotations is hereby announced." Three "rounds" were printed in subsequent weeks and the clippings filed away against the day he would further develop the idea. It did not come for thirty years, but like everything else in "The Free Lance" it appeared, eventually, bound and annotated for the public he had begun to accumulate, as a shopkeeper accumulates customers, during his first years in the business.

Somewhat reluctantly, Mencken had been caught up by the literary life of New York. He hated the place as a country boy hates the city, but, like the yokel, he was somehow drawn to the lights and noise of the wide streets, where fashionable women promenaded and great writers took their ease. As a literary critic, he did well to keep his home in Baltimore; certainly he could not avoid frequent trips to *The Smart Set* offices for editorial conferences. He might, as he did, ride over to Washington for an afternoon at the Army-Navy Club with an aged Major Ambrose Bierce, discussing the grim phenomena of exploding corpses, of crematories that had caught fire and singed the mourners, and of widows who guarded the fires all night to make certain their husbands did not escape. But he could not forget that New York was the writing capital of the nation and that his place was rightly there.

Once a month he made the proper arrangements at the *Sun* office, advertised that he was going home to press pants —"a swell crease, that's a big city"—and set out with a stack of books for the station. In New York he registered at the Algonquin, just across from Nathan's home in the Royalton, and telephoned across the street. "Well, here I am in your goddam town. What's new?" Nathan would order him to cross the street for cocktails in the bizarre, disheveled, and, to Mencken's mind, highly insanitary apartment he occupied. A Martini in his chubby fist, Mencken would salute himself, sip appreciatively, and hold forth on the idiots, boobs, and numskulls with whom he had had to ride during the long trip up. Nathan, looking like a prince of fantasy in the setting of tapestried walls, theater masks, and subdued light, gently smiled and sympathized. Then, his drink down, Mencken would explode, "Let's get out of this French whorehouse," and they would be off on a gourmet's spree—orange blossom cocktails at Sherry's, Taverns at the Beaux Arts, Rhine wine at the Kaiserhof, long-tailed clams and spring onions at Rogers washed down with Pilsner, ale at Keens, and Castel de Remy at the Brevoort. Soon or late they always would up at Luchow's on Fourteenth Street, listening in a "sort of fever" while the dean of their school, old James Gibbons Huneker, sat under his white, curling, and be-feathered hat, monologuing on the lives and works of Berlioz, Tschaikovsky, Nietzsche, Flaubert, Conrad, Liszt, Shaw, and Wagner. The young men sat, open-mouthed, while Huneker, now in his last years, held forth on the intimate lives of great men he had known, his theory of aesthetics, and his charming and utterly individualistic version of Manhattan cosmopolitanism.

But if Mencken was still learning, there were those who had come to regard him as a critical leader in his own right, as the man best equipped to carry on where Huneker's age had forced him to stop—more, as a champion with all of Huneker's charm plus a zest for combat the feathered chapeau never had. Bierce, gabbling away in the Army-Navy Club before his last trip to Mexico, saw it; the readers of *The Smart Set*, shipping manuscripts eastward, saw it; Dreiser, munching pumpkin pie at Hollins Street and listen-ing to a diatribe against comstockery, saw it. Subtly, relations between Dreiser and Mencken changed; the contributor to an older man's magazines became the counsellor and editor. When Dreiser became queasy over *Jennie Gerhardt*, he sent the proofs to Mencken; when Mencken, in reply, wrote "What I really want to say is just—'Hurrah!' You have put over a truly *big* thing," Dreiser worried no more. The next year *The Financier* went under Mencken's scalpel and was cut in half; Dreiser, with a publisher at his back, became panicky when he could not find Mencken for advice, and, finally locating him, wrote, "Lord, I'm glad you're back . . . for Heaven's sake keep in touch with me by mail. . . ." So successful was Mencken's editing of *The Financier* that, de-spite his rather lukewarm review of the book, he read the galleys of *The Titan* at Dreiser's request, suggesting cuts, ad-ditions, and variations before publication.

In his own generation, Mencken's most promising admirer, with the exception of Nathan, was Willard Huntington Wright. Young, handsome, athletic, Wright had been drawn to Mencken through a mutual admiration for German literature. As literary editor of the Los Angeles *Times* he had written "Los Angeles—the Chemically Pure" for *The Smart Set,* and Boyer, at Mencken's suggestion, had taken him on as editorial assistant. Brash, enthusiastic, and supremely his own man, Wright was already conspiring for the editorship of the magazine in 1911, and he sat fascinated while Mencken and Nathan spun their dream of a "knock-em-down quarterly" with an *American* motif, to be patterned after a suggestion in Wells' *The New Machiavelli* and titled, at Nathan's suggestion, the *Blue Review.* They talked of the project incessantly. Once they broached the subject to Thayer, but he, disillusioned by *The Smart Set,* put them off with vague promises.

But if Mencken and Nathan could not persuade Thayer to found a new magazine, Wright, on another tack, was more successful. A trip abroad, he suggested, would broaden his background as *Smart Set* editorialist and might, if he were charming enough, bring them the wares of the better-known European writers. With magazine articles in mind, Nathan agreed to tag along. So did Mencken—in his own fashion. To victual and drink with his friends in New York was one thing; a trip to Europe was quite something else again. He would meet them in Paris, he promised, but if he were to travel abroad, it must be with Baltimoreans. Wright, enthusiastic, and Nathan, blasé, went about their preparations in New York while Mencken rounded up Ed Moffett and A. H. McDannald, a *Sun* political reporter, and made his own plans. Passage was booked for April 11, 1912; Cook's tour agents along the route were alerted; and Mencken, studying his bankbook in his third-floor study, added and subtracted to figure how he might make the junket and return solvent. It wasn't easy going. The trip, he figured, would cost six hundred dollars, plus fifty-five dollars for insurance. Against this, and the two hundred dollars McDannald was short, he had but five hundred and fifty dollars in the bank. Ordinarily he kept a bank balance between seven and eight hundred dollars, but the bills for his sleeping porch, a two-week trip the previous fall, and the inevitable medical bills had cut him down. He debated whether to borrow one hundred dollars from his mother or to hock some of his Ibsen books. He decided in the end to practice thrift, and on Good Friday, 1912, a somewhat worried and nearly broke Mencken departed Baltimore with Moffett and McDannald for the mysteries of the Old World.

His *Smart Set* articles to the contrary, Mencken did the conventional things on his first trip abroad. His party landed in Gibraltar on a lovely spring day, "all in pastel shades, like the backdrop for a musical comedy," went on to spend the traditional two or three dollars at Monte Carlo, and then headed for Italy. From Naples they worked their way up to Rome, where they photographed one another at historic sites and managed, by luck and stealth, to tag on the end of a pilgrim file and kiss the Pope's ring. They had one bad moment on this adventure. As the Pope approached them, Mencken noticed that Moffett's Masonic charm was dangling over his trousers. He nudged him violently and Moffett, spying the charm, quickly shoved it into his fly. (On their return, Mencken told everyone the Pope had seen the charm and, turning to a cardinal, had asked, "What the hell is that?" When the cardinal replied "A Masonic emblem, Your Eminence," Mencken solemnly related, the Pope exploded, "That's a helluva thing to have in here!")

From Rome they traveled, under Cook's direction, to Florence, Venice, and thence to Bremen and Munich, "all in one day, with the apple trees in bloom." Munich, to Mencken, was the garden spot of the trip. He drank beer in the Hoftheatre Café ("perfect beer, beer *de luxe*, super beer"), fell in love with a waitress named Sophie ("Ah, those elegantly manicured hands! Ah, that Mona Lisa smile! Ah, that so graceful waist! Ah, malt! Ah, hops! *Ach, München, wie bist du so schön!*"), and chatted knowingly of the cellar with the long-coattailed, side-whiskered proprietor. He lounged in Ibsen's old chair at the Café Luitpold, drinking his *vahze* of Löwenbräu and reading his papers as old Henrik had. This was the Germany of which he had dreamed, the Bavaria his grandfather had described, and he was loath to leave it. Everything was as it should be—the gnarled old peasants in tapestry waistcoats and country boots, the corseted Bavarian lieutenants with their monocles and artificial restraint, and the Gargantuan old women, the "Munchenese of a rhinocerous fatness." When at last Moffett —who hated Munich—dragged him away, Mencken had so pledged his soul to his dream of Bavarian culture that no war, not even a Hitler, could ever shake him awake.

They rode the quaint European railroads of that long-ago, pre-Sarajevo day through Lucerne and Interlaken, and in Paris moved into a little hotel Cook's had found them just around the corner from the Opera House. Nathan popped up from the Continental nearby. Wright was living in a tiny room built around a piano, and there, on a glorious April day, they held a singing reunion. Wright, however, was not long for Paris. His scheme had somehow backfired; Thayer, who had a house in town, showed up and demanded some-one meet him in Carlsbad. Mencken and Nathan, as free agents, refused; Wright, as Thayer's employee, reluctantly went and spent a miserable week suffering in mudbaths by day and dinner jackets by night. Once Mencken had seen the Eiffel Tower and the other popular sites, the party eschewed what Nathan called "the Paris of New York." They relished Parisian food—caneton à la bigarade, ham boiled in claret and touched up with spinach *au gratin*—and strolled leisurely down the Allée des Acacias, the Boulevard Montparnasse, and the Rue de la Gaité. Paris was to Nathan what Munich had been to Mencken, but Mencken, tired by now of Europe and homesick for Baltimore, could not see it. Toward the end of their stay, the two young critics walked along the Champs Elysées one evening. Lights twinkled along the way and in the air was the warm, soft smell of a Paris May. "Isn't it magnificent?" asked Nathan. "You can have it," Mencken grunted. "I want a good American drug store, where I can get a first-class toothbrush."

After seven weeks abroad, Mencken returned to Baltimore. He celebrated his return by visiting August, hospitalized with pneumonia, and, shortly thereafter, by going under the knife himself to lose his tonsils, which had miraculously survived his thirty-one years.

In New York, meanwhile, Wright had gained editorial

control of *The Smart Set*. Thayer, dissatisfied with the rather dispirited editorship of Mark Lee Luther, had approached Nathan and Mencken, but Mencken had already returned his irreversible judgment against ever leaving Baltimore, and Nathan was too preoccupied with other magazine work. When Thayer called for suggestions, Mencken proposed Wright, who plainly wanted the job. Approached, Wright asked for an unheard-of contract: double salary for the editor, an ample budget for manuscripts, and the startling provision that Thayer have nothing to say about the control of his own magazine. It was a bold move, and it paid off. Thayer, perhaps remembering the verve of his own early career, signed without a murmur, and Wright was free to publish the authors he, Mencken, Nathan—and few others— admired. The first issue under his editorship appeared in June, 1913. Significantly, *The Smart Set* slogan was changed from "A Magazine of Cleverness" to "Its Prime Purpose Is To Provide Lively Entertainment for Minds That Are Not Primitive." Mencken, interested in his protégé, came to New York more often, and Mencken, Nathan, and Wright poured into *The Smart Set* the ideas which had been set aside for the *Blue Review,* now a fleeting dream. A new department, featuring absurd epigrams and debunking the country's creed, was introduced. Headed "Pertinent and Impertinent," it appeared under the signature of one Owen Hatteras, and its contents, like the spurious byline, were the product of the triumvirate jointly assembled. Mencken launched a new campaign for the Russian realists in his book department and contributed a series of biting articles on "The American." Nathan sent along his satirical "Scenes from the Great American Drama." And all three wrote up their recent European adventures in a series on the continental capitals— a series subsequently turned into the book *Europe after 8:15,* with illustrations by an unknown artist named Thomas H. Benton whom Wright admired.

The greatest contribution of *The Smart Set* under its new editor, however, lay in its outside writers, and since all blame went to Wright when the ax fell, it seems but fair, in retrospect, to give him full credit for bringing out, for one year, the magazine now considered a literary milestone.

For the first time the work of D. H. Lawrence, James Joyce, and Ford Madox Ford was printed in this country. Dreiser, Frank Harris, Max Beerbohm, George Bronson Howard, and Barry Benefield became regular contributors; the poetry of Joyce, Kilmer, Louis Untermeyer, and Sara Teasdale replaced the insipid verse Luther had printed. On college campuses, in newspaper offices, and along the winding streets of Paris, writers and connoisseurs of the best English writing became aware of a new and vital publishing force. At Princeton a wide-eyed young Edmund Wilson read it; in Chicago Burton Rascoe, then a prodigy on the *Tribune,* pored over it, and in Boston the *Transcript* wrote glowingly that *The Smart Set* "has been gathering laurels unto itself as a unique magazine for those who desire to keep abreast and ahead of modern literary currents."

But Wright, for all his farsightedness, was headed for the rocks. He was extravagant, he treated the censors cavalierly, and he held Thayer too strictly to his hands-off bargain to suit the owner. *The Smart Set* had become too erudite for many of its subscribers and nearly all its advertisers. The former wrote sarcastic letters; the latter, in the clubs Thayer frequented, advised him his magazine was printing material that was either incomprehensible or immoral or both. In some instances they canceled contracts. Thayer brought pressure on Wright; Wright, the contract in his pocket, thumbed his nose, and the inevitable falling out resulted. Mencken, anxious to settle the differences, appeared in the role of conservative. When Thayer insisted that Owen Hatteras, that impertinent fellow, be thrown out, Mencken advised Wright to let him go. "Why have a row every month," he wrote him, "all to no purpose?" Again, when the censors began to clamor: "Be careful with the sexual stuff, at least for the present. There are knockers on the warpath." He even suggested his own manuscripts be cut: "Don't make yourself an advocate of this stuff. It is far more serious than I ever expected it to be. If it doesn't fit your other plans, don't hesitate to say so. And if you detect any conspicuous rot in it, I depend on you to point it out."

Unhappily, Wright heeded neither Mencken nor Nathan, who protested he was "mussing up the magazine with pornography." Thayer, sensing an ally in Baltimore, came down for advice, rousing a testy Mencken from his sleeping porch. Mencken suggested that Thayer, unless he could work out a satisfactory arrangement, bounce Wright at the end of the contract. Wright, hearing of this, accused Mencken of double-crossing him and received, in the return mail, a protest: "Thayer seems to have convinced himself that the only magazine that has a chance is one appealing to all the right thinkers. . . ." In the end, Thayer did cashier Wright, running a candid editorial blithely asserting that "no magazine is really successful unless sufficient readers bring to it that support which gives a fair return on the investment." Wright, with a recommendation from Mencken, went to the New York *Evening Mail* as columnist. *The Smart Set*, under Boyer, settled back into its old rut, becoming, Mencken disgustedly wrote Dreiser, "as pure as the Christian *Herald*."

But not for long. Thayer's essential stupidity, face to face with a real crisis, produced the debacle which had awaited him throughout his ownership. For some time *The Smart Set* had been losing subscribers. When, in the summer of 1914, war loomed in Europe, Thayer decided to recoup his losses with what he regarded as a brilliant stroke. He dressed up the September cover with a panorama of men dying in battle, thinking to cash in on the war fever. The clientele Mencken, Nathan, and Wright had gathered laughed it off the newsstands; the circulation sagged from sixty to fifty thousand. Thayer, in a panic, decided to unload on one of his creditors, Eugene F. Crowe, head of the Perkins Goodwin Paper Company and owner of *Field and Stream*. Crowe named Eltinge F. Warner, who had been running his other magazine, as publisher. The fate of everyone on *The Smart Set* was in the balance; *Europe After 8:15*—probably the worst-timed book in publishing history—had gone the way of Thayer as the Germans attacked Liége, and Mencken and Nathan were in an unsettled state. Wheels within wheels were turning, whispered negotiations were carried on, and by August 11 Mencken, he darkly wrote Dreiser, was "at work on a plan which may give me complete editorial control of *The Smart Set*. . . . The chances, at the moment, are rather against success, but I am hanging on, and may know the result in a day or two. George Nathan is with me. He, in fact, is doing all the final negotiations."

The plan, such as it was, grew out of an absurd coincidence. In so far as it had any author, he was a London tailor who probably never heard of H. L. Mencken or *The Smart Set* and was, in that eventful year, as much a toy of fate as were they. Warner and Nathan, as it happened, had returned from Europe on the same liner. The men were strangers on embarkation, but it chanced they had gone to the same tailor in London, and Warner, spying a duplicate of his own overcoat on deck, approached Nathan and struck up a conversation. When Nathan introduced himself, Warner remembered him as a contributor to the magazine Crowe had just assigned him. A shipboard friendship grew, and Warner, who had no intention of editing *The Smart Set* himself, asked Nathan if he would like the job. Nathan agreed, providing Mencken come in as co-editor. "Who," asked Warner, "is *Mencken*?" After some haggling, with Crowe sitting in on negotiations, an arrangement was reached. Mencken and Nathan, as editors, were to have complete editorial control—not, as Wright had had, for one year, but for good. They were to put up virtually no cash, but were to receive one half the profits. Their first issue was to come out the following November.

Chapter 4

Mencken, Nathan, Und Gott

(1914–1918)

THE NEW EDITORSHIP certainly began inauspiciously enough. Circulation was dropping, advertisers were canceling subscriptions every day, and, to ice the cake, Norman Boyer committed suicide. Boyer had been filling in as interim editor while the Crowe management got established. When he learned Mencken and Nathan were to succeed him, he supposed, for a reason never learned, that he would be cashiered and so shot himself. The tragedy acted as a sort of cathartic; it swept out the past and prepared the way for badly needed economies. At Mencken's urging, the plush quarters Thayer had affected were abandoned and editorial offices re-established in a thirty-five-dollar-a-month room. Everyone save a Miss Golde, an efficient stenographer, was fired; she, Mencken, and Nathan were to form the office staff henceforth. A rigid division of labor was set up: Nathan was editorial head, Warner, business manager, and Mencken, editorial adviser, with the main job of gunning for manuscripts. From the beginning Warner proved his usefulness. However little he might know of literary matters, he did know a fifteen-thousand-dollar debt when he saw it, and, what is more, what to do with it. He pushed the English *Smart Set* edition, solicited advertising, and rebound old copies two-by-two, shipping them out to slow train territory as *Clever Stories*, a bi-monthly. *Clever Stories* was an immediate hit; the first number netted nearly twelve hundred dollars, and before long advertising contracts for six, eight, and even twelve months were coming in. In six months advertising jumped 33 per cent, circulation was up twenty thousand, and by April 1, 1915, Mencken was writing Dreiser, "I begin to believe we'll put it over. But what a sweat!"

On the editorial side the sweat was real enough. It rolled from the brows of Mencken and Nathan throughout the historic autumn of 1914 and on into the winter and spring.

Under the new arrangement they matched drop for drop. It was a unique editorial method which permitted Mencken to stay in Baltimore, laid responsibility with equal weight on each editor, and was possible only because of their complete compatibility. It worked this way: Nathan, in New York, cast his eye over manuscripts as they came in, rejecting those which were written in colored ink, or scented, or began with soliloquies into a telephone, or, for some reason, offended his aesthetic sensibilities. The rest were expressed, twice a week, to Hollins Street, where Mencken read them the evening of arrival. Those he disliked were returned to the authors in the morning mail; those he approved were expressed back to Nathan with "Yes" scrawled across them. If Nathan agreed, they were purchased at once; if he disagreed, back they went to the authors and that was the end of it. Two ayes were needed to get a given piece in; one nay threw it out. It was as simple as that. There were no story conferences, no arguments, no doubtful manuscripts. A veto from either editor meant the death of an article. The system had two further advantages. If the author were a friend of Mencken's, it went back with the explanation that Nathan, who was a dreadful boor, had thrown it out; if he were a fellow alumnus of Nathan's, Mencken, who hated college men, had said no. In the case of mutual friends, they had a stock explanation: Nathan had opened the office safe and lo! a whole raft of manuscripts on the subject, purchased by Boyer—dead, poor fellow—had been found hiding in a corner. And if a story were lost they could truthfully say that no record of having received the manuscript could be found, since none was kept.

They guarded their meager funds as a nun guards her chastity, and for the same reason: loss meant ruin. The one hundred dollars a month they had been receiving for their critical articles still came, but the fifty dollars a week they theoretically got for their editing often remained *non est*, and even Mencken's expenses for his now more frequent trips to New York came out of his own baggy pocket. Salaries were to be taken, they had agreed, when the money was in the drawer, and during that first year the drawer was always empty. Authors were paid fifty dollars for a short story, sometimes less. The editors had calculated, and, as it turned out, rightly, that the sort of material they were after could not be printed elsewhere, and that the authors, long without a market, would be glad enough of the prestige of appearing with others of their kind. To counterbalance poor pay, they decided to be always extremely polite to contributors, to accept or reject their contributions promptly, and to ask as few rights as possible. In a business where, normally, the author is expected to know everything and the editor nothing, they set a precedent in courtesy and helpfulness. A pamphlet for contributors was printed, with do's and don'ts carefully listed. Stories about authors, newspaper reporters, and spies; epigrams embodying puns; plays about death or the year 2000 A.D. were discouraged. Novelettes, one-act plays, prose poems —"in brief, anything that is novel and that the other magazines are not printing"—were encouraged. They wrote as much of the magazine as possible themselves, under pseudonyms—Mencken's favorite was the Duchess de Boileau—or under their own names, in pointless but characteristically clever conversations between the editors. Every friend, every contact was ruthlessly exploited: their first issue was largely given over to a novelette by a Philadelphia protégé of George M. Cohan, and later Nathan persuaded Cohan himself to write a one-act play, in which all the characters were detectives. The climax, which was Cohan's touch, brought all the detectives on stage waving American flags.

The chief solicitor of manuscripts, however, was Mencken. In this, as he wrote Ellery Sedgwick, he was "helped by the fact that my book articles for six years have put me on good terms with the very authors—e.g. Dreiser—that we want to cultivate." Like a salesman opening his own shop, he alerted his former clients that Hollins Street was ready for business and a gracious hand would be extended one and all. "You are constantly coming in contact with aspiring authors," he wrote Dreiser. "Why not spread the following whisper: that I'll be glad to see the manuscripts of any ambitious new one, buck or wench, and to give them my prompt and personal attention? This may develop something and so help both the magazine and the authors." Nor was he above making overtures to other magazine editors. "Our policy, I needn't say, is to be lively without being nasty. On the one hand no smut, and on the other, nothing uplifting. A magazine for civilized adults in their lighter moods. A sort of frivolous sister to the Atlantic. . . . If you see anything that we might use and you can't I'll be grateful for the tip. And maybe I can repay it in kind."

For all his protests that he refused to give letters of criticism, each morning's mail from Hollins Street was choked with long critiques to authors with scant hope of making *The Smart Set,* and nothing was too good for an author of talent. When he was in New York, authors departing for Europe were sure to find boxes of Uncle Willies in their staterooms. Authors hospitalized would find a bouncy Mencken in attendance and, after he had gone, a jug of Maryland rye by the bed. Letters were shot out to every corner of the country, asking for novelettes and including, always, a typical Menckenian touch—a pamphlet on modern dress reform, say, urging the correspondent to see II Cor. 13:5 for the evils of immodest dress, or a circular from the Anti-Tobacco League, with the plea "Fight the cigarette. It is subversive. The battle against it is the battle for civilization." Meeting an author by chance on Broadway, he became a combination greeter, door knob salesman, and smiling Lothario. "The other day, in New York, I met Ed Howe, the Kansas sage. . . . You should have heard the exchange of compliments when we met—gigantic explosions of tallow bombs, oleomargarine grenades and neats foot oil shells. Two master greasers."

There was literally nothing, up to and including the imperiling of his precious chastity, that he would not risk for a good manuscript. One day a magnificent novelette, written on blue, lined paper, reached Nathan from Sheepshead Bay. Nathan sent it along, covered with exclamation marks, and Mencken, concurring in his judgment, decided to find out more about the author. She turned out to be the beautiful daughter of a gambling tycoon. Despite protestations from both Mencken and Nathan that she had genius, the girl announced that she didn't want to write: all she wanted was love. Nathan assigned Mencken to woo her, and Mencken, in this unique project, was for a time successful. In the end, however, he failed. After he had cuddled and murmured four more stories out of her, she ran away with an impoverished shoe salesman and was heard from no more. Such pleasantries tended to tighten relations between editors. "My assignment to make love to lady novelette writers in order to get decent novelettes for the magazine is proving altogether too strenuous," Mencken complained.

> Last week, as you know, I took out three different literary wenches, bought and drank at least $50 worth of alcoholic liquor, made enough love to inflame at least two dozen Marie Corellis, didn't get home until dawn, and what will we get? Not a damned thing worth printing! And my health is gone! It's your turn, my boy!

To which Nathan acidly replied, "You are drinking too much. This means more work again for me."

From the very first, this new editorial attitude brought results. For six years the thin ranks of American realists had looked to *The Smart Set* for work of their fellows. Once they had learned of Mencken's new position and his eagerness to be hospitable, they flooded the office with manuscripts. Cabell appeared in *The Smart Set* for the first time as playwright, and at Mencken's suggestion he submitted the story "Some Ladies and Jurgen," the germ of his later novel. Lord Dunsany, after a wild, riotous night in New York with Mencken and Nathan, gave them his one-act paraphrase of *Faust*. They brought out Thomas Beer, Eugene O'Neill, and Sherwood Anderson. Ernest Boyd, then British consul to Baltimore, pressed upon Mencken tales of Dublin life a friend had sent him, and Joyce, who had been forgotten after his brief appearance under Wright, became a fixture in *The Smart Set* and so founded his American vogue. Through his swelling correspondence, Mencken became the close friend and adviser of authors he had never seen and, in some cases, never was to see. Writers of stamina were persuaded to turn out better than a story a month, thus joining the Duchess de Boileau. Ben Hecht, then a Chicago police reporter, shipped eastward as many as four pieces each month; he was joined by one of Mencken's prize discoveries—Ruth Suckow, an Earlville,

Iowa, beekeeper whose first timid contribution, "Just Him and Her," had caught his eye.

What most endeared Mencken to his contributors—apart from the unheard-of promptness with which their manuscripts were processed—was that, like them, he was a writer, privy to the same humors which plagued them and thus capable of understanding where understanding, with other editors, had always been lacking. Accustomed to the terse, businesslike letters of Harvey of the *North American Review*, Davis of Munsey Publications, or Towne of *McClure's*, they were delighted to receive personal and amusing letters from an editor who had obviously read and evaluated their work. When Joseph Hergesheimer began his long friendship with Mencken after a *Smart Set* review of *The Lay Anthony* and ventured—impertinently—to protest that no creed had moved him in its writing, he got back what amounted to a second review, concluding,

You are, of course, quite wrong. . . . You got an idea into it whether you wanted to or not, and what is more, it was a good one. You cannot depict humanity without having some idea about it—that is, without viewing it in some specific manner, seeing some specific drama in its actions, setting it in some sort of opposition to an ideal. The baldest description of anything so complex as a man must needs be nine-tenths opinion.

Tacked on was the usual request for a novelette. Each letter was so written as to strike exactly the right mood in the author: for the first time in the memory of anyone, an editor was concerned with the impression he made on his contributors. When, for example, his letter to Hergesheimer on the publication of *Three Black Pennies* seemed too heavy, the charming signature was appended:

HEINRICH V. MENCKEN
Lt. d. Res. a. D.

(Seal)

Subscribed and sworn before me, a notary public in

the Ste. of Md., in the presence of God, SS. Mark, Luther, and Budweiser, and the Hon. the Holy Ghost.
(signed)
Hyman Hartoffelsuppe
My commission expired Jan. 1, 1915

There is no satisfactory substitute for money, however, and for all the conscious effort to be patronizing and charming, *The Smart Set's* limited budget subjected its editors to certain indignities. Frank Harris, solicited for an article on "How I Discovered G.B.S.," sent it along, and an issue was prepared with the author's name and the title gaudily displayed on the cover. Just after the press run, the editors discovered, to their dismay, that their article was appearing in another magazine already on the stands. Asked about it, Harris airily replied that he thought it good enough for two appearances. Max Beerbohm, condescending to send them articles, felt free to scribble "Not one thing to be changed!" across the top of his first pages, and Conrad, despite the great boosting Mencken had given him in this country, felt obliged to send nothing at all. Mencken wrote Conrad, discreetly mentioning the economics of *The Smart Set* and asking that a nominal price be set on contributions. For a long time he heard nothing at all; then a letter arrived from a London literary agent, with the information that a Conrad story was available for six hundred dollars. Mencken shot back the cable, FOR $600 YOU CAN HAVE THE SMART SET.

Because of their low word rate, the imposing list of discoveries made by Mencken and Nathan may be traced to nothing but the taste and sagacity of the editors. They got the unknowns, the disreputable, the unorthodox and unwanted manuscripts after everyone else in New York had had a crack at them. It was to *The Smart Set* that Charles Hanson Towne, acting as agent for Somerset Maugham, came when every other editor, beginning with Ray Long of *Cosmopolitan*, had turned down one of Maugham's lesser efforts—lesser, that is, in the opinion of everyone concerned, including Maugham, save Mencken and Nathan. At that time Maugham was getting from fifteen to twenty-five hundred dollars for everything he sent to this country, and *The Smart Set* had never paid a tenth of that. The editors read the story; their eyes bulged; they eyed one another, and finally consulted the office safe. Two hundred dollars was all they could afford, even with stinting at Luchow's. Towne, convinced he would find no other market, snapped it up, and "Miss Thompson" appeared in a subsequent issue of The Smart Set. Later it appeared on the stage as Rain—after Maugham had refused to dramatize it, or even to attend rehearsals, on the ground it was certain to fail.

Every third week end a stoop-shouldered, bowlegged, rotund little man wearing a long black funeral director's overcoat alighted at Pennsylvania Station and pranced up the stairs. Cab drivers saw a chubby forefinger beckoning them and heard a gravelly voice chirp "hack! hack!" Inside the car, the passenger perched upright in the very center of the rear seat, a size 7½ felt hat squarely on his head and quizzical, innocent blue eyes—so wide they seemed to arch his very forehead—full of unspoken questions to passers-by. At the Algonquin he registered with Mitchell the clerk, had his scarred little bag taken up to the suite that was always his, and then strolled over to The Smart Set editorial office, grimacing at every street scene and passing reflections that would have received the nihil obstat of a rural evangelist preaching against the sin of the city. To Mencken New York was the ugliest of towns, the seat of hideous architecture, grotesque monuments, alien peoples, and swindling shopkeepers. "Totentanz," he called it; "the lurid dance of death." "To find a parallel for the grossness and debauchery that now reign in New York," he told gasping Baltimoreans in the Evening Sun, "one must go back to the Constantinople of Basil I." The city was "shoddily cosmopolitan, secondrate European, extraordinarily cringing"; its spirit, "for all the gaudy pretentiousness of the town" was one of "timidity, of regularity, of safe mediocrity." A brightly painted woman, her skirts swishing rakishly against her calves, passed the dumpy little man, setting his skin bristling against his B.V.D.'s. He whipped out a stubby pencil and a slip of copy paper from his side pocket and made note against a new article on New York: "At no time and place in modern times has harlotry reached so delicate and yet so effusive a development." This done, he had arrived at *The Smart Set*. After a self-conscious glance at his newly creased trousers and a pleasant thought to the frolic coming, he made his way to the rendezvous with Nathan.

Nathan liked having an office, but it cannot be said he did much to deserve it. His prolific work was largely done in the unkempt den at the Royalton, and despite his desk and cable address—NATHGENE—he swore each time an office caller was announced by Miss Golde. When Mencken was in town they put in more time at the office, but it certainly was not spent more profitably. For two hours in the morning, and an hour and a half in the afternoon, they sat at facing desks, each arguing that he was the bigger fool and both, to Miss Golde's way of thinking, succeeding. The office, indeed, was never meant for work. It looked far more like a penny arcade than a place of business. The walls were decorated with colored portraits of Follies girls; by Mencken's desk sat two enormous brass spittoons, brought from Baltimore for his comfort "and nine-tenths of the poetry submitted." But the most imposing property was a large marble slab which Mencken had found in a local cemetery. The sign above identified it as the Poet's Free Lunch; spread along the marble were pretzels, smoked herring, olives, and cheese, for the victualing of the poor devils in Greenwich Village who struggled along on the twenty-five cents a line *The Smart Set* paid. But the victualing could not go too far: in the closet a shotgun of ancient make was hauled out whenever a poet —the chief offender was Harry Kemp—had gone too far, and down the stairs the luncher would go, a swearing and gesticulating Mencken behind him. Warner's Philistine imagination was outraged by this unseemly show, and on his rare visits to the office the slab was covered by a great tapestry with a gilt lion in the center and the spittoons discreetly draped in black cretonne.

In retrospect Miss Golde (they never knew her first name) assumes heroic proportions. She it was who dealt with the creditors, subscribers, and indignant poets when Mencken was in Baltimore and Nathan off on his interminable lunch. What records there were, she kept; what letters there were, she wrote; what crises arose—and on such a magazine they were arising continually—she handled in her own very special way. Telephone calls from censors, clergymen, and other such undesirables were treated according to a set formula: Mr. Nathan was in Hollywood, having turned screen actor, and Mr. Mencken had just sailed for South America to hunt snakes. The formula was infectious. During the grim days when paper mills were calling for their money and authors for their misplaced manuscripts, Nathan often found himself saying Mr. Nathan was in Hollywood, having turned screen actor, and Mencken expressed regret that Mr. Mencken had just sailed for South America to hunt snakes. There were times when Miss Golde, as a mortal, came near losing patience with her posturing young employers, who zealously guarded their dwindling fare on the marble slab one moment and, in the next, talked airily of wanting "the dollar of no man who has degraded himself by earning it." But it is in the record that she never boiled over.

Their idiotic posturing at the office did not mean no work was accomplished when Mencken was in town, however. The tone of the magazine, story rates, and details of the articles they were writing together were all settled during those long week ends—but not at the office. The fate of *The Smart Set* was settled at the Beaux Arts, or Luchow's, or Beneduci's, where a magnificent dinner with wine could be had for eighty cents, or on long Sunday afternoons in Nathan's apartment, with the host at his broad, flat-topped desk and Mencken, certain he had picked up another dreadful disease in this unhealthy hole, perched on the Victorian sofa under the heap of books. And each division was punctuated by a new prank at the expense of their friends. They went to simply extraordinary lengths to bedevil and outrage everyone they knew, and Mencken's visits were looked forward to with fearful anticipation by everyone concerned but Nathan. To Tom Smith, at the *Century*, they dictated letters at ten-minute intervals during the busiest hour of his day, signifying acceptance of dinner invitations never tendered. Harry Kemp, coming for advice on how to get his poems before the public, was told to paint them on the side of the Brevoort Hotel. When Kemp, again, gleefully told them he had found a restaurant owner willing to take his IOU's, they told him he was a fool, that the restaurant was giving him a dollar meal and selling his autograph for two dollars—and sent him off in a rage. And when Frank Crowninshield expressed interest in the work of Owen Hatteras and thought to solicit manuscripts from him, they gave him a fictitious address in France; no answer, of course, followed Crowninshield's letter, and the word was passed that Hatteras was too proud to write other than for *The Smart Set*. Even their colleagues on the magazine were not exempt; when Warner or Crowe objected to this or that feature as unacceptable to *Smart Set* readers, Mencken alerted the chain of correspondents he had built up, and for the next week Warner would be bombarded with letters heaping praise on the feature under fire.

Their favorite goat, however, was Dreiser. Dreiser had become something of a nuisance. His eternal fretting over money forced them to draw up contracts—a major operation in *The Smart Set* office—and even then he was unsatisfied. He began mocking the magazine, writing Mencken that under the new editorship it had become "a light, non-disturbing periodical of persiflage and badinage," given to "gay trifles." Moreover, his manuscripts grew progressively worse. He took to sending them abstract one-act plays of the supernatural, composed by candlelight in the miserable little West Tenth Street apartment he now occupied, with windows covered by red hangings and the same three Russian records playing constantly. In some cases they were so pornographic as to be unacceptable, and whenever they were rejected, Dreiser was furious. He had become a great partisan of Village movements—the very word made Mencken and Nathan shudder—and was forever delivering speeches on behalf of unwed mothers or hanging around Isadora Duncan's studio, his great humorless face agog over some new and perfectly ridiculous cause.

Nevertheless, Mencken still entertained some affection for Dreiser, as a symbol if not as a man, and he and Nathan undertook to lighten the older man's dreary life with the buffooneries at which they had now become expert. They stuffed his mailbox with small American flags, Black Hand threats, hot dogs tied with red, white, and blue ribbons, beer bottle labels, Armenian menus inscribed by Harold Bell Wright, and letters from Woodrow Wilson, urging him to come to Washington for a confidential talk. Dreiser, in his plodding way, tried to follow the lead. The trouble was that he could think of only one countermove—to present his wild-eyed friends with the paper-bound works of Bertha M. Clay. Mencken, tired of reading Dreiser's "poetic meditations," dug deeper. "Why don't you get out of the tenement and dirty undershirt atmosphere for a change?" he told him. "Do us a society story—something swell and tony. Get a butler in it." Dreiser took him seriously. He produced a story with literally dozens of butlers, red velvet settees, and a dialogue which would have set Newport howling. When he found that the editors, reading the piece, were overcome with mirth, he was offended to the point where he refused ever again to believe Mencken or Nathan. Some months later, when they came up with a bona fide proposal—that he pose writing at a desk for a forthcoming motion picture, the honorarium to be two thousand dollars—he declined, convinced it was another gag.

But for all the gaiety of his tri-weekly harlequinade, Mencken could not, or would not, learn to like the town. He remained, as he was known in the Village, a Monthly Hick, who never shook the manners of a shy provincial and spent much of his time eying strangers suspiciously or checking his wallet. He simply could not adapt himself to the hotel life which suited Nathan so admirably. Each night at the Algonquin, as he eased his shapeless body—now up to 195 pounds—into a cold bath, dressed in flashy new striped pajamas, bought for the occasion, and turned in to read himself to sleep, he fervently wished he were at home on his spiffy sleeping porch. He tried: he bought expensively tailored suits and dress clothes in New York, but he could not wear them. He stuck to his baggy blue suit, cleaned his fingernails with a jackknife, and never learned to tie a bow tie. His happiest moments in New York, indeed, were spent shopping for Saturday Night Club scores—full parts for five Haydn symphonies, or four-hand piano parts for the gay waltzes—or, if the season were right, Christmas presents for Charlie Mencken's little daughter Virginia. His Christmas shopping began in November, and much as he protested—"Let the Goyim celebrate their damned Christmas. It costs me $9 or $10 every year for presents to stenographers, salesladies, chambermaids, manicures, fancy women, etc. etc. I almost wish the Yiddish had let the late redeemer go"—it afforded him such pleasure as he had when Nathan was busy with the theater and he was left on his own. When Christmas was far off and the club's music library well stocked, he swiped Gideon Bibles by the score, sending them to his friends in Baltimore elegantly inscribed, "With the regards of the author."

Astonishing as it may seem, his editorial chores, plus his work on the paper, did not exhaust his energies in these years: he had enough left to produce two books. They were not, it is true, completely divorced from his other work; indeed, they were largely made up of excerpts from his "Free Lance" and *Smart Set* articles. With them he began a custom to be followed thenceforth. He would sit down with a pile of his published articles, have at them with a pair of shears and a pot of paste, and with a few weeks of odd labor, presto! He had written a new book. Despite the scissors-and-paste character of *A Book of Burlesques* and *A Little Book in C Major,* however, the cutting and pasting did take time, and it is remarkable that he found time to do them at all. They appeared, under the John Lane imprint, in 1916 and were received with delight by the book reviewers of the country. "Unholy yet innocent cleverness," said the Chicago *Herald* of the *Burlesques;* "the cleverest offering of recent years," commented the Boston *Herald. The Artist* was included in this little volume, together with a dozen others, including his introduction to *Europe after 8:15,* the complaints of a magazine editor, and, naturally enough, a litany for hypochondriacs, including, among his new illnesses, rose cold, dropsy, and dumdum fever. *A Little Book in C Major* was made up of two hundred-odd epigrams from *The Smart Set* ("Love is the delusion that one woman differs from another"; "Pensioner: a kept patriot"), and virtually every newspaper in the nation, with the sour exception of the Springfield, (Massachusetts) *Union,* which was already suspicious of anyone with a

German name, found it scintillating and clever. Both books had a small sale, and Mencken began to look around for a new publisher.

He found him a former office boy for Mitchell Kennerley, a book publisher who specialized in better fiction and who, for his pains, was forced out of business shortly after the war began. Late in 1913 a downy-cheeked youngster named Alfred Knopf had called on Mencken at the *Sun*. He had, he explained, read Mencken's reviews of Conrad and wanted to talk about him. Knopf, who had studied under the rebel Spingarn, seemed a likely fellow, and when Mencken learned he was going into business for himself in June, 1915, he hunted him up. Nothing definite developed at first, for Mencken felt bound to Jefferson Jones at Lane. When 1916 came and his two little books sold poorly, he became restive. He had a big project in mind, a book of essays on American literature, and wasn't at all sure Jones would go for them. Jones didn't. He couldn't. Late in 1916 his company folded, throwing him out of work for two years and leaving without a publisher, among others, Mencken's book and Anderson's *Winesburg, Ohio*. Mencken was anxious that *A Book of Prefaces* go well; the last chapter, born in an *Evening Sun* piece titled "Notes for a Proposed Treatise upon the Origin and Nature of Puritanism," was calculated to deliver a crushing blow at the high command of American letters. With Jones out of the picture, he vacillated between Knopf and Little, Brown. Influenced, finally, by Knopf's book jackets, reminiscent of those of Fischer Verlag, in Vienna, he sent the manuscript to him. But of this, more later.

The Smart Set was now prospering. Mencken and Nathan were drawing cash salaries now and then, and this money, added to his other income, gave Mencken something of a nest egg. He decided to splurge a little of it. A reducing cure had brought him back to normal weight, and he thought he had had just about enough of walking and trolley cars. Accordingly, he bought a four-cylinder open Studebaker with flappy canvas curtains, parked it in front of the house, and rushed upstairs to write Dreiser enthusiastically, "My new jitney bus makes at least 12 miles an hour on level roads. . . ." His pride in it became reflected in all his correspondence:

"Let me know when you set out and my jitney will meet you," he wrote Hergesheimer on an impending visit, or, "When you head this way let me know in advance, so that I may have my car washed and gasoline put in." It was a pride short-lived, and justly so.

He was, by all accounts, the most outrageous driver known to automobile history, not excluding Bernard Shaw. His mother refused to ride with him, and those of his friends who did found their loyalty sorely tested. Four days after he bought it, he called Theodor Hemberger and invited him along for a drive in the country. It was probably the most terrifying experience in that shy, philosophical little German's life; nothing that came later, when America was at war, could compare with it. Once the car was in motion, Mencken seemed to forget he was at the wheel. He talked enthusiastically, turned to face his rider for long periods, ignored the road, waved both arms to illustrate a point, and drove at erratic speeds that had little to do with the shape of the road. In heavy traffic, he would have been killed instantly. Fortunately, there were few other cars, and thus he was free to roll from one side of the road to the other, and sometimes onto nearby fields and in ditches. Moreover, he insisted on loading the car with everyone who would ride with him, despite August's warnings that the four-cylinder Studebaker was a temperamental car and could not be treated cavalierly. He developed what was known as "hind-end trouble"; the jack shaft in the back, constantly overloaded, broke down whenever strain was put on it, necessitating a complete overhauling and rebuilt back. His complete lack of mechanical knowledge was totally unable to cope with this emergency. Repair bills mounted, and the car became the despair of his bankbook.

The climax came one snowbound night late in 1917, when he went to call on Harry Black's wife and her sister. After a pleasant supper and a long evening, he made his farewells, and despite their advice to go *this* way, went *that* way—and buried himself and his automobile in an avalanche of snow. To his humiliation, his hostesses had to bundle up and escort him to the nearest streetcar stop. Shortly after that, he sold the car. He immediately announced loftily that he was "perhaps the first American ever to give up automobiling, formally and honestly," and devised all sorts of elaborate reasons for the sale—that he rebelled against parking regulations, that he got tired of taking guests home after parties, that the unattached man who kept an automobile in an American city was insane, and that Maryland had passed a law forbidding the transportation of working girls by auto for natural purposes. The plain fact—that he had been completely routed in a fair fight with the machine age—was quite ignored.

At the *Evening Sun,* Mencken was on the ropes. From the very beginning of the war, he had been outspokenly pro-German, both privately and publicly—not, as the myth of the Twenties had it, a mocker of war and patriotic sentiment. His support of Germany was marked by the emotionalism of a patriot, combined with an affected Prussian coldness in the Nietzschean tradition. "The old aristocracy of birth and vested rights has given place to a new aristocracy of genuine skill, and Germany has become a true democracy in the Greek sense," he wrote Sedgwick.

That is to say, the old nobility has taken a back seat and . . . is now governed by an oligarchy of its best men. And with this new cult of efficiency has come a truly Nietzschean disdain for all merely theoretical "rights."

Scarcely a letter passed without some panegyric to the Kaiser. His closest correspondents were Untermeyer and Dreiser—Germans like himself—and each note ended with "May all Englishmen roast forever in hell! A pox upon the English!" "The Kaiser must and shall win!" or "Hoch der Kaiser! Hoch von Hindenberg! Dreimal hoch!" As early as October 13, 1914, when Mencken had suggested doing a piece on Europe, Sedgwick answered, "A paper from you on the war, and there would not be one stone of the *Atlantic* left upon another. . . ." Mencken knew the war was cutting him back steadily. His book on *The American,* which had grown out of the pieces written for Wright, had been killed, and he had withdrawn a piece on Nietzsche from the *Atlantic* after the *Lusitania* went down because, "I do not want to appear a spokesman for Germany, for I am an American by birth and the son of native-born Americans."

But in the *Evening Sun* he was a spokesman for Germany, and an arrogant and offensive spokesman at that. "The Free Lance," which he may have thought could never be taken away from him, became little more than a pro-German tract and a study in the bad guesses of an amateur war strategist. Each week he predicted afresh the coming victory of the Germans, laughed merrily over the "pious, beery slobbering over Belgium," and ended each column with the cry "In Paris by Thanksgiving!" or "In Paris by Christmas!" The arrogance of Germans, he told his readers, was the natural result of a conquering nature. They were proud—proud because they *were* Germans, proud because they were living up to the German ideal. They were, to believe Mencken, constantly defeating their enemies with smaller arms. The English—sniveling, running to the Pope to stop a war which they were losing—the English, who had perpetrated the outrageous Waterloo and Crimean myths, would lose, for all their vaunted sea power. And once the Germans had won, let every sniveling Englishman beware! Wilson became anathema. He was denounced as an Anglomaniac who offered America an "ethical sugar-teat" and at whose urging America was rushing hysterically into preparations for war. "We laid out money on the wrong horse; there was wretched guessing in august quarters. Let boobs rejoice! Hurrah, hurrah! Our foreign commerce has been sacrificed to make the arms manufacturers rich. Now the taxpayer will be sweated to make them rich a second time!"

Baltimore had learned to take much from "The Free Lance," but this it could not take. Nor could the *Sun,* which had become a powerful administration organ since its successful support of Wilson's candidacy in Baltimore. Mencken had become embarrassing to the paper. What could be done with him? No one knew. He had become a fixture in the editorial offices, the most brilliant and most active of its writing men. More, his *Smart Set* work and his books had not been lost on his Baltimore colleagues; he was a man to be proud of, the sort of newspaperman of which a paper likes to boast. But . . . "pious, beery slobbering over Belgium!" Wilson offering an "ethical sugar-teat"! "In Paris by Christmas" indeed!

Abruptly, without explanation, "The Free Lance" ended on October 23, 1915. Two days later he was set to work writing "on various subjects" under two-column heads on the editorial page. But to the disconcertion of everyone at the office, he refused to be shut off, and if the variety of subject matter in the new department differed from that in "The Free Lance," no one could perceive it. If possible, he grew more violent. Wilson was hauled to the rack daily; the "slobbering ethic" and "childish faith" of "mobs, majorities, and messiahs" was ridiculed, and the very saboteurs now hard at work blowing up arms factories were defended as "simply gentlemen who try to do what they may, even at the risk of their own hides, to reduce the heavy odds of their brothers overseas." He affected a maddening arrogance toward "the professional Anglo-Saxons" with their "pious shibboleths and their tarletan truculence" and extended an even more maddening pity to their unprofessional constituent, now the joke of the world. ("Who could hate him in his last hour of agony?") He had become, as he boldly described himself, a "volunteer attorney for *kultur*."

The gang of Wilson cheerleaders who had succeeded Grasty at the *Sun* were at their wits' end. Useless it was to argue with Mencken; his ruthless and rigid mind was set and he would not, no he *would not* change it. The vision of Sophie, with her laughing eyes, and the corseted Bavarian lieutenants of Munich before him, he did what he could for the fatherland. The editors tried to lead him down other paths. Thinking to explore the pedagogy deep in the Mencken blood, they set him to work on a new style sheet for the paper, but he would have none of it. He tried half heartedly to reach an agreement among the news editors and, encountering resistance, reported failure. The style sheet was abandoned. A month's leave of absence failed similarly, and he was assigned to cover a week's performance of Billy Sunday, when that phenomenon floated into Baltimore for six colossal nights in April, 1916. For a week this worked splendidly; Mencken grew excited over the approach of "the eminent amateur Jesus,"[1] and wrote glowingly of the "gladiatorial shows of the Rev. Dr. Billy Sunday, the celebrated American pulpit-clown" and of "Men of all ages in enormous numbers . . . swarming to the altar; loudly bawling for help against their sins," but the diversion was temporary. Next week he was back punching lustily at Wilson and the English and sounding his brassy *hochs!* for the Kaiser.

In the end, it was Mencken's sound common sense—the hallmark of a German middle-class spirit—that solved the problem. As 1916 progressed and America's entry into the war appeared certain, he retired from the scene. His thunderings echoed more and more distantly on the horizon and eventually were heard no more. Privately he remained unreconciled, but his opinions, for the first time since his debut in "The Free Lance," were kept among friends and family and not aired before all Baltimore. Yet, for all his pious resolutions, he could not stay out of controversy; it stuck to him as Heywood Broun's undershirt stuck to Broun and, like that venerable garment, was with its creator for life. It was as if a malicious, but not unaffectionate, star hovered over him and directed his most innocent labors to the battlefield, whether he willed it or not. Certainly controversy was farthest from his mind in those unseasonably warm days when he struggled, among the welter of books and *Smart Set* contributions in his cluttered study, over the manuscript of Dreiser's latest book, hacking out great sections to give it form. And yet, though neither Mencken nor Dreiser were aware of it, controversy never loomed more certainly.

The "Genius," when published, received indifferent reviews. It seemed likely to pass on to the expanding graveyard of Dreiseriana when, early in July of 1916, the minister of the Ninth Baptist Church in Cincinnati was roused by an anonymous caller who objected to certain parts of the book. The minister hung up, bought a copy the next day, and read the cited passages. Events moved swiftly; the Western Society for the Prevention of Vice was notified, seventy-five pages

---

[1] A reporter asked Sunday what he thought of Mencken. Sunday answered, "Mencken? Mencken? I never heard of him, but he's some cheap jack trying to get a reputation out of attacking me."

were labeled as "lewd" and seventeen "profane," and *The "Genius"* was removed from Cincinnati bookstores. Simultaneously, John S. Sumner, executive secretary of the New York Society for the Suppression of Vice and a consistent target of *The Smart Set*, received in the mail a number of pages from the book torn from a library copy by an indignant citizen. Sumner read them, went to Jefferson Jones, and threatened court action unless the book were withdrawn.

Dreiser rushed off in all directions at once. Since the suppression of *Sister Carrie,* he had feared just this sort of thing, and he had long eyed the New York comstocks—who had banned, among other books, Horace's *Odes, The Wandering Jew,* and *The Three Musketeers*—with trepidation. His already meager income was threatened, and he began issuing statements to the papers, attacking the "band of wasp-like censors," and demanding that Lane—whose American branch was in shaky condition—take action. He was, he wrote Mencken, willing to go to jail; "It will save me living expenses." The comstocks everywhere took up the challenge, and in San Francisco a Catholic priest candidly explained their position when he told the United Press that unless he misunderstood the American public, "it will guard the morals of the people even at the sacrifice of the liberty of the individual. In other words, we do believe in censorship."

Mencken advised caution; the war was approaching, and overt action by Dreiser might fan nationally the anti-German sentiment he saw growing in Baltimore. His own soft-pedaling in the *Evening Sun* had begun, and when Jones suggested compromise, Mencken advised Dreiser to tag along. But Dreiser intended to do no such thing. The most exculpable characteristic of the man—he was, as Mencken noted, "solid, granitic, without nerves"—had been aroused, and he refused to yield an inch. He had, as he was fond of pointing out, nothing to lose by defiance. Besides, this was a cause, and Dreiser loved causes. Mencken felt he had a moral obligation to Dreiser, as editor and adviser, and when it became clear that the author would not backtrack, he allowed that some sort of resistance might scare Sumner. Just what form the resistance might take was not at first clear; Lane was the publisher, and Jones, as his agent, obviously intended to sit tight. Copies in his stockroom were left there, and bookstores which had not yet sold theirs were asked to return what they had to New York. Somewhat reluctantly, he did agree to go with Mencken and Dreiser along the one avenue of counterattack left open: a public protest.

On August 9, 1916, Mencken swung into action, writing the Author's League of America to ask if it would join in a defense of Dreiser. The League agreed, and by August 24, Mencken and John Cowper Powys had drafted protests for writers and artists to sign. Jones wrote London for support from English authors. Pamphlets supporting Dreiser were circulated, Wright debated the issue publicly with Sumner in New York, and Ezra Pound threw the support of his *Egoist* against the comstocks. Harold Hersey, a Dreiser admirer, did the heavy work while Mencken wrote the more conservative and famous authors and persuaded Dreiser to keep the names of his "tenth-rate Greenwich Village geniuses" off the list, lest they alienate those he was most anxious to enlist. His pleas were confined to the basic controversy. He wrote the conservative literary figures

Perhaps you believe, as I do, that "The 'Genius' " is anything but a great novel. But here we have a battle that involves an issue far greater than the merits or fate of "The 'Genius' ", and that is, the issue of freedom in letters. I know Dreiser to be an honest man, and I think he deserves to be let alone. His case is the case of all of us. We should at least support him as firmly as the authors of France supported Zola.

There were some who refused to sign—William Lyon Phelps, William Dean Howells, Brander Matthews, and Hamlin Garland—but the final list was imposing. Knopf, Nathan, William Rose Benét, Robert Frost, Edwin Arlington Robinson, Willa Cather, William Allen White, and James Montgomery Flagg were among the hundreds who signed in America, and in England they were joined by Arnold Bennett, Hugh Walpole, and H. G. Wells. When the Dreiser protest, as it came to be known, was all drawn up, the immediate objective was as far away as ever: Sumner not only refused to back down;

he actually stiffened in his straight lace. "We need," he wrote, "to uphold our standards of decency more than ever before in the face of this foreign and imitation foreign invasion." But the immediate objective, so important at the start, had been all but lost along the way. In its place had come a purpose far more telling, and one which, in the end, was realized: to make the acceptance or rejection of Dreiser the yardstick by which a given literary figure was judged. The protest, despite its ostensible failure in 1916, served to draw together more tightly the advocates of the new spirit in American letters and to establish Dreiser as chief artist and Mencken as high priest of the awakening. The "Genius" battle became the flag to which these forces rallied, and the most formidable aspect of the case was probably its interminability. Throughout the war, Dreiser pressed Lane to release the book and finally, in the spring of 1918, his case was thrown out of court. All other attempts to get the copies out of the stockrooms ended in frustration until, in 1923, Liveright reissued it to a well-primed public. By that time Jones, the Cincinnati origin of the suppression, and even the protest itself had been forgotten. Mencken and Dreiser had grown apart, partly because of Dreiser's forlorn attitude—noting that he took to the ouija board when things went downhill, Mencken began to suspect "that the old boy secretly hopes for a verdict against him, that he may wrap himself in the bed-tick and play the martyr"—and all that remained were the two symbols: Dreiser, the persecuted artist, and Mencken, his intrepid champion.

Mencken wound up the Dreiser protest November 30, 1916, and set to work packing his bags the following day. At the paper he had become more and more disgruntled. "Conditions at the office, in truth, are so unpleasant that I seldom go there myself," he wrote Wright on November 14. Cognizant of this, and still undecided what to do with its *enfant terrible*, the *Sun* tried a new tack: Mencken would go to Germany as a war correspondent. This delighted him. Since Wilson's hairbreadth victory earlier in the month, he had been in a terrible state of mind over the war; a little action, a close view of the war itself, would be welcome change from the impossible situation which had developed for him at home. Even *The Smart Set* contributors were now touched by war fever. "I get at least 50 war poems a day from the hog-meat and hominy belts," he wrote Untermeyer,

> Worse, in every one of them the Kaiser is called a——! Well, maybe he is, but I am for him all the same. Once he has Europe by the neck, insurance on the hides of all you Socialists will go up by 50 guineas per cent. But what a day for us arrogant, sniffish, malty Dutch Junkers! As for me, I am going to revive my ven, and have a couple of scars cut across my right cheek—or is it left?

He sailed for Denmark on December 28, 1916, with high hopes of getting into Germany "in time to see the English cross the Rhine." His trip over was smooth, if quite cold. He was, as always, the first passenger to the rail whenever land was sighted, his baby-blue eyes arched with wonder at the sight of the little town of Kirkwall, in the Orkney Islands, "in a mid-Winter mist, flat and charming like a Japanese print," or Christiania, with the snow-clad statue of Ibsen "looming through the gloom like a ghost in a cellar." New Year's Eve was spent five hundred miles off the coast of Greenland, and on January 14 he landed in Christiania, there to hang around while his papers were cleared for the Reich. Christiania he thought an awful dump; the sun rose at 9:30 and set at 3, and the over-all effect, to Mencken, was about as inspiring as "a Pennsylvania railroad town in the dead of winter." He visited Copenhagen briefly, liked it somewhat better, and was there when word arrived that Germany was open to him.

In Berlin he shook hands all around and was immediately bundled off—a sweatered and overcoated roly-poly figure, all eyes—to the Riga-Dvinsk sector on the eastern front. He was enchanted by the countryside—the charming lakes, beautiful forests, and lovely little towns of Estonia. Near Vilna, he joined General Eichhorn's army and was shuttled up to the front lines. It was bitterly cold; the action was indifferent, and everywhere was the dreamy unreality of a sleeping war. The Germans had constructed elaborate front-line trenches on a series of hills that approached no man's land, and in one of the most elaborately furnished of these Mencken—who was not unknown to his hosts—was quartered. For three weeks he lived the lordly life of a V.I.P. at the front, chatting amiably with the Junkers and running out of his snug hillside home occasionally at night to see the signal lights flaring out gracefully over the Russian lines. The Russians were there, as he discovered unhappily by inadvertently sticking up his head during the daytime, but they surely were not troublesome. In the front trenches, German privates peered across the waste between armies through perforated steel plates; when they noted undue activity across the way, rockets were sent up and minor artillery duels followed. On one occasion he saw a man with a severe lung wound carried to the rear, but what impressed him most was that in 40-degree-below-zero cold, German soldiers should walk around with their heads and ears uncovered. "Don't they," asked a muffled voice from behind five scarves, "catch cold?"

Between excursions to the front he bunked in the charming little town of Novo Aleksandrowsk, a few kilometers behind the lines. He was, indeed, far more impressed with the multitudinous business of supplying the army—"the endless hauling and building, the setting up of saw mills, slaughterhouses and other supply stations, the extraordinarily complex and yet extraordinarily efficient system of getting up men and munitions"—than with such fighting as he saw. In the town's *Offiziere Heim,* he slept on straw pillows under army blankets, ate boiled eggs and sausage, and made his rear echelon headquarters. From there he adventured out to inspect the town. Lovely little Lake Ossa, he discovered with a shudder, was frozen to a thickness of three or four feet, but on its shores the German army had set up steam baths, and in one of these, each time he returned from the front, a naked Mencken pranced and whooped while his clothes were disinfected by live steam. From the steam bath—necessarily his first stop— he wandered into the little schoolhouse where the commanding officer had established compulsory education, there to note the resemblance to Knapp's Institute—"the same long wooden benches, the same illustrated charts on the walls, the same blackboards, the same elevated platforms for the teachers. Even the pictures on the charts were the same—birds with their names, geometrical figures, all that sort of thing."

On his last evening in town, he was feted in the officer's casino, a large, one-story building, once the home of some Novo Aleksandrowsk dignitary. The musicians—a pianist and a violinist—were anxious to play something in his honor, but they didn't know "The Star-Spangled Banner." They compromised on "The Stars and Stripes Forever" and some rather brassy cakewalks. Next morning, clutching a certificate testifying that he was free of smallpox and cholera, he was shipped back to the west.

On January 21 he arrived in Berlin, and there began a series of incidents so bizarre that he himself, returning to America, could find no details upon which to elaborate. America and Germany had broken off diplomatic relations, Ambassador Gerard and his staff were packing their bags, and, interestingly enough, the cooling-off period required of correspondents just back from the front had been stretched from two to eight weeks by the all-powerful Ludendorff. This meant Mencken, fresh from the lines, would probably be interned for the duration. Brooding over his situation with a dozen other war correspondents at the Hotel Adlon bar, he decided to make representations to the powers. The Germans he found agreeable enough, but the food situation was terrible, and his stomach was rebelling against a diet of watered Martinis. He strolled over to the Military Bureau and there approached a clerk. "Waive the rule," he demanded.

"Impossible," came the indignant reply.

"Why impossible?" asked Mencken.

"The rule," came the impressive reply, "was made by Excellenz Ludendorff himself!"

Or, as Mencken later wrote it in *The Atlantic Monthly*, "'The rule' (pianissimo)—was made by (crescendo)—'Excellenz Ludendorff' (forte)—'Himself'—(fortissimo, subito, sforzando)."

Here was a situation which called for the most astute lobbying. He again made representations, this time to members of the Reichstag, and his fellow correspondents at the Hotel Adlon bar were sent hustling. Somewhere a magic string was pulled, and a few days later Mencken was hauled out of bed and ordered to the Military Bureau. Shivering, breakfastless, and frostbitten, he hurried to the appointed place—

"and behind the door I heard the Awful Name again. Excellenz had stooped from his Arctic alp. I was free to go or stay; more, I was a marked and favored man. All the way to Zurich I paid no fare."

He departed Berlin two hours after the official American party and arrived in Paris via Berne. There he found Gerard in a blue funk. Because of the U-boat danger, all sailings from North European ports had been canceled. The only avenue left was Spain. Gerard and the other correspondents sent wires to Madrid, but the French censors held them up, leaving the uneasy official American party in a beleaguered French capital. Leaving them—but not Mencken. Quietly in the night he slipped away from his hotel and entrained to Madrid, setting up headquarters in the Palace Hotel and looking around for Ernest Boyd, who had last reported from Spain and who, if he could be found, would surely know how to get passage on a Spanish liner. Boyd could not be located. He left him a note ("Once we meet again, and my glottis is oiled by appropriate malt, there will be a tale to tell to curl your eyebrows. In eight weeks I have lived 10 or 20 years") and cast around on his own hook. The American embassy proved helpful. He secured passage on the Spanish liner *Corunna,* due to sail in five days; lolled around the Palace Hotel for a week, reading of the revolution in Cuba; cabled the *Sun* of his arrangements, and sailed on schedule, beating Gerard and the other correspondents out of Europe by a week.

Aboard ship, he set to work on his notes and had rapped out fifty thousand words when a wireless arrived from Baltimore, directing him to stop in Havana and cover the uprising there. Heavy censorship, it seemed, had thus far made the truth about the revolution impossible, and the New York *World,* as well as the *Sun,* was eagerly awaiting Mencken's report. As it happened, he was again in luck. Captain Asmus Leonhard of the Munson line, a Baltimore friend, was in Havana; Mencken wired him from aboard ship, and he replied immediately, with instructions to look for his launch at disembarkation. Leonhard knew the bigwigs of the government and, just to make the whole thing incredible, in a nearby stateroom a contact with the revolutionary leaders popped up——Dr. Hermann M. Biggs, former Health Commissioner of New York, who was returning from a study of tuberculosis in the French Army.

The assignment was thus virtually completed before he ever arrived in Havana. The revolution was typical Latin comic opera; without exercising himself overmuch, he followed Leonhard to the official headquarters and Biggs to the pretenders' hotel and evaded censorship with the help of Key West-bound ferry passengers. Within a week the rebels were crushed and Mencken took the Key West ferry back to an America on the brink of war. The holiday was over.

America declared war on Germany April 6, 1917. Six months later Stuart P. Sherman declared war on H. L. Mencken.

The occasion was a review of Mencken's newly published *A Book of Prefaces,* but the attack itself was not occasional. It had been building up since his debut in *The Smart Set,* and when it came at last it took a form so vindictive, so cruel, so coldly malicious that his friends suspected Sherman's sanity and no one ever again doubted the breadth of the schism which had split American letters. Professor Sherman represented a different philosophical school than Mencken, but there was nothing philosophical in "Beautifying American Literature." It was, indeed, a savage and deliberate onset through the back door of ancestry, calculated to wipe out an ideological enemy through the promotion of wartime prejudice. Mencken, avoiding muckers as enemies, had been sought out by a prime blackguard. Thus his lethal attack:

Mr. Mencken is not at all satisfied with life or literature in America, for he is a lover of the beautiful. We have nowadays no beautiful literature in this country with the possible exception of Mr. Dreiser's novels; nor do we seem in a fair way to produce anything esthetically gratifying. Probably the root of our difficulty is that, with the exception of Mr. Huneker, Otto Heller, Ludwig Lewisohn, Mr. Untermeyer, G. S. Viereck, the author of "Der Kampf um deutsche Kultur in Amerika," and a few other choice souls, we have no critics who, understanding what beauty is, serenely and purely love it. Devoid of esthetic sense, our native Anglo-Saxon historians cannot even guess what ails our native literature. For a competent historical account of our national anesthesia one should turn, Mr. Mencken assures us, to a translation from some foreign tongue—we cannot guess which—by Dr. Leon Kellner. Though a lover of the beautiful, Mr. Mencken is not a German. He was born in Baltimore September 12, 1880. That fact should silence the silly people who have suggested that he and Dreiser are the secret agents of the Wilhelmstrasse, "told off to inject subtle doses of *Kultur* into a naif and pious people." Further, Mr. Mencken is, with George Jean Nathan, editor of that staunchly American receptacle for *belles-lettres,* "The Smart Set."

He is a member of the Germania Männerchor, and he manages to work the names of most of the German musicians into his first three discourses. His favorite philosopher happens to be Nietzsche, whose beauties he has expounded in two books—first the "philosophy," then the "gist" of it. He perhaps a little flauntingly dangles before us the seductive names of Wedekind, Schnitzler, Bierbaum, Schoenberg and Korngold. He exhibits a certain Teutonic gusto in tracing the "Pilsner motive" through the work of Mr. Huneker. His publisher is indeed Mr. Knopf. But Mr. Knopf disarms anti-German prejudices by informing us that Mr. Mencken is of "mixed blood—Saxon, Bavarian, Hessian, Irish and English"; or, as Mr. Mencken puts it, with his unfailing good taste, he is a "mongrel." One cannot therefore understand exactly why Mr. Knopf finds it necessary to announce that Mr. Mencken "was in Berlin when relations between Germany and the United States were broken off," nor why he adds: "Since then he has done no newspaper work, save a few occasional articles." Surely there can have been no external interference with Mr. Mencken's purely esthetic ministry to the American people. . . .

"Presently," Sherman concluded, "one begins to suspect that his quarrel with American criticism is not so much in behalf of beauty as in behalf of a *Kultur* which has been too inhospitably received by such of his fellow citizens as look to another *Stammvater* than his."

The essay was reprinted in the New York *Tribune* under the headline WHAT H. L. MENCKEN'S "KULTUR" IS DOING TO AMERICAN LITERATURE, but its significance lies in its first appearance in *The Nation,* then edited by Paul Elmer More. More was one of the twin chieftains of reaction for whom Sherman fronted in the *Prefaces* review and in his equally deadly attack on Dreiser in *On Contemporary Literature.* The other was Professor Irving Babbitt of Harvard, whose impact on Sherman, then a young graduate student, had in 1904 paved the way to the war-within-a-war of 1917. Between them, More and Babbitt represented a spirit that was medieval, a mysticism that was fascistic, and a theory of letters in violent reaction to everything Mencken and the tender band of writers he was nursing held basic.

More and Babbitt had first met at Harvard in 1892, when they constituted Professor Charles R. Lanman's class in Sanskrit for a semester, and since that time they had formulated and propagandized, through parallel series of books, a philosophy based on More's theory that all life existed in two realms, of pure grace and evil, and that to all evil the Humanist, as they called their chance disciple, must answer an uncompromising No. Useless it was to argue for victims of cruelty and injustice; the Humanist who failed, by his creed, to exercise his "inner check" was blaming society, not the victim's absence of grace, and was thus weakening that victim's chance of recognizing his own responsibility for his fate. It was this rigid Calvinism which led Babbitt to scorn the starving prostitute as a bastard of Rousseau and produced More's defense of the Colorado strikebreakers in 1914 on the ground that property rights, to the civilized man, are more important than the right to life.

They had actively entered the critical arena shortly after Mencken's meeting with Nathan in 1908, and their target, curiously enough, had been the same popular novelists who were anathema to him. Their attack on the old-maidishness of current fiction had just begun, however, when the powerful surge of realism forced them into a protective alliance with the old maids who were, after all, far less dangerous than what Babbitt called "art without selection." Even more alarming was the spread of the realistic revolt to the colleges. In 1910 Professor Spingarn of Columbia, a disciple of

Benedetto Croce, delivered his epic lecture "The New Criticism," defending the right of the artist to create a work governed only by its own laws. The alliance of the Menckens and the Spingarns was too much; the Babbitts and the Mores were rapidly put to flight. Suddenly, as Mencken noted, "the old houses of cards came tumbling down, and the professors inhabiting them ran about in their nightshirts, bawling for the police." But the bawling, as befitted professors, was discreet until the war, despite Van Wyck Brooks' hostile comments of 1915. Then Sherman, restive at the University of Illinois, saw his chance to knife the two chief bugbears of the new literature and went after Mencken and Dreiser with a calculated vengeance.

The object of his attack was a somberly bound little book containing four essays, on Conrad, Dreiser, Huneker, and "Puritanism as a Literary Force." The most powerful, most revolutionary, and, to Sherman, most offensive was the last. The basic trouble with American culture, Mencken wrote, was the Calvinistic obsession of a hypocritical people who were, in everything smacking of sex, "God-crazy." Because of this, "the only domestic art this huge and opulent empire knows is in the hands of Mexican greasers; its only native music it owes to the despised Negro; its only genuine poet was permitted to die up an alley like a stray dog." He scorned all "sane," "clean," "inspiring," and "glad" books, wrote that Twain's nationality "hung around his neck like a millstone," laid Richard Harding Davis, with his 'ideals of a floor-walker," Gene Stratton Porter, with her "snuffy sentimentality," and Robert W. Chambers with his " 'society' romances for shop girls" squarely at the door of comstockery, and concluded that no other country presented "so wholesale and ecstatic a sacrifice of aesthetic ideas, of all the fine gusto of passion and beauty, to notions of what is meet, proper and nice." Conrad, he declared, could never have written in America under the "huggermugger morality of timorous, whining, unintelligent and unimaginative men," and he singled out, interestingly enough, one Stuart P. Sherman, because of Sherman's attack on Dreiser, as the "archetype of the booming, indignant corrupter of criteria, the moralist turned critic."

The national press picked up *The Nation* hymn, and presently Mencken found himself everywhere denounced as an enemy alien seeking to undermine Sherman's dictum that "Beauty has a heart of service." The Springfield *Republican* wrote bitterly of "an American critic of alien race," the New York *Evening Post* paraphrased Sherman's sarcasm, and even the *Sun* printed an absurd and meaningless notice. The *Prefaces*, despite its several score reviews, received only three favorable notices and one was from the Socialist New York *Call*, itself suspected of treason. The other two were in the loyal Boston *Transcript* and Burton Rascoe's book page on the Chicago *Tribune*. In the light of what later happened, Rascoe's piece is significant. It was by far the most forceful of the three; it appeared, under the three-column etched head "Fanfare," at a time when to speak out as it did was dangerous; it was the first indication that Mencken's work had penetrated beyond the Atlantic coast. Rascoe reviewed the whole range of Mencken's work to date, stuck himself far out on the limb in echoing the book's sentiments, and wrote of "a bellicose extravagance, arising to meet a peculiarly American need." The rare character of the review was reflected in a touching letter of thanks from Mencken; "As George Cohan says, I thank you; my family thanks you; my valet, Rudolph, thanks you; my Bierbruder, George Nathan, thanks you; my pastor thanks you; my brother, Wolfgang, thanks you; my chauffeur, Etienne, thanks you; my secretary, Miss Goldberg, thanks you; my accompanist, Signor Sforzando, thanks you."

Rascoe followed his review with a terrific blast at Sherman, but he was, after all, but one man, little read beyond Chicago. Sherman, not content with his first piece, wrote "The Lotus Eaters," which was, if anything, more vicious than the *Prefaces* review. Mencken was in a corner, and he knew it. "Once the war is over," he wrote Rascoe, "it will be possible to tackle the Puritans head on, but as things stand they can simply wrap the Grand Old Flag around them, and the game is called. I do not offer mere thanks, but I shall not forget." His own view of his position was characteristically dispassionate; he was, as Sherman had labeled him, a pro-German, and the patriots had a right to defend their own country. What chiefly roused him was the attack on Dreiser, who then had no interest in politics, and who certainly had enough troubles without calling down his German ancestry on his head. Dreiser, however, was little affected by the Sherman attacks—he was, in 1917, almost beyond hurting—but Mencken was. Warner was uneasy over his pro-German views; the New York *Evening Mail,* to which he had begun to contribute articles, was wary; and Knopf was badly frightened. He was just getting started, and the Sherman assault was something with which to reckon. He quarreled with Mencken over the book. Mencken heatedly told him he might withdraw it whenever he pleased, vowed Knopf would never get another of his works, and ended by breaking off relations entirely. Down to January 1, 1919, the book had sold but 1,257 copies, and Mencken, the following March, dismally wrote Boyd that the one hundred and eleven dollars Knopf owed him in royalties was "about all I'll ever get."

The break with Knopf was directly responsible for Mencken's brief publishing, and long personal, relationship with Philip Goodman. They first met at the old Hofbräu, on Broadway near Twenty-third Street, while lunching with Nathan and John D. Williams, the theatrical producer. Goodman, working his way through an enormous beefsteak and four or five sandwiches, outlined a pet scheme: to sell books nationally through drug stores. The idea attracted first Nathan, who gave Goodman his *Bottoms Up!,* and then Mencken, who hauled out his paste pot and shears and put together *Damn! A Book of Calumny* in one week and *In Defense of Women* in six. Goodman's plan fell through—*In Defense* sold less than nine hundred copies—and his tardy royalty payments soon left Mencken drifting back to Knopf. For all his charm, which was considerable, Goodman eventually went completely busted as a publisher and turned to the theater, a milieu he found far more satisfactory.

In Defense of Women, as is generally known, was anything but a defense; it was, instead, a delightful lampooning of the more ridiculous aspects of relationships between the sexes, and was inspired, Mencken told his friends, by thoughts which came to him while lying abed with cuties. Its

1918 edition, pasted together in late February and March with fingers numb from the cold, created a certain uproar in the suffragette magazines,[2] but Mencken had no hankering for more of Sherman's race-baiting, and the book which became famous in the Twenties was a revised and lengthened version of a much milder edition, written with a sharp eye on the new censorship law. Probably because of its title which Goodman had slapped on over Mencken's protests, the little *Damn!* book got a rough going over from the disciples of what Ernest Boyd called Ku Klux Kriticism, however, The Albany Knickerbocker *Press* called it "too bizarre, too shocking, too altogether immoral"; *The New Republic,* "hackneyed, stupid, conventional, swine-like," and the Macon (Georgia) *News* wrote bitterly of "the Mazurian marsh he calls his brain." Shortly after publication, it was furiously beset by patrioteers who demanded its suppression; letters were written the Justice Department, complaining that the author had accused George Washington of fornication, and Mencken, happening to be in New York when Edward A. Rumely of the *Evening Mail* was arrested for concealing the German ownership of his paper, found himself shadowed for four days. "I am glad George is not alive," he wrote Boyd, now in Ireland. "He would probably sue me for making a Methodist out of him."

The disappointing show of his books, wartime prices for *The Smart Set* paper, and the lack of a steady income combined to dwindle his bank account and send him casting about for new work. Since his return from Germany, the *Sun* had offered him no job, "save gingerly and indirectly," and he began to suspect, as he wrote Rascoe, that the paper was trying to live him down. He became desperate for money; when Goodman wrote delicately of hack work to be done in New York, he answered, "Why ask me if I am willing to do a little whoring? Tell me what it is and I'll do it. If necessary, I'll do a piece proving that William G. McAdoo is the Son of God." He fished around, received

[2] An exasperated reviewer for the London *Vote* wrote, "Oh, the things that an evolved woman could say but for realizing the cheap easiness of being smart per medium of destructive criticism!"

tentative offers from a fearful publishing world, and finally signed a contract with the New York *Evening Mail*, calling for three articles a week, chiefly against prohibition.

The *Mail* arrangement proved stormy on both sides, and throughout its turbulent, wartime life, relations were broken off at least once by both sides. Trembling under the censorship act, the *Mail* returned article after article, usually on the ground that the contents were unpatriotic. At one point the *Mail* abrogated his contract and a quarrel developed over four hundred and fifty dollars Mencken felt was due him. He finally settled for two hundred and fifty dollars to avoid an expensive suit. A new management came in, he began to write again, and again the articles came back to Hollins Street, this time with the explanation that the writing was immoral. "This," he tartly wrote Rascoe, "is a refreshing variation on the usual charge that it is German propaganda." When at last the war ended the arrangement, both sides heaved long sighs of relief.

Curiously, much of his most enduring prose was written for the *Mail* "The Sahara of the Bozart," so important to the Southern renaissance of the Twenties, appeared there; so did his history of *Sister Carrie's* suppression and his famous Bathtub hoax. In the Twenties, turning with his scissors and paste pot in search of *Prejudices* articles, he repeatedly came back to the *Mail* material, and when, thirty years later, he essayed to select his best out-of-print writing, the *Mail* was represented far out of proportion to the number of pieces printed.

However restive he might become under his *Mail* contract, Mencken had little choice. The war fever mounted daily, and he might consider himself lucky to have a platform of any sort on which to express his original, and hence subversive, ideas. In Baltimore, a pier built over defective wiring flared up, and German aliens all over town were rounded up. In New York, Wright, editing an encyclopedia, was brought to the rack for pro-German views expressed before the war. And in Chicago, Rascoe, editing his book page, printed selections from *Areopagitica* under the simple byline "John Milton"—and received scores of letters denouncing Milton as an un-American apostle of Prussian *kultur*. Dreiser lay in his rat-infested New York apartment, penniless and ill, cut off from his royalties by the comstocks; Mencken's book on his experiences in Germany, *The Battle of the Wilhelmstrasse*, lay in a safe, never to be published, and its author wrote Untermeyer with bleak confidence, "All men with names like yours and mine will be jailed before Sept., 1918." Even the harmless articles the *Mail* printed stirred up the flag-wavers. Anonymous threats and denunciations came every day with the post, and the paid spies of Washington and the unpaid spies of the American Protective League contributed to his fattening Justice Department file. It was variously reported he was in the Kaiser's pay, was slated for a high Junker decoration after the war, and was an intimate personal friend of "Nitsky, the German monster" and Captain Paul Koenig, commander of the German U-boat *Deutschland*.

In this atmosphere of hysteria and fascism, Mencken's friendship with Nathan grew and was strengthened. Nathan simply bypassed the war. His interests, he argued dispassionately, lay in the theater, literature, the arts, and magazine editing; of what concern were the quarrels of nations to him? In peacetime he scarcely knew who was president of the United States; now, the terrible autumn of 1917, he was dimly aware of an unpleasantness in Europe. Whatever, he wondered vaguely, had become of the Viennese dance girls he had found so enchanting? "On that day during the world war . . . when one of the most critical battles was being fought," he later wrote calmly in *The World in Falseface*, "I sat in my still, sunlit, cozy library composing a chapter on æstetics for a new book on the drama. At 5 o'clock, my day's work done, I shook and drank a half dozen excellent apéritifs."

To Mencken, with his battle maps and pins, this was sublime idiocy, but he found it refreshing, after a week in his third-floor study, to sit in Luchow's with Nathan, far from his battles with the *Mail* and the patrioteers. Nathan, seeing his friend's discontent, led him to the charming ivory tower where he dwelled, talked glowingly of a new day after the war, and persuaded him to join in an attempt to recapture the gay, idyllic mood of their prewar fancies. For Knopf, before the *Prefaces* blow-up, they prepared *Pistols for Two*, a delightful little publicity pamphlet on the character of the *Smart Set* editors, written, of course, by the prolific Hatteras. That done, they turned to a play, *Heliogabalus*, and a commentary on American superstitions, *The American Credo*. *Heliogabalus*, with its omission of everything save traditional "theatrical buncombe," was never presented, though the playwrights received overtures from such notables as William Gillette and John Barrymore for the next twenty years. Bit by bit, musical comedy writers pirated such inventions as the Big Bed, which was Mencken's contribution. The *Credo*, brought out by Knopf in 1920, consisted of a long introduction by Mencken and an exhaustive listing of Credo items by Nathan—"That oysters are a great aphrodisiac" and "That when one takes one's best girl friend to see the monkeys in the zoo, the monkeys invariably do something that is very embarrassing." Even more amusing was a privately printed appendix which Mencken and Nathan sent their friends as Christmas gifts. Included was the doctrine that "coitus interruptus causes locomotor ataxia in the husband and adultery in the wife."

The Smart Set had continued to flourish on the eve of America's entry into the war, but once the fever was on it began to limp. By the fall of 1917 it was paying its editors no salary, appearing on poor paper that cost astronomically, and being kicked from pillar to post by government agencies. The mails were forever delivering it to the wrong towns—a corporation of "idiot Chinamen" could outshine the Post Office Department, Mencken decided—and even its colorful office was taken over by the Creel Press Bureau, forcing it, to Nathan's delight, to 25 West Forty-fifth Street, a few steps from the Royalton. The war, which had begun its purge of periodicals with *Harper's Weekly* in 1916, was forcing it to the wall, and only the most drastic economies, it soon became clear, would keep it on its feet. Mencken and Nathan turned out what they could under a new barrage of pseudonyms, and Hecht tagged closely behind them with as many as eight stories in an issue, five of them under such Mencken christened bylines as John Henslowe Saltonstall, the Rev. Dr.

Peter Cabot-Cabot, and Ethan Allen Lowell. Even Louis Untermeyer came to learn of the stock of Boyer-bought poetry
hiding in the safe, though the quality of authors still contributing was certainly low; of the Europeans, only Dunsany
and Joyce still wrote, and the best Joyce could send from
Switzerland was three poems. Harry Black was recruited for
a page of epigrams, and to the astonishment of everyone—
chiefly that of Harry Black—they turned out to be very good.
For a time, when costs were soaring and their pressmen
were on strike, Mencken almost longed for a half pound of
lead; "My one regret," he wrote Boyd, "is that I am not
eligible for military service on account of my albuminuria."
But somehow, with caution and a complete avoidance of
controversy, they managed to hang on month after month
without corrupting the magazine, confident that an end of the
war would bring a new tide. "Nathan and I are so convinced
of this," he told Boyd, "that we are sticking firmly to our
resolution to print nothing about the war. When the reaction
against alarms and headlines comes we'll pick up the circulation we now lose."

What saved the magazine in the end was just what had put
it on its feet four years before: the astuteness and ability of
its editors. *The Smart Set*, they reasoned, would never make
money during wartime; it was not that kind of magazine.
The answer, therefore, was to start a sideline of new magazines, which *were* the right kind. After conference with
Crowe and Warner, they began, with one thousand dollars
capital, *The Parisienne*, a cynical and successful attempt to
exploit the pro-French feeling of the time. Whatever the
locale of a submitted story, it was changed on general principle to France. *The Parisienne* was an enormous success.
Selling for fifteen cents, it was soon returning four thousand
dollars a month, and in six months Mencken and Nathan,
having realized their objective, sold out to Crowe and
Warner. Old Colonel Mann, meantime, had been bitten by
the pulp bug, and his *Snappy Stories*, supporting the same
long, swirling S's that were the trademark of *The Smart Set*,
appeared on the market. In answer, Mencken and Nathan
brought out *Saucy Stories*, which, after a quick sale to their
partners, survived until 1925. Their final venture in the pulp

field was *The Black Mask*. It still appears. Crowe bought it after six months, giving them an excellent price, and that return, combined with proceeds from the other two, put them on easy street and assured the future of *The Smart Set*.

Real though they were, however, Mencken's money difficulties were the least of his worries during those war months, and their alleviation helped little to ease a troubled mind. Sitting in his lonely room, shut off from the newspaper he loved, he struggled ineffectively with his creative moods, poured out his heart to Boyd, and asked peevishly in the *Mail*, "What is the precise machinery whereby the cerebrum is bestirred to such abnormal activity on one day that it sparkles and splutters like an arc-light, and reduced to such feebleness on another that it smokes and gutters like a tallow dip?" The shipyards had recruited all Baltimore's furnace men, and between his frantic labors, he puffed his way down four flights of stairs to have at the coal pile in the cellar. As a furnace man, he was a total failure, largely, he claimed defensively, because of the mass of slate which now appeared in wartime coal. Whatever the reason, the temperature at Hollins Street was never right; at times, it pushed 85 degrees, rolling the sweat down his moonish face. Other times, it dropped to 45 degrees, sending him storming downstairs or rooting in his closet for a warmer set of B.V.D.'s. And when the furnace failed, the chill winds of the harbor seemed to blow more furiously. "The damndest weather ever seen is still raging here," he wrote Boyd in January, 1918. "There is constant snow, great cold, and hence much suffering. Coal is short, food is high, and every day seems to be meatless, wheatless, beerless, porkless, or sugarless. It is almost impossible to get a drink on Monday. I almost long for peace."

Saturday nights were still spent with the club, despite its depletion from enlistments, and on warm afternoons he walked in the country with Theodor Hemberger, singing the German soldier's song, *Ich hatt' einen Kameraden,* complaining of his renascent piles, and planning a home in the country. He talked endlessly of the books he would write after the war—a book of prejudices, a book for men only, a history of the American effort to maintain neutrality in the war, complete with an analysis of documents, a series of small aphoristic books on democracy, war, and Christianity, and the new review he dwelt on more and more. Whenever Hemberger, who was in despair over the fate of German-Americans, grew disconsolate, Mencken reminded him grimly, "Don't worry, Theo. They'll have to feed us."

The war had cut him off from two of the three friends he saw in New York, and despite Nathan's charm, Mencken missed them terribly. Dreiser, with his unusual sensitivity, had been deeply wounded, first by Mencken's digs at *The "Genius"* in his *Prefaces* essay—digs which were, as Edmund Wilson later pointed out, skillfully designed to spike the enemy's guns by admitting Dreiser's technical faults—and then by Mencken's attempts to dissuade him from following through with "The Hand of the Potter," the drama of a sexually depraved young man, on the ground that it would bring the censors down on his head with new fury. And Dreiser's numbness under attack, his retirement into a world of ouija boards, Russian records, and candlelight, became irritating. When Dreiser wrote that he had already framed his last words—"Shakespeare, I come!"—and asked Mencken what his would be, Mencken replied acidly, "I regret that I have but one rectum to leave to my country."

Wright he was destined never to see again. The war hysteria had conspired to drive them apart; the break, curiously enough, resulted from mutual German sympathies. Wright had become nettled by an *Evening Mail* stenographer who, unbalanced by the spy scare, refused to write down dictated German book titles and took to making off with copies of his correspondence. Finally, in a rage, Wright deliberately dictated a suspicious letter calculated to inflame her, introducing whatever names came to mind. Once it was finished the girl, in a sweat, ran out to the street and hailed the nearest policeman. The police accepted Wright's explanation, but the attendant publicity lost him his job and, ultimately, his health. What outraged Mencken was that among the names in the letter—which was printed everywhere—was that of a mutual friend. The friend was investigated by the Secret Service and subjected to all sorts of indignities, and Mencken, with his quaint sense of loyalties, blamed Wright for the whole affair. Wright, he reasoned, had got both his *Smart Set* and *Evening Mail* jobs through him. Now he repaid this service by injuring him indirectly. Therefore—he would never again see Wright, and he never did. "To put such burdens on innocent friends in crazy days such as these is an unforgivable offense," he wrote Boyd. ". . . I myself was not mentioned, but what he did to Leeds in his childish folly he might have done to any of his friends." In the years that followed, when Wright was down on his luck and ailing, Mencken refused to see him or even to answer his letters. The man, he was convinced, was through. This was not quite true. Under doctor's orders, Wright was later permitted, for a long period, to read nothing heavier than detective stories. He became fascinated with them, tried them himself, and in time made quite a name for himself as S. S. Van Dine.

Note, if you please, the tone of Mencken's letter to Boyd. It was written by a man who had been hurt beyond belief by those he scorned and had sworn to give them no further excuse to attack while the war continued, not even if he must deny his friends and leave unscarred his critical targets. However much the patrioteers might later regret it, they had temporarily shut him up. For as long as the crisis continued, he had resolved to devote himself to neutral matters or to books to be published after the war. He plunged into a translation of Nietzsche's *Der Antichrist* with this in mind and began, in the spring of 1918, to work on a project which "should get me an LL.D. from some negro college." It was an outgrowth of earlier *Smart Set* and "Free Lance" articles on the peculiarities of the English language as spoken and written in the United States. His interest was fanned by a wartime friendship with Harry Black's wife, a native-born Englishwoman. Black was away in the Navy, and Mencken, in one of his regular visits to Johns Hopkins, came to visit Mrs. Black, laid up with a severe hemorrhage following the removal of her tonsils. After her release she invited him out to their house to spend an evening with her and her sister, who had just come over from England. Mencken interviewed them on British origins of the American vulgate or, as he chose to call his new manuscript, *The American Language*.

He worked rapidly that summer, against time, for he was faced with a new threat, this time not idealogical. He was thirty-seven, unmarried, and hence supremely eligible under the new draft bill. Between paragraphs on the Corona, his mind wandered to the training camps. Where would he go? "My experience fits me for the medical department," he wrote Boyd, "but that is already overcrowded so, as a bachelor, I'll probably draw the infantry." Nathan was also eligible, and Mencken feared for the future of *The Smart Set*. But not Nathan. He announced grandly he was already studying the bass piccolo and would become a field musician, aware that the medical board would, as it did, reject him because of his eyes. "George is palpably unfit physically," Mencken told Boyd, "but I suppose my own gaudy physique will fetch me despite my asthma, piles, tongue trouble, hay fever, alcoholic liver, weak heels, dandruff, etc." On September 4, with the new bill a law, this was followed with the intelligence that he would register on September 12, his thirty-eighth birthday. "What will follow, God alone knows. If they take my with my asthma my barks will at least alarm the Hun." On September 12, as the law required, he did register, and was awaiting the call when the end of the war came. But by that time he had submerged his troubles in new projects, determined to turn over as much completed work as possible to a reconciled Knopf.

Armistice Day found him in the third-floor rear at Hollins Street, bowed over a welter of proofs for *The American Credo, Heliogabalus,* and *The Antichrist,* miserably awaiting the draft board's call, sublimely unaware his hour had struck.

Chapter 5

Hoisting the Black Flag

(1918–1925)

LATE SUMMER, 1918.

In an officer's club full of smoke, conversation, and rattling newspapers, Lieutenant F. Scott Fitzgerald worked away at *The Romantic Egotist,* preparing another chapter for shipment to his Princeton typist. . . .

In a jammed little Italian hospital, young Ernest Hemingway shifted his smashed leg and reread the slip of paper on which a British officer had written for him: "By my troth, I care not: a man can die but once; we owe God a death . . . and let it go which way it will, he that dies this year is quit for the next. . . ."

At Chaumont, France, Sergeant Edmund Wilson stuck pins in G.H.Q. maps and reread *A Book of Prefaces.* . . . E. E. Cummings sweltered in a French concentration camp. . . . Private John Dos Passos of the U. S. Medical Corps, notebook in hand, wearily traced his newsreel of death and terror back through the years in Italy, at Verdun. . . .

Late summer, 1918.

In Baltimore, that morning's *Sun* had carried five and a half columns of death notices, and even now, as twilight deepened, the mournful roll of Army trucks could be heard outside on nearby Lombard Street, carrying the day's dead to outlying cemeteries. Nathan lay ill at the Royalton; his brother was dead; and in Baltimore Charlie Mencken, down for a minor operation, could find no hospital bed. The great influenza epidemic of 1918–19 was at its height. The week's toll for the city approached fifteen hundred.

But if the disheveled man upstairs noted this, or even heard the muffled rumbling outside, there was no indication. Hunched over his tiny portable, hands well scrubbed, he studied the blank sheet before him. Restive, he glanced at the completed typescript on the pivotal bookcase, then swigged lustily from the glass of tap water beside him. Now the last

137

truck rolled down Lombard Street into the gathering darkness. Now the house lay quiet beneath him. Now he pulled long and heavily at the cigar in his well-muscled jaw, the lengthening ash approaching his face at a quarter-inch clip. And now two fingers shot out toward the waiting keyboard.

The aim of this book is best exhibited by describing its origin. I am, and have been since early manhood, an editor of newspapers, magazines and books, and a critic of the last named. These occupations have forced me into a pretty wide familiarity with current literature, both periodical and between covers, and in particular with the current literature of England and America. . . .

He stopped, swore softly, and, laying the cigar aside, wrote *"into a familiarity* with the current literature" over the line. Then, settling back, he wrote on.

. . . It was part of my daily work, for a good many years, to read the principal English newspapers and reviews; it has been part of my work, all that time, to read the more important English novels, essays, poetry and criticism. An American born and bred, I early noted, as everyone in like case must note, certain salient differences between the English of England and the English of America as practically spoken and written—differences in vocabulary, in syntax, in grammar. And I noted, too, of course, partly during visits to England but more largely by a somewhat wide and intimate intercourse with people in the United States, the obvious differences between English and American pronunciation and intonation. Greatly interested in these differences. . . .

He had been greatly interested in these differences since one evening thirteen years before, when he wandered into the Pratt Library and there found the file of a small, erudite journal titled *Dialect Notes,* describing the origin of words. In the years that followed, words of the vulgate, words with which to spice his reviews and columns, became a sort of hobby, and shortly after the establishment of the *Evening Sun* it occurred to him that others might have a like interest. Stuck one afternoon for a column to plug the editorial page, he wrote "The Two Englishes." The subject proved surprisingly popular; a number of subscribers asked for more, and in the weeks that followed, he printed "Spoken American," "More American," "American Pronounced," and "England's English." Inauguration of "The Free Lance" ended the *Evening Sun* series, but from his clippings he found time, in August, 1913, to write a *Smart Set* article on his accumulated findings. Another batch of correspondence followed, this time from a more widely scattered audience, suggesting leads, enclosing information, and inspiring the decision to write still another article. Early the next year he actually wrote Ellery Sedgwick, asking an opinion on the *Atlantic Monthly's* hospitality toward an article "on certain peculiarities of the American language." Sedgwick was friendly enough, but before the piece could be turned out Thayer sold *The Smart Set,* Mencken became co-editor, and the ensuing struggle left no time for philology. Sometime in late 1915 or early 1916 he wrote a long article for future placement, and now, with the public hostile to all other offerings, he rewrote it into book form. In the beginning the work was desultory, but as the summer came on and the war became more and more impossible, he sunk into a sort of pedagogical coma. He had, in that furious manner of his, wolfed down most of the existing books on the subject, and as autumn neared and the draft pressed closer, he traveled far into the lands of scholarship, exploring the wherefores of the nation's language: the historical move to the West; the preservation of Elizabethan verve in speech and the paralleling triumph of Puritan dogmatism in England; the development of Americanisms; the powerful influence of regionalism on American speechways. On October 14 he had finished the draft of his text. Those sections of his newspaper and magazine articles which were to go into the book were pasted together and the manuscript shipped to Knopf; he then plunged into the index. By the time that was done, the galley proofs and the end of his bitter wartime vigil were at hand. The following year *The American Language* was published.

The impact of the book was terrific. With one powerful

stroke he had hewed in half the umbilical cord which philologically bound this nation to England. Later strokes were to come—and he was to deliver them—but the immediate effect of that first edition, coming as it did with the dying echoes of rifle fire in France, was tremendous. Even the pedagogues were stirred. The New York *Sun,* alarmed, asked "Can English be saved?" "Never," said *The New Republic,* "has the flourishing personality of H. L. Mencken been so happily exercised as in this big book on the living speech of America." The *Atlantic Monthly* acclaimed the "opening up of a new line of research," and even Brander Matthews, lately an ally of Stuart Sherman (who was greatly upset by this attempt to "split asunder the two great English-speaking peoples"), approved it in the New York *Times* as "well planned, well proportioned, well documented, and well written." In the circles where language is written and taught, the battle was on; Dr. Louise Pound at the University of Nebraska and Frank Moore Colby, editor of the *New International Encyclopedia,* were Mencken's chief defenders, and Sherman and his band of schoolmarms were the attackers. Nor did the storm blow over; as late as the fall of 1924 an entire convention of the National Council of Teachers in St. Louis was devoted to denunciations of *The American Language.*

Mencken was astonished. He had conceived the book as an innocuous diversion during troubled times; once it was off his hands, he thought it "a heavy indigestible piece of cottage cheese. . . . I thus purge my blood of inherited pedantry." He used it as a lance to prod a moonish Dreiser—"My ambition is crowned: I have written a book longer than *The 'Genius'.* It will be at least five inches thick"—and heartily agreed with Knopf that so small a public awaited such a work the edition should be limited to fifteen hundred copies. When the bookstores, their stock exhausted, demanded more; when Rascoe wrote from Chicago of the enthusiasm there; when the resale price soared from five dollars to ten dollars to twelve-fifty, he was bewildered. Why the uproar? "I have never been a scholar and have never pretended to be one," he protested. "I'm just a sort of scout for scholars. I accumulated the material and tried to put it into a readable form, so people could understand it, and dug out of it whatever human juices there were, and there were plenty, and my hope and idea was that the material I had accumulated would be used by actual philologists." Information poured in from all over the world—notes for the revised work his correspondents were sure would follow—and Mencken, dazed and confused, began organizing against the new edition Knopf was trumpeting in New York. But he couldn't understand it. Something had happened.

Something had happened. A war had ended, but more: a new era had begun. The day of the American Protective League, of the war saboteurs, of the *Evening Mail's* pussy-footing and Theodor Hemberger's terror, the day when to be German was to be suspect, when Wright could be cashiered and Dreiser and Mencken gagged—that day had passed. Its last vestiges were fading that summer as the *Language* mail flooded Mencken; fewer were the parades down North Charles Street, with bayonets gleaming in the sun and the bands playing "There's a Long, Long Trail A-Winding"; fewer were the flashes of khaki and French blue along Baltimore Street. A war had ended, but the nation's appetite for excitement had not, as the success of Fitzgerald's *This Side of Paradise* was presently to testify. Skirts were going up; young women were painting their faces and puffing defiantly, if awkwardly, on cigarettes; and on the horizon was heard the harsh, plaintive wail of the saxophone. Woodrow Wilson, back from Europe, geared himself for the Senate fight and the long trip to Pueblo and paralysis; Attorney General Palmer headed into the Reds; the New York *Daily News* began its astonishing climb along the highways of sensationalism. And along the streets of many an American town a discharged soldier, haunted and lonely, tracked down an elusive job. It was 1919. The Twenties were on the threshold. And so was H. L. Mencken.

Mencken voted for Harding the following November and sat back to enjoy the show. It looked like farce, and farce was to his taste. He voted for Harding—and then, through the short months that pathetic figure had to live, subjected him to a merciless and withering fire. On March 4, 1921, he pressed his pants, rode over to Washington, and sat perched on a folding chair for the opening act of the comedy. Back in

Baltimore that evening, he wrote Carl Van Doren: "Harding's speech was the damndest bosh that even he has perpetrated. It almost brought me to tears. Was it for this that George Washington was frost-bitten and Grant put his feet into that mustard-bath at Appomattox?" He hung up his pants, squatted before his littered desk, and began the overture: "No other such complete and dreadful nitwit is to be found in the pages of American history. . . ."

That year the lines were drawn. All over the nation the forces of ignorance and reaction rallied to put down the threatening insurrection of those they had successfully throttled during the war. The censors stripped off their masks. In Knoxville, Tennessee, Miss Mary Boyce Temple, whom Joseph Wood Krutch nominated as "the perfect censor," advocated the suppression of *Rain*. She had, she admitted, never seen it, never read it—had, in fact, never heard of Maugham's short story. But, "We of the D.A.R. and the United Daughters of the Confederacy have had the advantages of education and travel and have been prepared for such things. Such a play would not injure us; it would only disgust us. But there are women who have not had these advantages. . . . It is our duty to protect those who have not had our advantages." On the floor of the U. S. Senate, Reed Smoot, of Utah, cried, "I would rather a child of mine take opium than read one of these books. . . . I would rather keep out a thousand, than have one mistake made." And in New York, John Sumner moved toward the suppression of Cabell's newly published *Jurgen*.

But this time the revolt was not confined to the literati alone. Insurgents were popping up in almost every household, mascaraed, half dressed, and nicotine besotted. Everywhere— ideologically, socially, sartorially—a generation was in revolt. Fanned by warmed-over war fevers, the alarm against the threatening revolution spread. Designers of the "moral garment" began their bizarre campaign for modest dress among women. Preachers took the stump for celibacy. And everywhere—in Centralia, Washington; Albany, New York; and South Braintree, Massachusetts—an indignant citizenry moved against the Reds. Something, quite definitely, had happened.

Mencken certainly did not approve of the younger generation. The new freedom of American women scandalized him
quite as much as it did his neighbors. Companionate-marriage
advocates, he felt, should be hanged. "I lament the spread of
carnality in the fair republic," he wrote Rascoe. "Even the
great city of Washington, I hear, is full of fornicators."
"One wonders, indeed," he whispered in *The Smart Set*, "what
women now talk of to doctors." Jazz he thought abominable.
The saxophone fetched "vulgarians, barbarians, idiots, pigs";
its addicts inhabited "the sewers of the bozart." Night clubs,
coming into vogue with prohibition, moved him to great
sorrow and an acid description of the "sideshow murals on
the walls . . . middle-aged couples bumping and grunting over
the dance floor like dying hogs in a miasmic pen . . . crooners
bawling maudlin jingles. . . ." But the contest lured him, all
the same, and his principal target, as always, was the
established and accepted, not the new and insurgent. He had
been opposed to the established order for too long to line
up with it. It was not a question of choosing sides. There had
always been just two sides: Mencken's and everyone else's.
It never occurred to him that his fight against intolerance
would be interpreted by the victims of that intolerance as a
friendly act. Had anyone told him he would be considered
radical by the Mary Boyce Temples and Reed Smoots, he
would have agreed instantly; but had he known he would be
considered a liberal by the young flappers in shortening skirts
and their baggy-trousered escorts, he would have been amazed.
Not even his friends thought any such thing in that first year
of the Harding regime, and certainly he was far too busy to
reflect on it himself.

Now the pages of *The Smart Set* were set humming with
the accumulated horsepower of the war years. Free as he
had never been before, liberated quite as much in his way as
were the flappers in theirs, he let go one mighty blast after
another, leveling, for his readers everything which had been
sacred under the now dying Wilson. It was not revenge
he sought: Mencken's compulsion was not that simple.
Revenge implies a personal relationship which never existed
between him and his enemies. His billingsgate was surely
personal enough, but the motivation turned on an abstract

hatred of what his adversaries represented, not a man-to-man dislike. He preferred, indeed, not to know his targets; better, he felt, they should remain to him the caricatures they became to his readers. Sherman he would not meet, despite Carl Van Doren's attempts to bring them together. He was, it seemed, afraid he might, knowing him, get to like him.

The end of the war meant more than a supercharged Mencken. It brought also a rechanneling of his energies. The prejudices—he began so to describe his attitudes—fevering him broadened immensely. His interest in the national scene, apart from its literature, had necessarily grown during those long months of enforced silence. Now, in his writing, the attitudes of "The Free Lance" swept up those of *The Smart Set* criticism. He began, as he wrote Van Doren, to "sicken of belles-lettres" and became entranced with general imbecilities of the American people. He peered out across the country, took in every aspect of the developing era, and gloated. Absurd newspaper items were clipped for reprinting in *The Smart Set;* pamphlets from booming businessmen and subversion-conscious Legion posts were filed away against future articles. His interests, significantly, stopped at the national borders. All he knew, or pretended to know, of Europe was that "In the Balkans, as everyone knows, there are wars at the regular intervals, regardless of probable cause. Once in so often the Bulgars simply begin to butcher the Serbians and the Serbians the Bulgars." Moreover, he was not, as were some, disturbed by the hysteria of the Red-baiters or the smugness of the comstocks. He regarded these as part of his own peculiar concept of what America should be—an arena where the more amusing morons performed. When Harold E. Sterns began the exodus of American intellectuals in 1922, Mencken obligingly wrote a section on politics for *Civilization in the United States;* yet he himself remained, "on the dock, wrapped in the flag, when the Young Intellectuals set sail."

. . . here, more than anywhere else that I know of or have ever heard of, the daily panorama of human existence . . . is so inordinately gross and preposterous . . . that only a man who was born with a petrified diaphragm can fail to laugh himself to sleep every night, and to awake every morning with all the eager, unflagging expectation of a Sunday-school superintendent touring the Paris peep-shows.

As the nation turned toward normalcy, Mencken greased his long idle bore, primed his high-explosive shells, sighted in, and . . .

WHAM!

"Wilson: the self-bamboozled Presbyterian, the right-thinker, the great moral statesman, the perfect model of a Christian cad."

WHAM!

"Gamaliel the Stonehead."

WHAM!

". . . if they [Sacco and Vanzetti] are electrocuted it will be because they are radicals and not because they have been actually connected with the murders."

WHAM!

"In so foul a nest of imprisoned and fermenting sex as the United States, plain fornication becomes a mark of relative decency."

WHAM!

"The mob delight in melodramatic spectacles, thus constantly fed and fostered by the judicial arm of the United States, is also at the bottom of another familiar American phenomenon, to wit, lynching."

WHAM!

"It is still socially dangerous for an American man to have the reputation of being virtuous. Theoretically, he who preserves his chemical purity in the face of all temptations is a noble and upright fellow and the delight of the heavenly hierarchy; actually, he is laughed at by women and viewed with contempt by men."

WHAM!

"All government, in its essence, is a conspiracy against the superior man: its one permanent object is to oppress him and cripple him."

WHAM!

"On the evening of that same day that an American Legionary has his wages reduced to 40 per cent and his hours of labor increased 25 per cent, he goes out at his own risk and expense and helps to tar and feather some visionary who tries to convince him he has been swindled."

WHAM!

"What ails the beautiful letters of the Republic, I repeat, is what ails the general culture of the Republic—the lack of a body of sophisticated and civilized public opinion, independent of plutocratic control and superior to the infantile philosophies of the mob—a body of opinion showing the eager curiosity, the educated skepticism and the hospitality to ideas of a true aristocracy. This lack is felt by the American author, imagining him to have anything new to say, every day of his life."

WHAM! WHAM! WHAM!

Like a great peal of thunder, his invective rolled across the nation and broke with a tremendous roar, sending the self-appointed policeman of our moral and political standards scampering about to see what was the matter. He lumped the Ku Klux Klan, the American Legion, the Anti-Saloon League, and the Department of Justice together—"all great engines of cultural propaganda"—and spread before them the proposition that the one way to find the truth about anything in America was to take a vote on it. The Klan, he said, was just what it pretended to be—an order devoted to the ideals most Americans held sacred. Those who opposed it were hypocrites. The triumph of the Ohio Gang he interpreted to mean that the people of the United States were not against robbing the country—that every individual hoped for his chance at the drawer, praying his share of the swag would be greater than the amount he would have to pay the bank. The Just Government League? Swell. The cops would be kept on the jump, the newspapers would be filled with "gaudy and pornographic stuff," and the bootleggers would be given a breathing spell. Female suffrage? Wonderful. Now adultery would replace boozing as the chief amusement of politicians. Social work? Magnificent. Without it, humanity would be disgraced "by the spectacle of hordes of lady Ph.D.'s going to work in steam-laundries, hooch shows and chewing-gum factories."

Criticism and progress, he had written a friend, "must be done boldly, and, in order to get a crowd, a bit cruelly." Certainly he was cruel enough. There was little properly describable as pity in his railing "Gamaliel the Stonehead"—while poor Harding, lost in his job, fornicated clandestinely in a White House coat closet. The crowd was not far behind. In the newspapers, in the pulpit, and from the lecture platform, the pattern set down in Baltimore a decade before was repeated nationally. He was denounced as a mangy ape, a dog, a weasel, a maggot, a ghoul, a jackal, a tadpole, a toad, a tiger, a howling hyena, a bilious buffoon, a cad, a British toady, a super-Boche of German *Kultur*, a cankerworm, a radical Red, and a reactionary. "Shocking," editorialized the Brooklyn *Eagle;* "Improper," said the Nashville *Banner;* "Insulting," wrote "Outraged" to the Chicago *Tribune*. A minister preached he was grateful he had been raised with a hickory stick, not on Mencken; another said Mencken "could only deal in boorish vituperation, with a vocabulary borrowed from Billingsgate and the Bowery." The Los Angeles *Times* stormed, "This admirer of Prussian Kultur seems to be afflicted with a fatal world-belly-ache only to be cured by a descent into the warmer air of Gehenna." A North Carolina woman cried "Away with the inhibition of inferiority this clever Hebrew would wish upon us!" G. K. Chesterton summed him up as "A clever and bitter Jew in whom a real love of letters is everlastingly exasperated by the American love of cheap pathos and platitude." His philosophy, to believe Chesterton, was a sort of nihilistic pride which belongs "to a man with a sensitive race and a dead religion."[1] In Los Angeles he was described as an "eighteen carat, twenty-three jewel, thirty-third degree, bred in the bone and died in the wool moron." To a lady writing a Middle Western newspaper, he was rude and insulting—"He *might* speak of our mental deficiencies in a more restrained tone," she said indignantly. Enterprising newspapers hired analysts to study his photograph, his handwriting, and an X-ray of his head; they concluded that he really wanted to join the ranks of the respectable, that he would soon enlist in a Methodist congregation, that he needed to get married. In Chicago a college professor demanded of his simpering class,

[1] The delusion that Mencken was Jewish persisted throughout the decade, and he did nothing to correct it. He was, for many years, listed in the Jewish *Who's Who* and was seized with a fit of mirth whenever the book came out.

"Cannot America produce someone who will knock Mr. Mencken into a cocked hat, or at least smack his sassy face?" America apparently had no one. But one attempt was made in these years to shut him off. It happened in the hot summer of 1921, and it came from Arkansas.

In the August issue of *The Smart Set*, Mencken—who, though America did not know it, was just getting up steam— had written a full-fledged attack on the state of Arkansas under the inviting title "The South Begins To Mutter." He described the "miasmic jungles," the "dead brains," the "idiotic patriots" and the "brummagem mountebanks" of "a state almost fabulous." To Arkansas, this seemed offensive. The Little Rock *Daily News* led the attack, demanding, the week the magazine hit the newsstands, that action be taken against the writer, whose name the paper was pleased to spell "Menneken." He was, the *Daily News* informed its readers, the "one remaining relic of the Kultur Klub of the one-time Kaiser Bill." The editor reprinted much of the article and demanded to know if this sort of fellow was to be permitted to run loose. Answers came swiftly. Correspondents denounced him as a scoundrelly Yankee, a Bolshevik Jew, and an agent of the Wilhelmstrasse. *The Pythian* Herald described the piece as ". . . the vilest slander of the Southern people and the Christian religion that has ever been spewed up from the slimy sewers of a diseased brain and a putrefied soul." The *Herald*, it appeared, thought Mencken had syphilis. But the *Little Rock Trade Herald* put every other paper in the state to shame. Indeed, though its editors never knew it, it nearly killed the offender by producing apoplexy. "In the words of Scott's immortal hero," spluttered the *Herald*, " 'Lay on Macduff, and damned be he that cries "Hold, enough!" ' " Prodded by a group of Arkansas clergyman, Virgil C. Pettie, president of the Arkansas Advancement Association, issued a statement proclaiming that Mencken—who was assumed to be an alien —had "made himself sufficiently obnoxious to a majority of the American people to warrant deportation." Washington ambassadors from the miasmic jungles were asked to look into the matter. Unhappily, it was discovered, Mencken was a native fellow countryman, eligible to stick around as long as he liked.

In the midst of all this pother, Robert Bridges, Poet Laureate of Great Britain and a philologist, arrived in New York to take a chair at the University of Michigan as professor of English poetry. He was received by an august deputation from the American Institute and the American Academy of Arts and Letters at the dock, seen to his quarters, and asked, as a point of etiquette, if there were any names he cared to add to a prepared list of greeters. Bridges waved away the lists. "The only man I want to meet in America," he said, "is H. L. Mencken." As Burton Rascoe noted, from the expressions on the hosts' faces Bridges might just as well have said, "I am badly in need of a whore. Will you please get me one for the night?"

The medal had another side; it always has. The very violence of the attack on Mencken stemmed from concern over his widening and sympathetic audience, and if he had more vilifiers than ever before, he certainly had more admirers. As Rascoe observed, "With startling suddenness, he who had been outside the pale for so long was quoted everywhere with approval." The editors of the *Liberator* and the *Yale Review*, for whom Mencken had never before existed, now quoted his praise of them freely; *The New Republic,* despite editorial disclaimers, was delighted to get his copy; Villard's *Nation* made him contributing editor, with no duties beyond the holding of the title. A swarm of writers hustled to review his precepts— Vincent O'Sullivan in the *Mercure de France;* Frank Harris in *Pearson's Magazine;* Lawrence Gilman in the *North American Review;* Aldous Huxley in the London *Athenaeum;* Percy Boynton in *Freeman;* Spingarn in the London *Nation;* Ernest Boyd in the *Athenaeum* and *Freeman,* and Edmund Wilson in *Dial* and *The New Republic.* Stuart Sherman, startled to find the ghost he had laid so alive and vigorous, lashed at him again, first in the New York *Times,* then in the *Atlantic Monthly* and his book of *Americans.* But Sherman's hour had passed; Mencken now could dismiss him in a single sentence:

> The Iowa hayseed remains in his hair; he can't get rid of the smell of the Chautauqua; one invariably sees him as a sort of reductio ad absurdum of his fundamental theory— to wit, that the test of an artist is whether he hated the

Kaiser in 1917, and plays his honorable part in Christian Endeavor, and prefers coca-cola to Scharlachberger 1911, and has taken to heart the great lessons of sex hygiene.

With justification, Mencken wrote that the Goths and Huns were at the gate of Humanism, and that as they battered wildly they threw "dead cats, perfumed lingerie, and bound files of the *Nation,* the *Freeman,* and the *New Republic* over the fence." With reason, More protested bitterly he was "the least read and most hated author in America."

Why the hubbub? Had Mencken changed so greatly? He had not. He was, as noted, bolder than before, but neither his style nor his basic tenets had shifted appreciably since 1908. It was intellectual America which had changed. Just as the Civil War had directed all the reform movements of the 1840's and 1850's into a crusade against slavery and secession, so had the war just passed channeled the idealism of Roosevelt and Wilson into a noble battle for democracy. When the bust of the League of Nations came,—"the old Peruna bottle," Mencken called it—and the wartime patriotism turned into Normalcy, the jailing of Debs, and the rewriting of schoolbooks to conform with the fiats of the Ku Klux Klan and the D.A.R., the reaction set in. Doughboys returned to a culture whose hero was Theodore Roosevelt, whose philosopher was William Jennings Bryan, whose high priest was Comstock, and whose religion was Don't. Their literature they found to be dominated by old women, mummies, and dry-as-dust fifth-carbon-copy Ralph Waldo Emersons, who worshiped everything English and thought Macaulay the last decent stylist. And they rebelled. As Harold Stearns wrote in a blistering attack on Sherman, "the kernel of truth, of course, is in the depiction of the younger generation as in revolt against the right-thinkers and the forward-lookers. It is in revolt, it *does* dislike, almost to the point of hatred and certainly to the point of contempt, the type of people who dominate our present civilization, the people who actually 'run things.'. . ."

Thus did the Twenties come to Mencken. The champion of intellectual unrest, of disillusion, he tapped this new vein with a flourish and zeal that staggered the Philistines and brought the jaded literati flocking. In the gaudy covered *Smart Set* and in his stream of books and magazine articles, they found their unspoken thoughts brilliantly couched. When he beheld, "sweeping the eye over the land . . . a culture that, like the national literature, is in three layers—the plutocracy on top, a vast mass of undifferentiated human blanks bossed by demagogues at the bottom, and a forlorn *intelligentsia* gasping out a precarious life in between," the raccoon-coated aesthete saw himself perfectly described. When he ascended to the levels "where ideas swish by and men pursue truth to grab her by the tail," the raccoon coat floated up with him. And when he cried, in his introduction to the revised *In Defense of Women*, "If I knew what was true, I'd be willing to sweat and strive for it, and maybe even to die for it to the tune of bugle blasts. But so far, I have not found it," the raccoon coat, mournfully sipping bathtub gin, sobbed, "Neither have I."

He was compared to Juvenal, Dryden, Swift, Voltaire, and, in the Glasgow *Herald*, to Sam Johnson. Overnight, it seemed, his fame became international. The Sydney, Australia, *Times* praised his honesty, the *Deutsche Rundschau* his satire, the Caracas, Venezuela *El Universal* his power, and the Cartagena, Colombia, *El Porvenir* his erudition. Defenses came from the famous—Hugh Walpole and Aldous Huxley—and from the obscure—a Chicago businessman and an editorial writer on the Fargo, North Dakota, *Tribune*. He was translated into Spanish, German, Russian; in Moscow an article telling of his fight for Russian realism was accompanied by a sketch of a square-jawed giant bearing the caption, "H. L. Mencken." In Greenwich Village a red-haired girl gained great favor by announcing she had been sleeping with Mencken for six years. In the first-edition market—which Dreiser now led —he climbed steadily, past Poe, Kipling, O. Henry, and the field. The final release of The *"Genius"* built his defense of Dreiser into a legend, and for his single letter in the *Jurgen* suppression, he was credited with leading the battle. Alfred Stieglitz's photograph of a horse's buttocks, titled "Spiritual America," was attributed to his inspiration, and it was whispered his attacks had led to Wilson's stroke. By June, 1921, a correspondent of the Detroit *Times*, hitherto regarded as a crank, protested that "as Menckenism spreads in this country, I have difficulty in maintaining my position as one of the original Menckenites," and F. Scott Fitzgerald, running ahead of the Twenties for once, lamented that Mencken, like Aristides, would soon be exiled because one was tired of hearing his praises sung.

All this delighted him, though he took it with small seriousness. The terrific publicity he welcomed as advertising—an author, he noted, was most admired by those who had not read him but had merely heard of him. In 1922 he began subscribing to Romeike's clipping service, carefully pasting the sheaves of newspaper articles in numbered scrapbooks. His audience he carefully cultivated. The name "H. L. Mencken" he cherished as a trademark; his friends were advised that "Henry L." was proper only in indictments, income-tax returns, passports, "and other criminal documents." *Ventures into Verse* became something of a problem: the popularity of his first editions swept it into the first rank of rare books, and its harmless Kipling imitations, agreeable enough from an adolescent poet, became embarrassing to a famous critic. All requests for it, even from his closest friends, were turned aside with vague references to the bank vault where it was supposed to be kept. The *Sunday Sun,* when it began reprinting poems from it, received a cease-and-desist order from Hollins Street. In later years he strenuously protested that he never bought up copies in the secondhand book market, but at least one New York dealer who knew him remembers that he did. Inexplicably, one of the two copies in the Library of Congress disappeared.

As a celebrity, he was subjected to certain annoyances. He generally took them good-humoredly; even the spurious Greenwich Village mistress amused him, and the persistent reports of his coming marriage, always attendant on a bachelor's entrance into the limelight, delighted him. He usually admitted there was some truth to the story—in these years, there was none—or turned it off with protests that it had killed his chances with another "fair creature" whom he had wooed to the brink of the altar. ("After all," he told Hergesheimer, "it is hard to prove that one is *not* married. I'll have to hand her lawyers transcripts from every parish register in the United States since the year 1886, when I attained to puberty.") His only protests over adulation were levied at the telephone callers who plagued him endlessly. One can scarcely blame him. The telephone was downstairs, the steps were steep, Mencken was overweight again, and the callers, almost invariably, were persons of no consequence to him or were, as he preferred to put it, "swine."

Beyond that, he had no complaints. Business was booming, for obvious reasons: "Imprimis, that the war has greatly improved trade for me. Why has no one noticed that before? I hate to think of it, but it is so." None of his admirers had "ever shown the slightest sign of understanding, or even suspecting" his feelings, but that was to be expected. The strategy, then, was clear: produce more wares. Accordingly, he rolled up his sleeves, sat down at his work bench, and turned out items for his showcase. Early in 1919, at the suggestion of Richard Laukhuff, a Cleveland book dealer who had asked Knopf to collect *Smart Set* book reviews every two years, he pasted up *Prejudices, First Series*. The book had been received enthusiastically that fall, and now he plunged into *Prejudices, Second Series,* dealing not only with the Humanists "and other such grave and glittering fish," but with the whole range of American culture which now interested him. After all, he had reasoned, "Every normal man must be tempted, at times, to spit on his hands, hoist the black flag, and begin slitting throats." Why confine the *Prejudices* to book reviews? Edition by successful edition, literary criticism was forced from the series, until, in 1924, but one of the seventeen essays in *Prejudices, Fourth Series* dealt with letters. Mencken thought the books "tripe," but they served a useful purpose—the solidifying of his month-by-month opinions between covers—and certainly they contained much of his best writing. Between *Prejudices* he worked on introductions for *The Free Lance Series,* a project of doubtful feasibility from its inception. The scheme called for handy-sized little philosophic books, each prefaced by Mencken, tied together with the title of his memorable column. E. W. Howe, Edwin Muir, Pío Baroja, Nietzsche's *Anti-Christ,* and James N. Wood were brought out between 1919 and 1921. The last of the series—the revised *In Defense of Women*—had an excellent sale, but the plan had proved a failure and so was abandoned. He then turned to a revised edition of *The American Language.* Edmund Wilson and E. A. Hecker were recruited to write an A.E.F. glossary, the cargos of material voluntarily sent him were sorted and organized, and Knopf, over his stiff protests, was persuaded to print the result on the thickest paper obtainable, so as to present an imposing product—"fat as a bible." The book sold extremely well, despite Knopf's vow it was a typographical monstrosity, and Mencken, to his horror, saw yet a third edition looming before him. The pedagogy was deeper in his blood than he had thought.

For six weeks after his influenza attack, Nathan was in indifferent health, and the responsibility for getting out *The Smart Set* lay largely in Mencken's hands. That October the pressmen went on strike, and no sooner had arrangements been made to print the magazine in Albany than second-class mailing facilities went berserk, cutting off whole towns from periodical literature. The mess cost *The Smart Set* fifteen hundred dollars for one month alone, and Mencken began to consider inaugurating more "louse magazines" to raise money. As it turned out, this was not necessary. The funds built up by the three wartime pulps held out, the spreading fame of *The Smart Set* brought a Famous Players contract for permission to display its epigrams on the screen, and Mencken, who had bought no Liberty Bonds during the war, enjoyed the amusement of picking them up on the stock market at 83. The financial crisis passed quickly, but it brought him to New York at a time when intellectual America was seething with the new excitement. He had not yet begun his trend away from literature; he was still regarded, and still regarded himself, as primarily a literary critic, and the swarms of young and promising authors drew him irresistibly to the city more and more. This social activity conspired to cut sharply into his Hollins Street activity. Owen Hatteras had won a majority and the D.S.O. in the war, and the necessity for pumping material into his new department, "Americana," meant the constant culling of provincial newspapers for absurd news items. Hatteras's patriotic pretensions, it developed, were not so absurd as his creators had thought; his demands on his creators' time temporarily turned aside, in late 1920, what was meant to be the most damaging book on democracy ever written. Mencken simply had no time for it.

Steadily, the lure of the city increased. He remained the Monthly Hick, but New York was now teeming with hicks who had something to say, and the cosmopolitan tone of the literati, combined with the tremendous esteem in which that literati now held him, served to temper his painful self-consciousness. Goodman, a Philadelphian, had the same love of German culture and good food which were Mencken's; his Broadway projects—*The Old Soak* and *Poppy*—kept him in New York as a powerful attraction. Rascoe, Boyd, and Thomas Beer were now there, and Knopf, eager for publishing suggestions, drew them together at luncheons whenever Mencken was in New York. Peace had been patched up with Dreiser, and Mencken got a tremendous enjoyment out of running into a bookstore with him, bowling the dumfounded clerks off their feet, and proceeding to autograph every book in sight. His suite at the Algonquin was thrown open to late parties for Huneker, Rascoe, Boyd, Goodman, and Nathan, with illegal hooch and subversive statements carrying them through until dawn. Nathan, once back on his feet, was as delightful as ever. Together, he and Mencken redecorated *The Smart Set* walls, tacking up a Hoover-for-President poster, a one-sheet of Louis Robie's *Crackerjacks,* and a batch of temperance posters Edna Ferber sent them from Paris. They sent out requests for a gilt chair which would collapse if a fat lady poet sat in it, photographs of the late Czar Nicholas, Archbishop Manning, and Lillian Russell (in tights), and a concrete bust of a leading reformer. When delighted friends responded, they promptly announced themselves as candidates for the Republican Presidential and Vice-Presidential nominations in *The Smart Set,* publishing a platform including promises to take the Statute of Liberty out beyond the three-mile limit and dump it, to wear no cutaway coats and plugged hats, to abolish the Y.M.C.A., to establish enormous arenas in which to turn clergymen loose upon one another, and to turn the Philippines over to Japan. Word of the announcement spread, to the indignation of Harding bigwigs, and even in London there was a brief, solemn flurry of interest over the "surprise candidates." In the New York *Sun,* Berton Braley pretty well summed up the attitude of their contemporaries to all this with his satirical "Mencken, Nathan, and God":

There were three who sailed away one night
Far from the maddening throng
And two of the three were always right
And everyone else was wrong
But they took another along, these two,
To bear them company,
For He was the only One ever knew
Why the other two should be.
And so they sailed away, these three—

Mencken,
Nathan,
And God.

And the two they talked of the aims of art,
Which they alone understood,
And they quite agreed from the very start
That nothing was any good,
Except some novels that Dreiser wrote
And some plays from Germany.
When God objected, they rocked the boat
And dropped Him into the sea,
"For You have no critical facultee,"

Said Mencken
And Nathan
To God.

The two came cheerfully sailing home
Over the surging tide,
And trod once more on their native loam,
Wholly self-satisfied.
And the little group that calls them great
Welcomed them fawningly.
Though why the rest of us tolerate
This precious pair must be
Something nobody else can see

But Mencken,
Nathan,
And God!

No issue was serious to them, no figure exempt from the harlequinade. Every topic of importance, it seemed, wound up on the vaudeville stage as a sort of burlesque of itself. Nathan, who loved the theater, and Mencken, who hated it, spent much time defending their respective positions, but when the difference reached the dignity of debate, it was slapped down mightily by Nathan. He had, that season, discovered a play by Dario Nicodemi which, in sheer awfulness, surpassed anything ever seen on the New York stage. Indeed, so terrible was the performance that, fascinated, he sat through the last curtain. Back at the Royalton he wrote Mencken, with great seriousness, that however much a man might dislike the theater, he should not miss the greatest drama since Ibsen's debut. Mencken was doubtful, but if Nathan said so. . . . Up he came to New York, dressed to kill for the great occasion. Nathan tipped off John Williams, then Charles Frohman's right-hand man, and the three took a box at the Morosco. Mencken was placed in the center. There he sat, bolt upright, looking, as Nathan told him later, like Harding, while his hosts, during the performance, murmured ecstatically to one another, "Oh, this scene!" . . . "Isn't it tremendous?" . . . "What a speech!" etc. Mencken at first said nothing—Nathan was a drama critic, he ought to know—but as the farce wore on, he murmured over and over again, more and more loudly, "Pishposh!" At the very end, he caught on, eyed Nathan and Williams with great severity, and lustily croaked, "PISHPOSH!" And the dignified debate was over.

His reputation, like himself, was most stimulated among other aliens in New York, or among writers in other parts of the country. The intellectual masturbators of Third Avenue —the "Tenth-rate Village geniuses"—found it impossible to imagine that a man so Philistine in his personal habits could be more than an impostor. His New York friends, like himself, were strangers to Broadway; for them, New York was sort of no man's land where they might cavort, free from the taboos of the home town. His most enthusiastic followers lay in the provinces, and their number seemed to increase in direct proportion to the ridicule directed at rural regions. All over America the reaction against patriotism had set in, and if the local boomers fumed when a specific locale was singled out for *Smart Set* abuse, the local literati flourished. No more violent attack was printed in these years than the revised "Sahara of the Bozart," and none stirred up greater enthusiasm among the Bozart's poets. The South, Mencken wrote, was "that stupendous region of fat farms, shoddy cities and paralyzed cerebrums . . . that gargantuan paradise of the fourth-rate" which stretched, "a vast plain of mediocrity, stupidity, lethargy, almost of dead silence," between "senile" Virginia and "crass, gross, vulgar and obnoxious" Georgia. Contemplating its letters, Mencken thought of "Asia Minor, resigned to the Armenians, Greeks and wild swine, of Poland abandoned to the Poles." Shortly after the essay appeared in *Prejudices, Second Series,* young Emily Clark of Richmond brought out her first issue of *The Reviewer.* Included was a laudatory review of the book, pleading guilty to the charges. Mencken, who was reading virtually every regional periodical, received it enthusiastically and offered his assistance to Miss Clark. To its pages he brought the names of Hergesheimer, Rascoe, Boyd, Ellen Glasgow, Frances Newman, and the work of an obscure Greensboro, North Carolina, editorial writer named Gerald W. Johnson. His deep conviction that literature should be "a particular outgrowth of its particular soil" inspired him to refer all talented Southerners to *The Reviewer;* indeed, so distinguished did its writing become that, on reconsideration, he was obliged to write "Violets in the Sahara," an answer to his own attack. Coming to Richmond to visit Cabell, he met Miss Clark, and their friendship grew.

In that masculine society he had built around himself, she was unique. There were many women in Mencken's life in these years, but their position was sharply defined and almost extra-human. They provided admirable decoration at New York parties—bright, waxen figures who might stay only if they giggled appreciatively and kept their mouths shut—but they did not alter his flippant view of love and marriage. He insisted that he remained single only because no attractive woman had ever attempted to marry him, or because those who had had used toothpicks in public, or suffered from acne, or offered "the subtle but quite inescapable suggestion" they were wearing soiled underwear. The fact was he had no time for the intricacies of romance and had to take his pleasure as best he could. He keenly felt the lack of any solid feminine companionship, particularly in New York, when he was away from the domesticity his sister and mother provided. "I'll bet you don't think I have any fun," he told Burton Rascoe's wife one evening, adding, wistfully and defensively, "I've got a girl."

His social energies were devoted to cultivating and whooping up the young talent which had sought out *The Smart Set*. Characteristically, he met the new excitement with great industry and constant grumbling. He acknowledged that "a hundred thousand second-hand Coronas rattle and jingle in ten thousand remote and lonely towns, and the mail of every magazine editor is as heavy as the mail of a get-rich-quick stock broker," but the manuscripts pouring in from every direction, he wrote Boyd, were "mainly crap." It may be that he actually thought so, but if so, his interests had suddenly and completely turned to the soliciting, reading, and purchasing of crap. Every young man who approached either Mencken or Nathan was cordially received and his talents thoroughly investigated. When a bacteriologist named Paul de Kruif sat down one afternoon in the old Hotel Pontchartrain in Detroit and wrote Mencken, asking if he could combine science and writing, he was invited to *The Smart Set* for succor. When a playwright named Eugene O'Neill timidly ventured to cross recognized dramatic horizons, his plays were printed and he was urged to go still further.[2] And when three young Princeton graduates—John Peale Bishop, Edmund Wilson, and F. Scott Fitzgerald—stormed the Royalton one morning after the war, they were wined, victualed, and warned by Nathan that failure to submit stories to the magazine would be taken as a personal affront. Sometimes the

[2] From West Point, New York, O'Neill wrote on May 1, 1919, "Dear Mr. Nathan: I am sending under separate cover, for Mr. Mencken and yourself, two volumes of my book which has just appeared. I hope you will accept them as small remembrances that I remember how much of gratitude I owe both of you for your encouragement and constructive criticism. I feel that in great measure the book is already yours since you published three of the plays and had the very first peep at one of the others. . . ."

manuscripts, even after repeated rewriting under direction, proved unacceptable. Such was the fate of Wilson's first sex story, "The Devil." Other times their acceptance gave the author his entree into the publishing field, as with Fitzgerald's "Babes in the Woods," which had originally appeared in *The Nassau Lit* and for which he was paid thirty dollars.[3] It was this critical tutelage, given the first faltering steps of nearly every major writer of the Twenties, which accounts for Mencken's elevation to critical sainthood by the first war generation. For almost a decade there was scarcely a major writer in the country who did not trace his career from a first acceptance by *The Smart Set*.

Mencken and Nathan still avoided literary parties, partly because of the people they drew, but also because they had no time for such frivolity. In the first year after the war, they were lured to but one such affair. It turned out to be the most ghastly experience of their careers to date—and by all odds the most profitable. Tom Smith of the *Century* insisted they drop by "just for one drink." Mencken complained vigorously in the cab, and as soon as the door opened he knew he had made a dreadful mistake. They were greeted by a tall, skinny redhead, obviously quite drunk, who wrapped one arm around Mencken's neck and another around Nathan's. Resistance was quite useless; he had them by the esophagi, and as Nathan groaned and Mencken grunted pitifully, this apparition from another planet yelled into their flinching eardrums, "So you guys are critics, are you? Well, let me tell you something. I'm the best goddam writer in this here goddam country and if you, Georgie, and you, Hank, don't know it, you'll know it goddam soon. Say . . ." There was no escape, at least not for the present. While Smith shrugged and the other guests, amused, looked on, the summit of their fears held forth on his own abilities and the necessity for favorable notice in *The Smart Set*. At the end

---

[3] He surveyed the one hundred and twenty-two rejection slips pinned to a frieze in his room and went out to buy a pair of white flannels—not, as he once said, a fancy fan for Zelda, his fiancée. At this time, however, Mencken's name had little meaning for Fitzgerald. A year later it had so grown that the author inserted it into the proofs of *This Side of Paradise*. It had the right air.

of a half hour the door of the flat opened and Mencken and Nathan, wild-eyed, fled down the stairs and into the first cab that passed, sympathizing with one another and vowing never again to come within shouting distance of Smith's place. But their troubles with "the louse," as Mencken called their persecutor for want of a name, were not over. Next morning, dropping by the office on his way back to Baltimore, he was amazed to find the proofs of a novel by the redhead, together with a note from the publisher, thanking him for the praise he had allegedly bestowed on the author at Smith's party. Disgusted, he was about to toss the sheets in the wastebasket when he suddenly remembered he had nothing to read on the train. In Jersey City he became interested. In Philadelphia he was fascinated, and back at Hollins Street that afternoon he excitedly wrote Nathan, "Grab hold of the bar-rail, steady yourself, and prepare for a terrible shock! I've just read the advance sheets of the book that *lump* we met at Schmidt's wrote and, by God, he has done the job! It's a genuinely excellent piece of work. I begin to believe that perhaps there isn't a God after all. There is no justice in the world."

The novel, as many will have guessed, was *Main Street;* the drunk, Sinclair Lewis, or, as Mencken came to know him, "Red." His performance that first night had not been out of character, but Mencken had learned to be tolerant with men of talent, and once he and Nathan had extracted a promise to "keep your goddam hands off our goddam necks," they got along famously. Lewis, in fiction, had precisely the same aims Mencken had in criticism, and his peculiar behavior was but another manifestation of the urge which prompted Mencken's evangelical letters to friends. Between them, on Mencken's visits to New York, they gave bar patrons as bizarre a show in the perversion of American mores as even that jaded audience had ever seen, with Mencken quoting from prohibition pamphlets and Lewis delivering a lecture on the merits of Rotary or a sermon on the beauty of the Church of God. By January of 1922, Lewis was looking to Mencken for critical tutelage as Dreiser had a decade before. "You ask about the new novel—which won't be out till next September," he wrote from London.

It's curiously associated with yourself. A year ago in a criticism of Main Street you said that what ought to be taken up now is the American city—not NY or Chi but the cities of 200,000 to 500,000—the Baltimores and Omahas and Buffalos and Birminghams, etc. I was startled to read it because that was precisely what I was then planning, and am now doing. But your piece helped me to decide on this particular one as against one or two others which, at the time, I also wanted to do.

I think you'll like it—I hope . . . you do. All our friends are in it—the Rotary Club, the popular preacher, the Chamber of Commerce, the new bungalows, the bunch of business men jolliers lunching at the Athletic Club. It ought to be at least 2000% American, as well as forward-looking, right-thinking, optimistic, selling the idea of success, and go-getterish.

The central character is a Solid Citizen, one George F. Babbitt, real estate man, who has a Dutch Colonial house out on Floral Heights. . . .

Throughout the Twenties, as Harding's Normalcy gave way to Coolidge's "The Business of America Is Business" and Hoover's Rugged Individualism, the staccato Mencken-Lewis hammering grew through *Babbitt* and *Elmer Gantry,* through issue after issue of Menckenian declarations that the whole bag of tricks of the businessman, America's new hero, represented but superficial accomplishment—that their acquirement put "little more strain on the mental powers than a chimpanzee suffers learning how to catch a penny or scratch a match." To the horror of the Montparnasse deadbeats, who fancied themselves the Only True Enemies of America's crass and vulgar culture, Mencken and Lewis became the champions of the insurgent young men, of the Mooney, Billings, and Debs partisans, and the chief targets of the Philistines. Later, in 1922, Lewis formally announced the entente in a press conference, declaring, "If I had the power, I'd make Henry Mencken the Pope of America. He spreads just the message of sophistication that we need so badly"; thereafter, in country papers all over rural America, it became the custom of the Twenties to read stories beginning:

WRITERS ARE TERMED
MERE "ICONOCLASTS"
H. L. MENCKEN AND SINCLAIR
LEWIS DENOUNCED AT FIRST
CONGREGATIONAL SERVICE
BAN ON LIQUOR LAUDED

While the storm raged about H. L. Mencken in many a farflung pulpit, H. L. Mencken laid bricks and played with pet turtles. His back yard—that narrow stretch of ground between the rear door and the old pony stable—had become, late in the war, a sort of private pasture to which he might retire with his thought, and he was now engaged in throwing up a sturdy brick wall on either side to insure privacy. The wooden fence on the north side of the yard was first torn down, and Mencken, trowel in one hand and cement can in the other, dug into a pile of bricks while his mother watched anxiously from the window. With the thoroughness which touched everything he did, he took to dropping in evenings at nearby Linder's Saloon, the hangout of Baltimore's bricklayers; now, with the information there gained, he went about the simple business of laying one brick on top of another. At first he did the thing very badly. His square, chunky hands— bricklayer's hands, they had told him down at Linder's—were forever getting in one another's way or under a downcoming brick and became, under this constant mauling, all but unfit for weekly piano playing. After a few weeks he got to be expert, however, and slowly the wall rose, solid and erect, not an inch out of line. Still he was unsatisfied. He decided to become fancy. Persian tiles were set into the brick, and a concrete fountain, his masterpiece, was lugged in from the back alley and installed. Visitors to 1524 Hollins Street were first shown the slackening of his convex waist, then led through the house to the back yard to see the fountain—"It actually works. Isn't that amazing?"—and the wall which would be standing "when the rest of Baltimore is dust," the long mass of bricks which was walling Mencken in and his neighbors out.

The turtles came in 1921, when August's dog Tessie, "fifteen years old, and a virgin," died. Mencken mournfully buried her in the yard, set a bronze plate in the wall overhead, and brought the new pets. Of an evening, before beginning the night's work, he would squat in the back yard with his prize, General Sawyer, escorting him in and out of his little pen. A month or so after his acquisition, and to the great embarrassment of his owner, General Sawyer scandalized the family by laying three eggs. Next day he was renamed Mrs. Mary Baker G. Eddy.

Mencken's income had now stabilized at six thousand dollars a year, and much of it was sunk into improving the home he never intended to leave. In the early 1920's he had the house virtually rebuilt. New floors were put in, a larger kitchen was built on, the heating system was replaced, every new appliance which would lessen the burden of housekeeping for his sister and mother was installed, and in the third-floor workroom a washstand appeared, to facilitate the furious hand-washing sessions which always punctuated an evening of writing. Mencken particularly admired new plumbing: "I wouldn't swap an American bathroom for the Acropolis," he wrote Emily Clark. He tried, unsuccessfully, to redeem the house's ground rent—a medieval Baltimore levy which exacts annual rentals from home owners. Anna, now in her sixties, erect and dignified, presided over the house as matriarch. All her sons, and particularly her eldest, adored her. After a stag party downstairs, before going to bed, he scrupulously swept the floor, dusted the furniture, and washed and dried the dishes that she might not be annoyed in the morning. To his everlasting amusement, both his sister and his mother maintained that he was like all writers—absent-minded, careless, and quite without ability to cope with the smaller businesses of life. "They never speak of my workroom save in terms of horror, though it is actually the most orderly room in the house. Weekly I am accused of having lost all my socks and handkerchiefs, though they are in my clothespress all the while." Monthly, plans were made to organize his life, and he solemnly went along with the scheme, vowing to behave himself in the future—to keep a record of where he left his undershirts, to abstain from dropping cigar ashes on the floor, to keep the floor visible in his office. "On my death-bed, I dare say, I shall carry on the masquerade. That is to say, I shall swallow a clinical thermometer or two, upset my clam-broth over my counterpane, keep an ouija board and a set of dice under my pillow, and maybe, at the end, fall clumsily out of bed." Anna, for her part, preserved a customary in-sulation from the world beyond Union Square. A friend asked her what she thought of an article her son had written. "I haven't read it," she replied. "I never read anything he writes. That's his business." But there was small doubt of her supremacy within the handsome new vestibule. One Christ-mas, while his mother was entertaining guests in the living room, Mencken quietly wandered in and began to fuss with a vase of flowers. Anna stopped in the middle of a sentence and turned around. "Harry!" she snapped. "Stop that!" And Harry, after a perceptible start, backed away from the vase and meekly sat down.

To the third floor each morning now came his secretary, Miss Alice B. Deering, crisp and neat, notebook and pencils in hand. His enormous correspondence and the self-imposed need for answering each letter, no matter how absurd, in the return mail had made her necessary. The study had changed little; all four walls were lined with books now, and pictures of Cabell, Bismarck, and his Leipzig ancestors—the product of two years' research by a firm specializing in tracing ancestry—stood behind his desk. The letters were shorter now, however close a friend the correspondent; there were too many, even with dictation. Otherwise, they were un-changed. He voiced the usual physical plaints: a tumor had been dug out of his foot, he was off to St. Agnes Hospital to have a folded membrane in his rectum investigated, or, de-pressed, was merely shipping out samples of his urine to all known pathologists. (A note of desperation here: "I begin to believe that in the end, as the hearse approaches the crema-tory, I shall rise up and give three cheers.")

The preposterous flights of fancy, his chief refuge in moods of artistic depression, were brought up to date. He organized a spurious golf club, placed it near Richmond, had stationery printed, and recruited prominent Southerners to membership. The organization over, he sent out word that the club's pro— hitherto referred to only as "Sandy McTavish"—was a Negro. He spread the rumor that Knopf was investing his money in taxicabs, chrome yellow, with green stripes and purple spots and a douche bag in every cab. A Saturday Night Club member, he reported, was making a fortune with literary toilet paper. "He prints pornographic serials on it. As the passions rise the bowels move." He stoutly defended Boyd, who, he said, had been accused by Goodman of violating the person of his nigger wench. "I doubt it. Boyd never goes beyond pinching the buttocks." And when, during the course of the Fatty Arbuckle case, the history of Miss Rappe's bladder was spread throughout the land, Mencken wrote all his friends he understood they were involved, asked them to write and tell him all about it, and promised, in any event, to do his best to keep their names out of the papers.

He made small concessions to fame. Invitations to speak—even a thirty-thousand-dollar six-week lecture tour offer, made jointly to Mencken and Nathan—were spurned. In Baltimore he consented to appear twice yearly, at City College, a public high school, and at Goucher College for women, and then he agreed only with the understanding that the talks would approach the absolute in informality. His addresses at Goucher, which began in 1923, were advertised among the students as esoteric comments on this or that philosophy, but the topic was always the same: How To Catch Husbands. He treated such occasions far more lightly than the least of his family obligations—hunting down a hairnet for little Virginia Mencken, say, or attending to the needs of his sister-in-law, at Johns Hopkins for a minor operation. Life at home had stabilized for the first time since his father's death, and Mencken, a strong believer in the family circle, meant to see that the wants of each member were attended to. Charlie and August, after years on the road, had settled down: Charlie at Pittsburgh, and August, after one last trip to Havana, at home. The house had never been fuller, and Mencken, shut up in his workroom, was somehow happier to know that downstairs were his sister, his mother, August, and, on holidays, Charlie and his family. He brought them presents, held forth at the table, and entertained them with stories of the morons in New York. Once, he almost blew them up.

The explosion—it seems no exaggeration to call it that—

came as the climax of a long series of events, directly connected with, and in flagrant violation of, the Eighteenth Amendment. The great drought, or, as Mencken was pleased to call it, The Horror, began on January 16, 1920, but his concern with it began long before that. To one so given to the pleasures of good liquors, the approach of the noble experiment loomed as a ghastly and indescribable thing. He kept mum in *The Smart Set*, unable to find words apt to the crime, and watched the distillers like a cat. Presently he sent a dispatch to Goodman, who was equally concerned, that the brewers were "taking time by the foreskin"—were closing down their plants and converting them to oleomargarine factories. That week Goodman slipped out of New York, bound for Europe in quest of a magic yeast, and Mencken headed north to rally Nathan and Tom Smith for the trying days ahead. Smith hired the biggest automobile he could find in Greater New York, and he, Mencken, and Nathan toured the liquor stores systematically, buying everything in sight. Smith stocked his flat, Nathan his apartment, and Mencken, back in Baltimore, filled the house so completely "that the bottles clink every time I walk across the floor." He did more. One corner of his cellar was set aside for wines, and he began at once to import the cheap synthetic stuff which already issued from Hoboken, New Jersey. In late January, 1920, a Baltimore wine dealer went out of business, and Mencken, who arranged to be on hand at the right moment, bought up his stock of Rhine wine and French red wine labels. These were pasted on the Hoboken sewage, giving him a cellar with an imposing look if a metallic taste. The Saturday and Sunday Night Clubs met in joint session at Hollins Street to mourn the closing of the bars and debate the future. A rapid inventory disclosed they had enough gin to last two years and some seven hundred bottles of beer. The Rennert, for obvious reasons, was eliminated as a meeting place. Hildebrand's violin shop was similarly out. At length they decided to go underground. Future meetings would be held at the homes of individual members, with shades drawn and each host responsible for the evening's refreshment. Did anyone know how to brew beer? Everyone looked at

Mencken. He was the great hymner of Pilsner. Besides, he was a graduate of the Polytechnic where, someone vaguely suggested, you learned how to do things. Well *did* he?

Sure, he blustered. Nothing simpler. Leave it to Heine. Forthwith he bought a vast number of bottles, retired to the kitchen, and began mixing and stirring, mixing and stirring. When the beer had fermented for what seemed a reasonable time, and after an examination by "Gustav Kabernagel, the well-known urinalysist," he bottled it and—this from a graduate of the Polytechnic, mind you—put it *out in the back yard.* He had, August told him later in a post-mortem, made two major mistakes: he had bottled it too soon and had left it precisely where the early summer sun would strike it most sharply. The day of the catastrophe, he alerted all members of the club to be on hand for a swell treat. Later in the day, the first thirsty arrivals rang the bell by the old brass door-plate. As they entered the vestibule, a muffled thunder, followed by a tinny rattling, as of shrapnel, came from the back yard. Everyone flinched. Mencken stood motionless. Then, as he turned toward the inside of the house, another explosion followed, and another, and then another. Hard by Tessie's memorial, a few feet from the wall fountain, all hell had broken loose. Everyone took cover; then, as the sounds of battle rolled away, August, wearing boxing gloves and carrying a screen before him, went out to investigate. The entire batch, save for a few bottles, was ruined. It was on this evidence that Mencken, writing his memoirs, claimed, "I was, so far as I have been able to discover, the first man south of the Mason Dixon line to brew a drinkable home brew. . . ."

Steadily, his liquor stock dwindled, until in January, 1922, after a devastating visit by Red Lewis, he had touched bottom. In Richmond he and Hergesheimer were reduced to White Mule Whisky; in New York the walls of the Royalton were treated to the bizarre spectacle of Mencken and Nathan discussing Joyce over cocoa cups. No more did the bottles clink as he walked across the floor; indeed, it took long, awful minutes of persistent searching to turn up anything at all. Then it was he decided to build a *real* cellar, fit to cope with any emergency. Concrete, a foot thick, was poured; the walls were covered with skulls and crossbones, and on the door was written the legend: "WARNING: Tampering with this gate will release chlorine gas under 250 pounds pressure." In desperation, he spent his mornings building shelves inside and his afternoons decanting, filtering, doctoring, labeling, and tasting the precious little that was left. But succor was on the way. In Union Hill, New Jersey, he and Nathan found an excellent drinking place, and once Goodman was back, things eased up considerably. Goodman had a genius for discovering first-rate speakeasies, it developed, and turned up some excellent places in Hoboken and Manhattan. More, he had returned from Munich with a genuine Löwenbräu dry yeast. Mencken turned the yeast over to Max Broedel, who had it purified in the Johns Hopkins bacteriological laboratory, where it survived until the end of prohibition, a constant source of Saturday-night joy. Meanwhile, Mencken contacted every reliable bootlegger in Baltimore and set up a satisfactory arrangement with a Philadelphia author for shipments of bathtub gin. He seemed to get a tremendous pleasure out of guarded telephone conversations with his suppliers, and went so far as to procure a false nose for security while trafficking with their agents. In *The Smart Set* and *Prejudices*, he waged a campaign to solve the problems of the human race by getting everyone gently stewed. The bootlegger became a mock hero to his readers. "Think of him," he wrote,

creeping in his motorboat on Christmas Eve, risking his life that the greatest of Christian festivals may be celebrated in a Christian and respectable manner! Think of him soaked and freezing, facing his exile and its hardships uncomplainingly, that his mother may escape the poor farm, that his wife may have her operation for gall-stones, that his little children may be decently fed and clad, and go to school regularly, and learn the principles of Americanism! . . . on the roaring deep there are still men who are colossally he, and when the bugle calls they will not fail.

The club's progress underground was remarkably smooth. Save for the necessity of permitting women in the household to sit in on the meetings, which had been held in Hildebrand's completely masculine shop, and Hildebrand's purchase of a dozen cellos, one for each member's house, to avoid toting the one around, there were few changes in the weekly evenings. The Rennert, its respectability unable to cope with the new era, was abandoned even as a mid-weekly meeting place for club members. Schellhase's Restaurant on Franklin Street had cornered the market on the best of the new beer, and there it was Mencken met his friends at noon or after a session of bricklaying. The turning to Schellhase's was but one of the major changes prohibition wrought in Mencken's solidified personal life. He began, early in the Twenties, to participate in annual Terrapin parties at Easton, Maryland, held for the purpose of gorging seafood and drinking applejack in its native state from gourds. These Oktoberfests always resulted in bitter physical complaints, ("My liver is swelled to the thickness of seven inches, and I have spiders in my urine"), but they served for him the same peculiar function that all-night country-club gin parties were serving elsewhere. Like everyone else, Mencken was drinking more, and home did not quite seem the proper place to lose control of oneself. On a somewhat higher lever, he began to attend the Moravian Bach Chorus festivals in Bethlehem each spring with Knopf, largely because he enjoyed the B-Minor Mass, but also because genuine Helles was for sale for a dime a glass over the public bars and nearby was stationed a convenient church against which he could relieve himself when the long sessions brought discomfort. Joseph Hergesheimer, who sometimes tagged along to Bethlehem, was now living at his colorful old Dower House in nearby Pennsylvania, and there, of a week end, Mencken would travel for two days of pleasant, alcoholic talk. Professionally, his violent attacks on the Drys brought him his first close political friends: sardonic Senator James Reed of Missouri, and Albert C. Ritchie, the powerful governor of Maryland, both vehement enemies of prohibition. Mencken's political naïveté was never better demonstrated than in his admiration for these two men, each of whom had gained power through the very public posturing he so scorned. But in 1923 both were in favor of repeal, and that, for Mencken, was enough.

His final adjustment from war to postwar tempo came late in 1919, when he rejoined the *Sun*. Deeply hurt by the hands-off treatment he had received from the paper after his return from Cuba, he spurned all overtures after the Armistice, including an offer to return full time at one hundred fifty dollars a week—just three times his salary in 1916. He believed he had outgrown the paper, and in this he was quite right. But powerful forces of habit were working on him, and his old cronies at Baltimore and Charles Streets were anxious to please. After some haggling, he agreed to act as general editorial adviser, with a fat retainer and the understanding his work would involve no more than a few hours a month. Successful in this, the *Sun* pressed him to write some articles. Mencken wobbled slightly. ". . . I doubt that they could either stand the doctrine or pay the price," he wrote Boyd. "I shall not make an arrangement that does not include absolute freedom of *all* subjects and very good pay." He was finally won over by the prospect of Wilson's retirement from the political scene and the consequent reversion of the *Sun* to an anti-administration organ, a role far more suited to Mencken's liking, and by the advent of a new management in the Sun Building. Kent had been managing editor of both morning and evening papers, but Kent was primarily a political writer, not an editor, and there was some feeling he had been filling the papers with politics, to the annoyance of those with other interests. After a brief period of reorganization, Paul Patterson, the business manager, was named publisher. Patterson, with definite ideas of the sort of direction the *Sun* should take, received advance warning of his new position and cast around for counsel. He asked Mencken and Harry Black to join him in setting the papers' pattern. The three met, night after night, at Black's house, emerging at length with the blueprint which has governed the *Sun* papers ever since. The evening and morning papers were given separate managements, make-up and typography were changed, and the front pages were cleared of advertising. Henry M. Hyde, former star reporter for the Chicago *Tribune,* was brought out of retirement, and to the *Evening Sun* as managing editor came J. Edwin Murphy, a newsroom tornado admirably suited to that paper's new tone of pertinacity, persistence, and irony. Most important, from Mencken's point of view, was the decision henceforth to cover the national and international events with staff men—most important because he was to be one of the chief workhorses in the new system.

Since he had had a hand in shaping the policy, he became more hospitable to the *Sun;* became, indeed, one of the major props of the editorial department. He began writing essays for the Monday editorial page of the evening paper after the manner of his *Smart Set* editorials and in the vein and style of the old "Free Lance," and when Patterson, determined to cover the 1920 conventions as they had never been covered by any other paper, proposed to send him along with the crew of *Sun* men, he was quite agreeable. He was—but of the rest of the crew, it developed, many were not.

Woodrow Wilson lay broken and dying in Washington, but in the offices of the *Sun* he remained to some the same warrior of idealism who had triumphed so splendidly in Baltimore eight years before. Men like John Owens, political reporter, and Adams were extremely sensitive about the President's defeat in Congress and viewed the return of so rude and outspoken an enemy of the New Freedom as Mencken with grave misgivings. They were willing he should come along to Chicago for the Republican convention, however, until the week before the trip was to begin. On that Monday, Mencken, with sublime indifference to the feeling against him, wrote a bitter piece describing the President as a "congenital liar." For Owens and Adams this was too much. They stormed into the front office, white-faced, and threatened to resign unless Mencken's name were withdrawn from the convention roster. Open rebellion seemed at hand, and Patterson called in Mencken to talk it over. Mencken offered to retire from the trip—pointing out, however, that the *Sun* had been under no obligation to print the piece—but Patterson would have none of it. Everyone, he decided, would go along. In addition, he would send a case of 100-proof hooch. An armed truce arranged, Patterson left for the convention. The others were to follow.

The hooch turned the trick—that and an absurd little jingle Mencken chanted in rhythm with the humming of the Pullman's wheels. On the train Owens refused to speak to him at first, but once the suitcase was opened and the singing begun, Wilson, the treaty, and the New Freedom were forgotten. Mencken, the battered old portable by his seat, his shirt open, threw back his spherical head and let go:

Sing, Oh Sing! Of Lydia Pinkham, Pinkham, Pinkham
And her love of the human race, race, race
She can cure all female weakness
And the pimples on your face.

In Chicago Patterson called the hotel to find out what had happened on the train. Owens answered the phone. "Is everything quiet?" asked the publisher. "Quiet!" came the answer. "My God!" And in the background came the swelling refrain,

Sing, Oh Sing! (Yes, singosing!) Of Lydia Pinkham,
Pinkham, Pinkham
And her love (altruistic love!) of the human race,
race, race
She can cure (bio-log-i-cally!) all female weakness
And the pimp-les on your god-damned dir-ty face.

Wilson lived three and a half years, but that was merely a social blunder. So far as Mencken was concerned, he died in that boozy Chicago hotel room.

Mencken returned from the Chicago convention on the same car with Henry Cabot Lodge, whom he admired enormously, and laid away whisky against the Democratic show in San Francisco. As it turned out, this was unnecessary. The San Franciscans had taken care of that and everything else admirably, and his week there, for Mencken, was a superb circus. The weather was delightful—it had been terribly hot in Chicago—the liquor was abundant, and the women were most amiable. His most amazing adventure while there was to wake up one morning in an unfamiliar bed with a strange but not unlovely woman. Thinking her to be a cheap tart he had picked up during the hazy evening, he jumped into his spacious pants and fled down the stairs. Later in the day, however, he discovered her to be a respectable San Francisco woman, a Democrat who had seen him floundering in a pitiable condition and had decided to care for him "in a Christian manner." Mencken promptly betook himself to the nearest florist's shop and sent her a large and fragrant bouquet. At the climax of the convention, the band broke into a series of tunes honoring Al Smith, and Mencken, singing with the convention, pounced up on a chair, grabbed a baton, and waved time enthusiastically to the strains of "East Side, West Side," "Little Annie Roonie," and "Tammany." The breakdown of reserve in the midst of political chicanery was to him a wonderful thing, and those in attendance remember him best on that chair, waving the baton, tremendous joy written on his face. All, that is, save the respectable woman Democrat who cared for him in a Christian manner.

His Monday articles continued in the *Evening Sun,* a source of constant controversy in Baltimore, and between his magazine work and other writing he sandwiched in out-of-town assignments and editorial suggestions. He covered the Dempsey-Carpentier fight in Jersey City ("Clout, clout, clout!"), the Washington disarmament conference of 1921-22, and brought to the editorial page such contributors as Harold Stearns, Lewis Mumford, and Vincent O'Sullivan. His note to Patterson that a cartoonist named Edmund Duffy was loose in New York brought Duffy and, eventually, three Pulitzer prizes to the paper; correspondence with Gerald Johnson, in North Carolina, eventually landed Johnson in the *Sun's* editorial rooms as a staff member. In August, 1922, he sailed from New York for an extended three months' tour of Europe for the paper, this time under far more pleasant circumstances than had surrounded his last junket. Britons were generally hostile to him on arrival, but a trip to Manchester with Jim Bone, of the *Guardian,* and a long songfest in the press club there changed all that. From London he crossed to Holland, spending a day with the German Crown Prince on his lonely island there. He traveled through hectic Berlin, visited, in Pilsen, Czechoslovakia, the celebrated cellar of Pilsener-Urquell, "the cradle of the human race," and returned to Munich for the Oktoberfest, which he thought stupendous, and in which he joined enthusiastically, sweating freely and happily with forty thousand soused Müncheners. Germany confused him, he wrote Patterson. "Outwardly, everything looks serene (the communist outbreaks reported are chiefly no more than drunken fights) but every intelligent man looks for a catastrophe. If it comes, then there will be a colossal massacre of the Jews." He stopped in Leipzig briefly, then sailed from Bremen for home.

He was anxious to get back. The time, he had decided, was ripe to resurrect his old dream of the *Blue Review*—to give American intellectuals of the Twenties the magazine for which they were yearning.

For some time he had been anxious to get rid of *The Smart Set*. For one thing, the title was distasteful. To him and, he felt, to many of his readers, it meant a fashion magazine. More, its shady past under Colonel Mann, he believed, still clung to it and discouraged subscribers. Since the days when he and Nathan had dreamed of the *Blue Review*, he had nursed plans for a new magazine with an American motif, and when Knopf brought up the idea on his own hook, Mencken fairly seethed with enthusiasm. There was but one obstacle. Mencken's talk of a periodical dealing with the political ramifications of the national scene found Nathan, who was little interested in such ramifications, lukewarm. Literary and artistic interests were quite enough for him, and he viewed as alarming Mencken's increasing absorption with things political. Knopf was acceptable—eminently acceptable —as a publisher, but if Knopf wanted a magazine, why couldn't it be *The Smart Set*? Mencken, dubious, approached Knopf, and Knopf, after huddling with his father, business manager of the firm, returned their verdict. It was No. A new magazine or none was Knopf's position, and Nathan, somewhat dubious, was drawn into the scheme. Nor were Nathan's doubts his alone. Alfred had seen, as Mencken had not, the growing breach between the editorial enthusiasms of the two editors, and a new politically minded magazine, he believed, would be best edited by Mencken alone. But Mencken's sense of loyalty balked at this. Nathan had always been with him, and, he vowed, Nathan always would be. There had to be two editors for the new project, and they had to be Mencken and Nathan. Thus it was that two of the three sponsors for *The Smart Set's* heir—Nathan and Knopf—went into the inaugural conference with grave misgivings.

The first squabble developed over a name. Mencken and

Nathan liked the *Blue Review,* probably for sentimental reasons, but Knopf vetoed it. Then a long series of prospective titles was proposed: *The Twentieth Century, The Capitol, The Defender, The Sovereign, The Regent, The Chancellor, The Portfolio, The Pendulum, The Other Man's Monthly, The Gray Monthly, The Colonnade, The Inter-Continental Review, The Athenaeum, The Colonial Review,* and *The New Review.* Finally, Nathan suggested *The American Mercury.* Mencken protested at once; it would, he argued, be interpreted as an imitation of the London *Mercury,* the *Mercure de France,* or the *Mercurio Peruano.* Knopf, however, voted in favor of *The American Mercury,* and *The American Mercury* it became.

Next came the problem of *The Smart Set.* Before any sort of contract could be written between the publisher and his editors, Mencken and Nathan must first get rid of their *Smart Set* stock. Hearst was approached, but refused to buy. Mencken suspected that he was really interested, however, and after a conference with Warner, an ingenious scheme was devised. Warner was to handle the stock, with the understanding that if Hearst buy within a year, the editors should share in the proceeds. Warner agreed, the sale was transacted, and sure enough: in a few months, Hearst was nibbling. He bought *The Smart Set* and turned it over to a sub-editor, who for six years turned out a sleazy product which honored Colonel Mann's memory. This done, Mencken and Nathan signed with Knopf, assuming complete editorial responsibility and the ownership of one third the magazine. Offices were to be in Knopf's headquarters at 730 Fifth Avenue.

Throughout 1923 Mencken and Nathan shaped the details, conferring with Knopf over problems of typography and format and writing prospective contributors, asking for manuscripts which might fit the tone of the *Mercury.* The magazine, designed by Elmer Adler, was to be green-backed; the type, Garamond—again, over objections from Mencken, who was afraid it would look "too damned Frenchy." Letters went out each week to such men as Upton Sinclair, Dreiser, Hergesheimer, Johnson, Gamaliel Bradford, Jim Tully, a newcomer to *The Smart Set,* and Dr. Raymond Pearl of Baltimore, whom Mencken then knew only as one of the scientific writers he was patronizing. Later, as Pearl contributed more and more frequently to the *Mercury* and became a member of the Saturday Night Club, he became also one of Mencken's closest friends, but in August he was simply "Dear Dr. Pearl:

> I am preparing to set up a new monthly review in New York, and turn to you in the hope that you may be interested in it. Described briefly, it will represent an attempt to cover the whole national scene—not only politics, government, and the fine arts, but also the sciences—and to bring a realistic habit of mind to the business. A very diligent effort will be made to avoid the obviousness and formalism which mark the existing reviews; I am trying to get together a group of collaborators who at least know their subjects and may be depended upon to tell the truth as they see it. For example, Lowie in anthropology, Chafee and Pound in law, Grant La Farge in architecture, Watson in psychology, and so on. . . .

To Sinclair he wrote more frankly:

> I shall try to cut a rather wide swathe with it, covering politics, economics, the exact sciences, etc., as well as belles lettres and the other fine arts. I have some promises of stuff from men who have something to say and know how to write, and I hope to stir up the animals. In politics it will be, in the main, Tory, but *civilized* Tory. You know me well enough to know that there will be no quarter for the degraded cads who now run the country. I am against you and the Liberals because I believe you chase butterflies, but I am even more against your enemies.

Certain features were carried over from *The Smart Set;* Owen Hatteras's "Americana," Mencken's literary article, Nathan's drama criticism, and the column of observations on the human comedy, written by Mencken and Nathan in *The Smart Set* under the heading "Répétition Générale," henceforth to be known as "Clinical Notes" and written by Nathan alone. It was a time which augured well for infant publications—*The Reader's Digest* was founded in 1922, *Time* in

1923, and *The New Yorker* in 1925—and Mencken and Nathan were full of high hope that fall as they put the finishing touches on the first issue.

It was hope well justified. The opening number, for January, 1924, came out just before Christmas, and was swept off the newsstands. By December 28 they were on the presses with the second edition of the issue, and Knopf excitedly sent Mencken word from New York that the circulation department was already 670 subscriptions behind.[4] Within a month the number had been reprinted a second time and the February issue was headed for a twenty-five-thousand circulation—this in a fifty-cent magazine which its editors never expected to go over twenty thousand. So rapidly did the subscription lists mount that the printers, who had taken credit for the first few numbers, were paid off at once and the *Mercury,* in effect, had financed itself. Nor was the end in sight. An average monthly circulation of 38,697 in 1924 soared to 77,921 in 1926, and never dropped below sixty-five thousand until the depression. Knopf's business department, stunned at first, immediately plunged into advertising in the big cities, whence most of the subscribers came, and in the college towns, where circulation seemed to approximate population. Mencken was jubilant. "Prayer still has its old power," he wrote Van Doren.

In the *Mercury* office he was regarded with a mixture of awe, respect, and affection. Knopf had set aside a tiny room for the magazine, and this was divided by a partition, with Mencken, Nathan, and Edith Lustgarten, their editorial secretary, on one side, and ten advertising and circulation workers on the other. These ten worked at extremely close quarters, huddled among great piles of figures, bills, and copy layouts, and to reach the editors visitors had to step warily between them. Once through to the other side of the partition, they found a bare and only slightly less crowded closet furnished by three desks and one of the great brass spittoons Mencken had rescued from his gaudy *Smart Set* quarters. To this office

---

[4] "Knopf has bought 30 new yellow neckties," Mencken wrote Goodman, "and has taken a place in Westchester County to breed Assyrian wolfhounds."

he now came on his tri-weekly visits to New York, beginning Monday morning and extending through Wednesday afternoon. All his outstanding business in the editorial offices, which Nathan was running as he had *The Smart Set's,* was settled Monday. Letters were dictated and the few authors who had to be seen were interviewed. As a general rule, he and Nathan avoided the company of writers outside the office, and lunch hours and evenings were spent with such old friends as Tom Smith, John Williams, Fitzgerald, and, less frequently, Dreiser. Often, just as Mencken had settled down to some particularly absorbing editorial chore at the *Mercury,* the phone would ring: Knopf, anxious to show off his prize dog, had a distinguished visitor in his office. Mencken would swear a bloody oath—part of Miss Lustgarten's necessary equipment, she had been told, was a pair of asbestos ears—and after methodically washing his hands he would trot off to the front office to humor the "visiting fireman."

At the office each day arrived between fifty and sixty letters, from authors, aspiring authors, admirers, and, more often, assailants of the *Mercury.* "I have just read your magazine, and it certainly is nothing I would want my fourteen-year-old daughter to read," a matron would write, or "If you don't like the good old U.S.A., the boats are still sailing for Russia, buddy." At first, their terrific labor brought the editors small financial return; despite the *Mercury's* soaring circulation, the initial expenses soaked up most of the income, and Mencken found himself working at a frantic pace with little difference to his bankbook save the money drawn out for New York trips. "The increasing business of The American Mercury is working me to death," he told Gamaliel Bradford. "I find that I am now a business man in active practice, with many of the duties that also belong to the pants business." The 1924 Democratic convention, which he spent sweating naked in a New York hotel room, furiously editing *Mercury* articles between *Evening Sun* editions, nearly broke his health, and he began to cast around for help.

He found it in a wide-eyed young product of the Boston slums, fresh out of Harvard and full of desire to crash the magazine business. Charles Angoff had submitted examples of his work to a number of magazines, the *Mercury* among them. A correspondence with Mencken prospered, they met in New York, and ultimately he was offered the job of assistant editor. It was a bid half of young intellectual America might have snapped at, and Angoff took it without a question. Twenty-four hours later, he found himself, terrified and confused, in complete charge of the magazine: Mencken, sick of routine, had introduced him to the office staff and then blithely left for Baltimore on the next train. Angoff's only instructions were to answer all letters the day they arrived and to return all manuscripts within twenty-four hours. There was, he had been told, no excuse for not doing either. Angoff proved capable, however, and henceforth he handled most of the correspondence and made up each month's issue. In matters of detail, he found, Mencken was completely irresponsible; indeed, his irresponsibility was at times alarming. When, during his first weeks on the *Mercury,* Angoff received a formal request for the magazine circulation, and asked Mencken what it was, he was told it hovered at two hundred twenty-five thousand. The information was sent out; then he looked it up and came back to Mencken on the run. "It's under fifty thousand," he gasped. "Why did you say that?" "Well," said Mencken, with a nonchalant flip of his Uncle Willie, "it's a good round figure."

His *Mercury* work, as with *The Smart Set,* was done at Hollins Street. There he solicited and received manuscripts and there his critical articles and editorials were written. He remained, as always, the delight of authors exasperated with the cavalier manner of other editors. Rarely was a manuscript held over three days, and before it went into the magazine, authors were given the opportunity to inspect the proofs for error. His consideration of contributors was incredible. If, reading a contribution, he thought it might be sold to a magazine paying more money, the author was so advised, and Mencken offered to withdraw. Stories of promise which, for various reasons did not suit the *Mercury* were returned with notes suggesting magazines they *did* suit. And those authors who did sell manuscripts received, a month after publication, a notarized transfer of copyright, in the event they should want to publish the piece again. Should the *Mercury* find a foreign market and sell the article there, the author, in a forthcoming mail, would receive a check for the proceeds.

In return for this, Mencken asked his contributors to bear with him through the several revisions he asked of each manuscript before it saw print. "When it goes into The American Mercury," he wrote Tully after the *n*th rewriting of an article, "I want it to be perfect"—by which he meant an integral part of the expression of his personality which the magazine had come to be. Twenty years before, as city editor of the *Herald,* he had rewritten leads until the managing editor had ordered him to stop; now, with no managing editor over him, he rewrote incessantly, inserting the word or phrase which gave the piece the proper salting of Menckenese. Titles were changed constantly ("The Decline of the Negro Churches" became "Black America Begins To Doubt") for this same reason, and no suggestion for a projected article went out without detailed instructions for its writing. When, for example, he asked Benjamin DeCasseres to do a sketch of New York saloons which Nathan had suggested, he sent along a complete outline, including the saloons to be discussed, and named specific anecdotes for inclusion. Back the manuscripts would go, again and again, with notes describing Mencken's bouts with his editorial conscience, usually beginning "My eyes are streaming with tears as I write, but the bald fact remains . . . ," and winding up with an embellished request for another try. In the end, authors generally got the idea: everything which came under Mencken's pencil had to have something of him in it before it could get his stamp of approval. If it did not, the author wound up with the original story and the short note:

> Mr. Mencken has just entered a Trappist monastery at Gethsemane, Ky., and left strict orders that no mail was to be forwarded. I am returning the enclosed for your archives.
>
> Sincerely yours,
> Edith Lustgarten.

Such editorial conduct would have been inexcusable had it not succeeded so enormously. What his readers were buying, after all, was Mencken, and if the contents had strayed far from his interests, they would have doubtless been as disappointed as would he. The scraps of "Americana" printed each month—sweet tributes to Edgar A. Guest; news items of ministers wearing black ties presented by silk manufacturers, singing "Blest Be the Tie That Binds" and offering to eat their straw hats if the word of God were proven untrue— were surely not representative of America. They were representative only of the editor's absorption and of the vital, iconoclastic personality he was vending. Open a copy of the *Mercury* for these years—say that for December, 1924—and you find his stamp on virtually every page: in the essay on Bryan by Edgar Lee Masters; in the study of the jury system; in the article on patent medicine and fake food tonics; in the report of letters to congressmen by their constituents; in the James M. Cain attack on the blowsiness of statesmen; in the notes on the Ku Klux Klan, on Dr. Frank Crane, on journalism, on the ancient Greeks. Was it a one-man magazine? Not quite—not yet. Nathan still wrote his monthly theater article and the department "Clinical Notes"; to it he still brought authors who were his special protégés. But more and more, as Mencken threw himself into the enterprise with all of his unbelievable energy, it became a product of the peculiar maelstrom which he had created, and in which he now lived. Through its pages each month he brawled and bellowed with the gusto of a Norfolk whore, the finesse of a Spanish fencer, and the independence of a Maine farmer. "The news that the American Mercury is 'lacking in constructive points of view' is surely not news to me," he wrote Sinclair in answer to criticism; "If any such points of view ever get into it, it will only be over my mutilated and pathetic corpse. The uplift has damn nigh ruined the country. What we need is more sin."

Significantly, perhaps, Sinclair, who was one of the *Mercury's* sharpest critics, was also one of its greatest benefactors. Like many another established writer who disagreed with Mencken's basic tenets, he was moved to admiration for the tremendous energy and positiveness of his editorship, and so sent him the names of all young writers of talent who entered his horizons. It was this channeling of raw talent toward

Baltimore, combined with Mencken's sharp eye for merit in unsolicited manuscripts, which brought to the magazine so high a level of writing. As a quality magazine unafraid to make the common man respectable, the *Mercury* was working in a virgin field, and hence was untroubled by competition. Stories by jailbirds on penitentiaries, by prostitutes on whoredom, by vagrants on how to bum a meal—stories which could never have got beyond the slush heaps in the *Atlantic Monthly* or *Harper's*—found an eager reader in Mencken. From Ernest Booth, behind bars, came "A Texas Road Gang," "We Rob a Bank," "I Face a Jury of My Peers," and "Ladies of the Mob"; from Robert Tasker, another convict, came "The First Day." A young common laborer sent an impossible story to Hollins Street; Mencken, seeing an unusual sparkle in the writing, suggested new themes, and James Stevens rose to national fame as the author of "Paul Bunyan," "Brawnyman," and "Mattock." A dock worker in San Pedro, hearing of the Baltimore phenomenon, shipped him a manuscript, and Louis Adamic made his debut in print. George Milburn, writing obscurely in a regional anthology, came under the alert eye at Hollins Street and was invited to spread his talents before a national audience, and Mike Gold, who, as a communist seer, was later to make a career of attacking Mencken, was lifted from the shadows in his serialized *Jews Without Money*. Rightists, Leftists, genii, boobs—if they could write, it was enough. There was room for them between the Paris-green covers of *The American Mercury*.

Yet the most distinguishing characteristic of the *Mercury*, which gave it its very special flavor and for which it is best remembered, was not the quality of its contributions, not even the saucily edited articles on the Klan and the Babbitts, but the pieces from Mencken's own pen. While he tenderly cultivated budding talent and spread himself with courteous gestures before all authors, this other side of Mencken, this curious combination of Voltaire, Frederick the Great, Thomas Jefferson, and Main Street, thundered closer and closer, as the Twenties grew older, to an absolute in philosophical nihilism never before approached in America. His stupendous gift for invective had now reached heights so incredible, so breathtaking, so awe-inspiring, so terrible, that in its indictment of the national culture it wrung monthly gasps from sixty thousand readers and porcupined the hair of intellectuals, Army officers, bond salesmen, and garage mechanics in St. Paul, St. Louis, St. Joseph, and St. Cloud. How could so violent a hymn of hate be sung so jubilantly?

Hear it!

The normal American of the "pure-blooded" majority goes to rest every night with the uneasy feeling that there is a burglar under the bed, and he gets up every morning with a sickening fear that his underwear has been stolen.

Of the farmer:

No more grasping, selfish and dishonest mammal, indeed, is known to students of the anthropoidea; he deserves all that he suffers under our economic system and more.

Of the politician:

A good politician is quite as unthinkable as an honest burglar.

Of prohibition agents:

A corps of undisguised scoundrels with badges.

Of the motion picture industry:

Gilded pants pressers, decayed actors, and other such half wits.

Of the Bryan crusade:

. . . a jehad against what remained of American intelligence, already beleaguered in a few walled towns.

Of the war:

That combat was carried on, at least from this side of the

fence, in a grossly hysterical, disingenuous, cowardly, and sordid manner.

Of veterans:

How easy it was to turn the morons of the American Legion upon their fellow slaves!

Of religion:

The church itself, as it has grown more sordid and swinish, has only grown more prosperous.

Of the yearning of yokels to put down culture:

They dream of it behind the egg-stove on Winter nights, their boots off, their socks scorching, Holy Writ in their hands. They dream of it as they commune with Bos taurus, Sus scrofa, Mephitis mechitis, the Methodist pastor, the Ford agent. It floats before their eyes as they scan the Sears Roebuck catalogue for horse liniment, porous plasters and Bordeaux mixture. . . . This Utopia haunts and tortures them, they long to make it real. They have tried prayer, and it has failed; now they turn to the secular arm. The dung-fork glitters in the sun as the host prepares to march. . . .

And as he howled across the union, month after month, back came the answering refrain, from delighted college students, from posturing preachers, from disillusioned intellectuals, from hairy-faced matrons of the D.A.R.:

H. L. Mencken!

"He is one of the smart type who, having no constructive ability and lacking in depth—to judge from his writings— directs his energies to undermining and pulling down. His magazine misrepresents in the interest of the anarchists, supports subversive movements, and is widely circulated among the Reds." Thus Representative Blanton, of Texas, on the floor of Congress.

Students at Marshall College, West Virginia, protesting the withdrawal of the *Mercury* from their library, held a mock funeral by torchlight, wearing crepe on their arms and carrying the latest copy on a stretcher across the campus.

H. L. Mencken!

At a University of Virginia commencement, a professor of Romance languages declared, "Mencken and his *American Mercury*, the most widely read periodical on the university campus, are an indication of how low undergraduate thought has sunk."

At George Washington University, students debated whether the *Mercury* or *Captain Billy's Whiz Bang* was the more stimulating. In the vote, Mencken won by a yokel.

H. L. Mencken!

In Los Angeles, the president of a small Western college stormed, "Mencken's opinions are unsound, immoral, and un-American."

The Rev. John Roach Stratton, addressing four hundred students at Harvard, compared Bryan to Gladstone and opened an attack on Mencken. He was heckled to a halt by boys waving green-backed magazines. "Why are there lightning rods on church steeples?" shouted a sophomore. "God expects people to use their heads," stammered Stratton.

H. L. Mencken!

"These literary poseurs, Harold L. Mencken and Sinclair Lewis, mean little in the busy lives of 100,000 Rotarians," declared Alexander MacFarlane, international director of Rotary. "These high-brow writers attack Rotary because of its popularity, and it is their motto to attack everything that is popular."

The New York *Times* called him "the most powerful private citizen in America."

H. L. Mencken!

"The Y.M.C.A.," declared the Muskogee, Oklahoma, *Times-Democrat* primly, "teaches a man healthy fun rather than the lewd and suggestive thoughts that Mr. Mencken seems so eager to champion."

The tempestuous Gutzon Borglum, asking for an introduction, said, "Mencken is the only honestly free man in America, I believe."

H. L. Mencken!

Stuart Sherman, a thin voice from the past, indignantly protested Mencken was proceeding "at a hard gallop, spattered with mud . . . high in oath."

In the *Saturday Review of Literature*, Walter Lippmann called him "the most powerful personal influence on this whole generation of educated people."

H. L. Mencken!

"The buzzard of American literature says that 'one bold and intelligent editor could save Mississippi from the blight of Fundamentalism,'" wrote Frederick Sullens in the Jackson, Mississippi, *News*. "It is only wild-eyed, loud-mouthed jackasses like Mencken who seek to destroy mankind's faith in the fundamentals of Christianity. By cutting through six inches of fat and drilling through four inches of bone one might possibly find Mencken's brain cavity—but he would not discover any grey matter there."

Coed debating teams from Stanford and the University of California argued whether Mencken was fit to associate with nice people. They decided he was.

H. L. Mencken!

"If a buzzard had laid an egg in a dunghill and the sun had hatched a thing like Mencken," cried the Rev. Dr. Charles E. Jones in the *Gospel Call*, "the buzzard would have been justly ashamed of its offspring."

In the *Peninsula Daily Herald* of Monterey, California, appeared the advertisement: "Wanted—Young woman would like position as housekeeper for single gentleman of simple tastes. Subscriber to *The American Mercury* preferred."

And throughout the Republic, in shabby Kansas city rooms, one-building colleges, and I.B.M. offices; along San Francisco docks, Main Street drug counters, and Broadway bars; behind Vermont barns, stockyard fences, and Westchester hedges; in twenty-room mansions and one-room shacks; under chandeliers and freight cars—wherever thoughtful men rebelled against the brassy, shoddy atmosphere of a Model-T culture—the name became a challenge and a talisman:

H. L. MENCKEN!

Chapter 6

The Infidel Scopes

(1925)

FROM EVERY CORNER of the republic the giddy ballyhoo rolled in via his clipping bureau and his spies; from Upton Sinclair in Pasadena and Marquis Childs in St. Louis; from Gerald Johnson in Greensboro and Emily Clark in Richmond; from Ben Hecht in Chicago and Percy Marks in Hanover; from Edgar Lee Masters wherever he might be and from *American Mercury* subscribers everywhere. It piled up in the central Baltimore post office, was shipped down Baltimore Street to Stricker, up a block to Hollins, and was dumped in the gleaming vestibule. There Mencken scooped it up and toted it, puffing, to his third-floor office where, gleefully pasting it in thickening scrapbooks, he pondered its significance. What did it mean, all this vaseline and all this bile? His following, he had always believed, was confined to men with superior intelligence but inferior virtue and a few of the better sort of women in public stews. Now, it appeared, the very sheep of the campus were deserting their bellwethers and flocking to his colors. Was it an unmixed blessing, this skyrocketing stock of his? He doubted it. For one thing, it rather put him in the class of the pompous best-sellerist, of the upright and the accepted. "The returns from the universities begin to make me sweat," he wrote Untermeyer. "The truth is that both of us are beginning to grow sclerotic and respectable. A few years more, and you will be Brander Untermeyer and I'll be Paul Elmer Mencken." For another, he observed, there was a disturbing lack of discrimination in his worshipers and his vilifiers alike. "There is something embarrassing about unqualified praise," he noted to Dreiser. "A man knows, down in his heart, that he doesn't deserve it. When he sees all his petty bluffs and affectations accepted seriously, the sole result is to make him lose respect for the victim." Quite obviously, neither side

189

understood him, but that wasn't his worry. He certainly wasn't going to turn away customers.

Yet as those customers multiplied he found that, out of respect for his sanity, he had to discourage some of them. They became terrific pests, hammering on his front door by day, calling him long-distance by night. Callers on the stoop could be ignored; a peek through the curtains of his mother's bedroom told him all he needed to know about a given visitor. But the anonymity of a telephoner until conversation had been begun was something else again. The telephone, indeed, became "the greatest boon to bores ever invented. . . . It is a great invention and of vast value to the human race, but I believe it has done me, personally, almost as much harm as good. How often a single call has blown up my whole evening's work, and so exacerbated my spirit and diminished my income!" He never got used to it; after forty years he still jumped with the first ring, thereby losing, sometimes for good, a pregnant train of thought. Exasperated, he began to envy the very Trappists, who, whatever the disadvantages of their calling, were at least untroubled by this fiendish menace. Friends proposed that he withdraw his listing from the directory, but that was dismissed with a snort. No prima donna he. Finally, when the situation reached the pathological stage, he hit upon a somewhat unsatisfactory solution: all callers were assumed to be drunk unless proven otherwise. This saved him a good deal of time at the telephone, since many of his admirers, especially in the colleges, *were* drunk when they called, but it did not serve to lessen the annoyance of the opening rings, now numbering twenty or thirty a day, and he continued to fret, thwarted by this absurd infelicity.

Now in the year of grace 1925—the graceless year in which the incredible Twenties reached their height— Mencken walked out of the wings and onto the kaleidoscopic stage that public life had become. Long had he remained in the pit, hooting and blowing spitballs; with the coming on of the mid-point in the era that was so rightly his, he stepped out on the apron and joined the act. The occasion for this significant move was the celebrated trial of John Thomas

Scopes, Tennessee schoolteacher, for violation of the state's anti-evolution law.

The case was widely advertised at the time as a bizarre incident, and it was surely that. But the gathering of mighty forces in Tennessee was no more incidental than were the battles of Saratoga and Gettysburg. It was, indeed, the very purposefulness of the clash which drew Mencken; in a sense the issues at stake were those on which the *Mercury* had been founded, on which his whole life had come to be based, and for him to have stayed away from Dayton that brassy summer would have been as unlikely as his enlistment in the U.S. Army seven years before. The die was cast, the wheel was set in motion. It was over such men as John Scopes that Mencken's star now hovered, not, as in the past, over such as Conrad, Shaw, and Dreiser.

Tennessee happened to be the scene of the monkey trial and Scopes happened to be the defendant. The verb is used advisedly. The struggle might have come in Kentucky—whose legislature had just defeated a similar bill by one vote —or in any other of the fifteen states where the Fundamentalist clergy was clamoring for the suppression of "Modernism," i.e., of any teaching in conflict with its own narrow theology. That it came in Tennessee may be credited to one John Washington Butler, a very honest, very sincere, and very ignorant country farmer inflamed by reports that the schools were debauching the state's young with a cock-and-bull story about man being a mammal and not, as Butler well knew, a divine creation of God. Butler was elected to represent his district in the legislature on an anti-evolution platform. On the morning of his forty-ninth birthday he composed the law. A secretary at the state capitol translated it into English, and at its next session the House of Representatives—believing, its leaders claimed, that the Senate would kill it—passed the bill overwhelmingly. The Senate, thinking the governor would veto it, did likewise, and the governor, to the astonishment of that body, signed it on March 21, 1925. Butler's theology, translated into English by a secretary, had been translated into law by the irresponsible canons of political chance.

The entrance of Scopes into the picture may be laid to one George Rappelyea, the thirty-one-year-old manager of the Cumberland Coal and Iron Company of Dayton. A native New Yorker, Rappelyea was appalled by the primitive religion which held sway in his new home, and when he heard that Butler's bill had become law, he decided to do something about it. Straightway he wrote Arthur Garfield Hays of the American Civil Liberties Union. Hays had announced the union's readiness to back any teacher who would test the law, and he replied immediately, agreeing to pay the expenses of the defense. This received, Rappelyea lit out for Robinson's Drug Store, where the best of Dayton's minds were in constant communication with one another. There he precipitated a first-class row over whether or not towheaded young Scopes, the local high school's biology teacher, was violating the law. As Scopes himself later told it,

> There was a crowd in the drug store one afternoon last month, and Mr. Rappelyea said nobody could teach biology without teaching evolution. I was playing tennis, but the dispute got so hot they sent for me. When I got there I said Mr. Rappelyea was right, that any teacher, even a high school teacher, was violating the law and that I was doing so. So Mr. Rappelyea said, "Let's take this thing to court," and we did—that's how it started. After the indictment the townspeople got excited about it.

The indictment, here reprinted for its intrinsic charm, read as follows:

> That John Thomas Scopes, on April 24, 1925, did unlawfully and wilfully teach in the public school of Rhea county, Tennessee, which school is supported in part and in whole by the public school fund of the State, certain theory and theories that deny the story of the divine creation of man, as taught in the Bible, and did teach instead thereof that man descended from the lower order of animals.

The fat was in the fire. Forthwith old William Jennings

Bryan, who had been watching all this anti-evolution pother excitedly, offered his service to the state of Tennessee as prosecutor. Bryan was now at the end of his long, desolate road. He had, in these boom years, made over a million dollars in Florida real estate, but power, not money, was what he pined for. He had been goaded beyond all sense of balance by ridicule, and now, with the very religion in which he believed under attack, he saw, or thought he saw, a chance to strike back. Could he but get an anti-evolution amendment tagged onto the Constitution—and such was his avowed intent—could he but turn Fundamentalism into a political force, he might be elected President by the assembled Christians of the nation and rout the despised atheists, all with one stroke. Such were the reflections of this three-time loser, this wet-turned-dry, this pacifist-become-soldier, when he laid his rusty but still powerful sword at the disposal of the forces of darkness. Very well. The Commoner would attack John Scopes. Who would defend him?

Mencken talked Clarence Darrow into taking the case. He and Hergesheimer were visiting James Branch Cabell in Richmond when Darrow, who had been turning the case over in his mind, came to pay his respects. They met there. "Nobody gives a damn about that yap schoolteacher," Mencken told him. "The thing to do is make a fool out of Bryan." Bryan's entrance into the case, he pointed out, had changed it from a purely local matter; Hays and Dudley Field Malone were already packing in New York. Darrow, Mencken insisted, was the logical opponent for Bryan. For one thing, they had battled one another on the evolution question two years before in the pages of the Chicago *Tribune*—Bryan, it may be noted, withdrew speedily when a showdown loomed—and for another, they hated one another powerfully. Darrow saw the point. From Richmond he wired Dayton, volunteering his support to the towhead Mencken was already calling "the infidel Scopes."

Mencken was enormously interested in the trial. For *The American Mercury* it was the choicest piece of Americana since the magazine's founding, and in Baltimore the *Evening Sun*, fascinated by the cultural lag of the Middle West, had put up Scopes' bond. Bryan's crusade for a Fundamentalist amendment was something into which Mencken could sink his jagged teeth; he had long contended that the American people were almost unanimously against free speech—as witness the assaults on communist leaders in New York—and here was an example without parallel. He conferred with the defense attorneys, oiled his shabby Corona, and issued furious bulletins—that Bryan was the worst citizen ever heard of in the United States, that Darrow was the Antichrist mentioned in the Book of Revelation, that he was rooting for God, etc. Malone came down from New York to discuss strategy; after he had gone, Mencken fell on eight *Mercury* articles, polished them off, and laid plans for the trip to Tennessee with Kent, Hyde, Fred Essary, and Duffy, all of whom were coming with him to represent the *Sunpapers*. At first he was hot for staying in Chattanooga; Dayton, he feared, would be choked with bootleggers, hookworm, and Chicago whores. But this, it turned out, was impractical, and so they made arrangements by mail with the local gentry. He and Kent were to room together in the home of the town dentist. Finally the schedules were set, and Mencken, on the eve of his departure, wrote Tully gaily, "I am off to Dayton, Tenn. to hear the trial of the accursed infidel who flouted Genesis. My pen is at the disposal of the sainted Bryan."

Chattanooga, they discovered, was a clean, prosperous city of one hundred twenty-five thousand, with a large business center of tall, clean buildings and hundreds of tiny, one-story bungalows on the circling hills. There was little interest in the trial there—yet—and they amused themselves by walking through the town while arrangements were made to hire an automobile. Chattanooga was already jammed with the international press. The trial was still two days distant, and the visiting reporters were looking for copy. One of them ran into Mencken as he stood before a bookstore window, wherein were displayed a group of Bryan's books. "Why don't you buy a Bible?" suggested the reporter. "I don't have to," he replied. "The Gideons furnish me with them." Finally the hired car arrived and he climbed in. They crossed the wide river under a hot and pitiless sky, with the huge gray bulk of Lookout Mountain looming to the west; they passed the high green bluffs of the bank and struck smooth oiled macadam on the far side. And there, hard by the road, appeared the first outpost of the enemy.

Plastered on a huge, sagging circus tent was the glaring sign:

BIG DICK

THE WORLD-FAMOUS ENGINEER EVANGELIST

NIGHTLY REVIVAL MEETINGS

INSIDE

Beyond lay Dayton, Tennessee.

As they crawled along the dipping, turning road, following the outline of the foothill, the signs and portents increased. "Prepare To Meet Thy God," read the lettered warning on the side of a barn; "Your Sin Will Find You Out," announced a billboard on the outskirts—scarcely distinguishable from the inskirts—of the town of Daisy. On the main street of the coal-mining village of Soddy a second canvas tent dipped weirdly; outside, a barefoot boy bashfully allowed as how the Baptists were holding a revival inside. All told, it took them an hour and forty minutes to make the forty-mile drive—an hour and forty minutes of orchards, watermelon patches, sweet potato fields, and, of course, theological billboards, which seemed to increase in geometric progression as they neared the end of their trip. "Where Will You Spend Eternity?" asked one barn door starkly; "You Need God in Your Business," briskly declared a sign on an old oak tree. Lastly, as they started to climb the final height leading to the village, they passed a dilapidated wooden sanitarium, which announced in huge, blood-red letters that it followed "The True Indian Method of Treatment."

Dayton turned out to be an attractive, thriving little community of some two thousand people, with a main street bordered by neat two-story buildings and pleasant, comfortable homes sitting in shady yards. Ordinarily, town life revolved around two foci: Robinson's Drug Store, the local Coca-Cola oasis; and the courthouse, a large, well-built structure surrounded by shade trees. To these two a third had just been added. Across from the courthouse and within spitting distance of a sign advising the passer-by to read his Bible for a week was a yellow frame cottage, now the scene of diverse and frantic activities. Half the cottage had been occupied by the press corps, whose two hundred-odd members availed themselves of the facilities provided by the Chattanooga *News*. The other half was dominated by a white-haired, wild-eyed apparition who described himself as T. T. Martin, field secretary of the Anti-Evolution League. Martin —*Dr.* Martin, Mencken insisted on calling him—was a product of Mississippi. His battlecry was "Drive Hell out of the High Schools," and he exhibited a street stand chock full of religious books, explaining the urgency of his message. On the way, he added, was a Mississippi-built set of portable bleachers, the better to hold the remarkable crowds he was attracting each night in the grove before the courthouse. Mencken and Dr. Martin held a long and confidential conversation about the mysteries of theology and the menace of the Reds. Then they parted, Mencken further to inspect the town, Martin to await his bleachers, which as it happened, never arrived.

Mencken had scarcely navigated half a block before he was nearly knocked down by a small yellow car manned by the very schoolteacher he had come across the country to see. Johnny Scopes had just driven over to Chattanooga to pick up his father, an elderly railroad machinist from Paducah, Kentucky, who wanted to be on hand for the show. Scopes was as yet unaccustomed to the thickly populated streets, it appeared, and Mencken, brushing himself off, damned all yaps and yokels and set out to track down bigger game: William Jennings Bryan. He found him surrounded by local theologians in front of the cottage he was to occupy during the trial, his bald head covered by an enormous white pith tropical helmet, his striped linen shirt tucked under his neck, his great catfish mouth turned up in a leering smile. A few weeks before the *Nation* had carried "In Tennessee," in which Mencken had argued sarcastically that the truth or falsity of Scopes' teaching was irrelevant, that the only important thing was whether or not his employers approved of it. Mencken, somewhat astonished by Bryan's merry greeting, thought at first he had been mistaken for "some Baptist clergyman ruined by drink," but when it developed that Bryan had swallowed the *Nation* piece for what it was not, he bowed to Bryan's bows and purred in answer to Bryan's purrs. They parted, he noted, in the manner of two Spanish ambassadors.

Dayton was seething with activity, all of it religious, most of it incredible. Shortly after Scopes' car had whisked by it was followed by another, carrying a party of Seventh Day Adventists, including a very pretty girl. The automobile was plastered with signs announcing that the end of the world was at hand, that "Selfishness Is Sin," and that a performance of the "She-Devil"—obviously the girl—would be held each night under canvass during the trial. Tied across the rear of the Ford and anchored to the top was an enormous banner demanding that the pedestrian "Get Right with God." The She-Devil, it developed, was to get lively competition from a rival organization. This outfit, which went by the name of The Methodist Volunteers, was to present a motion-picture portrayal of the life of Christ, including his birth, his works and miracles on this earth, the Last Supper, the Crucifixion, Resurrection, Ascension, "and many other such incidents" in the high school auditorium for a week. Everywhere street hawkers were peddling pamphlets, written by themselves, on the evils of Modernism; under the big court-house yard maples moved a constant procession of country women and small children, each carrying a life-size cloth monkey in natural colors. On a nearby corner a blind mountaineer sat at a small organ, playing and singing gospel hymns in a thin, wavering voice while around him a hundred mountain men chewed tobacco and wove their shoulders back and forth in time with the music. It was impossible to find anyone uninfected with the bug. Mencken, stopping natives, finally found one pasty-faced youth who hesitated when asked his church. "I don't belong to no church," he finally said, adding, with perfect seriousness, "I'm a sinner."

Most of the zealots, he discovered, were not Daytonians. Many, like the gifted Dr. Martin, were as far from home as he was. But for the most part they were from the surrounding mountains; Fundamentalists to a man, they had come to Dayton to see their champion, Bryan, and to witness the ignominious defeat of the forces of the Devil. Dayton itself was not lacking in religious fever. The town had nine churches, and most of the bull sessions in Robinson's Drug Store turned on such hair-splitting questions as whether Jesus lived to save the world or died to save the world. No, Dayton was no citadel of enlightenment. But it was rather civilized and tolerant. Most of the local citizens were friendly, mild-tempered, and good-humored; they watched, amused, as newspapers rushed in radio equipment and sent up airplanes to observe their homes from the air; they were interested, but not upset, by the furious statements Darrow and Malone were issuing in reply to each outburst from Bryan. Dayton was proud of its tolerance, apparently with good reason.

The Klan has never got a foothold here, though it rages everywhere else in Tennessee. When the first kleagles came in they were given the cold shoulder, and pretty soon they gave up the county as hopeless. It is run today not by anonymous daredevils in white nightshirts, but by well-heeled Freemasons in decorous white aprons. In Dayton alone there are sixty thirty-second-degree Masons—an immense quota for so small a town. They believe in keeping the peace, and so even the stray Catholics of the town are treated politely, though everyone naturally regrets they are required to report to the Pope once a week.

To the men and women of the mountains—the instigators and passionate defenders of the anti-evolution law—Dayton was, indeed, a sort of Babylon, to be viewed much as a bumpkin from upstate New York would view Broadway. The religion of the Freemasons they regarded as tame and, after a fashion, sinful; the approach of Scopes' defenders set their spines tingling. Surely, they felt, Darrow would be fetched by a lightning bolt before the trial was ended. Indeed, to believe Mencken, the night Darrow arrived in Tennessee "there was a violent storm, the town water turned brown, and horned cattle in the lowlands were afloat for hours. A woman back in the mountains gave birth to a child with hair four inches long, curiously bobbed in scallops."

As the clamor grew louder, as the crowds of visiting crackpots doubled and doubled again, as hysteria mounted, even the soberer of Dayton's citizens began to share their apprehension. The trial had not yet begun, but already it was apparent it would not take the turn for which the town promoters had hoped. When the indictment was first handed down, the Freemasons had entertained ideas of a great Boost Dayton carnival; some of the prominent visitors, it was believed, might even take to the countryside and come to settle in Rhea county. With this in mind the Progressive Dayton Club laid plans for "monkey medals," to be presented to the participants; in this spirit, J. R. Darwin decorated his Everything-To-Wear store with a gigantic banner proclaiming "DARWIN IS RIGHT—inside." When it developed that the trial would be a grim and bitter battle and not, as hoped, a pleasant farce, the promoters began to get panicky, and it was on this disillusion that Mencken keyed his first dispatch.

On the eve of the great contest Dayton is full of sickening surges and tremors of doubt. Five or six weeks ago, when the infidel Scopes was first laid by the heels, there was no uncertainty in all this smiling valley. The town boomers leaped to the assault as one man. Here was an unexampled, almost a miraculous chance to get Dayton upon the front pages, to make it talked about, to put it upon the map. But how now?

Today, with the curtain rung up and the worst buffooneries to come, it is obvious to even town boomers that getting upon the map, like patriotism, is not enough. . . .

I have been attending the permanent town meeting that goes on in Robinson's drug store, trying to find out what the town optimists have saved from the wreck. All I can find is a sort of mystical confidence that God will somehow come to the rescue to reward His old and faithful partisans as they deserve—that good will flow eventually out of what now seems to be heavily evil. More specifically, it is believed that settlers will be attracted to the town as to some refuge from the atheism of the great urban Sodoms and Gomorrahs.

But will these refugees bring any money with them? Will they buy lots and build houses? Will they light the fires of the cold and silent blast furnaces down the railroad tracks? On these points, I regret to report, optimism has to call in theology to aid it. Prayer can accomplish a lot. It can cure diabetes, find lost pocketbooks and restrain husbands from beating their wives. But is prayer made any more efficacious by giving a circus first? Coming to this thought, Dayton begins to sweat.

Work done, he and Kent roamed the town, looking for edification. They found it in the cupboard of the local prohibition leader; mixed with Coca-Cola it got down somehow, but one slug was all a city man could take, and they wound up with the rest of the press corps in Robinson's, hashing over Scopes' chances, which were generally conceded to be small. Mencken turned in early, after writing Pearl, "This is far worse than anything you could imagine, even under the bowl. Every last scoundrel in sight is a christian, including the town Jew. I begin to realize what life must have been like in Judea 1925 years ago. No wonder the Romans finally bumped off the son of Joseph."

He arose Friday morning in the fiery furnace of a new day, strolled briskly past the shaded homes of the Dayton gentry, past the courtyard signs "Be a Sweet Angel" and "Read Your Bible," climbed the little flight of stairs to the courthouse, and took his place on one of the press benches. Around the brown wooden railing that enclosed the bar were rows of roughly built pine tables, and by 8 o'clock some fifty out-of-town newspapermen were at their seats. The three hundred spaces for spectators were filling up rapidly, and by 8:30, when Judge John T. Raulston, a plump, red-faced man of middle age—who had been born in a tiny mountain community called Fiery Gizzard, and whose mother had led him to school on muleback by day and read him the Bible by night—arrived, no room was left. At quarter to 9, Scopes arrived with his father, shortly followed by Malone, sleek and fat. Shortly thereafter there was a stirring in the back of the room; in strode Clarence Darrow, his shoulders bowed, his scanty hair tousled, his broad face broken by a hundred wrinkles. Soiled suspenders crossed his pale yellow shirt, and an old blue coat dangled from the crook of his arm. He looked like a mountain lawyer—which is, of course, precisely how he wanted to look. At 9 sharp a burst of applause was heard in the courtyard; William Jennings Bryan, in full sail, with sickly young William Jennings, Jr., in tow, stomped down the aisle. Darrow and Bryan shook hands, glared, and went to their corners. The monkey trial was about to start—in its fashion.

A seedy-looking Fundamentalist preacher led off with a long-winded prayer, asking that the trial be so conducted as to give the greatest possible glory to God. Then Darrow, Bryan, and all the assistant lawyers rushed to the bench, to pose in various positions while photographers and movie cameramen ordered them about for fifteen minutes. This done—"Any more pictures, gentlemen?" asked the judge hopefully—Darrow, Malone, and Hays were assured that all "foreign" lawyers would be treated as politely as the local counsel. The first order of business was to select a new grand jury. The original indictment, it developed, had been imperfectly drawn up; a new bill was necessary. This farce was carried out without protest from Darrow. But one man was challenged by the defense. Darrow, tipped off, asked the prospective juror if he had ever preached against evolution. "Yessir," said the man, waggling a tangled white head, "I preached against evolution. I stand strictly for the Bible." "I'll excuse you, Brother Massengill," said the judge, and down stepped the candidate, to a tremendous burst of applause from the spectators. The prosecution challenged another man simply because he did not belong formally to any church, and Darrow, who didn't give a hang about the new indictment anyhow, passed fanatic after fanatic into the box, some of them, as Mencken noted, "glaring at him as if they expected him to go off with a sulphurous bang every time he mopped his bald head." Inspecting the chosen, Mencken silently congratulated himself on his day's lead.

The trial of the infidel Scopes, beginning here this hot, lovely morning, will greatly resemble, I suspect, the trial of a prohibition agent accused of mayhem in Union Hill, N.J. That is to say, it will be conducted with the most austere regard for the highest principles of jurisprudence.

Judge and jury will go to extreme lengths to assure the prisoner the last and least of his rights. He will be protected in his person and feelings by the full military naval power of the State of Tennessee. No one will be permitted to pull his nose, to pray publicly for his condemnation or even to make a face at him. But all the same he will be bumped off inevitably when the time comes, and to the applause of all right-thinking men.

The real trial, in truth, will not begin until Scopes is convicted and ordered to the hulks. Then the prisoner will be the Legislature of Tennessee, and the jury will be that great, fair, unimpassioned body of enlightened men which has already decided that a horse hair put into a bottle will turn into a snake and that the Kaiser started the late war. What goes on here is simply a sort of preliminary hearing with music by the village choir. For it will be no more possible in this Christian valley to get a jury unprejudiced against Scopes than it would be possible in Wall Street to get a jury unprejudiced against a Bolshevik.

I speak of prejudice in the philosophical sense. As I wrote yesterday, there is an almost complete absence of bitterness in these pious hills, of the ordinary and familiar malignancy of Christian men. If the Rev. Dr. Crabbe[1] ever spoke of the bootleggers as humanely and affectionately as the town theologians speak of Scopes, and even Darrow and Malone, his employers would pelt him with their spyglasses and sit on him until the ambulance came from Mount Hope. There is absolutely no bitterness on tap. But neither is there any doubt.

The grand jury filed out and court recessed until 11 A.M. Mencken spent this hour in the courtyard, sweating profusely, listening as nasal-voiced evangelists sang gospel hymns, and arguing with the Bible Champion of the World, who performed before a blackboard with his title painted on the back of his canvas coat. The recess over, the veniremen handed down a new bill, the old indictment was quashed,

[1] Maryland prohibitionist and leader of the Anti-Saloon League of America.

and Attorney-General Stewart announced that the defense's bid for the introduction of scientific testimony on the nature of evolution would be fought bitterly by the State. Court then adjourned until Monday morning, to give the defense attorneys an opportunity to map their strategy. Darrow, Malone, Hays, *et al.* retired to The Mansion, a commodious, rococo building on the outskirts of town which had been reopened by Rappelyea, who, like every other principal in the trial, was as much a showman as an idealist. Mencken went to the mat briefly with the Bible Champion over theological doctrine; then, wilting under the mighty heat, he walked slowly back to the dentist's home with Kent to write his dispatch. Dayton, he had discovered, was admirably suited to his taste. The longer he stayed there, the better he liked it. It was, in a sense, an issue of *The American Mercury* brought to sparkling life. In these delightfully absurd hills of Zion were all the caricatures, all the half-baked dogma that typified rural America to the *Mercury* subscriber—the boomers, the yokels, the shysters; the propositions that a minority had no rights, that the Old-Time Religion was superior to cultivation of the intellect, that the local scene, however shabby and pathetic, was a far finer place to be than the eastern citadels of sin. Bryan—the genius of bigotry, the master pettifogger, the tarnished emblem of American politics—might have stepped full-blown out of a *Mercury* editorial. And Judge Raulston—could Major Owen Hatteras, D.S.O., digging through the thick files of "Americana," have found a better birthplace for him that Fiery Gizzard, Tennessee? Even Darrow, about whom Mencken had no illusions, fitted perfectly. Darrow's passion for truth, after all, was "exactly comparable to what a man feels for an amiable maiden aunt. What he really loves is to make men leap." Dayton, therefore, in July, 1925, was a Menckenian Utopia, a sort of ideological dream, where the turning of each corner brought perspiring proof of a philosophical dictum, where each street scene was, in effect, a tableau illustrating the profound truths on which his magazine had been founded. So he pranced along Market Street, his blue eyes sparkling, his florid face glowing happily in the heat, button-holing Freemasons who thought Sergeant Alvin York, born in the neighboring hills, the greatest man the country had produced, or chatting with odd pilgrims to the trial—a Nebraska farmer who had traveled night and day at his own expense to tell Bryan how his wife had been turned into a stone statue, perhaps, or an Arkansas evangelist with absolute proof that the reigning Pope was a keeper of bordellos. And after a turn about this bizarre town, what was more natural than that his *Evening Sun* dispatches, hammered out in the steam bath that was Dentist Morgan's home, should take on the flavor of a choice *Mercury* editorial?

To call a man a doubter in these parts is equal to ac- cusing him of cannibalism. Even the infidel himself is not charged with any such infamy. What they say of him, at worst, is that he permitted himself to be used as a cat's paw by scoundrels eager to destroy the anti-evolution law for their own dark and hellish ends. There is, it appears, a conspiracy of scientists afoot. Their purpose is to break down religion, propagate immorality, and so reduce man- kind to the level of brutes. They are the sworn and sinister agents of Beelzebub, who yearns to conquer the world, and has his eye especially upon Tennessee. Scopes is thus an agent of Beelzebub once removed, but that is as far as any fair man goes in condemning him. He is young and yet full of folly. When the secular arm has done execution upon him, the pastors will tackle him and he will be saved.

. . . A clergyman has the rank and authority of a major- general of artillery. A Sunday-school superintendent is believed to have the gift of prophesy. But what of life here? Is it more agreeable than in Babylon? I regret that I must have to report that it is not. The incessant clashing of theologians grows monotonous in a day and intolerable the day following. One longs for a merry laugh, a burst of happy music, the gurgle of a happy jug. Try a meal in the hotel; it is tasteless and swims in grease. Go to the drug store and call for refreshment; the boy will hand you al- most automatically a beaker of coca-cola. Look at the magazine counter; a pile of *Saturday Evening Posts* two feet high. Examine the books; melodrama and cheap amour. Talk to a town magnifico; he knows nothing that is not in Genesis.

He protested, of course, overmuch. If the theological orgies of Dayton had grown monotonous and intolerable, it was only because he hankered to see the culmination of all this moaning and praying, the end product of what Westbrook Pegler once called the God business. The opportunity, unparalleled, lay four miles outside Dayton, just beyond the little village of Morgantown, and he meant to improve upon it. There, for the course of the trial, Brother Joe Furdew, boss demagogue of twenty thousand Holy Rollers in the hills, was holding nightly revivals under a great huckleberry tree. Those in the press crew who had gone pronounced the show excellent, though the more squeamish had been unable to stay through to the end. This, of course, was precisely what was wanted. That Friday night he rounded up Kent and Hyde. They were as enchanted with the idea as he was, and once darkness had settled down upon the mountains they piled into their automobile and bumped and rumbled along the tortuous, narrow road that led along the ridges, past Morgantown. At length they glimpsed, in a far-off glade, a winking mote of light. That, they had been told, was Brother Joe's signal to the faithful. Accordingly, they parked by the road, disembarked, and began to sneak, as skirmishers, along the edge of tangled cornfield.

In a few minutes they were within shouting distance, and since that is just what brother Joe was doing, they were able to unravel fragments of his feverish message. "And I'm a tellin' yu," he chanted hoarsely, "Glory to God!—the Lord'll cast down the high kings into the dirt—Glory to God!—I'm tellin' yu—the king of Greece-y, what kivers the hull yearth an'—never tetches the groun'—Glory to God!—the Lord'll cast him down into the dirt—He certainly will—Glory to God!—there are mighty men in the churches—Glory to God!—who displeasure the Lord more than some that ain't in—Glory to God!—for Jesus was a humble feller—Glory to God!—an' when the great day comes—Glory to God!— what kin any of 'em do but jump up an' say—Glory to God!

—I ain't nothin' Lord, I ain't nothin'—Glory to God!—
Glory to God!—Glory to God!"

It was an insidious rhythm, was Brother Joe's chant; like
the pitch of a violin which, repeated often enough, can collapse a bridge, it played upon the nerves relentlessly. By now
they were close enough to see the preacher, and because of
the thick darkness they could, for a time, see no one else.
From the limbs of the great tree hung three small gasoline
lamps, lighting the weird scene; under them, tall and lanky,
Brother Joe, in blue jeans, paced back and forth under the
smoking flames, waving his arms and bellowing fiercely. The
three heathen edged yet closer, until they could see the congregation. Encircling the preacher were rows of rough benches,
and on them sat his customers—bespectacled old men,
thumbing worn Bibles, mothers suckling their babies, pig-
tailed little girls, monstrous mountain women in one-piece
gingham dresses, all rocking steadily in rhythm to the sermon.

The preacher stopped at last and there arose out of the
darkness a woman with her hair pulled back in a little
tight knot. She began so quietly that we couldn't hear what
she said, but soon her voice rose resonantly and we could
follow her. She was denouncing the reading of books.
Some wandering book agent, it appeared, had come to her
cabin and tried to sell her a specimen of his wares. She
refused to touch it. Why, indeed, read a book? If what
was in it was true, then everything in it was already in
the Bible. If it was false then reading it would imperil the
soul. Her syllogism complete, she sat down.

Next a fat mountaineer led a hymn; he was followed by
Brother Joe again, who attacked the debauchery of Dayton—
even of Morgantown—and denounced all education. When
he had finished, with a spirited defense of the gift of tongues,
the woman took over again, jumping and screeching. This
went on for a time, punctuated by hymns, as Mencken,
Hyde, and Kent approached the perimeter of the audience.
Just as they reached the outer ring of benches, the mood of
the revivalists changed perceptibly. A hymn ran overlong; it
turned into a pulsing canticle; Brother Joe beat upon his

Bible, keeping time. Suddenly a young girl with bobbed hair jumped out of the congregation and flung herself upon the ground.

"This sister," said the leader, "has asked for prayers." We moved a bit closer. We could now see faces plainly and hear every word.

What followed quickly reach such heights of barbaric grotesquerie that it was hard to believe it real. At a signal all the faithful crowded up to the bench and began to pray —not in unison but each for himself. At another they all fell on their knees, their arms over the penitent. The leader kneeled, facing us, his head alternately thrown back dramatically or buried in his hands. Words spouted from his lips like bullets from a machine gun—appeals to pull the penitent back out of hell, defiances of the powers and principalities of the air, a vast impassioned jargon of apocalyptic texts. Suddenly he rose to his feet, threw back his head and began to speak in tongues—blub-blub-blub, gurgle-gurgle-gurgle. His voice rose to a higher register. The climax was a shrill, inarticulate squawk, like that of a man throttled. He fell back headlong across the pyramid of supplicants.

A comic scene? Somehow, no. The poor half-wits were too horribly in earnest. It was like peeping through a knot-hole at the writhings of a people in pain. From the squirming and jabbering mass a young woman gradually detached herself—a woman not uncomely, with a pathetic home-made cap on her head. Her head jerked back, the veins of her neck swelled, and her fists went to her throat as if she were fighting for breath. She bent backward until she was like half a hoop. Then she suddenly snapped forward. We caught a flash of the whites of her eyes. Presently her whole body began to be convulsed—great convulsions that began at the shoulders and ended at the hips. She would leap to her feet, thrust her arms in air and then hurl herself upon the heap. Her praying flattened out into a mere delirious cater-wauling, like that of a tomcat on a petting party.

I describe the thing as a strict behaviorist. The lady's subjective sensations I leave to infidel pathologists. Whatever they were they were obviously contagious, for soon another damsel joined her, and then another and then a fourth. The last one had an extraordinary bad attack. She began with mild enough jerks of the head, but in a moment she was bounding all over the place, exactly like a chicken with its head cut off. Every time her head came up a stream of yells and barkings would issue out of it. Once she collided with a dark, undersized brother, hitherto silent and stolid. Contact with her set him off as if he had been kicked by a mule. He leaped into the air, threw back his head and began to gargle as if with a mouthful of BB shot. Then he loosed one tremendous stentorian sentence in the tongues and collapsed.

By this time the performers were quite oblivious to the profane universe. We left our hiding and came up to the little circle of light. We slipped into the vacant seats on one of the rickety benches. The heap of mourners was directly before us. They bounded into us as they cavorted. The smell they radiated, sweating there in that obscene heap, half suffocated us.

So it went, for another hour, until even powerful five-cent cigars were futile antidotes against the immense odor steaming from the writhing, sweating bodies. They arrived back in Dayton shortly after 11, and that week end was spent in Chattanooga, patronizing the town's one beer emporium down by the river. Mencken wrote his account of camp meeting Sunday afternoon, in a boiling Chattanooga hotel room, naked save for a pair of shorts. It was the longest of his Tennessee dispatches and was, with the lonesome but magnificent exception of the last piece on Bryan, the finest of his Dayton-inspired writing. In Baltimore Murphy cut it out, tacked it on the *Evening Sun* bulletin board, and ordered his staff to read it. "That's reporting," he said.

By Monday, when court reconvened, Dayton was a raging madhouse. Gangs of fakirs, pit-show men, and circus-stand promoters exhibited great apes in cages on Main Street; on Market Street corners barkers stabbed themselves with fake knives and screamed with simulated agony to attract crowds of prospective suckers; policemen from Chattanooga patrolled the town, arresting wandering harebrained atheists drawn to the trial to prevent them from being harmed by hysterical Fundamentalists. That night a great, gaudy truck, flaming with electricity, rushed up and down the streets for two hours, its sides covered with huge signs praising "The life of Christ, the Ascension, the Resurrection," while a man in the back bawled through a megaphone and the driver incessantly rang a large bell. The trial was approaching its droll climax.

John Neal, a Tennessee jurist who technically led the defense, opened with a plea that the indictment be thrown out of court on grounds of unconstitutionality; he was followed by Hays and Malone, with similar arguments, and that afternoon Darrow took the floor. Darrow was out for blood—Bryan's blood. The relentless sun had turned the jammed courtroom into a melting pot again, and Bryan, his bald head glowing like an enormous red egg, sat grimly by his can of cool buttermilk, fanning furiously as he heard himself bitterly denounced as the evil genius of "this most wicked and malicious act." Darrow attacked the law as a deliberate attempt to set back Western civilization, as a calculated effort of one branch of the Christian church—and a backward branch, at that—to put down all rival faiths. The mountaineers sat stunned in the back of the hall; Judge Raulston listened attentively; after it was over, Ben McKenzie, one of the prosecutors, told Darrow he thought it the greatest address he had ever heard anywhere, any time, on any theme. But, as Mencken noted,

> The net effect of Clarence Darrow's great speech yesterday seems to be precisely the same as if he had bawled it up a rainspout in the interior of Afghanistan. That is, locally, upon the process against the infidel Scopes, upon the so-called minds of these fundamentalists of upland Tennessee. You have but a dim notion of it who have only read it. It was not designed for reading, but for hearing. The clangtint of it was as important as the logic. It rose like a wind and ended like a flourish of bugles. The very judge on the bench, toward the end of it, began to look

uneasy. But the morons in the audience, when it was over, simply hissed it.

Such pleasantries Mencken found amusing, but rather beside the point. Unlike Darrow, he held little hope that Raulston would rise above his narrow background and declare the law invalid. His main interest was in the expert testimony; if it were admitted, the spectacle of twelve men, at least one of whom could neither read nor write, listening to the testimony on mutation of species and Haeckel's law would be well worth attending. As it happened, both possibilities went out of the courtroom window. Wednesday afternoon the judge declined to quash the second indictment and the State, with seven Dayton high school boys as star witnesses, presented its case in less than two hours. The following day came the showdown on the scientific evidence and Bryan's formal entrance into the case. His mouth a thin line —he had taken a terrific beating in the press—he rose and announced he could no longer tolerate the presentation of "pseudoscientific" opinion before the court. He attitudinized; he gesticulated; his great voice filled the hall. And, in the end, his speech was a vast disappointment, even to his admirers, spotted as it was with such gassy epigrams as "Evolution begins with nothing and ends nowhere." As he finished, a motion-picture machine fell with a crash in one corner of the room. Malone, who followed him, did far better; for all the partisan nature of the audience, he got twice the applause of Bryan. When he had finished his long, cogent, and vehemently expressed argument, a score of admirers crowded around him, eager to shake his hand. Mencken walked over, and Malone, aware that praise from him would be praise indeed, looked up expectantly. "Dudley," said Mencken reverently, mopping his forehead, "that was the loudest goddam speech I ever heard."

Raulston broke the back of the defense Friday when, in a briefly written opinion, he refused to let the jury hear the expert testimony. Thinking to lighten the tense atmosphere, he added, in an aside, that he hoped the evolutionists would at least substitute "ascend" for "descend" in their future arguments. Darrow, his face like a ruined city, rose. "Descent of man," he pointed out, meant starting with a low form of life and finally reaching man. "We all have dictionaries," remarked Attorney-General Stewart. "I don't think the court has one," snorted Darrow. A few minutes later, when he asked for time to reorganize his case, Raulston turned him down. Darrow blew up. He demanded to know why his every request was rejected. "I hope you do not mean to reflect on the court," said Raulston. "Well," snarled Darrow, hunching his head between high-shrugged shoulders, "your honor has the right to hope." The following Monday he was cited for contempt of court and, after an apology, was released by the judge in what amounted to a theological discourse on the blessings of forgiveness.

Friday's action settled Mencken's mind. Manuscripts were piling up in Baltimore and New York and *Mercury* business generally was crying for his attention. The show, he decided, was over; that night he left Dayton. He therefore missed one of the greatest spectacles of the decade, when Darrow put Bryan on the stand as an expert on evolution and, to the astonishment of two thousand people massed on the courthouse lawn where Raulston had moved the proceedings, literally massacred him. Yet it may be he unwittingly saved his skin by leaving early. In later years he pooh-poohed the suggestion that any violence against him was brewing in Dayton, but the dispatches of his fellow newspapermen there indicate otherwise. His stories on the trial came closer to syndication than any other reportorial mission of his career; managing editors all over the country, familiar with his growing reputation, had besieged the *Sun* with requests to buy his correspondence as soon as they had learned he would cover the trial. One, the *Daily Oklahoman* of Oklahoma City, acceded to the demands of outraged subscribers in the midst of the proceedings and declined to print his latest dispatches on the pious ground that "Mr. Mencken in his attacks on intolerance himself went beyond the limits of reasonable and tolerant criticism,"[2] and in Dallas the *News* dismissed his

[2] The campaign against Mencken was led in Oklahoma City by the Rev. Lincoln O'Donnell, whose watchword was "Better to live and die in deepest ignorance than study evolution and become a follower of agnosticism."

account of the Holy Roller fiasco on the ground that the mountaineers must have been Negroes—that no white assemblage could so conduct itself. But most of the clients showed more editorial courage than the *Oklahoman* and less precipitancy than the *News,* and the articles, widely printed, naturally were widely discussed.[3]

Since they were appearing daily in the nearby Chattanooga *News,* Daytonians got in the habit of reading them; reading them, they seethed with anger; angered, they debated action. Some, like the Rev. A. C. Stribling, of Dayton's Cumberland Presbyterian Church, let off steam by writing the *News*— "Let your gourd seeds rattle, Buddy; they don't sprout"— and others, like the assembled Methodists of the town, took out their indignation in wild talk of taking him "into an alley." But there were some for whom wild talk was not enough and who did not know how to write. After a week of hearing themselves described as "morons" and "yokels," members of this civic-minded element decided to avenge the insult to their town and, according to A. P. Haggard, president of the American National Bank in Dayton, their plans came perilously close to fruition. Haggard was walking home past a Dayton store one evening in the second week of Mencken's visit when he saw a light burning in the rear of the building. Noting the lateness of the hour, he decided to investigate. Inside he found a score of bearded mountain men, dressed for combat. They had, it appeared, just finished plans to ride their critic out of town on a rail "and mebbe a little more." Haggard persuaded them to give up the idea and Mencken thus escaped what would have been, at best, an unpleasant mauling. There were other murmurings from the more outraged of Rhea county's citizens, but none reached the point of execution. For one thing, the leading citizens of the town were determined that the trial should not get farther out of hand than it already had. For another, T. T. Martin —he of the "Hell in the High Schools" battlecry—had become extremely fond of Mencken during their theological

[3] In Baltimore, the executive secretary of the Association of Commerce wrote the *Sun,* complaining that Mencken's "unjust characterization of people in the South" had hurt the city's business with that part of the country.

debates, and he served as a powerful friend among the Fundamentalists, discouraging physical violence. The possibility of assault remained right down to Mencken's last hour in Dayton, however; the night he left town some thirty men gathered around the flagpole at the junction of Main and Market Streets, figuratively tearing him limb from limb while the hooting traffic backed far up the road toward Morgantown.

On the morning of July 26, 1925, William Jennings Bryan breakfasted in Chattanooga with three evangelists and drove back to Dayton with Mrs. Bryan and a friend. For the past four days, since John Thomas Scopes had been found guilty and fined one hundred dollars, he had been writing and re-writing his answers to Darrow's final charges. The completed manuscript was to serve as his opening gun in the fight against Modernism, the keynote in the campaign for an anti-evolution amendment to the United States Constitution, and, perhaps, an anti-evolution political party, with him as its presidential candidate. It was, he believed, his finest effort since the famous "Cross of Gold" speech, now a tarnished memory. The night before he had tried excerpts from it on audiences in Winchester and Jasper, with gratifying results, and arrangements were now complete for its publication. He had, he believed, won a great victory in Dayton. Other, greater victories were to follow.

Has it been marked by historians that the late William Jennings Bryan's last secular act on this earth was to catch flies? A curious detail, and not without its sardonic overtones. He was the most sedulous fly-catcher in American history, and by all odds the most successful. His quarry, of course, was not *Musca domestica* but *Homo neandertalensis*. For forty years he tracked it with snare and blunderbuss, up and down the backways of the Republic. Wherever the flambeaux of Chautauqua smoked and guttered, and the bilge of idealism ran in the veins, and Baptist pastors damned the brooks with the saved, and men gathered who were weary and heavy laden, and their wives who were unyieldingly multiparous and full of Peruna—

there the indefatigable Jennings set his traps and spread his bait.

He knew every forlorn town in the South and West, and he could crowd the most remote of them to suffocation by simply winding his horn. The city proletariat, transiently flustered by him in 1896, quickly penetrated his buncombe and would have no more of him; the gallery jeered him for 25 years. But out where the grass grows high, and the horned cattle dream away the lazy days, and men still fear the powers and principalities of the air—out there between the corn rows he held his old puissance to the end. There was no need of beaters to drive in his game. The news that he was coming was enough. For miles the flivver dust would choke the roads. And when he rose at the end of the day to discharge his Message there would be such breathless attention, such a sweet rustle of amens as the world had not known since Johanan fell to Herod's headsman.[4]

In Dayton, Bryan led the congregation of the Southern Methodist Episcopal Church in prayer; then, after a post-service gab with the elders on the coming battle, he and Mrs. Bryan retired to the cottage they had rented for the trial. They dined grandly, as was their custom, early that Sunday afternoon. The enormous meal stashed away, the Commoner leaned back in his chair and fanned himself contentedly with the palm leaf he had affected throughout his Tennessee visit. His wide carnivorous mouth—which had fallen into such hard lines during Darrow's merciless attack—curved in a smile; he turned to his wife. "I've never felt better in my life," he said. "I think I'll go upstairs and take a nap." He climbed slowly to his room, his alpaca trousers swishing softly in the still summer air; he stretched full upon the groaning mattress. Moments later, he was asleep.

There was something peculiarly fitting in the fact that

[4] The quotations on Bryan are from Mencken's obituary of the Commoner which appeared as his editorial in the October, 1925, issue of *The American Mercury*.

his last days were spent in a one-horse Tennessee village, and that death found him there. The man felt at home in such scenes. He liked people who sweated freely, and were not debauched by the refinements of the toilet. Making his progress up and down the Main street of little Dayton, surrounded by gaping primates from the upland valleys of the Cumberland range, his coat laid aside, his bare arms and hairy chest shining damply, his bald head sprinkled with dust—so accoutred and on display he was obviously happy. He liked getting up early in the morning, to the tune of cocks crowing on the dunghill. He liked the heavy, greasy victuals of the farmhouse kitchen. . . . His place in the Tennessee hagiocracy is secure. If the village barber saved any of his hair, then it is curing gallstones down there today.

But what label will he bear in more urban regions? One, I fear, of a far less flattering kind. Bryan lived too long, and descended too deeply in the mud, to be taken seriously hereafter by fully literate men, even of the kind who write schoolbooks. . . . When he began denouncing the notion that man is a mammal even some of the hinds at Dayton were agape. And when, brought upon Darrow's cruel hook, he writhed and tossed in a very fury of malignancy, bawling against the baldest elements of sense and decency like a man frantic—when he came to that tragic climax there were snickers among the hinds as well as hosannas.

Upon that hook, in truth, Bryan committed suicide. He staggered from the rustic court ready to die, and he staggered from it ready to be forgotten, save as a character in a third-rate farce, witless and in execrable taste.

At 4:30 Mrs. Bryan felt her husband had slept long enough. She summoned James McCartney, the family chauffur. "Jim," she instructed him, "go up and wake Mr. Bryan." Up went Jim, first to call softly, then to shake gently, and, finally, to dash, white-faced, down the stairs his employer had climbed so serenely two hours before. The Commoner had passed away in his sleep, the victim of an apoplectic stroke. Mrs. Bryan took the news calmly, but her husband's admirers did not. A politician to the last, he had died on a Sunday, thus assuring a great play in the Monday papers, and all over the South and West, as the word spread, the elements of his incipient Fundamentalist party mourned him blatantly. Telegrams and long-distance phone calls flooded the Dayton cottage; the men in the hills held council with one another, debating their next move. Bryan was dead, but his death, they were determined, should not stop the great crusade against Modernism. Nor, for a time, did it.

Heave an egg out of a Pullman window, and you will hit a Fundamentalist almost anywhere in the United States today. They swarm in the country towns, inflamed by their pastors, and with a saint, now, to venerate. They are thick in the mean streets behind the gasworks. They are everywhere that learning is too heavy a burden for mortal minds, even the vague, pathetic learning on tap in little red schoolhouses. They march with the Klan, with the Christian Endeavor Society, with the Junior Order of United American Mechanics, with the Epworth League, with all the rococo bands that poor and unhappy folk organize to bring some light of purpose into their lives. They have had a thrill, and they are ready for more.

Such is Bryan's legacy to his country. He couldn't be President, but he could at least help magnificently in the solemn business of shutting off the Presidency from every intelligent and self-respecting man. The storm, perhaps, won't last long, as time goes in history. It may help, indeed, to break up the democratic delusion, now already showing weakness, and so hasten its own end. But while it lasts it will blow off some roofs and flood some sanctuaries.

In its original and considerably emasculated form, Mencken's obituary of Bryan appeared on the editorial page of the *Evening Sun* the day after the Commoner's death. In an effort to counterbalance the terrific blast, Gerald Johnson was told to write a sober, dignified account of Bryan's life, without praise but also without vilification. It appeared beside Mencken's piece and, as Johnson himself noted, was read by no one; for all the mollification it accomplished, it might just as well not have been printed. Baltimore's tenderhearted swamped the paper with letters, denouncing the bad taste of the article and demanding censorship or boycott if Mencken were not suppressed. Locally, at least, this squall blew off more roofs and flooded more sanctuaries than the great Fundamentalist storm brewing when Bryan died. That quaint movement was throttled the following year, when the Tennessee Supreme Court, in a masterpiece of diplomacy, reversed Judge Raulston's decision on the technicality that he, and not the jury, had fixed the amount of the fine. The *Evening Sun's* one hundred dollars were thus refunded and Scopes was free to eat ice cream sodas, on which he doted, if not to teach evolution, which little interested him. But this ending, for Mencken, had little real significance. His purpose had been achieved that sleepy Sunday afternoon in Dayton, when Scopes' chief prosecutor ate too much and ruptured a blood vessel. Years later, when Darrow was in Baltimore, Johnson showed him a cadaverous looking life mask of Bryan, wrapped in a newspaper. "He looks better that way than any other way I ever saw him," Darrow remarked drily.

Shortly thereafter Mencken was asked his view of the case in retrospect.

"Well," he said, "we killed the son-of-a-bitch."

On December 13, 1925, died Anna Abhau Mencken, aged sixty-seven. She had been suffering incessantly from arteriosclerosis for the past two years; there were times when she could not sew or hold a book to read, and she was utterly unable to sleep without drugs in her last weeks. Mencken had been greatly distressed by her illness and was fearful of seeing her helpless and in great pain for a long period. Curiously, it was a chance disease, totally unrelated to her long-standing trouble, which took her in the end. On December 12 she fell victim to a severe case of tonsillitis, accompanied by a high temperature. The infection spread to the glands of her neck; surgical relief was necessary; she was taken to Union Memorial Hospital. She bore the operation well, but remained very ill. She died believing she was getting well. In an unrecognizable and almost unreadable scrawl, Mencken wrote Madelaine Boyd, "My mother died at 6 o'clock tonight—very peacefully. It was a mercy. The alternative was long suffering." As head of the family, he made arrangements to take Gertrude and August to Pittsburgh for a dreary Christmas with Charlie's family. Afterward, they were to come back to Hollins Street. "My mother wanted the house to go on," he wrote simply. That the house could not go on properly without her—that her death had removed a pivot in his life which could never be replaced—this discovery, with all its implications, lay in the future.

Chapter 7

Banned in Boston

(1926)

MENCKEN WAS not only unsurprised by the Watch and Ward attack on the *Mercury* in the spring of 1926; he had actually anticipated it, and was at first amused when the news, so startling to a nation, came out of Boston. From its inception two years before, the magazine had been calculated to arouse the very rancor which moved J. Frank Chase, secretary of the Society, to his historic decision. The religious press had repeatedly asked its ban, and despite its harmlessness, the *Mercury* had actually been ruled off the newsstands in a few intolerant rural communities. The flavor of "Americana" and the tenor of Mencken's editorials, together with the reputations of its contributors—Darrow, Cabell, Margaret Sanger—moved the village Baptist, adventuring through its pages, to a helpless rage. Personally, of course, Mencken was anathema to the censors. His actions on behalf of *The "Genius"* and *Jurgen* had marked him, in many a ladies' auxiliary, as the Antichrist personified, and there was, in the far-flung Western towns where grass grew knee-high on Main Street, a constant marveling that he had not been struck down from above.

Moreover, he had excellent reason to expect reprisal from Chase in particular. His absorbing interest in the opposition had led him to question all Bostonians he met on the Chase consorship technique; fascinated by what he heard, he decided, early in 1925, to run a piece on Watch and Ward methods, and chose one A. L. S. Wood, of the Springfield (Massachusetts) *Union,* to write it. "Keeping the Puritans Pure" appeared in the September, 1925, *Mercury,* and within a few days word reached Mencken from J. J. Crowley, a Boston magazine agent, that Chase was beating his breast in anguish and promising his friends the *Mercury* was in for trouble. Three months later Angoff wrote "Boston Twilight," depicting the decline of Boston as a cultural center and mentioning Chase. Scarcely had this wound begun to heal before, in April,

1926, Chase appeared for a third time, in a derisive piece titled "The Methodists," written by Angoff under the pseudonym "James D. Bernard." That did it. Three days after the *Mercury* appeared in Boston on March 28, word came from Crowley that Chase was rising to meet the challenge.

Fate could have chosen a more adroit opponent for Mencken than J. Frank Chase, but it could have found none better suited to his purpose. A Methodist preacher in his youth, Chase had become secretary of the Watch and Ward Society in 1907. He quickly perfected a pattern of terrorism among the arts that won the envy of the great Anthony Comstock himself. Like the god of his calling, Chase was an incurable collector of the smutty literature he professed to abhor and loved to show it to friends on the side. On one occasion he had written an obscene ode to the night clubs of Boston and read it before a committee of the state legislature; on another, he told reporters, he spent a glorious evening lying in bed on the Fall River-New York boat, reading pornographic novels. As early as July 11, 1916, he had been accused by a New Bedford paper of various offenses against morals. In person he was the prototype of the censor: burly, superficially genial, with thin-rimmed glasses, thin lips, and a luxurious mustache. Mencken liked to describe him, through the course of their relationship, as a "Pecksniff."

With the Watch and Ward behind him he was all but invincible on home ground. The Society had been founded in 1876 when Comstock was gaining his own support, and claimed among its supporters much of Boston's élite. Backed by the Catholics and Puritans who lived together there in uneasy virtue, Chase held the whip hand over every bookseller, magazine vendor, and theatrical producer in the city. In censoring he seldom went to court. He merely notified the Boston Bookseller's Committee or the Massachusetts Magazine Committee that he "believed" there were certain "passages" in a given work which were illegal. He never named the passages. He never had to. Aware of his influence in the courts, the book sellers and magazine vendors quietly shelved copies of the questionable work, returning them to the publisher or selling them under the counter to known friends. Chase never appeared publicly, the publishers and authors were never given a chance to be heard, and Boston became a Sahara from which, among others, Cabell, Anderson, Dreiser, and Huxley were excluded. Even the newspapers, aware of his power, dared not criticize the omnipotent censor.

Small wonder, then, that he felt secure, that last day in March, 1926, in notifying John J. Tracey, chairman of the Massachusetts Magazine Committee, that the April *Mercury* —the one in which "The Methodists" and Chase appeared— was "objectionable." The wonder is that he felt obliged to depart from protocol and name the objectionable piece. Perhaps he anticipated the charge of animosity. Whatever the reason, he notified the Boston papers April's *Mercury* was unfit because an article entitled "Hatrack," by one Herbert Asbury, a reporter on the New York *Herald Tribune,* attacked the clergy. Tracey passed the word on down the line, and, since the issue had nearly run its course, magazine sellers from Concord, New Hampshire, to Fall River, Massachusetts— Chase's influence extended that far—hastily unloaded their stock. One, a dealer named Felix Caragianes, was actually arrested at his Harvard Square stand.

Mencken was in his third-floor workroom when a United Press reporter called with the news. He unloaded a few characteristic quotes for the public (Chase was a "buffoon"; the "wowsers" and "swine" in Boston never read the *Mercury* anyhow; they preferred *Hot Dog*) and returned to his labors, inclined to dismiss the whole thing. Boston was a poor magazine market in the mid-Twenties, and the *Mercury*, its circulation zooming, could easily do without it, for good if need be. Besides, the April number, aided by the Chase dictum, was all but a sellout in Boston. If the incident were repeated, it would be time to act.

Sucking his corncob pipe, however, he began to reflect on the whole thing—Chase's obvious reprisal, his dictatorial methods, and the harmless nature of "Hatrack." Asbury's story, a chapter from a forthcoming book, *Up From Methodism,* recounted an incident from his childhood in Farmington, Missouri. It dealt with an amateur prostitute held in her avocation by the snubs of the town churchgoers and with the aphrodisiac effect of revival sermons. Would not Chase, if unchecked, go on to greater censorship? And would not the other censors, the Methodists throughout the South and Middle West who hated the *Mercury*, be encouraged to imitate Chase?

In New York he talked the whole thing over with Alfred and Blanche Knopf. They advised counsel, and Mencken, remembering Arthur Garfield Hays from Dayton, suggested him. Consulted, Hays asked if Mencken would sell a copy of the banned book on the Boston Common and defy arrest. The plan, he observed, had certain advantages: Mencken could defy Chase in open court, those Bostonians who regretted Chase would be aroused, and, as a citizen of Maryland, he could appeal in Federal court for relief against an assault on his good name and property. Chase, Hays pointed out, could probably name his own judge and win a first conviction, but Mencken stood an excellent chance of winning on appeal, since "Hatrack" obviously was harmless. "If I lose?" Hays was asked. "You can get two years in prison," he answered. And Mencken, influenced by Anna's death in December and his consequent relief from responsibility, replied, "I'll go."

In Hays' office the four worked out details. He and Mencken were to meet on the Boston Common April 5 and sell a copy of the April issue to Chase himself. They would settle for no one else. If Chase refused to appear, they would sell dozens of copies to the crowd that was sure to gather, thus turning the Watch and Ward's power into a sham. The press associations were told of the arrangement on April 3, and the following day Mencken, after a conference with Patterson, set out for Boston with W. A. S. Douglas, a *Sun* reporter. At 7 A.M. they disembarked and went immediately to the Copley-Plaza to meet a gang of Boston reporters. Hays, meanwhile, was in conference with Herbert B. Ehrmann, his Boston associate. Ehrmann had talked with Chase and told him of the plan. Chase asked for an extension of time—until April 7, while he consulted his colleagues on the Society—but Ehrmann held the threat of a general sale on the Common over his head, and the censor finally gave in. The place agreed upon was Brimstone Corner. The time was to be 2 P.M. In the afternoon papers Mencken repeated his charge that Chase's ban was a reprisal against the *Mercury* articles about him. Chase told reporters "Hatrack" was "bad, vile, raw stuff."

Ehrmann told Mencken he must procure a peddler's license. Supremely happy, he rode over to the Boston Health Department and took out a certificate entitling him to sell everything except fish, fruit, or vegetables. He declined a license permitting him to peddle bones, grease, and refuse matter. Hays later wondered if this were a mistake, considering the current status of the April *Mercury* in Boston.

A tremendous crowd, mostly Harvard students, had gathered on Brimstone Corner by shortly before 2 o'clock when Mencken, with Douglas, John J. Mullen, Knopf's chief book agent; and three copies of the *Mercury*, arrived. The mob milled around, forcing him against a building. Hays drove up, with fifty copies of the magazine in a bundle, ready to carry out the general sale threat if Chase reneged. Mencken exchanged pleasantries with the Harvard boys, springing up occasionally in a vain attempt to peer over their heads and see if Chase were coming. A youth stepped up, identified himself as Chase's assistant, and offered to buy a copy of the April number. Mencken refused. The man offered credentials, proving he was a member of the Watch and Ward Society. Still Mencken refused. The young man went away.

At length those on the outskirts of the crowd shouted, "Here he is! Here he is!" and through the crowd, slowly pushing his way, came J. Frank Chase, until he arrived *vis-à-vis* with the peddler.

"Are you Chase?" asked Mencken.

"I am," Chase replied, depositing a silver half dollar in the editor's palm.

And Mencken, for the ages, bit it.

"I order this man's arrest," cried Chase, grabbing the proffered *Mercury* and turning to Capt. George W. Patterson, chief of the Boston vice squad. Oliver W. Garrett, a young plainclothesman, tapped Mencken on the arm, and the march began through the milling, sympathetic mob to police headquarters in Pemberton Square, four blocks away.

At the police station the drama turned into a farce, with

Captain Patterson, who had been upset by the crowd's hostility to Chase, as chief clown. The density of the mob delayed Ehrmann; by the time he arrived at the station house, Mencken and Hays were already inside. Ehrmann found his path blocked by Patterson. One lawyer, the vice squad leader said, was enough for the likes of Mencken. The lawyer took issue with Patterson, they wrestled briefly at the door, and Ehrmann left in disgust.

Meanwhile, on the second floor, Mencken was being booked on charge of violating Chapter 272, section 28, of the Public General Laws, by possessing and selling obscene literature. He found the cops, with the exception of Patterson, a genial lot and chatted amiably with them over the absurdity of the whole business. Returning to the first floor to await arraignment at the Central Muncipal Court, he was greeted by a strange scene.

Patterson, his bellicosity but slightly appeased by his triumph over Ehrmann, had turned on Douglas, who as a foreigner and a literate, seemed fair bait. Douglas was standing off to one side, with a copy of the *verboten* issue under his arm, and Patterson, spying this, let out a yell. "He's got the filth in his hands!" he shouted, rushing over and placing the amazed Douglas under arrest. Over the meek protests of his assistants, and the violent protests of Douglas, Patterson insisted his charge be booked. This had just been completed when Mencken arrived. Chase, to his credit, joined Mencken in arguing that since Douglas was a reporter, there only to cover the event, he should be released immediately. Patterson was stubborn. Finally he hit on what seemed to him a brilliant solution. He agreed to rebook Douglas as a suspicious person, provided the reporter sign a paper absolving him from legal responsibility for laying the original charge. Anxious to file against the late editions of the *Evening Sun,* Douglas agreed; after the cops had painfully drawn up the absolution document and he had signed it, he was let loose.

One item remained to complete the day's business: Mencken had to be arraigned. After considerable delay, a judge appeared, and he pleaded not guilty to both charges. Patterson—probably at Chase's suggestion—moved the trial be delayed one week, but Hays protested on grounds of hardship. He pointed out that the only evidence necessary, the magazine, was on hand, and that no witnesses not immediately available were needed. After some haggling, trial was set for 10 o'clock the following morning. Mencken was released on his own recognizance, with surety fixed at five hundred dollars. He then went to Ehrmann's office to talk to reporters.

Ehrmann and Hays, in the meantime, had drawn up a bill of complaint, asking an injunction to restrain Chase from further interference with the April issue and fifty thousand dollars damages. They took it to Judge George W. Anderson of the Circuit Court and asked for a hearing before him. Anderson was skeptical. He was anxious to get back on his circuit and was afraid of delay.

Mencken had remained outwardly calm during the whole of a trying day, but inwardly he was troubled. Conviction the following day seemed certain; the more powerful the authorities, the more hostile they were to him. The Boston newspapers, with the exception of the *American* and the *Transcript*, were extremely unfriendly. Chase, he was certain, could name his own judge. It hardly seemed likely he would survive the following morning without a conviction. Leaving Ehrmann's office, he wired the Fidelity and Deposit Company in Baltimore for bail money and returned to the hotel.

Three wires awaited him. One, from Maury Maverick in San Antonio, gave enthusiastic, if ineffectual, encouragement. The second, from the graduate secretary of the Harvard Union, asked him to be the Union's guest for lunch at any time during the next ten days. The third was from Murphy, Hamilton Owens, and Harry Black. It read:

STRAW VOTE TAKEN HURRIEDLY AT 2:15 TODAY SHOWS THE FREE STATE SOLIDLY BEHIND YOU WITH THE EXCEPTION OF CRABBE DAVIS AND KELLY STOP IF NECESSARY WILL SEND COLONEL BOWIE TO RESCUE YOU FROM THE UPLIFTERS STOP INDIGNATION MEETING IN MARYLAND CLUB STOP FREE STATE FLAG COMING BY SPECIAL DELIVERY.

The flag was Mencken's idea. At the time he had no specific

use for it save, perhaps, as a talisman. He counted on a use developing. It did.

Except for the wires, an invitation to the Brahmin St. Botolph Club, and a few calls from Bostonians who professed shame for Chase, the evening was disquieting. Throughout dinner at Ehrmann's, Mencken was nervous, and his nervousness was not allayed by the dismal prophecies of Mullen later in the evening. Asbury had just arrived from New York, and he, Mullen, Mencken, and Hays discussed their chances at the coming trial. Mullen, a Bostonian, was pessimistic. The judges were impossible—it was unheard of for a Municipal Court judge to find a Watch and Ward defendant not guilty. A jury trial would be no better; Thomas C. O'Brien, the district attorney, was rabid on the censorship question and had threatened to pack any jury against Mencken. The "Boston Twilight" piece, Mullen said, was deeply resented in some quarters. One prominent bookstore manager was offering fantastic odds on conviction and openly speaking against him. Against this, a nightcap was useless. Mencken slept little that night.

The following morning he arrived at the court shortly before 10—and found himself without lawyers. He began to sweat. Chase, he learned, had got his way with the Bench. The judge named was a notorious supporter of the Watch and Ward Society and was looking forward to the coming fiasco with relish. Mencken fumed and bounced and consulted his pocket watch, shaping barbed epigrams on the subject of lawyers, judges, court catchpoles—but principally lawyers. Ten o'clock came and went, and Hays and Ehrmann remained *non est*.

They were closeted with Anderson, wrangling his consent to an injunction hearing a week later, and it was probably their tardiness that saved their client. The court officials, like the cops the day before, were sympathetic to Mencken's cause. On the rather flimsy excuse that his judge's docket was crowded, they moved him to the calendar of one Judge James P. Parmenter. They knew nothing about Parmenter, they told Mencken, but unlike most of his colleagues, he was not definitely known to be sympathetic to Chase. Having accomplished this—the most important stroke of the whole case—without his counsel, Mencken rested a little more easily. At quarter to 11 Hays and Ehrmann hurried in. The trial began a few minutes later.

It was a strange hearing. The courtroom was packed, but since the evidence was supposed to be obscene, the judge moved over to a corner with Chase, Mencken, their lawyers, and a few reporters, and ordered that all testimony be conducted in a whisper. It was a verse right out of "Americana," and Mencken, for all his natural awe of courts, had a hard time suppressing his mirth.

John W. Rorke, Chase's lawyer, produced a brief which had obviously seen hard service and began by denouncing (in a whisper, of course) Mencken's corruption of youth. He followed with his evidence. It consisted largely of Patterson's testimony that Mencken had sold more than one copy of the magazine, which was not true, and Chase's assertion that the trial case was Mencken's idea and that he, Chase, had gone in against his better judgment, which probably was.

Hays then put Mencken on the stand as editor of the *American Mercury*. His magazine, the witness pointed out, sold for fifty cents a copy; its clientele was for the most part well educated. Moreover, its contributors were among the most distinguished men in the nation; included in their number were bishops and senators. The *Mercury,* he argued, never published obscene matter, and his sole purpose in coming to Boston was to challenge Chase's unfair methods, which menaced his own property and reputation.

He was followed by a young Boston lawyer, who testified to the value placed on the *Mercury's* legal articles at Yale Law School; by Douglas, who got in a few licks at Patterson before Rorke woke up; and by Asbury, who told of his youth in Farmington, Missouri, and testified to the truth of the story he had written. There was some discussion of his relationship to Francis Asbury, the first Methodist bishop ordained in the United States. To Mencken's delight, the reporters garbled this, writing that Asbury was a direct descendant of the bishop, to the great distress of the Methodist clergy which was well aware the bishop had never married.

After Hays had concluded with a whispered defense of freedom of the press, Rorke replied, *sotto voce,* that license was not liberty and that its high price did not exempt the *Mercury* from the Massachusetts statutes. Hays then came to the inevitable climax of the hearing. He asked Parmenter to read "Hatrack." "Your honor," he said, "must discover in your own mind whether reading it tends to arouse lascivious thoughts." Rorke then admitted the language in "Hatrack" was not obscene and turned, without previous announcement, to Nathan's "Clinical Notes" in the issue, which argued that sex was a diversion, that "civilized man knows little difference between his bottle of vintage champagne, his Corona-Corona, his seat at the Follies, and the gratification of his sex impulse." It was so like Nathan, to break into a solemn discussion with a statement of absolute triviality.

The judge, whom Mencken had regarded uneasily throughout, realizing that the whole case rested on him, interrupted but once, to uphold a prosecution contention that intention was no defense. At the conclusion of testimony, he cleared his throat and said he would read "Hatrack" and "Clinical Notes" that evening and announce his decision the following morning at 9:30. Mencken left the courtroom reconciled to a guilty verdict. Most of Boston agreed with him. That night he dined at the St. Botolph Club and turned in early, hoping for a good night. Again, he was disappointed.

A small crowd, made smaller by the surprise absence of Chase, greeted Judge Parmenter the following morning. The judge arose and immediately began his decision. Assuming he would be found guilty, that the best he could hope for then was the reference of his case to criminal court, Mencken was surprised to find Parmenter disposing, one by one, of Chase's contentions. He had just begun to wonder how the verdict would be justified when the judge concluded:

"The article 'Clinical Notes' merely points out that sex is not nearly so important a matter in life as it is often assumed to be.

"As to 'Hatrack,' the main article in question, I cannot imagine anyone reading it and finding himself or herself attracted toward vice.

"I find for the defendant."

There was a long silence while Rorke, alone in defeat, blinked and swallowed. Then the clerk turned to Mencken and said, "You are free to go. Your bail is vacated. Next case."

The verdict had been extemporaneous, and the judge declined to dictate it for the record. Finally, somewhat testily, he agreed to read and approve a version drawn up by Ehrmann and Douglas from memory. Mencken, pinching himself, left the courtroom.

In Ehrmann's office, facing a hostile Boston press gang, he decided to carry the war to the enemy. Hinting broadly at libel suits, he asked the reporters about Chase's property and took elaborate notes on their information, well aware they would carry the news back to a troubled censor. He sent for a copy of the society's annual report, expressed great interest in its endowment of one hundred and sixty thousand dollars, and questioned his questioners closely on the financial status of Charles W. Eliot, the retired president of Harvard and a vice-president of the society. Then, having turned gracefully from interviewee to interviewer, he pleaded the pressure of an engagement and left the baffled reporters in Ehrmann's office.

His engagement was for lunch at the Harvard Union. The day before, anticipating a conviction, he had taken advantage of the Union's invitation, expecting the luncheon to act as a bracer after the bad news in court. Now, exonerated, he rode across the Charles River, escorted by a committee of Harvard men, to a jammed Union living room, packed with students who had not yet heard the morning's news and who were met to protest. The living room, built to accommodate six hundred, held nearly two thousand young men, massed along the walls and in the gallery, prepared to show their idol there were New Englanders who supported him the more enthusiastically in defeat.

Mencken entered, whispered the news to Felix Frankfurter —who jumped up and announced it—and was greeted by a deafening roar of approval. Then he made one of the few speeches of his career. It was short and characteristic. He referred to "my colleague Chapman"—Gerald Chapman, who had been hanged at Wethersfield, Connecticut, the day before and had vied with Mencken for front-page space that morning —praised Harvard, and took a slam at the "cow colleges" and, of course, Chase. Then he sat down. After the luncheon he presented the gaudy Maryland flag, which had been rushed up from Sun Square, to the Union, and heard the Harvard cheer sounded three times lustily in his honor. He was immediately descended upon by scores of autograph-seeking students and made his escape only after a re-enactment of the flag presentation for the photographers and the newsreel cameramen.

Back at the hotel, he found another wire from Murphy. It read:

CONGRATULATIONS VIRTUE EVER TRIUMPHS SUN SQUARE NOW ECHOING WITH STIRRING STRAINS OF MRS. BROWN.

That night he and Mullen polished off a pint of the best bootleg whisky available and enjoyed a lavish dinner on the train. In New York he registered at the Algonquin, rehashed the victory with Hays and the Knopfs, and slept well for the first time since the Sunday before.

The next evening, while dining with H. E. Buchholz in Hoboken, he picked up a copy of the New York *Graphic*. A three-line item out of Washington announced the banning of the April *Mercury* from the United States mails.

Chase had anticipated Parmenter's decision. On the night of April 5 he had slipped down to Fall River and taken the boat to New York. The following morning, while Mencken was being acquitted in Boston, he had seen New York's Postmaster John J. Kiely, an old friend, and convinced him of "Hatrack's" faults. Kiely referred the matter to Horace J. Donnelly, solicitor to the Postmaster-General in Washington, who, in turn, spent the better part of a day examining the issue. Donnelly, a former stenographer, was undecided until the following morning, when Harry S. New, the politically conscious Postmaster-General, received a resolution passed by the Farmington Chamber of Commerce asking the magazine be banned. Donnelly took his cue; at 4:40 P.M. he wired

Kiely, instructing him to permit the mailing of no more April *Mercurys*. The news was announced in Washington simultaneously.

It was an incredible move. Mencken had been sent no notice and permitted no hearing. He had learned of it, ironically enough, through the pages of the New York *Graphic,* a publication which, under the most lenient censorship rules, was of questionable propriety. Moreover, the ruling was obviously futile and was, in a sense, a reflection on the system the Post Office Department had set up for the inspection of printed matter. The whole issue had gone through the mails by March 20, after a rigorous examination by postal inspectors ("smellers," Mencken called them) in Camden, New Jersey, where the *Mercury* was printed, and in New York City, where it was published. Under postal laws, four copies of each issue had to be submitted to Federal offices in each of the two municipalities. Nor were these "smellings" mere formalities. Many a New York publisher had been called before the New York office to answer for questionable passages, and Nathan, a few years before, had spent several hours justifying a *Smart Set* cover to a postal clerk.

It was a challenge which must be met, but for the moment it had to wait. The injunction hearing was coming up in a few days, and the *Mercury* office had been flooded with correspondence which Mencken, with his scruples, could not ignore. And the press, hostile and misinformed, had to be dealt with. Most of the papers had assumed the Boston trial was a publicity stunt, calculated to raise the *Mercury's* circulation. Mencken prepared a careful statement, pointing out that despite the enormous demand for more copies of the issue he had not, and would not, replate. While he struggled with the enormous pile of letters in his office, Hays sent his partner, David A. Buckley, to Washington to arrange a hearing. Donnelly at first insisted on a date which would have conflicted with the injunction trial, but agreed, after some bickering, to the morning of April 15.

Meanwhile, Mencken had run into fresh trouble. In the May issue, then rolling off the Camden presses, was an article by Bernard DeVoto under the pen name "John August" dealing, harmlessly enough, with the popular belief that promiscuity was rife among college girls. DeVoto's contention that the rumors were exaggerated was well backed, but the title, "Sex and the Co-ed," was aphroditic. Mencken showed the article to Hays, who advised against publication, pointing out that a second Post Office ban would permit Donnelly to suspend second-class mailing privileges on the ground that the magazine had missed two consecutive issues and was not, therefore, "of continuous publication." This, of course, would wreck the *Mercury*. Mencken debated the matter and decided to substitute a sterile piece entitled "On Learning to Play the Cello." The replate cost eight thousand dollars and held up publication two days, but it was probably a wise move; between Boston and Washington, he and Hays had their hands full, and further difficulties they could not handle.

Even this proved unsatisfactory. News of the substitution reached the papers, who erroneously reported that Knopf had made it over Mencken's protests. The *Mercury* printers, after dutifully filing copies of the May issue in Camden and New York, were told they must accept full responsibility for the content. The Post Office Department demanded advance issues of every publication, but declined to pass final judgment. Passage by its inspectors was no guarantee against a later barring of mailing privileges, as the April issue had graphically illustrated.

The injunction hearing was held, as scheduled, on April 12, but Anderson had transferred the case to Judge James M. Morton, Jr., explaining that he wanted to hold himself in reserve should the decision be appealed. Rorke had been replaced by a far better lawyer, one Edmund A. Whitman, but Whitman was no match for Hays; indeed, it was an almost unbelievable error on his part that probably carried the hearing for the *Mercury*. After a motion to quash the plea had been taken under advisement and Whitman, at the judge's request, had specified the objectionable sections in the issue—"Hatrack's" discussion of prostitution in small towns and the "Clinical Notes" section—Hays put Chase on the stand.

Chase pointed out that all copies of the issue had been

distributed and charged that "my adversary wants advertising." Hays countered this, informing the court that despite the demand for a million more copies, none had been, or would be, reprinted. Then Whitman addressed the judge and provided Hays with the opening for which he had waited, in vain, all through the trial before Parmenter.

"If they," he said, "will submit to us the May number in plenty of time, we will notify them whether it is objectionable or not."

Hays was on his feet instantly.

"That is an outrageous presumption," he roared. "That is what I object to—that we should have to submit our magazine to these people to find out whether we can distribute it in Massachusetts. It shows the whole situation. They want to be censors of our business, and they have no right to it. We will put in what we want, and we ask you to have us arrested if there is anything improper, and nothing more."

"Not even," ventured Whitman, "if we give you a warning?"

"No!" bellowed Hays. "We don't want the warning!"

During the whole of this outburst Judge Morton smiled broadly, making no attempt to check Hays' wrath. Two days later he granted the injunction and sustained the full fifty-thousand dollar damage claim, should the *Mercury* choose to press it. It was a terrific beating for the Watch and Ward, and was taken anything but gracefully. Later that same day, in a Cambridge district court, Felix Caragianes, the Harvard Square magazine vendor, was found guilty of peddling obscene literature—proving, if anything, the college boys are more corruptible than the general citizenry—and Whitman, who prosecuted, took occasion to attack Mencken personally on his prohibition stand and observe that "if Judge Parmenter had been married, he would never have dared go home after the 'Hatrack' decision." The following day Chase told an unsympathetic Harvard Liberal Club that "a whole high-school class of unwedded mothers may be the result of a lascivious book."

The Post Office hearing, of course, was foredoomed. Donnelly (who turned out to be the image of Calvin Coolidge) served as both defendant and jury, and since the *Mercury* would have had excellent grounds for suit had he decided against himself, there was no doubting the outcome. Its main value to Mencken was as a basis for injunction proceedings. The Knopfs went along for the ride and did not regret it, for Hays and Mencken displayed their best pyrotechnics. After a brief dispute over whether reporters should be admitted—Mencken agreeable and Donnelly opposed, Mencken winning out—Hays and Donnelly plunged into an argument over the value of Judge Parmenter's decision. Getting no results, Hays turned to Mencken and suggested he say something for himself.

He did. He protested the lack of a hearing before the ban and bitterly denounced Donnelly's "attack from the rear." Donnelly answered chastely that he had nothing to do with it —the magazine itself was to blame. He then used the time-worn bomb metaphor, citing the futility of waiting for a hearing before removing an explosive from the mails. Mencken pointed out that there was no parallel—the bomb was clearly dangerous, all were agreed on that, but the controversy over "Hatrack's" danger called for equity. He added that even "cancer quacks" were entitled to such hearings. Donnelly brought up the case of a disreputable California weekly which had reprinted "Hatrack" and without the *Mercury's* permission. Did Mencken make any distinction between the weekly and his own magazine? Mencken protested Donnelly was using a *Mercury* plagiarist as evidence against it. Donnelly read a letter from an anonymous Middle Westerner who protested the *Mercury's* reprinting of the Norphelt, Arkansas, adultery statute, and Mencken pointed out there was, and could be, no law against the printing of other laws. And so it went.

Midway through the hearing Donnelly acknowledged, somewhat testily, that Mencken's intervention on behalf of a Johns Hopkins University professor, who had run into trouble when he ordered a copy of *Ovid* through the mails, had stuck in his craw. At the conclusion of the session, which had been marked by his refusal to answer Mencken's more pointed questions, the solicitor told Hays he had not changed his mind. A week later he put this in writing, and four days later Hays filed suit against Donnelly in Federal District Court, asking an injunction against the solicitor's ruling.

Mencken's reputation had suffered greatly through the series of trials, and a hostile press was chiefly to blame. His treatment in Boston has been noted. The chief offender there was the *Herald,* whose vitriolic attacks were softened only after broad hints at libel suits. In New York the papers were split, the *Times* and the *World* friendly and the *Herald Tribune* and the *Sun* critical. The *Sun,* in particular, was bitter. The same war psychosis which had motivated Stuart Sherman a decade before lingered on in the editorial rooms there, and Mencken's stand was interpreted as a manifestation of the "Prussian" influence. In the South, where he was remembered for "Sahara of the Bozart," he was attacked from the Richmond *Times-Dispatch* to the Memphis *Commercial Appeal.* Josephus Daniels, publisher of the Raleigh *News and Observer,* called him an enemy of "the home, the church, the law, and order," and added, somewhat primly, that he had never read "Hatrack" because "I never deliberately soil my soul."

Cartoons depicted him as a grotesque ape. Editorial writers in the East compared him to Earl Carroll, who had recently been arrested for indecent exposure of his Vanities girls. In the West he was ranked with the unspeakable Sinclair Lewis who, on April 22, stood in a Kansas City church and successfully defied God to strike him dead. In Denver the Rev. William O'Ryan of St. Leo's Catholic Church, called "Hatrack": "Unredeemed dirt, an open sewer, without even the iridescent scum that half invites and half excuses a glance," and in Farmington the town banker stopped a public reading of "Hatrack," shouting, "Stop reading that! We should not listen to such an immoral recital!" With but few exceptions—the Kansas City *Post,* the Omaha *World-Herald,* the Cleveland *Press,* the Indianapolis *Times,* and, curiously enough, two religious weeklies—opposition to Mencken was virtually solid. Even the *Sun* papers were split; Hamilton Owens, of course, was behind him all the way, but the morning *Sun,* while opposing "Hatrack's" ban, deplored the story itself.

Mencken was bitter over this almost universal reprobation from the source where he should have received his greatest support. The accumulated animosities of years were being emptied upon him, he felt; he was being caricatured as a sort of racketeer when, in fact, he was fighting a battle in which the nation's press had a very real stake. His courting of an objective appraisal met with little success; a reprinting of "Keeping the Puritans Pure," describing Chase's methods, and his prepared statement, already mentioned, swung few papers. What support there was came from *Mercury* subscribers—there were few cancellations—and from the legal profession, with an avalanche of free counsel offers. Among the literati, his chief succor came from Lewis, who sent him wires, praised him in press conferences, and dedicated *Elmer Gantry* to him.

The first copy of the April issue seen in Farmington had been brought by Marquis Childs, then a roving United Press correspondent out of St. Louis. The town was in a state of near hysteria at first; no one was able to give Childs a coherent statement. Later, the citizens calmed down enough to send the Postmaster General the wire that probably swung Donnelly's decision. Childs, after filing a story on the Farmington reaction (to which Asbury wrote a counterblast), wrote Mencken, advising him he had found the original Hatrack living in a state of destitution and offering to send him affidavits to that effect for use in damage suits. Mencken himself found the Middle West to be full of Hatracks. He received scores of letters saying the harlot had been ascribed to the wrong town, and one pathetic note arrived from a woman who signed herself "A Hatrack" and praised Asbury's comments on the self-righteous prudes who govern small towns on the prairie.

In general, the newspaper opposition (and that of the clergy, which was, of course, virtually unanimous) did just what Mencken had hoped to avoid by going to Boston: it encouraged the censors. In small towns everywhere, politicians saw a bandwagon and jumped on it. In Lansing, Michigan, an office-seeking prosecuting attorney ordered the issue off the stands in Ingham County. It was banned in Poughkeepsie, New York, and in countless towns throughout New England. North Carolina unearthed a curious statute forbidding the sale of any magazine which had been banned from the mails. And in libraries beyond number the April issue was withheld from the public because demand for it caused a nuisance—the inevitable result of censorship. Librarians reported copies were stolen from California to Paris.

On April 28 Judge Julian W. Mack reheard the evidence by now known to schoolboys throughout the nation and granted Mencken his injunction against Kiely, the New York postmaster. Kiely's defense was interesting: since the April issue had already gone through the mails, the *Mercury* should not be granted its injunction, he claimed. "In short," Mencken commented tartly, "the Post Office Department cannot be restrained from inflicting an injury that can have no conceivable utility."

Even more interesting was an affidavit from a postal inspector who reported he had written, under a pseudonym, to a bookseller advertising in the issue. In the return mail, the astonished Judge Mack was told, the inspector learned he could buy such obviously lewd books as the works of Boccaccio, Rabelais, Casanova, Montaigne, the Enfield edition of Charles Lamb, and Walton's *Compleat Angler!*

Thus far the judicial decisions had favored the *Mercury*, but Mencken was by no means satisfied. The newspaper misrepresentation, the loss of advertising, and the tremendous cost of the case had had a telling effect; with but two years of success behind it, such a magazine could easily be ruined. He considered retaliation; the Boston injunction had left the door open for damage suits, and certainly Donnelly's behavior was not above reproach. Plans were made, statements were drawn up, and he was confident, for a time, that his position would be further vindicated.

Somehow all the plans fell through. He debated with Hays the filing of a petition to Postmaster-General New against Donnelly. They doubted that New would prove sympathetic, but counted on the attendant publicity to upset the solicitor. Hays advised waiting until the government filed its inevitable injunction appeal; unfortunately, when this came, on July 1, he was in Europe, and Mencken therefore abandoned the scheme. Any Boston action would be difficult. Federal suits are always hard to press, and in civil court chances of success were small. Mencken had gone to Boston voluntarily, the Watch and Ward Society was incorporated as a charitable trust, and it would be almost impossible to get those advertisers who had withdrawn support from the magazine to admit "Hatrack" as the cause. Moreover, complications had arisen in Boston since the Morton decision.

For one thing, the stature of the Watch and Ward Society had suffered terribly since Chase's double defeat, and the secretary was widely blamed for it. The Boston police commissioner had issued an order, specifying no official support be given Chase without sanction from his office, and the Boston *Telegram* had openly called Chase a "faker." The loss of Caragianes' appeal, which Chase had expected to bolster public opinion in his favor, had boomeranged, for the newsdealer was generally considered a victim of circumstances. At the same time, the *Mercury* paid Caragianes' fine and thereby gained public esteem. At first blush, all this would seem to have benefited Mencken, but it worked just the other way. The powers in the Watch and Ward Society chose to sacrifice Chase for the reputation of the Society, and Mencken, if he filed against the Society, stood to lose on the ground that the agent, not the trust, was at fault.

Moreover, the censors and the *Mercury* were shyly shining up to one another in anticipation of a forthcoming event: Knopf's publication of Asbury's book. Knopf naturally wanted no trouble, and the Watch and Ward, having been burnt once, was not anxious to try again. At first there was some talk of a public apology by Chase, but the chief source for this seems to have been unreliable. Then Whitman came forth with an offer to send no more Society "advisement" letters and to refrain from challenging Knopf publications, including the *Mercury*, save in open court. His price was the vacating of the injunction. Mencken declined, on the ground that he liked that sword over the censors' heads. This march-up-the-hill-and-march-down-again correspondence continued until early November when Chase, who had fallen ill two weeks before, contracted pneumonia, had a relapse, and died.

Mencken was unsurprised and unshaken. He had become accustomed to the sudden death of his enemies, and the world, he felt, was well rid of one more moron and comstock. Nevertheless Chase, in retrospect, seems a pathetic character. His faults were common enough, but his willingness to battle for what seemed to him right was unusual, and certainly his tenacity, if nothing else, marked him from the mob. He had shown a woeful lack of shrewdness in the opening stages of the game, it is true, but his overnight trip to New York and subsequent dealings with the Post Office Department were anything but stupid; indeed, in the end they defeated Mencken, as will be shown presently. Apart from the concepts of justice involved, the case was interesting for the conflict of strong personalities, and while Chase had lost the battle in Boston, his fight, as a fight, had not been without merit. In his pre-"Hatrack" activity there was a ruthlessness and vigor which even Mencken, who had once paid Anthony Comstock tribute, could admire. There is something tragic about this man who rose up mightily to do battle against the Antichrist, fought fiercely, and died in battle, broken by worry over damage suits and the perfidy of his friends.

With his death, the Watch and Ward took heart, and Whitman's attitude became less and less conciliatory. He was still willing to backtrack somewhat, for the injunction remained a threat to the Society's position, but with Chase out of the picture he could afford to take a stronger stand. What little respect Chase had been accorded in life was now gone, and the Society had no remorse in making him the scapegoat for the whole affair. Whitman still insisted on the right to send advisory letters to booksellers, pointing out that the Catholic and Puritan traditions remained strong in Boston and that outsiders, another time, might not be so fortunate in their judges. There was some flurry when *Up from Methodism* first appeared, but eventually it died out, and the book, despite its tremendous free advertising, sold poorly. Both sides retired, letting the injunction run its two-year course.

The following May the government's appeal came up in

New York before the Circuit Court of Appeals, and the public, having lost interest in what was by now an academic question, paid little attention. Curiously, it was on the academical nature of the issue that both sides based their cases. Hays argued that since the issue had already gone through the mails, the Post Office action had simply damaged the *Mercury* before the country to no good purpose. The government argued, as before Mack, that since the issue had gone through the mails, the injunction was purposeless. In the end, the three judges—Manton, Hand, and Swan, liberals all—found for the Post Office Department, on the ground that equity offers a remedy only for continuing injuries. There was little ground for Supreme Court appeal, since no point of constitutionality was involved. In the last round, Mencken had been knocked out.

For all its injuries to Mencken, the "Hatrack" case actually benefited him. He lost, in the end, on a technicality, but his fight throughout had been magnificent, and he had dealt the Watch and Ward Society a blow from which it never fully recovered. It was the first determined attack on censorship in Massachusetts; others followed, and for the next decade there was scarcely a suppression trial in the country in which its legal arguments and decisions were not quoted.

And, however much Mencken might deprecate adverse newspaper publicity, the case *was* advertising, if not for the *Mercury*, then for him. Doubtless it hurt him in the eyes of the frumps who castigated him throughout, but he had never sought their good favor and would, indeed, have been dismayed had he gained it. His readers had always been drawn from the higher cultural levels of the nation, and however silent they may have been, they could not but vastly admire this man who had defied all that intelligent men hate. What did it matter to him if the prosecutor of Mary Ware Dennett challenged every juror who had read Mencken? Didn't the very fact that the opposition had crystallized against him mean he had become a symbol of everything it hated and he loved? It did, and though he denied it, at bottom he knew it was true.

The case had cost the *Mercury* some twenty thousand dollars, of which seventy-five hundred was in fees for Hays and his colleagues, but the magazine had a twenty-five-thousand-dollar surplus before the Boston arrest, and since it had never been considered a moneymaker, the effects there were not disastrous. Everywhere Mencken's name became identified with freedom and tolerance. In the House of Representatives he was mentioned as "America's foremost critic"; in the Senate, Reed of Missouri moved to abolish the preposterous Post Office censorship and establish a quasi-judicial body to pass on the mailability of printed matter. In Canada he was attacked in Parliament for an article on the spiritual and intellectual decay of England in the June, 1926, *Mercury,* and a censorship resolution came within an ace of passing, but his blistering defense of the magazine won out, and even there he was recognized for his independence and courage. And among America's younger generation, so in revolt against the established order, he rose to the stature of a god.

Chapter 8

At a Gallop, Mud-Spattered, High in Oath

(1926–1930)

IT ALMOST seemed to Mencken as though the Twenties had conspired against the finest product of his wartime reflections: the polemic against democracy. He had begun it late in the fall of 1920, confident he could match the damndest that had been said on the subject, determined to blow the super-patriots out of the water. Scarcely had the first chapter been begun than Nathan's illness and the demands of *The Smart Set* on his time pushed it to one side. There, to his annoyance, it had remained through successive editions of *The American Language* and the *Prejudices* and the establishment of the *Mercury*. After the Scopes trial he was determined to get it out of the way. The time seemed ripe: Angoff had relieved him of his major burdens in New York and no new commitments loomed. Knopf was told to plan on publication the following year. But he had hardly plunged into the mass of accumulated data than his mother's illness and death halted him. After the dreary Christmas in Pittsburgh he began afresh—and ran into new family troubles. Uncle Henry's health was failing, and it fell on his nephew, as head of the family, to make some sort of order out of his affairs. The last papers had just been signed when Chase moved against the *Mercury* in Boston, and that spring's litigation knocked out the last chance of producing a thoughtful book. Knopf was demanding manuscript, and Mencken, in desperation, bludgeoned his way through several pots of paste and a stack of copy paper, finishing his first and only draft June 3. That fall, *Notes on Democracy* was published.

The result was probably the worst of his books, largely a rehash of *Smart Set, Mercury,* and *Evening Sun* clippings liberally sprinkled with quotations from Nietzsche. The now familiar Menckenian charges appeared in badly organized chapters: that politicians were knaves, that their power stemmed from the swinishness of their constituency, that city dwellers were put upon by yokels, and that, in a democracy, no honor, no dignity, no integrity was safe from the boobs. He argued his points with the usual vigor, and many of the observations were delightfully put ("Public opinion, in its raw state, gushes out in the immemorial form of the mob's fears. It is piped into central factories, and there it is flavoured and colored, and put into cans"), but the day had passed when he could safely raid his periodical material for manuscript, confident that the overlapping public would be small. Too many buyers of *Notes on Democracy* felt cheated; they had, they protested, read all this before, and had clipped *Mercury* editorials to prove it. The loyal Boston *Transcript* declared, "At worst it is but common sense." Other papers, less constrained, decided at its worst it was tripe. "It is almost unbelievable," said the ordinarily friendly Chicago *Daily News,* "that a man of Mencken's undoubted learning and intelligence can write a book of 212 pages and say so little that is worth saying." Significantly, perhaps, in all Mencken's vast clientele the one man to enthuse over *Notes on Democracy* was the former German Kaiser, now of Doorn. Wilhelm, after reading a German translation, shipped to Hollins Street two photographs of himself, suitably inscribed. They were proudly hung in the third-floor workroom.

Yet in 1926 not even such a botch as this could materially affect Mencken's fame, or even slow his soaring star. He transcended, it seemed, the conventional standards by which a writer is judged and went ahead by some sort of supernatural power which multiplied his audiences and turned the very railing against him into a sort of deification all of itself, with no abetment from him it charmed. For all its admitted shabbiness, *Notes on Democracy* sold itself through a second reprinting in America and into German and English editions. For better or for worse, his future was tied to the heady, frantic Varsity Drag that was life in the Twenties; so long as it prospered—and it prospered mightily in 1926— his stock was safe. The concept of American literature for which he had fought so nobly and so well was now established and secure, with *The American Mercury* as its monthly Bible and Mencken as chief god. Its major authors—Lewis, Joyce, Dreiser—were, and acknowledged themselves to be, flowerings of his critical genius. No matter if Mencken himself had lost interest in literature and the very writers he had championed; no matter if his monthly editorials had become as ephemeral as the topics with which they dealt. To the thousands upon thousands who constituted America's art-conscious that year, his name signified philosophical greatness, and the chances that the superficiality which characterized *Notes on Democracy* could shatter that reputation were—in 1926—as remote as the odds that a fraudulent income tax could jail Al Capone.

In that year, and the three that followed, what Walter Lippmann called Mencken's "viscera to viscera" appeal reached its height. He had become, as had no other critic in American history, a national figure, a twentieth-century Voltaire. Between editorial bouts with him on the value of the American Legion, the D.A.R., the Rotary, newspapers printed hundreds of scraps of information about his personal life, about his influence, and these dovetailed in the public mind to produce the elaborate legend of evil genius which haunted many a Methodist minister, many a George F. Babbitt. That he smoked long black cigars, that he imported corncob pipes by the gross, that he liked to eat off lunch counters, that he enjoyed having his picture taken, that, of his own books, he read only *In Defense of Women* —these and scores of other incidental facts, true and untrue, were recorded in the daily press. When a Texas murderer, en route to the gallows, invited Mencken, as his favorite author, to attend the execution, the wire services picked it up and make-up men all over the nation gleefully played it on the front page. When he praised Henry Ford as a man who had willed his career, Ford distributors lifted the quotation for full page ads of the Model A, then about to make its sensational debut. Theatrical agents doubled and trebled their offers for *Heliogabalus; The American Language* went into an English edition and was translated in Berlin as *Die Amerikanische Sprache; The Artist,* which Mencken himself had all but forgotten, was exhumed and presented in Los

Angeles by the Little Theatre and in London by The Unnamed Society. *Selected Prejudices,* after its publication by
Knopf, went into English and Modern Library editions and
French and Swedish translations. Mayor "Big Bill" Thompson
of Chicago, waging a campaign against "pro-British propaganda" in public schools, sought help from Mencken as "a
guy with guts." Rudolph Valentino, troubled over an unfriendly press, came to him as the accredited wise man of
the time for advice. And in Baltimore a New York Representative who parted his hair in the middle, asked if he were
the editor of *The American Mercury,* replied, "Mencken?
No, I'm just a Congressman." It was in 1927 that Mencken,
walking down Fifth Avenue with Angoff on a rainy afternoon, pointed to a gray, somewhat stooped old man who
walked close to the buildings so as not to get wet, and was,
as a consequence, pushed about by passers-by. "Do you
know who he is?" Mencken asked Angoff. "He's a former
candidate for the President of the United States—John W.
Davis. There's no one so obscure as a former Presidential
candidate." And Angoff gasped with admiration as they
walked grandly on.

On the college campuses, as he wrote a friend, "The uproar
is in progress in all parts of the country. Never a day goes
by that I don't get news that some college or other has
broken into rebellion." Sophomores everywhere tried to
write like him, talk like him, think like him; as Cabell
caustically noted, Mencken himself was probably a very good
thing, but the disease of Menckenoids was certainly troublesome. In the larger universities he became virtually a member of the faculty *in absentia,* whose printed lectures no good
student ever cut, and whose teachings had an alarming way
of introducing themselves into other classrooms. The *Mercury*
won handily in favorite magazine polls at the University of
Kansas, the University of Georgia, and the Johns Hopkins
University; the Harvard Debating Union, holding a plebiscite
on whether or not Mencken were an enemy of American
culture, gave him a fifty-to-four plurality—which seemed to
be the proportion of his influence among brighter students.
Frantic attempts by the professors to put down the insurrection failed miserably. When Northwestern University students

put out a special edition of their campus magazine in imitation of the *Mercury*, its editors were threatened with expulsion. After they had been let off with the lame warning to "behave next time," the English faculty heard the disturbing sound of snickers from the back of its classrooms. A University of California professor of psychology, after announcing Mencken seemed to suffer from an inferiority complex, found her blackboard covered with obscene drawings, and Chancellor Frederick M. Hunter of the University of Denver, attacking the "pseudo-intellectualism" of the Mencken school, received marked copies of the *Mercury* in the mail. The Humanists were forgotten. When, on August 22, 1926, Stuart Sherman died in Michigan of a heart attack trying to swim after an overturned boat, the academic world little noted his death. Those who did recalled uncomfortably his feeble attempt at a *rapprochement* earlier in the year on the ground that Mencken had begun "to quote from good authors."

Easy it is to assume that Mencken's vogue—as Oscar Wilde once said of all literary schools—was founded on mere style. Certainly it is true that that Menckenian electricity which charged everything he wrote was a vital factor in his popularity. But the arrival of Mencken as a national figure, as noted, was as much a product of history as of the man himself, and as the Twenties grew older (with no noticeable sign of maturity), that merger solidified more and more, until the bull market of the *Mercury*, based as it was on the same national symptoms which bulled the Wall Street market, became the index of Mencken's career. It was a pity, for so tinsel a glory was unworthy of him. But it cannot be said he was without responsibility for it. Heretofore, that curious dichotomy which marked his political views—philosophical anarchism married to the rankest Toryism—had struggled along with neither facet gaining the full approval of its possessor. Now, however, as it became obvious that the strength of the *Mercury* lay in its younger, more liberal subscribers, the anarchistic views became more and more dominant, sweeping aside, as a generation of admirers grew to manhood, the deep-seated conservatism in which there was so much of Main Street. There were other reasons for the unbalance, of course: the shoddiness of Republican administrations in the Twenties and his congenital opposition to the party in power. But in so far as Mencken was affected as a national figure, and it is as such that we here consider him, it was the apparent liberalism of his political outlook which accounted for much of his following in the *Mercury* years. Once history shifted, and his philosophical scales had shifted with it, that following felt cheated and betrayed.

It was for this Waterloo Mencken unwittingly prepared himself as he repeatedly voiced progressive sentiments which, however genuine they might be, were still not *all* of him. He protested the farcical trial of Sacco and Vanzetti, inspiring Parisian rioters to printing his editorials on great placards—and neglected to add that he thought the defendants guilty and sublimely eligible for the chair. He wrote scathingly of the "California Babbitts" who kept Tom Mooney in jail—and passed over his utter contempt for all of Mooney's ilk. He scorned the deification of American business, of which "Judge Gary is its grand vizier as Cal is its chief eunuch"—and did not explain his admiration for such tycoons as Gary. He favored the recognition of Russia and scorned anti-subversive legislation because "The American moron's mind simply doesn't run in that direction; he wants to keep his Ford, even at the cost of losing the Bill of Rights"—and forgot to mention that should the moron's mind turn, he would be in favor of putting him down bloodily. His belief in free speech "to the last limits of the endurable" became a major issue in the *Mercury*. The Socialist in jail was a far better man than the judge who had put him there; the notion of a Comstock—that a good woman was "simply one who was efficiently policed"—was a joke. He continued to join furious battle with the censors, who were banning Dreiser's *American Tragedy* in Boston and Rabelais in Philadelphia and were lobbying for Heywood Broun's dismissal from the New York *World*. Protestants against the suppression of *The Well of Loneliness* and *What Happens* and the indictment of the author of a sex-education pamphlet found in him a powerful ally. Because the friends of the downtrodden and progressive social legislation saw in Mencken so brilliant a reflection of their major beliefs, they assumed he was one of them, unaware that to him all progressive social legislation, and particularly that for the downtrodden, was plain bunk.

But these considerations were far from his mind in the heyday the *Mercury* enjoyed after the "Hatrack" case. Mencken was having too good a time and thriving too well to consider a faraway future. Weary, it seemed, of broad assaults on the entire nation, he localized his invective and went after the boobs by districts. State by state he assaulted them; state by state he singled out their pet beliefs, their local idiosyncrasies, and held them up to ridicule. It was an extraordinary performance: here was an American citizen, sitting down with cold calculation, systematically taking apart the union! California was an "Alsatia of retired Ford agents and crazy fat women—a paradise of 100 per cent Americanism and the New Thought"; Mississippi was "a desolate area of nothing with the bottom out"; Minnesota had never produced a great artist, author, scientist, or statesman; even Maryland's Eastern Shore was the home of legislation conceived "in crossroad Bethels by thieving politicians." Everywhere, custodians of local pride found their most sacred beliefs attacked in the *Mercury* and in the two annuals of *Americana* which came out in these years. The reactions were typical, and pathetically ineffective. Governor W. I. Nolan of Minnesota reminded the Minneapolis Republican Women's Club that the state had produced Cass Gilbert, "who designed the St. Paul Capitol and many other beautiful buildings." In Arkansas a Y.M.C.A. leader and a former governor joined to organize a "Show Mencken" dinner, a great feast of strawberries, sweet potatoes, and country hams, designed to exhibit the state's products. In Helena, Montana, the *Independent* protested "Mencken should get acquainted with Bryan Cooney of the Butte *American*, whose 'Making the Grade,' week by week, is as good as the stuff of Whitman and Lardner." Governor Austin Peay of Tennessee, campaigning for re-election, took a full-page newspaper advertisement to quote Mencken's attacks on him; the Mississippi Ku Klux Klan invited him down to have his say publicly, and Eastern Shore newspapers proposed he be run out of Maryland. And at home the Association of Commerce, discovering that Baltimore was everywhere identified as Mencken's home town, was at its wits' end.

It is difficult to describe, and even more difficult to account for, the great wrath the *Mercury* inspired. A massive chorus of Rotarians, preachers, American Legion leaders, and college professors seem to have organized itself for Mencken's private amusement; he had but to say the magic words and the chorus responded in a spluttering, hysterical hymn of vituperation. He became, alike to the unwashed Fundamentalist preachers and the well-washed ladies of the D.A.R., the symbol of a common enemy. The illness was described in various ways—as "Mercurianity," "Menckenitis," and "Menckenism"—and was variously treated: by Southern professors who protested the *Mercury* was turning the national letters Red and by Rotarians who primly declared, "His criticism helps us. None of us is perfect." But that it was an illness, and that it needed treatment, few denied. Sometimes the choristers crossed signals and became involved in interfactional strife, as when the Rev. S. Parkes Cadman, president of the Federation of Churches of Christ in America, blamed "H. L. Mencken and his ghoulish crowd" for the "overfed and underworked college men"—and found himself under violent attack from the college professors on his left flank. Other times strange allies joined the respectable group, as when the San Quentin *Bulletin* set up a terrific howl over Mencken's statement that O. Henry was a "Jail Bird," citing great men—John the Baptist, John Bunyan, Tom Paine—who had spent time in prison. Publicly, Mencken generally kept his own counsel after each incident, content to chuckle over the more bizarre declarations ("Individualism?" cried a Legion commander in California. "Down with all Isms!") or to read with amusement of reports fathered by the Department of Justice, charging that he was a Bolshevik whose magazine was financed by Russian gold. On one occasion he did reply. Following reports of a number of college suicides, which the irresponsible jazz-age press described as an "epidemic," the president of Rutgers diagnosed the cause as "too much Mencken." Mencken answered that what was badly needed was a wave of suicides among college presidents, and announced he would gladly provide the knives and/or pistols for the purpose.

It was all grist for him. While the boobs hired halls, printed pamphlets, and spent their money in other ways to have at him, he blithely clipped their comments from the daily papers, pasted them in his scrapbooks, and issued *Menckeniana: A Schimpflexikon.*

It sold very well.

Mencken came closest to enjoying New York in these years. He still protested bitterly: "I got home this afternoon with one wing crushed, two blades missing from my propeller, and five or six pounds of carbonate of soda in my carburetor." But in New York he had fashioned a society of his own choosing, from which the barbarisms of the city were excluded. Angoff was by now buying material for the magazine regularly, and Mencken had but to write his pieces, shape policy, and deal with the authors he knew. He had set up a system to cope with creative ideas which came to him while in New York. In the past, the scraps of paper he stuck in his side pocket had often been lost or misplaced, to his annoyance. Now he kept a thick envelope by his desk in Knopf's offices, and another on his bedside table at the Algonquin, and these, when filled with mites of paper, were mailed to him at Hollins Street. Similarly, when in Luchow's or a Yorkville speakeasy, he carried letters addressed to himself, ready for mailing at an instant's notice. Moreover, he managed to bring to the city something of the atmosphere of Baltimore in the persons of Pearl, Patterson, Buchholz, Hemberger, and John and Hamilton Owens, one or more of whom could be found registered at the Algonquin, ready for consolation whenever he became homesick for talk of the *Sun* or this or that civic project at home. Thus ensconced, seated in the old haunts with friends of long standing about him, he felt almost at home in the New York he still regarded as the seat of carnality and communism, the capital of city slickers.

As the last of the great cultural editors, he was regarded with fear and respect in the other magazine offices of New York. Angoff, sent out occasionally to gauge the climate in their headquarters, found awed talk of the "new formula" among the businesslike, anti-cultural executives who ran established periodicals. That there was no formula save the systematic exploitation of Mencken's personality never occurred to these men. Seated in their plush offices, studying synopses of new novels prepared for them by underlings, they vaguely thought of the *Mercury* as a new gimmick—and were astonished to learn that its editor regarded them with contempt. They simply could not understand how one provincial lexicographer, equipped with a callow assistant, a brass spittoon, and an irascible temperament, could cut so sharply into their circulation. That the days of Johnson and Pope, when literature and philosophy were worth dying for, were undergoing a revival in the green-backed *Mercury*—this never crossed their minds.

Yet that, for many a young reader hungering after cultural counsel, was what *was* happening, and to be with Mencken on one of his long, lyrical excursions in New York *was* like being with Johnson, Boswell, Goldsmith, and Reynolds in their great days. There was the same feeling of reverence for ideas, the same gusto, the same intolerance of the mean and ignorant which had marked Johnson in his prime. When Mencken leaned back in his rumpled blue suit, his boylike face aglow with some new enthusiasm, a seidel of illegal beer in his capable fist, the table fell silent. And when he cleared the massive throat that hung over the high choker collar and began to speak, everyone leaned forward.

"They talk of war with Russia," he would begin. "Well, *I* certainly shall not volunteer. The eight wounds I got in the last war are not yet healed."

Or:

"Teapot Dome? Very amusing." (A gravelly chuckle.) "The only reason Sinclair went to jail is that he hired the wrong lawyer. Even Sinclair himself, I daresay, will laugh at it once he gets used to the lizards and has made arrangements with the jail bootician. He used to keep a drug store in Kansas, I'm told, and hence must be a cynic."

Or:

"La Snyder? What a woman! Still, the horsepower of sex is overrated, it seems to me. I daresay Gray himself overestimated it. That's why he'll fry."

Or:

"Coolidge? A remarkable man, a really *remarkable* man. Nero fiddled while Rome burned, but Coolidge only snores."

Or:

"The trouble with the Shermans and Mores of this world is that they live with the Holy Scriptures ever before them and die in the hope of a glorious resurrection. Such men, it seems to me, are not hard to understand. The poisons of piety still run in their veins, and they are never able to think quite clearly."

The key for these evenings was always C Major. They would begin in the Algonquin, with a few drinks from Mencken's first-aid supply and a general spiffing up. If there were to be women present, and there sometimes were, he would sweat in front of the mirror, plastering his straight hair down and inquiring anxiously of all present, "Think I'll make it?" Then everyone would climb into cabs and head for Luchow's, where Mencken would put away an enormous meal. His stomach, he maintained, was capable of digesting anything not actually metallic; if one of the party demurred over another course, Mencken would slap the table. "Defy your bowels!" he would cry. "Put a tooth in that ham. I knew the hog well—a sound Calvinist!" Then, after a dozen Pilsners, they might head for a cheap burlesque show on the Bowery, followed by a few more beers in a cheap dive and an all-night newsreel. Mencken—the champion of Nietzsche, the scorner of the rabble—vastly preferred Canal Street stumblebums to the "bronze duchesses" whose salons eagerly awaited him, and before taking a cab back to the Algonquin, he would stand under a street light, cud in jaw, discussing with some down-and-outer the art of bumming a meal or the techniques of alley sleeping. Then, with a flourish, the party would head homeward. Throughout the evening, they would argue the merits of Schubert's C Major, perhaps, or which of his symphonies—the second or the third—was the greater. Mencken, all of a sudden, and for no apparent reason, might launch into a recital of Keats' "St. Agnes Eve," or "The Seven Ages of Man" from *As You Like It,* or Kipling's "Recessional," or Othello's final speech. Angoff, impishly, would ask, "I thought you didn't like poetry." Mencken, with a gesture of dismissal, would answer, "Ah! I can't help it. It's singing through my head." So they went, from haunt to haunt, until 3 or 4 o'clock in the morning, when he stepped into the elevator, bought the morning tabloids, and read himself to sleep with stories of ministers raping women.

He saw much less of Dreiser—and of Nathan. The break with Dreiser had been long threatening; when it came at last everyone, save perhaps Dreiser, felt it was overdue. The end of Dreiser's struggle for recognition ended Mencken's feeling of responsibility toward him, and once Dreiser began fancying himself a super-naturalist, he thought it best they part. "A prudent man," he had written,

> remembering that life is short, gives an hour or two, now and then, to a critical examination of his friendships. He weighs them, edits them, tests the metal of them. A few he retains, perhaps with radical changes in their terms. But the majority he expunges from his minutes and tries to forget, as he tries to forget the cold and clammy loves of year before last.

The final snapping of relations between the two men seems to have turned on Mencken's review of *An American Tragedy*. It was Dreiser's first book in ten years and was very important to him. He sent Mencken an inscribed copy. It arrived during the mournful days that surrounded Anna's death, and Mencken, reading it, found he could not honestly praise it. In the March *Mercury* he tore into it with what seemed unnecessary bile, describing it as a "shapeless and forbidding monster . . . a vast, sloppy, chaotic thing of 385,000 words . . . dreadful bilge . . . a colossal botch." Dreiser was indignant. Other reviewers had received the book with far greater hospitality—even Stuart Sherman, in one of his last acts on this earth, had applauded it—and Mencken's review he regarded as an act of war. "Poor old Dreiser has been going around New York saying that I rushed my review of 'An American Tragedy' into *The American Mercury* in order to get ahead of Sherman, and so poison the wells," Mencken wrote Irita Van Doren. ". . . Dreiser, I fear, is a bit ratty." Dreiser may have been ratty, or he may have merely seen the handwriting on the row-house wall. Clearly, it was the

American Tragedy review which ended things between the two men. Dreiser's last letter before it had been a note of condolence following Anna's death. After that, Mencken did not hear from him for seven years.

The Nathan divorce proceedings dated as far back as the second issue of *The American Mercury*, when the conflict Knopf had dreaded had first broken out. The immediate cause was Eugene O'Neill's *All God's Chillun Got Wings*, and the dispute—with Nathan, who had persuaded O'Neill to do it for the magazine, favoring publication and Mencken vigorously opposing it—somehow symbolized the growing rift between the professional interests of the two editors. *All God's Chillun Got Wings* went into the magazine, but that solved nothing. It is doubtful, indeed, if anything could have closed the schism, based as it was upon so fundamental a split in enthusiasms. That it occurred is in no way remarkable; far more remarkable is the survival of the partnership, dependent as it was upon utter and unbroken harmony, for so long. Nathan, with the aesthetic intelligence that governed his very being, believed the *Mercury* should continue the mission of *The Smart Set* as a pioneer in the arts, encouraging the fresh talent of a new generation and eschewing the Baroque politico-economic developments of the American scene. To Mencken, whose interests were fanning out and away from literature, these developments were all-important; investigating and harpooning them, he believed, should be the commission of the *Mercury*. Thus they reached an impasse, each viewing the other's position as untenable and, so far as the magazine went, impracticable.

Under a preconceived understanding, Knopf was to arbitrate differences between the editors, but no one could arbitrate so basic a difference as that. Diplomacy was impossible, for ideologies were involved, and however fond of one another they might be, neither could compromise his beliefs. It was the first intimation of a difference between them in fifteen years, and neither knew quite how to treat it. Mencken was plainly upset, but his decision, as always, was irreversible. The only solution, it appeared, was for one of them to retire, and Nathan did just that. He amiably agreed to withdraw to the role of contributing and consulting editor, and the announcement was made, effective July, 1925. After Angoff arrived and began handling much of the routine which irritated Mencken, things eased up somewhat. Nathan moved his desk to another part of the office and continued his regular departments until March 1930, when Knopf, aware that the situation would never resolve itself, bought up Nathan's share in the property under an early agreement. By this time Mencken scarcely spoke to his old friend. The feud, as it was known in New York, continued on into the Thirties, and in 1933 Mencken refused to appear in *The Smart Set Anthology* on the ground that Nathan would appear there also. Actually, the word feud is not apt, since Nathan, on his part, refused to recognize any difference. The generally accepted explanation among Mencken's New York friends at the time of both the Nathan and Dreiser breaks was that he was going through his male climacteric. It may be so. There is really no way of telling, since he had been claiming the pangs of menopause for as long as anyone could remember.

Nathan's protests that the *Mercury* was veering from the cultural tone which had distinguished *The Smart Set* were not without justification. Mencken not only had lost touch with the older writers he had championed, i.e., Dreiser, Boyd, Anderson, Cabell, *et al.;* he had lost that very contact with borning fiction upon which his reputation as a literary critic was predicated. He had become completely the magazine editor and social philosopher and had, in so doing, defaulted a role for which, intrinsically, he was far better suited. His book reviews were no longer reviews of books; they had become, to the mounting indignation of their authors, sermons on the subjects under discussion. When, in 1927, the sixth and last series of *Prejudices* was published, literature was virtually excluded, and the best essay in the book—on Valentino—was, significantly, the most dated. By 1928, when John Erskine achieved success without Mencken's help, editorial writers jubilantly declared that the reign of "King Henry, literary dictator" was at an end. His reign had been over for some time, however, and the editorial writers' belated recognition of the fact merely served to make it official. *An American Tragedy* was not the first novel of prime importance whose merits he failed to gauge. On May 2, 1925, making his debut in the *Advertiser* of Montgomery, Alabama, Zelda Fitzgerald's home town, he had reviewed *The Great Gatsby*. The book, he wrote, was "no more than a glorified anecdote, and not too probable at that . . .

> The principal personage is a bounder typical of those parts —a young man with a great deal of mysterious money, the tastes of a movie actor and, under it all, the simple sentimentality of a somewhat sclerotic fat woman. This clown Fitzgerald rushes to death in nine short chapters."

This from the man who had discovered for America Shaw, Nietzsche, Conrad, Suckow, Dreiser, and Lewis! Incredible? Not at all. He had, as he wrote Marquis Childs, simply "lost interest in fiction"; moreover, he had lost sympathy with the very purpose exalted in the now forgotten days of *The Smart Set*. As Ed Howe pointed out, the *Mercury* was almost in the revolt against literature itself. Joyce he now thought a "crackpot." Important writers, of whom Erskine was the first, appeared throughout the late Twenties with no sign of recognition from the man who had anticipated the renaissance now at its height and who spurned the company he had craved fifteen years before. When recognition did come, it was always unfavorable; he who had once batted 1.000 now struck out each time he came to the plate. Hemingway, he said, would pass. "Only too often he runs aside from his theme to prove fatuously that he is a naughty fellow, and when he does so he almost invariably falls into banality and worse." Faulkner he could not understand. "I like clear sentences," he complained to Angoff. It was only by tireless arguing that Angoff could persuade him to print "That Evening Sun" in the *Mercury;* to Mencken, the story was pointless. Wolfe's stuff he couldn't even read; each time he attempted it, he said, he was driven away. Wolfe became, indeed, a sort of running issue between him and Angoff, who admired *Look Homeward, Angel* enormously. But Mencken would not give in. In this case, however, there may have been extenuating circumstances. Wolfe, be it remembered, was wont to write on any sort of paper that chanced to fall under his pencil. One day he sent the *Mercury* a manuscript written on grease-speckled butcher paper, and Angoff, busily preparing for a visit from Baltimore, stuck it on Mencken's desk. There the lumpy pile lay, gathering flies, when Mencken stuck his head around the partition for his usual cheery greeting. He glanced at his desk. His jaw sagged. "Get that out of the office," he cried, pointing a trembling finger at the manuscript. "It isn't even sanitary!"

It was this lack of interest in living literature, together with the feeble reverence with which he had come to hold all artistic *genre,* which made possible the remarkable resurgence of reactionary criticism in the late Twenties. In the early days of *The Smart Set,* when the successful campaign for realism began, the professors had regarded Mencken as a clown and had ignored him. Even Sherman's wartime attack, late though it was, had been thought unnecessary and in bad taste by his fellows. By the time of *Winesburg, Ohio, Main Street, This Side of Paradise,* and *Jurgen* it was too late; the floodgates were open. Mencken, securely belted in his ark on the very crest of the wave, was unassailable for eight years. Then copies of the *Mercury* began to filter into the damp cells where More, Babbitt, and other such creeps dismally fretted, and the word was passed: He doesn't care any more. While the Wolfes and Faulkners and Erskines bowed on and looked about for critical guidance, Mencken was busy proposing legislatures be chosen by picking names out of hats, defending flagpole sitting on the ground that it gave the sitters perspective, and attacking birth control because the country needed future generations to run its gasoline stations.

The *revanche* of the New Humanists, as they now called themselves, opened in January, 1928, when *The Forum* for that month issued an anti-Mencken manifesto attacking "the facile penman of *The American Mercury*" and asking for "another school of critics in America whose skepticism resembles that of Montaigne, in that they doubt out of a greater faith." Out of the wings came crowding the Mores and the Babbitts, the Norman Foersters and the Sherlock Bronson Gasses, nipping one another's heels in their anxiety to have at the Antichrist. Babbitt was the first to square away. In *The Forum* for February 22 he declared, "Mencken at his best is good intellectual vaudeville"; wrote that America, badly in need of a Socrates, had got a Mencken; and laid down his challenge: "The characteristic evils of the present age arise from unrestraint and violation of the law of measure and not, as our modernists would have us believe, from the tyranny of taboos and traditional inhibitions." The voices of the reactionaries—so similar, in their stridency, to those of the National Socialists abroad—grew louder. Seward Collins bought the *Bookman* and made it over into a New Humanist organ. The professors argued over a satisfactory definition of the movement—to Babbitt it was "a standard set above temperament"; to More "a moral law of character"; to Gass the cognizance that "the central problem and hence the central interest of life . . . is what to make of it, that is, what values to pursue in it." And Michael Williams in *The Commonweal* and others elsewhere argued for a marriage between New Humanism and the Catholic Church. The marriage was never consummated—though the Roman intellectuals certainly panted with lust—but through such spokesmen as More the movement took on strong overtones of the Vatican, the Syllabus of Errors, even of the Inquisition.

To the collected philosophy of Sherman's heirs—*Humanism and America*—the modernists answered with *The Critique of Humanism*, under the editorship of C. Hartley Grattan. Rascoe, Henry Hazlitt, Allen Tate, and Edmund Wilson did their best to stave off the tide which, as the decade ended, entered more and more into the vacuum created by the *Mercury's* nihilism. But the counterattack was truncated. Mencken, it seemed, little cared. "Let the professors bandage their singed arses!" he told Boyd. Humanism, he wrote, simply resulted from the agony of Babbitts' sons who found their values questioned. "I believe that Humanism, like its brother, Rotarianism, relieves that agony effectively, and is thus worthy of the support of all humane men.

It convinces them that, after all, the pastor at home is probably right—that papa, running his sashweight factory, is really a better man than Cabell or Dreiser—that the United States sought no profit in the late war—that the editorials in the *Saturday Evening Post* are profound—that Sacco and Vanzetti, being wops, got what was coming to them.

But such pleasantries were rather left-handed gestures, growing more out of a feeling of duty than from genuine interest. The Humanist-Anti-Humanist struggle grew as the country headed into the depression and a reassessing of values, but Mencken, through choice, remained in the background. More and Babbitt continued to spar enthusiastically in their jet black tights, with the cross of Rome gilded thereon, but their adversary never entered the ring.

His mother's death, the "Hatrack" case, and the last wretched struggling with *Notes on Democracy* and *Prejudices, Sixth Series* had left Mencken in a state of almost complete exhaustion, and Patterson, seeing him thus depleted, suggested a vacation. A trip through the South, he pointed out, would provide matchless opportunities to observe the Bible Belt. Hergesheimer, at the same time, was lobbying for a trip to California and the Gold Coast, and Mencken, who was anxious to meet some of his long-time correspondents, agreed. Patterson was to go with him to New Orleans; there he would train for the West Coast and a rendezvous with Hergesheimer. Detailed timetables were prepared in the *Sun* office, reservations were made all along the line, and Mencken, making last arrangements in the *Mercury* office, sent Patterson frantic advice (DONT SHE IS AWFUL BEWARE BEWARE) on how to deal with the avalanche of invitations that poured in from the sub-Potomac. At length, on the afternoon of Thursday, October 14, 1926, they were poured on the train in Baltimore for the beginning of the Grand Tour.

In Richmond they lunched sedately with Cabell and Emily Clark; after an evening of sober discussion, they headed for Raleigh and the University of North Carolina, where Mencken began a lifelong friendship with Dr. and Mrs. Fred Hanes, of Chapel Hill. After attending a Carolina-Duke football game, they departed for Greensboro, Atlanta, and Emory University in Georgia, visiting country editors along the way and deftly avoiding questions about local suppressions of the *Mercury*.

Mencken was at his most charming chatting with the local gossips, joining in damnation of the crass North, and praising the beauty of whatever countryside happened to be nearby. Occasionally he got out of hand—in Emory he insisted on standing silently and reverently before Wesley Memorial Hospital, his hat over his heart, out of respect for Asa G. Candler, the discoverer of Coca-Cola, who lay inside—but generally he behaved beautifully. On the train each night, as Patterson dropped into bed exhausted, he hauled out his Corona and banged out bread-and-butter notes by the score before turning in. At each station he left a wake of swooning United Daughters of the Confederacy behind.

A quiet trip, it would seem, wholly without color. Actually it was anything but that. Being Mencken, he had to add his own dash of spice to the tour—and spice from Mencken being Mencken was sure to come in large, powerful doses. It was simply a physical impossibility to project that lumpy, bubbling little mass of hormones on the dreamy South without something happening. What happened nearly ruined Southern politics that year.

He conceived the idea in Baltimore on the day of departure, and the more he thought of it, the more it tickled him. Governor Ritchie's militantly Wet statements had endeared him to Mencken more and more, and eventually the idea crept into his head, as it had into Ritchie's long before: how about the Presidency? Accordingly, he issued a patriotic statement booming Ritchie for the Democratic nomination. Ritchie for President! The reaction set off a splendid furor among Maryland Wets and Drys, and in Virginia the temptation mastered him. There he mounted the rostrum to praise Governor Harry Byrd as Virginia's gift to the Confederacy and the nation. Byrd for President! The uproar had just begun in Richmond when in North Carolina he met the press. Far be it from a magazine editor to interfere in local politics, but . . . Governor Angus W. McLean for President! Then, in Georgia, he singled out Major John S. Cohen, the state's Democratic National Committeeman, as the nation's hope. Cohen for President!

Incredible as it may seem, all the booms took hold, and as Mencken and Patterson contentedly snored their way over the Louisiana state line, four fledgling campaigns were flowering—Ritchie in Maryland, Byrd in Virginia, McLean in North Carolina, and Cohen in Georgia. In Maryland the pro-Ritchie statement was denounced as a diabolical *Sun* plot. In Danville, Virginia, the *Register,* a strong administration organ, praised Mencken as a "shrewd analyst of people and an even keener judge of existing conditions"; in Charlotte, North Carolina, the pro-McLean *Observer* went into the governor's chances with great editorial seriousness; in Winston-Salem the anti-McLean *Sentinel* sniffed, "The South has a way of picking its own candidates for President, whether native sons or otherwise, and it does not need the services of H. L. Mencken." Everywhere local bosses and bosslets committed themselves, committees were forming, and Major Cohen, greatly pleased by this boost from an unexpected source, was debating his next move when the Associated Press, noting a remarkable similarity in all the booms, put two and two together and let the cat out of the bag.

They were months getting it all straightened out.

Mencken and Patterson visited Zed Ballard at the *Item* in New Orleans, motored in the country with a Catholic priest who had been writing to Hollins Street for years, and attended an International Association of Fire Chiefs convention. The chiefs were so taken with Mencken they elected him Honorary Chieftain; to the horror of many a campus aesthete he stood meekly while they stuck a tin hat on his head and sang "For He's a Jolly Good Fellow." Then, after a six-hour creole dinner, Patterson trained for Baltimore, and Mencken, after sending Goodman the *n*th postcard reading, "This is a swell town. Having a swell time. Everybody is treating us swell. Wish you were here," headed West. He stopped briefly in Kansas City to boost Jim Reed for the Presidency, then pushed on to Pasadena, where Upton Sinclair and a curious citizenry awaited him. Sinclair had given out word he was coming, and local editorial writers had discussed the impending visit furiously, some protesting he was a Bolshevik and should be stopped at the city line, others proposing he be invited to harangue the Pasadena Rotarians. Somehow he managed to see Sinclair and avoid the press. Then, girding his staunch loins, he advanced on Los Angeles.

There he greeted reporters with the cheerful statement "Valentino must have a successor somewhere, and it might as well be me," and hunted up Joe Hergesheimer. Hergesheimer had taken a bungalow in the lush wilds of Hollywood. He was passing the time pleasantly, surrounded by Anita Loos, Aileen Pringle, and a score of film beauties when Mencken walked in with vigorous complaints of bronchitis. After the women were shooed out the door they sat down over a quart of hooch to chart their course through a maze of party and studio tour invitations. There were a good many. Joe had become increasingly popular since his first day in town when, greeted by a boorish actor who announced, "I have never read any of your damned books," he had replied, "And I have never seen any of your damned pictures—that makes us both Elks." Mencken professed to be amazed by Hollywood's respectability. Actually, he was scandalized. "It is at least ten times as bad as I expected," he wrote Pearl. "The movie dogs, compared to the rest of the population, actually seem like an ancient Italian noblesse." Early in his visit a young actress shocked him badly by quipping, after he had told of his adventures in Baltimore's sporting houses as a young reporter, "I thought your face was familiar."

The climax of his Hollywood adventures followed a bacchanalian feast given in honor of a celebrated bachelor about to marry a star of the silent era. All Hollywood's prize stallions turned out for the occasion, and after a half dozen drunken speeches, someone suggested adjournment to a bordello. Everyone, including Mencken, agreed enthusiastically except Tom Mix. Mix was squiffed but virtuous, and he refused. He did, however, insist on lending his snow-white Rolls Royce to Mencken—who proceeded to park it directly in front of Hollywood's only hook shop, with its "T.M.'s" embossed all over it and everything but a neon sign proclaiming its ownership. Inside, Mencken kept his hat on—the madam, he said, expected it—and headed for the joint's piano. There, for the rest of the evening, he squatted happily while the orgies raged about him, cigar in mouth, playing, *forte* and continually, "The Battle Hymn of the Republic." The groom, determined to lure him from the stool, offered one of the female faculty fifty dollars if she could persuade him to relinquish it for more comfortable surroundings. Mencken would have none of it. "Mine eyes have seen the glory of the coming of the Lord," he played frantically, trying to ignore the girl. "He is trampling out the vintage where the grapes of wrath are stored." The groom upped the ante to one hundred dollars. Mencken insisted he was impotent. Finally the lady, in desperation, pleaded, "Say, Mister, can't you give a girl a break?" But the indomitable pianist, tilting his hat to the back of his head, merely shifted pedals and broke into "Lead Kindly Light."

Before heading for San Francisco and home, he paid one last tribute to California: a visit to the shrine of Aimée Semple McPherson, the notorious female revivalist. He wired Goodman: WAS BAPTIZED BY AIMÉE LAST TUESDAY NIGHT YOU CAN HAVE NO IDEA OF THE PEACE THAT IT HAS BROUGHT TO MY SOUL I CAN NOW EAT FIVE BISMARCK HERRING WITHOUT THE SLIGHTEST ACIDOSIS. Actually, he sat meekly through the tabernacle service and retired discreetly when the baptisms began. Two years later, when Aimée claimed Mencken was one of her converts, he promptly nominated her for Miss America. ("Has Aimée got it? My God, has she! At least 6,000 horsepower.") A few days later he left the coast, gravely admitting he had been refused the leading role in *Little Lord Fauntleroy*. The San Francisco editorial writers, with great satisfaction, announced he had failed in the great test of sex appeal and that there was at least one realm of the arts Baltimore's *enfant terrible* could not crack—the motion-picture industry.

He arrived home December 1 without enthusiasm. Anna Mencken had been in her grave nearly a year now, but the memory of her still haunted her son. "I begin to realize how inextricably my life was interwoven with my mother's," he had written Dreiser in that last letter before the *American Tragedy* review.

A hundred times a day I find myself planning to tell her something, or ask her for this or that. It is a curious thing: the human incapacity to imagine finality. The house seems strange, as if the people in it were deaf and dumb.

In an effort to brighten the old home, he repapered all the

walls—and, almost immediately, regretted it. Any break with the past, any change in the pleasant, domestic routine which had left him so free for his work seemed intolerable. All civic improvements, everything which represented a difference from the Baltimore he had known as a boy, when his mother was young and busy about the house, he resisted fiercely. In his *Evening Sun* articles he struck out at those who would improve this thoroughfare or enlarge that viaduct, at those who took pride in the fact "that the General Electric Company is building a plant here, and bringing in 30,000 morons to man it, or that the Bethlehem Steel Company is enlarging its stink pots." On the mechanical improvements which, more and more, crowded the American scene, he frowned disapprovingly. Movies, air-conditioning, public-address systems, the replacement of streetcars by buses, the very passing of the Christian Endeavorists brought him to the point of tears. Soft collars came in, but he stuck to his high chokers. His persistent devotion to high shoes reached the point of absurdity, but to all protests from his friends he replied simply, if illogically, that if he wore the new-fangled low-cuts, they would fall off his feet. A friend, "seeking to improve my Americanism," gave him a radio, and he, out of courtesy, brought in a technician to install an aerial.

Since then I have made about 250 attempts to get something out of it that was worth hearing. But though I have tackled it from all hours of daylight to 2 A.M., and swept the pointer from end to end of the dial, I can't recall more than 30 occasions when I have got anything remotely describable as civilized entertainment. The height of comedy on the air is reached by the dialogues of Amos and Andy. . . . Music, if it be instrumental, is supplied mainly by gangs of union men sawing dismally away in the dining rooms of second-rate hotels. . . .

To relieve his depression, he sought out old friends more often than ever before. Week ends he rode to West Chester, Pennsylvania, where Joe and Dorothy Hergesheimer greeted him with a makeshift German band. After the Grand Tour, he and Patterson took to visiting Dr. and Mrs. Hanes in their

North Carolina home. To Hollins Street, now efficiently managed by Gertrude, came Jim Tully, to talk of books, and the Darrows, to reminisce of Dayton. He developed his domestic talents, laying more bricks in the back yard, and spent hours shopping for little gifts for Virginia or for Patterson's young son Maclean, whose godfather he was. His gallantry with elderly women, which had always approached the saturation point, increased still more. Gerald Johnson's mother-in-law, who was terrified of his reputation, chanced to ride to New York on the same train. Mencken collared a porter, had his seat changed to be beside her, and so entranced her that she immediately wrote Baltimore on arrival, "Mr. Mencken is *sweet!*" When, shortly afterwards, Nathan's mother lay dying in New York, he sat by the bedside for hours at a time, holding her hand and soothing her pain. But no yearning for the past, no cultivation of his mother's virtues could allay the pain in his heart. His physical complaints and bizarre correspondence grew in intensity: he had hiccups for three days straight, synovitis gripped his right wrist, and in the mail he shipped out packet after packet of Dr. Mencken's Hell Salts, Guaranteed To Cure Everything. Deeply and sincerely, he mourned.

He visited the *Sun* office every afternoon at 2:30 with critiques of the day's news coverage and sharp comments on the editorial policy—Patterson called him his Hairshirt—and continued his contributions throughout these busiest of years. His Monday articles, which were in effect an extension of the *Mercury* editorials, and which still kept nice old ladies in a homicidal frame of mind, were not enough. For the paper he covered all sorts of odd assignments—local hangings; the 1928 Pan American Conference, which, he told Mrs. Darrow, was "a sort of international Scopes Trial"—and, as the conventions came on, he oiled up his typewriter for another cross-country jaunt. It was not, as some supposed, a form of masochism which drew him to the press rail every four years; he actually enjoyed it, and always embarked with the eagerness and anticipation of a small boy off for the circus. The Republican convention that year was in Kansas City. Mencken, Hyde, and Patterson drove out, and in the hall they were joined by Knopf, who had decided to investigate

his number one stud's claim of vast entertainment in the
political arena and was rewarded with a *Sun* photographer's
badge. After the Hoover performance—which proved rather
dull—they left a disappointed Knopf and drove through the
Ozarks (which Mencken pronounced "one of the great moron
reservoirs of the United States" for the edification of local
reporters) and down to Houston. Mencken had some trouble
covering events outside the hall; he was regarded, with Jim-
mie Walker, Bugs Baer, and Will Rogers, as one of the major
celebrities to see, and was forced, finally, to pose dismally
with a local beauty beside him and a ten-gallon hat on his
sweating head. But in the press stall, with Patterson on one
side and Hyde on the other, he was supremely happy. Hyde
and Mencken functioned as a sort of perpetual-motion reportorial machine; one of them was on hand at all times,
and regardless of which byline appeared over the lead story,
the other was sure to have written part of it, as Baltimoreans
were told in frequent inserts—"Mencken batting for Hyde"
or "Hyde batting for Mencken." Mencken was delighted
when Bishop Cannon's Drys were shown the door. He
promptly announced he was for Al Smith "up to and including the neck, anyhow" and was, at his request, assigned to
cover Smith's campaign tour.

He had an enormous time. Smith was his idea of the perfect candidate: charming, shrewd, a Wet, and completely
without scruple. The trip through the South, with W.C.T.U.
sisters insulting Mrs. Smith and Baptist ministers bawling of
a Papal plot to seize the country, he thought particularly
amusing. But his biggest laugh of the campaign came in
Jefferson City, Missouri, where convicts in the state penitentiary lined the walls of the prison to cheer Smith's campaign
train as it passed. To Mencken, that was the ultimate in
American politics. And in 1928, it was.

His return from Hollywood had served as the signal for
a new and more vigorous crop of marriage rumors. Aileen
Pringle was the gossip columnists' favorite. It was reported,
widely and confidently, that he had presented her an expensive shawl—its value was variously estimated at fifteen
hundred and fifteen thousand dollars—and that the anounce-

ment was forthcoming. So authentic did the news seem, Sedgwick actually sent his congratulations to Hollins Street. When the Pringle rumors died out, a Washington opera singer was chosen as "the recipient of Mr. Mencken's long-deferred affections," and the columnists reached new and more feverish heights. In vain did Mencken protest he knew but one woman in Los Angeles, and she an aviator; that such reports annoyed his present wives and hence should be suppressed; that all the girls he knew were bankrupt and therefore unmarriageable. In vain did he send out counter-rumors that he was engaged to "Mrs. Bertha Kupfernagel of Hoboken, who was a beauty before she began to take on weight, and whose husband died leaving her $17,000." In vain did he argue that despite his belief that marriage was a highly sanitary institution, it was not for him, and that his escape from its benefits was no more his fault than was he responsible for "my remarkable talent as a pianist, my linguistic skill, or my dark, romantic, somewhat voluptuous beauty." The gossipmongers were out to get him hitched.

The curious thing about all these rumors is that they were dead wrong in one sense and dead right in another. Mencken *was* drifting into marriage in 1927—drifting slowly, to be sure, but drifting all the same. But of the six candidates publicly nominated that year, not one was even in the running. The columnists could not have known Mencken well, even by reputation, for it was unthinkable he should look beyond the city limits of Baltimore for a real woman, or that any short acquaintance, man or woman, could penetrate beyond that façade of ready-made hospitality in which there was so much reserve. None of his relationships had ever smacked of immediacy, and if nothing else was certain in his relationship with Sara Haardt—and certainly nothing else, in 1927, was—it remained that whatever he did would be done with great caution, after long contemplation.

For such was her name: Sara Powell Haardt, of 2109 North Charles Street, Baltimore. He had met her at that first "How To Catch Husbands" lecture at Goucher College, when his bright, anxious eyes, sweeping over the feminine audience, had first sighted her tall, delicate frame, her Camelia-like beauty, and the dark brown eyes that gently lowered over hollow—almost etched—cheeks. Next day, writing Goodman, he had described the phenomenon: "It greatly astonished me; I always thought education ruined the complexions of women." Through mutual friends at Goucher they met socially; he was enchanted to find her well-bred, witty, and extremely intelligent. Like so many of his new friends that year, she was of a younger, more flexible generation than his, better equipped to understand and appreciate his insurgent values. Moreover, she did this without the harsh militancy of so many of the female intelligentsia. She was a Southern lady, with all the charm and easy bearing of her birth, and Mencken, who had always been a traditionalist in his personal relationships, found this immensely appealing. So they met more often, first at Goucher or with Hergesheimer on his visits, then at Schellhase's, to discuss Emily Clark, perhaps, or Southern politics, or the brightness of the literary scene. Naturally enough, their friendship was, in its early stages, somewhat tempered by the background each brought to it. Sara was rather restrained by the massive reputation of her host, and Mencken's enjoyment of their evenings was, in turn, qualified by her youth. But with the passing of months, and then of years, an understanding grew to replace the timidity, and the friendship warmed under his congenial good humor and her merry, easy laughter.

Sara was an instructor in English at Goucher when he met her, an alumna of the college and the brightest star of its faculty. Seven years before—the fall of the Dreiser protest —she had come to the college at eighteen. Her home was in Montgomery, Alabama—the same Montgomery from which Fitzgerald had taken his bride—and as the descendant of an old and established family she had attended Margaret Booth School there. In her first year at Goucher she had stirred the campus by winning a short-story contest, and beginning in December her name appeared in the college literary magazine as editorial assistant. By her senior year, when she was graduated Phi Beta Kappa, she was editor-in-chief, both of the magazine and of *Donnybrook Fair*, the Goucher annual. Despite financial troubles—she paid for part of her tuition as college postmistress—she was a dominant figure on campus, the spearhead of a drive for political consciousness. At college she maintained a bulletin board listing the records of Presidential candidates in 1920, and in Montgomery, two years before, she had joined in an enthusiastic, if vain, suffragette rally. Yet even in these years she was, and considered herself, very much the lady; she refused to participate in any strenuous form of campus activity, on the ground that it was unbecoming to her position, and across the pages of her college annual was scribbled, at appropriate places, "I was never in dramatics! or athletics!" After graduation, she taught for two years at Margaret Booth School; then, at twenty-four she returned to Goucher as the youngest member of the staff. She was, when Mencken met her, dividing her leisure between fiction writing and work on an advanced degree at the Johns Hopkins University.

Sara's prose, like Sara, was gracious, charming, and completely at war with itself. Like her, it was a product of a deep conflict between traditionalism and liberalism, between the heir of Southern custom and the apostle of the new movements fevering her generation. In the early days of their acquaintance, she liked to point proudly to her grandfather's birth in the Rhein-Pfalz and to an ancestor who served on the Leipzig faculty with the two Menckens, but her escort, eying the long line of Powells, Treats, and Jeffersons on her mother's side, was dubious. She too was dubious; the enervation and sentiment ran too deeply in her blood; it could not be dismissed. This curious and very basic schism was reflected in everything she wrote, in everything she did. Sara was in revolt against herself, and whichever way the battle might go, she was hurt. She might take the stump for women's rights in Montgomery, to the horror of her mother's generation, but when she shopped, it was always with an eye out for the Victorian bric-a-brac she loved to collect. She might talk, long and convincingly, of Ellen Glasgow's talent, of William Faulkner's power; but when their books were shelved in her home, they stood cheek-to-jowl with heavy tomes on Victorian etiquette, and were read no more frequently. She might cry out against the seeds of death sown deep in Southern culture, against the reverent preservance of old legends, but when she attempted a biography of Lee she was forced to put it down because "It makes the general silly, and I can't bear to think of him as silly."

She might write:

Oh, no use talking, the South was sweet. But, it was a sweetness tinged with the melancholy of death. It was because beauty, somehow, is shorter lived in the South than in the North, or in the West; and beauty, more than mere survival, is the most poignant proof of life. How many times I have been reminded of death—of my own death —in the tropical flower gardens of the South.

But the truth was she had "lived the old war songs and the perfume of magnolias, like any other," and "could never escape, either to the North, or to the East, or to the West; I have lived in the eternal mystery of the tropics, the memory of tulip flowers wafting down in the fragrant dusk, the soft kiss of the mists as they rolled over." Like the Mary Julia of her "Twilight of Chivalry," she thought the Old South was wonderful, only she got a little sick of hearing about it sometimes—only she thought it was wonderful.

It was a conflict Mencken could understand, for in large part it was also his. For all the separation of years, they were much alike, these two: both enormously complicated personalities, both complicated in the same ways. Mencken's yearning for the past, for the old days in West Baltimore, for the dead reign of the Hohenzollerns, was echoed sharply in this dark-eyed, enormously sensitive girl who loved the Conferedate tradition she wanted to destroy and attacked the vestiges of decadence with the poise and bearing of a matriarch. There was something almost comical, and equally almost pathetic, in the spectacle of these two genteel rebels drinking illegal brew in Schellhase's, she gracious and charming, he courtly and cavalier; discussing their *avant garde* ideology enthusiastically, he in the literary English of a Congreve, she in the lilting, pleasant accent of old Alabama. It was, from its inception, a friendship of people ideally suited to one another, in weaknesses as in strengths.

Sara's college fiction, like his early stories, had concerned itself with faraway places, notably the battlefields of France. Once she had matured and learned to write out of her own background, she found markets readily enough. The first of her pleasant, sad little sketches of the South appeared in Emily Clark's *Reviewer* for July, 1922, and before long she was appearing regularly in the leading magazines of the time —*Bookman, Century, Virginia Quarterly Review,* and, after its founding, the *Saturday Review of Literature.* She had been hopefully sending stories to *The Smart Set* for several months before that first meeting at Goucher, and in October, 1923, Mencken printed "Joe Moore and Callie Blasingame," later to provide the theme for her first novel. It is in the record that he rejected "Miss Rebecca," one of her finest stories, in the first hectic months of the *Mercury.* Later, as she came to appear regularly in the *Mercury,* she turned her talents to new fields. Much of the work on Mencken's *Schimpflexicon* was done by Sara, digging through his thirty massive scrapbooks, and her frequent meetings with Hergesheimer when he was Mencken's guest brought an excellent fee for research on his *Swords and Roses.* In 1927 she embarked on a real adventure. Famous Players, of Hollywood, bought a film scenario from her and offered a contract she could not afford to turn down: expenses to the Coast and back and two hundred fifty dollars a week for five weeks. If she produced a usable film play, they were to get it for thirty-five hundred dollars. If she did two, they got the second for five thousand dollars. On September 28 she left, well-equipped with letters of introduction and advice from Mencken, who was really afraid Hollywood's debauchery would shock the poor girl to death. He accounted without her resiliency. Sara simply concluded everyone within the city limits of Los Angeles was, by definition, insane. She treated them so, with patronage but dignity. Office politics, she found, made work impossible, and on Mencken's advice, she sat tight, collecting her money under the terms of the contract. Early in January she returned to Baltimore full of marvelous tales, to rework her book, *The Making of a Lady,* then in one of its several revisions.

Her distaste for Hollywood was propitious. Had she remained in California grinding out stock dialogue, Mencken's affection for her would doubtless have diminished, or at least stabilized. Their compatibility, great though it was, would never have blasted him from his entrenched bachelordom had she not been conveniently nearby in these lonely months. Mencken's friends, noting his depression over his mother's death, had assumed that the great affection he pledged to her memory would make marriage impossible, but they reckoned without the man's great craving for domesticity and female companionship. He was, basically, a family man, whose role was rightly at the head of a bourgeois household. During the quarter century by which his mother survived his father he had functioned as such, and now, with her gone, there was a vacuum in his life aching to be filled. Even before Sara's Hollywood adventure, he had begun to primp and press his trousers before their meetings in the manner of a young blade, and in the late summer of 1926 had actually resorted to surgery to better his appearance. "I have had all my warts, moles, war scars, etc. cut off, and am full of plasters," he wrote Hergesheimer. "But when they drop off I shall be one of the handsomest men of modern times." When Sara left for Hollywood, he sent Jim Tully a letter, asking hospitality for her and describing her as a "special case." Now that she was home they met more often in Baltimore and New York, where she often traveled with her manuscripts. Sara had moved to an apartment near Edmund Duffy on Read Street, to be with Duffy's wife, whose great friend she was, and Schellhase's, more convenient than ever, saw them more and more often. Her own attitude toward him had passed from awe to respect, from respect to affection, and thence to still deeper affection. When, in Hollywood, another guest of Tully's had begun to criticize him, her austerity had vanished in an explosive "Heah! Heah!" and she would not, even among her oldest friends, hear a word against him. Thus did the friendship, so agreeable to both, prosper through the years that followed Anna Mencken's death.

Charming? Yes, charming—and also tragic. For Sara Haardt, like the old war songs that lured her young heart from the generation to which it rightfully belonged, was doomed. It is somehow appropriate that her first story in *The American Mercury* should have dealt with a tubercular, for Sara, though she did not know it then, had tuberculosis herself. It was the most deadly of the diseases which sapped her strength, but it was by no means alone. In her later, bedridden years, she traced her troubles to her wartime days, when a thinly lined pocketbook had forced her to eat ersatz food. Yet it is likely that even without this deprivation she could not have flourished; there was something in her wan, languorous constitution which forbade it. Shortly before the first Christmas of their acquaintance she had fallen ill, and the better part of 1924 was spent in a Maryland sanatorium. After partial recovery she went home to Montgomery and was not seen by Baltimore or Mencken for over a year. She was probably at her healthiest during the Hollywood trip and the spring that followed. That fall, shortly after a pleasant week end in West Chester with Mencken and the Hergesheimers, she was rushed to the hospital for serious surgery, and Mencken spent all the time he could spare between Al Smith junkets at her bedside. He pretended to treat her illness lightly—"Her first word, coming out of the anesthetic, was 'Gettysburg'. The Confederates never forget anything"— but he was really deeply concerned, and his concern deepened the following April, when she went back to Union Memorial with an infected kidney. Then it was, after removing the kidney, that doctors found the tuberculosis. She recovered very slowly, with high temperatures and great prostration, unaware of her plight. "What will follow, God alone knows," Mencken wrote a friend in desperation. He and Raymond Pearl dropped by daily with cheerful messages, and for weeks his correspondence was largely made up of little notes to mutual friends, asking they write or visit her. Two months later she was released, and after her convalescence he took her around to the old table at Schellhase's, there to outline, with great enthusiasm, his newest and, he was convinced, his greatest book.

Treatise on the Gods was finished on Thanksgiving night, 1929. Little Virginia, then fourteen, was visiting Hollins Street with her parents, and Charlie, his wife, August, and Gertrude went out for the evening. While they were gone he finished the last, powerful passage, and on their return they celebrated the occasion with a drink. Next day he began to pack for what, with a splendid snubbing of the Grand Tour, he called his first holiday in seven years. He was to cover the London naval conference for the *Sun* and jog around Europe while abroad. As always, he packed with furious speed and bitter complaints. "Now," he wrote Goodman, "I have nothing to do save write 3 months *Mercury* stuff in 2 weeks, and read and edit 10 Mss., beside having my underwear patched and begging my collars from the laundry." Finally he sailed just after Christmas, with a tender good-by to Sara and the usual idiotic assurances to his frends that he would bring them locks of Lloyd George's hair or a handful of excelsior from the beard of King George. The trip over was unexpectedly pleasant; his suite was "fit for the Harlot of Babylon—a private bathroom, electric heaters, a desk, cigar-lighters, etc.," and Dudley Field Malone, en route to his second marriage, was aboard. In Paris he visited Emma Goldman and the Philip Goodmans, and devised, while there, a unique gauge to test the civilization of a city. He calculated the number of cafés in the capital, multiplied it by the capacity of the human bladder, compared it with the number of pissoirs, and pronounced Paris an absurd town. When the civic leaders showed little interest in Mencken's Formula, he left for the Bristol Hotel in Vienna and a "Confederate reunion" with Paul Robeson. In London he covered the conference, attended Malone's wedding, and swilled beer with *Guardian* men. He returned home in excellent spirits, writing vast contributions for the ship's paper, including detailed plans for an enormous super-ship which, he announced, was being built. The Doppelschraubenpostexpressluxuskolossal-riesendampfer, as he insisted on calling it, had, among other things, a fourth-class for professors, a space for communists, single-taxers, birth controllers, and "other reformers," and a stadium seating two thousand.

He arrived in New York February 18 with a great glass receptacle to show the press—"the biggest beer mug in the world"—and a decided mind on the subject of Sara. After a brief stop at the *Mercury* office he rode over to Pennsylvania Station, bought a copy of the *Sun*, and climbed aboard a Baltimore-bound train.

The financial page startled him. Was it this bad? Well, let the boobs sweat. *He* hadn't bought any stock. It certainly didn't affect *him*.

Chapter 9

Sara

(1930–1935)

FROM TIME TO TIME, in his role as impresario of the *Sunpapers*, Paul Patterson entertained his chief lieutenants at soirées, and there was, therefore, no great surprise at the office when he issued such an invitation for the evening of August 1, 1930. Indeed, so commonplace did it seem to John Owens, playing host to Louis I. Jaffé of the Norfolk *Virginian-Pilot*, that he felt free to bring him along for what promised to be a pleasant gabble. The congressional elections were coming up, Hoover was making an ass of himself, and the future, for Democratic journals, looked agreeable. There were European adventures to hash over and the usual convivialities. Specifically, Hamilton Owens had brought along a delightful story. In Philadelphia the week end before, he had encountered the Hergesheimers, Emily Clark, and several other women who knew Mencken. All had demanded to know when Henry would marry Sara. Imagine Mencken married! Women were so unrealistic.

Promptly at 7 o'clock the various editors, managing editors, and other functionaries arrived and settled down before the fireplace in Patterson's study. A matter of policy important to both papers came up, and for the first hour it dominated the conversation, with Patterson, John Owens, and Bill Moore trying to argue Mencken down. At length they ran out of wind, he leered cheerily, and Patterson, reaching into his pocket, produced a sheet of copy paper. He handed it to Owens.

"John, I've got a statement to be published tomorrow. You're sitting by the lamp. Read it. See what you've got to say about it."

Owens laboriously fished for his glasses, found and polished them, and adjusted the lenses on his nose. The room quieted down as he cleared his throat:

"Special dispatch to the *Sun*, Montgomery, Alabama, August 2. Mrs. John Anton Haardt, of this city, today announced the engagement of her daughter, Miss Sara Powell Haardt, to H. L. Mencken, of Baltimore. The wedding will take place September 3."

"What!"

Patterson looked mildly surprised.

"What do you mean, 'What!'?"

"You say we're printing that?"

"We are indeed."

Owens sunk into a deep study and the room exploded into a barrage of "What! What! What!" Mencken puffed judiciously on his cigar. Ed Murphy, very sour, demanded, "I don't get it. What does it mean? What's the gag?" "No gag," Patterson replied. "It means what it says." The rest of the room joined Owens in stunned silence. For thirty seconds no one said a word. Finally Jaffé—the only stranger in the crowd—turned to the publisher. "Do I understand you are serious?" he asked. "Yes," Patterson replied. "It will lead the society column tomorrow." Jaffé rose and walked over to Mencken. "Then you are to be congratulated, sir," he said simply. That broke the ice. Everyone rushed to Mencken with extended hand—everyone, that is, save Patterson, who grinned merrily, and Owens, who had not changed expression or position since reading the document. Finally the crowd settled down, and Mencken, smoothing the wrinkles in his voice, began, "Now back to this matter we were discussing. . . ." He was interrupted by Owens, who leaped to his feet and stood rigid.

"Henry, Ill be damned!" he cried.

All Mencken's friends could be damned. It was unthinkable that the most ostentatious bachelor in America should marry—yet marrying he was. Patterson, first told during cocktails at his home, had nearly dropped his glass, and Hergesheimer, Pearl, and Goodman, notified by mail, had groped feebly for support after reading his letters. He certainly hadn't broken the news gently. Dorothy Hergesheimer, like Emily Clark, had suspected what was coming—had indeed, suggested the marriage three years before.[1] But Joe had no inkling until the letter of July 28:

If any scandal-mongers call you up and try to make you believe that Sara and I are to be joined in connubial bonds on August 27, don't deny it, for it's a fact. The solemn announcement will issue from Confederate G.H.Q. at Montgomery in about a week. Your congratulations I take for granted, for you know Sara, and so you know what a lovely gal she is. If you write her please say nothing of my heavy drinking, or about the trouble with that girl from Red Lion, Pa., in 1917. I still maintain I was innocent of any unlawful or immoral purpose.

The wedding will be very pianissimo, in view of my great age and infirmities. We are taking a swell apartment in Baltimore overlooking Mt. Vernon place and very close to Schellhase's kaif and several other excellent saloons. Wedding presents are absolutely forbidden, on penalty of the bastinado. I shall continue my book-writing business as usual. Sara also proposes to engage in literary endeavor, but I suspect that cooking, washing and ironing will take up a lot of her time. Her novel, by the way, has been taken by Doubleday, and will be published shortly. Thus in one year she gets launched as an author and marries the handsomest man east of Needles, Calif.

In this greatest of body blows to the serenity of his friends, he used precisely the same technique which had demoralized a generation of moralists and conservatives: the stating of the obvious in terms of the absurd. To Governor Ritchie, so stunned he could not answer for twenty-four hours; to Harry Black, fumbling for his Madeira 1854; to Goodman, unable to look a *bifstek* in the eye for days; to Broedel, who nearly forgot his cultivation of Goodman's yeast, he replied airily, "I have promised to let her call me by my first name," or "The bride is a lady from Alabama—(white.)" To those

[1] Mencken, giggling all over himself, had replied: "The idea is charming! Ah, that it could be executed! But I already have one foot in the crematory, and spies hint that she is mashed on a rich Babbitt in Birmingham, Ala."

who feebly asked where they would be married, he replied, "We shall follow the rite of the Church of England—after all, a very high-toned ecclesiastical organization, say what you will. I have rejected all evangelical bids." Inquiries about his established bachelor life were answered with the explanation that Sara had agreed he should spend five evenings a week at Schellhase's, "not counting anniversaries of the great German victories." They met, these friends, in huddled little groups, asking one another, *sotto voce*, what in the world had happened. Only Nathan preserved his indestructible poise. Notified by wireless on the *Aquitania*, he told a reporter, "I'm not the least bit surprised. H. L. Mencken is really a home man and he actually bellows with rage if he doesn't get his noodles by 6 P.M." To which Mencken replied with a promise that if Nathan weren't married by February 14, 1932, he, Mencken would undergo baptism by the Baptists, run for Congress as a Socialist, go to ten movies on ten successive nights, and read the complete works of Edgar A. Guest, E. Phillips Oppenheim, and Christopher Morley.

The press ran riot. As Edith Johnson wrote in the *Daily Oklahoman*, "No forthcoming marriage could possibly create so much excitement with the possible exception of an announcement that the Prince of Wales was about to take a bride." WEDLOCK SCOFLAW TO MARRY, wrote the copyreaders; MENCKEN JUST A "HOME BODY," BIBLE BELT GIVES BRIDE TO MENCKEN; MENCKEN, ARCH-CYNIC, CAPITULATES TO CUPID; ET TU, H. L.?; WHAT IS THIS, HENRY?; and OH, HENRY! Delighted editors hauled out their worn copies of *In Defense of Women* and pounced on his verdicts of sex, quite ignoring the dictum that "The marriage of a first rate man, when it takes place at all, commonly takes place relatively late . . . as a man grows older, the disabilities he suffers by marriage tend to diminish and the advantages to increase." In a year of depressing news and plunging salaries, word that H. L. Mencken was getting married was must copy in any newspaper office. It was played prominently—sometimes under eight-column streamers—and nearly every editorial writer in the country had his bubbling say. The Louisville *Times* suspected him of mellowing. The Des Moines *Tribune-Capitol* feared he might join the Anti-Saloon League. The Chattanooga *News* predicted that when he went out in the rain he would have to wear rubbers and carry an umbrella. The Fort Wayne *News-Sentinel* starkly depicted "the shades of Schopenhauer and Nietzsche chuckling—with their grim old heads together." The Hartford *Times* hoped he might have a few kind words to say about yokels, chiropractors, and realtors. The St. Paul *Pioneer Press* indicated an invitation to join the Fundamentalists might be forthcoming. The Columbia, Mississippi, *Commercial Dispatch* piously observed that "a southern girl as his wife should have some sort of refining influence in his life." The Memphis *Commercial Appeal* raised the possibility that he might "invite Paul Elmer More and Irving Babbitt to dinner, hug a Methodist bishop and announce for Dr. Hoover in 1932." Hardly were the last comments in the pressroom than the Montgomery Kiwanis Club elected him to an honorary membership and the running comment started afresh. The Oakland *Tribune* summed it all up: "The plain, every-day duffers whom he has long derided have the privilege of smiling."

For once Mencken was on the defensive. His first comments were a little shamefaced. He replied he saw no discrepancy between *In Defense of Women* and his decision to marry (there was none, actually), or that he had gained wisdom with years. But this reticence was most unlike him, and once he felt certain of his ground, he began spouting pronouncements in the grand manner. The origin of his love for Sara was quite simple: the Holy Ghost had informed and inspired him. Like all infidels, he was superstitious and always followed hunches. Getting married was really very simple. One had but to be polite. He was marrying one of the politest of women, and she, in return, was getting a husband whose politeness had "the high polish of a mirror." True, he and the bride differed somewhat on politics; it was his private belief that the Confederacy had never carried out the terms of the Treaty of Appomattox in good faith—he had it on the best authority, for example, that its army still held maneuvers every autumn in the remoter reaches of the Mississippi, and that more than one hundred thousand Negroes were still held in Alabama slavery. But while he deplored this as a liberal, as an anti-reformist he planned to do nothing about it. As for the formalities:

> I have no objections to honeymoons, nor to church weddings, nor to wearing a plug hat. In all matters of manners I am, and always have been, a strict conformist. My dissents are from ideas, not from decorums, and I do not favor wearing odd clothes, or living in an eccentric house, or making odd noises.

In short, he hoped to stand up to it as a patriot and a Christian. Marriage, like hanging, was, after all, a good deal less dreadful than thought. Sara, on her part, was less glib. She knew, she told reporters, all about her fiancé's marriage wisecracks, but they did not apply here. She did not remember anything he had said about women being inferior to men. And there she stopped. Happily, the reporters were far more interested in Mencken than his bride, and she was bothered little.

It was well for them they did not want more of her, for she was far too busy for such nonsense. They had taken the entire third floor of a stately brownstone house at 704 Cathedral Street, in the oldest residential section of Baltimore. Built in the 1880's, it had survived on the perimeter of the great fire, and despite the passing of a quarter of a century and the coming of the business district to its quiet neighborhood, had yielded little to the years. A carved stair rail wound leisurely under a stained-glass skylight, which, to Mencken's delectation, was said to have come from the smoking room of a German liner. And on the top floor, among the recessed windows, under the towering ceilings, Sara plied her musty arts.

Mencken spread it about that her main industry was devoted to the setting up of beer crocks, bottling machines, funnels, etc., for the brewery he planned to open after their wedding trip. She did a good deal more than that. Her long interest in the best Victorian taste now flowered in a home that was to express all the charm, and none of the frigidity, of the nineteenth century. She was, in that dreadful August heat, bustling about happily, buying carpets, putting in fly screens, and supervising the installation of bookcases in Mencken's office and in the hall which ran past their separate bedrooms. With Anne Duffy she shopped endlessly to gather the furniture proper to the period she exalted. The grimier the junk shop, the better Sara liked it: with a grand sweep of her skirts and a dainty mince she would step between the shopman and his newest wares, penetrating to the depths of the stock, where lurked the abandoned shield-backed sofas, tufted barrel chairs, and fifty-year-old bric-a-brac which delighted her. The shopping done, she turned to the upholstering—a difficult job, since most craftsmen insisted on overstuffing Victorian furniture—and the papering. She debated long over the living room walls and settled at last on a pale lemon paper to match the gold, rust, and green brocade of her chairs. By mid-August, she was ready for moving.

She did not, as her betrothed alleged, carry everything on her own back,[2] but for the effort she put into the job she might well have. Mencken's books, his booze, and the heavy mahogany files that bore his *American Language* notes had to be brought and installed, and once they were in, she turned her attention to the vast store of fusty gadgets she had been accumulating for years. In the bathrooms she hung her collection of framed old Valentines—all handmade and covered with hearts, silver lace, posies, and fervent inscriptions in delicate, sloped handwriting. Along the walls, in cases, with mirrors behind them, were set her hundreds upon hundreds of nineteenth-century pinboxes, shaped as organs, fruit, wheelbarrows, etc. On the dining and living room walls she hung her tinsel and mechanical pictures, and on odd tables were placed her glass bells, so popular a century before, ranging from tiny bulbs covering Madonnas to enormous shells over bird-like specimens. Mencken liked the funny pinboxes. He particularly admired a farmyard picture which was equipped with a mechanism that set cows to

[2] "Sara is moving the piano tomorrow—a heavy job for a frail girl in such weather," he wrote Goodman. "She tells me that Southern ladies were never expected to do such hard manual work. I reply that what goes in one place doesn't go in another."

stamping and chickens to pecking when released. He played with it constantly, rewinding and jiggling, chuckling to himself. His own contributions to the furnishings, apart from the books, liquor, and files, consisted of a brass spittoon and an enormous chromo of a pre-prohibition brewery which, to Anne Duffy's horror, he insisted on hanging in the dining room. But what most entranced him about the apartment was his neighbors. On one side loomed a Christian Science temple; on the other, the Knights of Columbus alcazar. "I live in a neighborhood so holy," he told a friend, "I can look out of my back window any night and see the Holy Ghost skipping across the chimney pots."

Finally the last valance was in place, the last Sandwich pitcher arranged at its station, and the little card "H. L. Mencken—apt. 3" posted downstairs. The event loomed nearer and nearer—somewhat nearer, indeed, than all but the closest friends of the couple suspected. The discrepancy between the formal announcement and Mencken's letter to the Hergesheimers had been real and intended. September 3 was the date given out, but in reality it was August 27; Mencken, fearful that the local Hearstlings would burst into the church with flash bulbs popping, had deliberately deceived his public.

Down to the last week he was too busy to worry. On August 18 Van-Lear Black, chairman of the *Sun* board, perished in an accident at sea, and affairs at the paper were in a great stew. Of less moment, but closer to him and Sara, was the fatal illness of Anna, senior waitress at Schellhase's. Between the two tragedies and his arrangements at the *Mercury* office —he ducked in and out of New York "like a burglar," fearful of recognition—he was kept well occupied. On August 21 he took out his license at the City Hall, telling bystanders only that he believed in preparedness, and settled final details for the ceremony. In Maryland there was and is no civil marriage, and since it was unthinkable they should marry other than in Baltimore, the problem of a preacher presented itself. Mencken settled on Dr. Herbert L. Parish of New Brunswick, New Jersey, a former Baltimore rector who had written a biting article on the state of the church for the *Mercury*. Sara, in her junk shop wanderings, had unearthed an ancient Currier and Ives wedding certificate, and this was filled out, ready for Parish's signature. The overture was at an end.

Mencken began to tremble. He could, he broadcasted, "almost hear the sheriff's stealthy step"; he asked all to pray for him. Pearl was greeted "from the brink of the precipice," and wild requests were sent out for a Prince Albert coat "with no moth-holes." Preposterous bulletins were dispatched to Goodman alleging that he wanted to get out of the ceremony and describing daily palavers with Sara's lawyers. Mencken was prepared to settle for under five thousand dollars, since it would cost him that much to get married, but the situation, from the first, was hopeless. ("Sara refuses to discuss matters with my attorney. She says the chance to marry the handsomest man east of Needles, Calif., comes once in a lifetime.") For a while it looked as though he would be excused. ("Sara now offers to compromise for $350,000.") But, in the end, all was lost. ("I have put in four solid days with lawyers. Sara's representative, Attorney Leon Greenbaum, demanded an anti-nuptial settlement of 86% of my entire resources. How he arrived at this figure I don't know. My own counselor, Otto Pagentecher, made a private offer of 65%, excluding my pornographic books and my private jewelry.") Greenbaum and Pagentecher, it appeared, fell to quarreling over points of law, and all hope of relief vanished. Mencken, he reported cheerfully, was a doomed man.

Shortly before 4:30 on the afternoon of August 27, 1930, an automobile drove unobtrusively to the side entrance of the Protestant Episcopal Church of St. Stephen the Martyr, North and Warwick Avenues, and Mencken and August alighted. Inside they joined Gertrude, Charlie, Charlie's wife, and Virginia Mencken. Sara, wearing a summer brown crepe dress and a dark felt cloche, arrived shortly thereafter with her mother, sister, and brother-in-law. She went up the aisle on her brother-in-law's arm a few minutes past the half hour. A few moments later she was Mrs. Henry Louis Mencken. The bride and groom were driven to the railroad station and boarded a train unrecognized. Aboard, Mencken dispatched a wire to Goodman: WE SHOOK OFF THE LAWYERS AND GOT AWAY SAFELY THE FINAL SETTLEMENT IS VERY FAIR

I GET A LIFE ESTATE IN ONE SIXTEENTH MY OWN PROPERTY
LESS COUNSEL FEES.

Much of the credit for a smooth ceremony and getaway
went to Patterson, who had volunteered for the role of public
relations counsel and general manager, and en route to
Montreal they wrote their thanks. The notes were typical.
Sara said: "It was a tedious business and you managed it
perfectly." Her husband wrote: "It was a masterpiece. No
publicity has been better handled since the Snyder-Gray
case." He also sent out postcards and letters to his friends,
advising them they were right—he *had* turned out to be a
perfect husband. In Montreal he was uneasy; his hay fever
tickled him somewhat, and they pushed on to Quebec, reaching there at the height of the Labor Day rush. Quebec,
he disliked enormously. The accommodations were poor,[3]
and the town he thought really dreadful. "The streets swarm
with tourists, and most of them look ripe for the guillotine,"
he wrote Patterson. "This morning I saw at least 100 head
of women who would butcher beautifully." Fortunately, they
ran into a Canadian Army officer—one of Mencken's ever-
present correspondents—and he and his wife produced some
excellent Scotch. But neither Henry nor Sara cared greatly
for the society of others that first week, and during most of
their stay in Quebec they sat pleasantly by their hotel window, watching the ferry boats dodge one another in the St.
Lawrence.

In Halifax, which they found far more suitable, Henry ran
into some of his friends from the New Orleans Fire Chiefs
convention, and they staged a reunion. From Halifax they
went on to Digby, St. John, across the Bay of Fundy by
boat, and thence back into the United States. Sara was greatly
taken with the Canadian mountain ash, and Mencken paid
fifty dollars duty on a bunch—unaware that it grew wild in
Maine, across the line. After a brief stay in Boston, they
trained for New York, and there, after three weeks of marriage, granted an interview to a United Press reporter. The

---

[3] "Jesus, what a swell hotel! *Two* Gideon Bibles—and *one*
towel!"

reporter found Sara, to her great consternation, with a wave net on her hair and Mencken demanding of a porter where the ice and mineral water were. Sara was somewhat reluctant to talk to the visitor ("She's gun shy," said her husband), but after some coaxing, she confessed the prime discovery of her first three weeks with him: he was a Victorian, though he wouldn't admit it. And a Victorian husband, to her mind, was ideal. "What?" croaked Mencken. "You with an ideal? What do you mean, an ideal?" Sara skirted over to her luggage and produced a copy of *The Young Lady's Toilet*, published in 1841. From it she recited the husbandly virtues: piety, contentment, moderation. "In drinking?" asked Mencken, startled. "In everything, Henry." "That's terrible." The reporter asked Sara about the possibility of household arguments. It greatly embarrassed her.

On their return to Cathedral Street, he hastened to make his report to the Rev. Mr. Parrish. A score of invitations awaited them, and Sara, with her great respect for appearances, insisted they attend. To luncheons in the *Sun* board room, to evenings at Willie Woollcott's they went, Sara in her immaculate summer finery, Henry in his usual summer costume—a flat straw boater and a baggy, tight seersucker that looked as though it had been slept in for at least a week. The Menckens, indeed, became quite sociable. To a certain degree, Sara's likes and dislikes affected her husband's former friendships—her objection to Dorothy Thompson notably cut him off from Red Lewis—but for the most part they saw the couples both had known before. Supper parties, to Sara's vexation, were impossible because of her husband's working hours, but she liked formal luncheons quite as much, and whenever the Darrows or McDannalds were in town they were sure to be so entertained. For a time, after the arrival of the Scott Fitzgeralds in Baltimore, they were intimate, but Fitzgerald's drinking had already become intemperate and Zelda had begun her trend toward madness; after one trying evening at Rodgers Forge, Mencken forbade Sara to have anything more to do with them. Generally he liked her bent for entertainment, however. He loved to play the host, pouring the first drops of wine in his glass and throwing them down an open gullet, explaining to the guests, "There may be some cork chips floating on top, or a dead fly, or some staphylococcus."

Under Sara's gentle but resolute prodding he came out of his shell. He sat for a portrait for Richard Reid, the Negro artist; spoke publicly on Lizette Woodworth Reese's seventy-fifth birthday; granted a radio interview on the American language, and, nervous and trembling, led a German band over the air. Reporters calling for public statements on stock occasions found him receptive for the first time; before the first Christmas of his marriage he astonished them by advising the world to "take to heart the verse from John XV, 12: 'This is my commandment: that ye love one another as I have loved you.'" He settled easily in the bovine tempo of middle-aged married life, strutting his stuff when such strutting was expected, retiring to the brocaded rooms of his apartment when it was not. The old brawling arguments with bachelors were past now. In Baltimore Sara and Constance Black entered into a pact to keep their husbands from lending money to the vagabond Boyd, and in New York Sara and her husband rested sedately at the Algonquin, eschewing the old Bowery dives he had once relished.

From the first they were sublimely happy in their marriage. Cathedral Street was peculiarly fitted to Sara's Victorian appetites, and when she was not writing in her rear room, she would wander over to Siegfried Weisberger's bookshop on North Charles Street, bringing review books for resale, or among the antique shops with Anne Duffy, adding to her vast and rather disorderly collection of Victorian knickknacks. Mencken, for his part, worked at his usual hours with Rosalind C. Lohrfinck, his new secretary, and after a session with his new Remington—he had, at last, abandoned the disintegrating Corona—would venture out to buy for Sara an ornate set of brass fireplace paraphernalia, wrestling with it all the way home, or stretch lazily on his bed, perusing one of her file of *Godey's Lady's Book* as he had his mother's long ago, marveling that so much novel and instructive information could appear in a woman's magazine. Both were exceptionally fond of children, and any visitor with a child in tow was sure to bring Henry from his study, beaming and clucking. On one occasion a little girl had, in the inexplicable manner of little girls, come to believe she was being brought to see Mickey Mouse. When Mencken appeared, she burst into tears. He, greatly upset, managed to find out what the trouble was and immediately jumped into his coat and out the door, returning shortly with a toy mouse. While the child, fascinated, looked on, he got down on his hands and knees, wound the mechanism, and guided the toy in a series of somersaults. When the little girl left with her mother, she told him shyly that she preferred him to the real Mickey Mouse. He was enormously gratified.

Shortly after that first Christmas, Sara told Mrs. Hemberger she never thought life could be as easy with anyone as it had been with Henry, and he, writing to Goodman on their first anniversary, admitted the fears he had taken to St. Stephen's Church and their ultimate groundlessness.

> Frankly, I expected to make rather heavy weather of the first year. I feared I'd be homesick for Hollins Street, and that it would be more difficult to work in new surroundings, eating purely Southern cooking-hams and greens, corn-pone, hot biscuits, etc. Nothing of the sort ensued. I am far more comfortable than I was in Hollins Street. Sara takes all telephone calls. The bills leave me $1.50 for Uncle Willies. Such is life with a really Good Woman.

Professionally, both were prospering. Sara's *The Making of a Lady* had received excellent reviews, and sales of *Treatise on the Gods*, despite the inevitably hostile notices, went beyond thirteen thousand before the end of 1930. It went into a dollar reprint form, and Mencken thereby lost a great deal in royalties. But the furious opposition stimulated interest, and one preacher—Father John E. Graham, a Baltimore Catholic—went so far as to write an entire book in answer. Life for Henry and his bride, it seemed, could not progress more happily.

And yet . . .

Shortly after their first New Year's Eve of marriage,

Mencken fell victim to an annoying siege of sinus trouble. His complaints had scarcely begun to gather momentum, however, when Sara succumbed to influenza, and her plight, unlike his, did not lessen after the first attack. Influenza was succeeded by pleurisy, and the fluid accumulated in her lungs, producing a racking cough and compressing her lungs so that she could hardly breathe. This, in view of her medical history, was serious, and she was taken to Union Memorial Hospital, where surgical drainage was established. Her temperature leveled at 103 for several days, then dropped slowly, persistently refusing to leave altogether. A half-degree fever lingered each night, and so long as it remained, her doctors refused to take her from the hospital. All told, she was away over a month, and Mencken, despite attempts at joviality and a stag dinner at Cathedral Street, was miserable. When she came home at last, he took her to Atlantic City for the week end. She was encouraged to put on weight, and she did, but minor afflictions continued to pursue both of them through the summer and fall, and he decided to take her to the West Indies on a rest cruise.

They sailed from New York January 9 on the North German Lloyd steamer *Columbus* and spent eighteen days lolling in deck chairs, soaking up sun and reading. The trip was a boon to both of them. Mencken reveled in the lengthy beer and wine lists of the *Columbus,* and Sara enjoyed the frequent stops—Jamaica, Havana, San Juan, La Guaira, Curaçao, and Panama. She returned in splendid health, plunged into work, and, by the following May, had written and sold four short stories and an article. Her husband, the day of his return, began on a new enterprise, *Treatise on Right and Wrong,* designed to round out the trilogy begun with *Notes on Democracy* and *Treatise on the Gods.* The work, he found, went very slowly. But what did it matter? No book—no conceivable book—could sell in 1932. Best let Sara raid the women's magazines, which were holding up remarkably in the declining market. When it zoomed again—then the public would be ready for his heavier screeds.

Superficially, it seemed that Mencken's vogue was holding up. Lewis, accepting the Nobel Prize at Stockholm in late

1930,[4] had saluted him as the critical genius of the age, and few literates outside the Bible Belt disputed it. He was still able to charm, and befriend, the more cynical of his enemies. Bishop James Cannon, Jr., the Dry tycoon, granting an interview in Washington, was delighted with him, and so enjoyed the resulting article he sought him out frequently. During the 1932 Democratic convention, Cannon virtually lived in the *Sun* press stall and refused to issue any statement without first consulting Mencken. And the old power to inspire wrath still thrived, as three incidents in 1931 eloquently testified.

In February Richard Reid was arrested in a New York cafeteria for insisting on eating with a white friend, and Mencken publicly advised him to sue the restaurant, announcing that "the whole thing sounds almost as if it had happened in Mississippi." The Mississippi press, led by his old friends in Clarksdale, set up a great whoop, declaring that he obviously was anxious to "Eat, sleep, and drink with a black man"; that "Water eventually seeks its own level." That same month the Arkansas boomers, who had been quiescent for several years, lighted on an *Evening Sun* article and turned in their best performance to date. The piece, titled "Famine," pictured Arkansas as the apex of moronia, a land so intellectually underprivileged that not even the Red Cross, with all its munificence, could prevent the inhabitants from starving to death through congenital stupidity. The legislature promptly passed a resolution censoring Mencken, and Dallas T. Herndon, Arkansas' state historian, and former governor Charles H. Brough sent windy replies to the *Evening Sun* forum. Called at home by an Associated Press reporter, he remarked, "My only defense is that I didn't make Arkansas the butt of ridicule. God did it." This set the yokels to hollering louder, and one legislator jumped to his feet and moved that the House "demand an apology from that jackass." On the motion of another, and more Christian, representative, the House decided to stand for a few mo-

---

[4] Four years before, he had turned down the Pulitzer Prize for *Arrowsmith* at Mencken's suggestion.

ments of prayer for the soul of H. L. Mencken. This was done gravely, and in Baltimore Mencken, queried again by the A.P., replied: "I felt a great uplift, shooting sensations in my nerves, and the sound of many things in my ears, and I knew the House of Representatives of Arkansas was praying for me again."

The loudest of the three ovations came from Maryland's Eastern Shore, a rural and backward peninsula sprawling seedily along the east side of the Chesapeake Bay. The Shore had nothing in common with Baltimore save its situation inside the same borders, and Mencken had long advocated it be forced out of the Free State. His repeated advice that the electoral system be revised to prevent the outvoting of the city's legislative delegates by "some half-witted oysterman" had long ago identified him there as the meanest and sickest of the automobile-riding, cocktail-drinking, book-reading louts of Baltimore. But the Shore, like Arkansas, had been ignored by Mencken of late, and its inhabitants had had small reason to think of him down to December 7, 1931.

Two months before, one Green Davis, a Worcester county farmer, his wife, and his two daughters had been found brutally murdered in their beds. Yuel Lee, an itinerant Negro laborer who nursed a financial grievance against Davis, was charged with the crime, and the Shore, always troubled with the foulest race prejudice, seethed through October and November. On December 4 came the spark for which the farmers were waiting. Matthew Williams, Negro, shot and killed his employer in Salisbury, twenty miles from Davis' home, declaring his wages to be too low. A few hours later a mob rushed a Salisbury hospital where Williams lay suffering from a pistol wound, dragged him to the courthouse green, and lynched him within plain sight of a dozen police officers. While the crowd howled with merriment the body was raised and lowered several times. It was then cut down, taken to the edge of Salisbury's Negro settlement, drenched with gasoline, and set afire. Several homes in the neighborhood were stoned and a score of Negroes, several of them women, were badly beaten as the corpse flared.

Three days later the *Evening Sun* printed "The Eastern Shore Kultur."

What the farmers had done to Williams, Mencken did to he entire Shore. It was, he said, the "stronghold of Prohibi- ion (and all the rotgut liquors that go therewith)" within vhose borders "tin-pot revivalism was making its last stand in Maryland." It had menaced the state before with its "swinish- less"; now it held Maryland up to the contempt of the nation ind the world by staging "a public obscenity worthy of can- iibals." Salisbury was the "Alsatia of morons," of "low- grade political hacks who flourish in such swamps," of 'ignorant and ignoble hinds"; the lynching was "the local noron's answer to the efforts of city men to get them to pehave with common decency."

The lynching of poor Williams, dragged to death blind and in bandages, was no more than a melodramatic dem- onstration that the brave fellows of the region were not to be intimidated. They proved it as such poltroons always do—at odds of 1000 to 1.

The leaders of the mob, he added, were known to every choolboy in Salisbury; they were "on public display at this noment, bathed in admiration."

For days no one on the Shore could speak coherently of he article. Duffy, who regarded the institution of lynching nuch as the lynchers regarded the National Association for he Advancement of Colored People, drew a number of his ne, biting cartoons, and the *Sun*, together with Mencken, ecame a target of abuse worthy of a Mississippi Baptist. he *Marylander and Herald* of Princess Anne charged Mencken with affiliation with "anarchist and communist roups, composed for the most part of men and women from he lowest strata of the mongrel breeds of European gutters." Mencken and Duffy, it concluded, were probably jealous be- ause they could not attend the civic pageant. Had they been n hand, they would have "danced with glee around the onfire of human flesh; could have easily imagined a bar- ecue was on hand; could have eaten the flesh of the carcass, nd smacked lips over the fine flavor of the gasoline." On ecember 11 the representatives of eighteen local firms met Salisbury and voted to do no business with Baltimore until Mencken, the *Sun*, and all the ministers of Baltimore had apologized for the outrageous piece. Alarmed, the Baltimore Association of Commerce apologized for its impetuous journalists, agreed with the Shoremen that the lynching was a local matter and should be settled in Salisbury, without outside interference, and begged the businessmen not to shut off trade with Baltimore.

The apology was heard but faintly. Salisbury was heaving with rage, and the life of Yuel Lee was actually in grave danger. An attorney for the International Labor Department, coming to defend him, was set upon by a mob and he and two colleagues, one a woman, were driven from the Shore. Then, on December 14, appeared Mencken's second article, "Sound and Fury." He reprinted the *Marylander and Herald's* attack, scorned the "low-down politicians, prehensile town boomers, ignorant hedge preachers, and other such vermin" who had made it, and brought up the matter of Williams' toes, which had been cut from his feet after the hanging. "No doubt," he wrote, "they now adorn the parlor mantel piece of some humble and public-spirited Salisbury home, between the engrossed seashell from Ocean City and the family Peruna bottle."

Now the animals were really stirred up. A former mayor of Salisbury, serving on the coroner's jury, threatened to subpoena the entire editorial staff of the *Sun* papers, "since they know so much about it." Mencken was actually preparing for a visit to the Shore when strongly worded advice to stay at home arrived from friends across the bay. Telegrams were arriving daily in Hamilton Owens' office, threatening to lynch any *Sun* man who set foot on the Shore flats, and the incident was fast developing into a small war. Two *Sun* papers trucks, en route to Salisbury, were ambushed by a mob, their contents dumped in the bay, and their drivers beaten. The Salisbury Lodge of the Tall Cedars of Lebanon met in special session to consider reprisals, and a large meeting of public-spirited citizens debated the question of secession from the state—a move Mencken had long advocated. Farmers by the thousands were outfitting their cars with large stickers reading "I am an EASTERN SHOREMAN and proud of it" and driving up to Baltimore, looking for trouble.

From every pulpit in the Shore's nine counties, clergymen were denouncing the city men for offering their opinions on something that was none of their affair.

Lee was moved to Towson, north of Baltimore, for trial, and after his conviction the noise died down. Mencken had one last round with the mobsmen the following March, after a coroner's jury had failed to bring indictments against any of the lynchers. "The lynching, it appears, was a sort of transcendental event, taking place in secular space but only dimly visible to mortal eyes," he wrote acidly. "A large crowd turned out to enjoy it, but no one could make out who was running it." He was genuinely indignant over the incident, and three years later, when the Costigan-Wagner anti-lynching bill came up in Congress, he rode over to Washington to testify in its behalf. On the Shore, feeling against him was slow in abatement and exists, indeed, to this day. In 1933 one J. R. Barnes, a war veteran who had adventured as far from home as Niagara Falls and the Mississippi, enjoyed quite a vogue after the publication of his pamphlet *The Spirit of the Eastern Shore,* which reached a feverish, if indiscriminate, crescendo with the passage:

> I love every flea, chigger, sand burr, corn stalk, and musk-rat trap on these level sandy shores. I thank whatever Gods may be that I was baptized by the spray of the Atlantic Ocean. . . . It was not serpentine venom that annoyed us. It was merely the secretion from a lowly skunk. And while the little winged god called Fair Play hovered overhead, enjoying a huge laugh, this skunk juice created quite a stink among the people of Baltimore.

Mencken serenely clipped every editorial, every news story, every broadside during the battle and pasted them in his scrapbooks, dating each item with his own hand. Business, his peculiar business, was still prospering.

And yet . . .

And yet it was not. Just as surely as if he had been a corporation listed on the New York Stock Exchange, Mencken's value sunk lower and lower and all but vanished as the great depression deepened. Ten years before he had ridden in on a wave of disillusion and irresponsibility, the surprised beneficiary of a changed society. Now that society had changed again and he was riding out, as helplessly the victim of the public's whim as he had once been its darling. Some of the factors in the decline were unconnected with the depression and would have brought him down a notch or two anyhow. More and more, as the Twenties rushed to their tragic end, a new younger generation had been indisposed to subscribe to a postwar despair it had not experienced, as the popularity of the New Humanists had testified. And Mencken's marriage would inevitably have driven away many customers who were attracted by the color of a militant bachelor. But his own private smash-up—and it reached those proportions as the bread lines lengthened and the Hoovervilles grew—was largely a result of the collapse of the jazz-age bubble. To the *Mercury* readers wearily walking from office to office, searching for elusive jobs; to the University of Chicago boys who passed, on their way to class, old men groveling among garbage cans; to thinking America, reading of farmers defending their farms from foreclosure with sharpened pitchforks, there was little sense or purpose to Mencken's belaboring of Kansas, his formation of an American Beard Association, his gleeful display of the world's largest beer glass. And sense and direction were what these readers suddenly wanted. For too long—for all of adult life, for some—they had lived the inebriation of the Twenties, and now, in the depths of the great hangover, they blamed the jolly bartender for their misery. Art for art's sake was dead, gone, finished. There was no room for a writer with nothing to say about the crisis gripping the world. There was no room for H. L. Mencken.

The shift was apparent in a thousand different ways, some of them but distantly related to Mencken, all of them pointing to the death of an era. When a dozen students at Bryan Memorial University in Dayton were expelled for bootlegging, the nation, which would have rolled on the carpet five years before, scarcely noticed them. When Joseph Hergesheimer set sail for Europe, "where a man doesn't have to take a drink unless he wants one," a lethargic public passed him by. Forthwith the caperings of the old entertainers had become absurd, foolish, and in intolerably bad taste. Mencken might draw public tributes from Sinclair Lewis and private tributes from Bishop Cannon; he might still stir up the animals in Mississippi, Arkansas, and on the Eastern Shore. But Lewis and Cannon, like him, were passé, and his rural vilifiers, after all, had constituted only a third of the show, of which Mencken was master of ceremonies and the city readers were paying customers. The yokels might holler, and the maestro might holler back, but the audience was *non est*. Not only was the audience staying away; the more articulate of its members were loudly disdainful. Mark Van Doren now took notice of a long-accomplished fact—that Mencken was "no longer writing in the sky of our new literary epoch." Gorham Munson, viewing the past decade from the perspective of April, 1930, wrote in the New York *World* that all its chief philosopher had contributed to the American scene was the pleasure of a few minutes' reading. *The New Republic* announced editorially that "most of his virtues have declined . . . all of his faults have increased," quite ignoring the fact that Mencken's attitudes and style had changed not one whit since the crash. And Henry Seidel Canby, who had once relished the Scopes trial stories, looked bleakly out at the sinking economic scene and wrote of the "burly self-satisfied discontent of H. L. Mencken."

What hurt Mencken most—and he was hurt, deeply, despite his protestations of indifference—was the turning against him in the colleges. As early as May, 1930, Irving Babbitt could smugly and safely claim that Mencken was a dethroned monarch so far as the Harvard boys were concerned. "Mr. Mencken rose superior to the Rotarians and Kiwanians and saw them all as boobs. Young men flocked to his standard, because it gave them a chance to look down from the heights on the 'booboisie', but they have become weary of just being superior." No longer did collegiate polls acclaim the *Mercury;* at Long Island University, journalism students went vigorously on record as *not* approving of Mencken. Many were at pains to write him at his new home, telling him he was a sophomore, and those writing in magazines attacked him with a fury that was suspect because of its very violence. Even V. F. Calverton, a Baltimorean, lashed out at "Mencken the myth, Mencken the vaudevillian," thereby betraying himself as one of the spiritual castrates. Senior orators, who had once embarrassed their old teachers with page-long quotations from the *Prejudices,* now delighted them with pious pledges to safeguard the maidenhead of scholarship. At the Georgetown University School of Foreign Service, the senior class president actually urged a curb on free speech for such as Mencken, and the valedictorian of the University of California '31, a hopeless New Humanist, challenged his "contemptuous negation of human values and human motives."

New Humanism was now at the height of its glory; like a withered old campus strumpet suddenly gifted with scarlet sex appeal, it paraded through the fraternity houses and library stacks, luring the children from their play. Abandoned was the chastity belt which had restricted clientele fifteen years before; it had become a flexible philosophy, all things to all men, and its supernatural perimeter attracted many a young searcher for truth who remained ignorant of the black reaction which was its core. All this contributed heavily to Mencken's retreat into the shadows, not only through the enlistments brought to More and Babbitt, still bellwethers of the movement, but also through a crippling of the liberals who were left. The controversy which had raged through *Humanism in America* and the *Critique of Humanism* had forced the defenders of realism into solidified beliefs; it was no longer possible merely to carp at the national absurdities; positive faith became necessary, and many of Mencken's greatest supporters were driven far to the left, to the dialectic materialism which produced such Marxist tracts as Granville Hicks' *The Great Tradition* and James T. Farrell's *Note on Literary Criticism.* This philosophic civil war left Mencken squarely in the middle, which is to say, alone.

The first casualty was *Treatise on the Gods.* The book sold well enough, but its popularity in the stores was simply a carryover of the massive reputation which had not yet begun to crumble publicly. The reviews told a somewhat different story. Attacks from the pulpit, from such as Michael Williams, who wrote in *The Commonweal* the book should be titled "Mencken's Bible for Boobs," were to be expected. But Irwin Edman's verdict that "It confirms the report of the death of one minor deity, its author," and the scathing reviews by younger men were not, and they rocked Mencken. He had done a terrific amount of research on the book and had tried conscientiously to make it a lucid, unbiased exposition of the history and psychology of religion. Perhaps the saddest aspect of its cold critical reception was that *Treatise on the Gods* was just about everything Mencken hoped it would be. It carried some of his most scintillant prose; it tackled a difficult problem with grace and finesse; it condensed the best that had been written on one of the most important and mysterious problems of civilization; it avoided billingsgate and unwarranted conclusions. "Whom did he write it for?" asked Huntington Cairns derisively—ignoring the obvious answer, that he wrote it for himself, as all great books are written; that he wrote it out of a need to put down, once and for all, the torture of doubt that he might some day awake and find the Bible to be true. "But it has been done!" cried Angoff, reciting the sources in Frazier, Tyler, and Andrew White, forgetting that it had been done before them and would be done again and that that was no gauge of its value. The young men were contemptuous of the book Mencken had conceived as his masterpiece. It missed, they said; it missed badly. It lacked the old jazz.

Two years later came *The Making of a President*, a dreadful mistake, and not altogether Mencken's fault. It was the pastiest of all his books, patched together at Knopf's insistence in thirty-six hours, made up of dispatches to the *Evening Sun* from the 1932 conventions, with a couple of *Mercury* editorials thrown in for transition. Convention prose is no test of any writer's ability, even in the reportorial field, and the hodgepodge that resulted was just what the Marxists and the Humanists were looking for. They seized upon it with joy and tore it to shreds. Most newspapers, aware of his shrinking stature, limited their reviews to a paragraph, and H. Allen Smith, book editor for the United Press, summed up the climate of opinion when he wrote, "Henry L. Mencken writes a profound apology for his latest book, 'Making of a President'. It needs one. His publishers charge $1.50 for his new book. If you've got $1.50, get it changed into nickels and take 30 rides on a street car. You'll have more fun."

Mencken's first reaction to the depression was to deny its existence. "The restaurants I go to are full, the streets are teeming with automobiles, and the theaters and music halls are doing a good business." When, after a long and stubborn resistance, he finally admitted there was some deprivation, it was only to add quickly that it was the product of interested parties—"communists, charity mongers, and the king of idiots who yell 'fire' in crowded theaters." He turned the "Hoover prosperity" into a gimmick for his booming of a Democratic President in 1932. But as for the unemployed: "The people who die aren't worth saving anyway. A few more slaves, a few less slaves, what's the difference?" He saw no need for extreme measures to deal with the problem. When Sinclair suggested radical steps, he was answered tartly, "As always, you are right—save in matters of politics, sociology, religion, finance, economics, literature, and the exact sciences." Storming into the *Mercury* office one day, Mencken turned wrathfully to Angoff. "I've just seen Fitzgerald," he fumed. "He says there may be something to socialism." "Well," said Angoff, "Fitzgerald's socialism is only a form of Wilson's New Freedom, and there is surely something in that." "Harvard," snorted Mencken. "Just like Princeton."

The economics of the crisis were wholly beyond his grasp, but he would not admit it. "What goes up must come down. A friend of mine in Baltimore told me that a few years ago, and it's all the economic theory worth knowing." When, in the very depths of the depression, he arrived in Pittsburgh for Virginia Mencken's graduation from high school and was asked what he thought of the situation, he said it was at an end. He had, he said, talked to a friend on the train; his friend's steel mills were reopening. What more conclusive evidence could a man ask? And when, in March, 1932, his long-awaited *Mercury* editorial on the depression came out, he sounded a cheerful note most of his readers found merely annoying.

What we suffer from, essentially, is only a gross and persistent Katzenjammer, the natural product of the grandest jag in the history of the modern world. . . . In actual values the country is still rich, and any man who owns any honest part of it still has that part, and will see it making money for him when the clouds roll by . . . once they discover the massive fact that hard thrift and not gambler's luck is the only true basis of national wealth . . . they will be as rich as any other people on earth . . . the United States is as sound as ever—probably a good deal sounder. . . .

Yet under it all he was as deeply touched by the national tragedy as he seemed *not* to be touched. When, in the bleak, chill winter of 1932, Angoff took him by Times Square to see the long, hopeless queues of hungry men, standing in threadbare overcoats, waiting for their bowls of broth, he turned his head to the wall and could not speak. A few days later, after he had returned to Baltimore, Angoff was called from his desk by a stenographer to greet a man who had come to see "the editor of the American Mercury." In the hall he found a frail and miserable tramp, wearing an overcoat which somehow looked familiar. The vagrant had come to thank the man who had talked to him encouragingly in Times Square and had ended by stripping off his overcoat and giving it to him.

It was Mencken's overcoat.

To the decline of his popularity he was contemptuous. "The diatribes and jeremiads of the young gentlemen who write for such magazines as the *Bookman* and the *Hound and Horn* are not to be taken seriously," he wrote Roscoe Peacock. "All they proved is that education cannot make a damned fool intelligent." When the Columbia University *Spectator* sent him a list of hostile questions, he replied, ill-naturedly, that college boys were all stupid. In the *Saturday Review of Literature* he sneered at the proletarian literature movement; it was, he said, to his misfortune that his father had been relatively well off, "since no man in America seems to be worth listening to unless he was born in a sweatshop." And despite his admiration for the craftsmanship of James T. Farrell, he rejected ten of Farrell's stories of Irish-American life in Chicago for every one he accepted. John Dewey, then enjoying his great vogue, he could not read. "His capacity for being uninteresting amounts to genius." The whole

American literary scene had rearranged itself, passing over Mencken and leaving him hurt and mute by the roadside.

Literature was only part of it. The entire world had shifted key, and C Major, the only tone he knew, was suddenly discordant and out of tune. In Germany National Socialism was rising, and when Mencken treated Hitler with his accustomed gaiety, he found, to his amazement, that some of his closest friends were contemptuous. "I have a postcard from Hitler saying that he is really not anti-Semitic at all," he wrote DeCasseres. "He tells me, in fact, that some of his best friends are Jews." When DeCasseres did not laugh, he was puzzled. Hitler was a joke, Mencken argued, and you cannot fight a joke. He was, he said, disappointed to hear that Hitler had burned none of his books. When it was suggested that Hitler was not a joke, and that his book burnings could not be treated lightly, he denied it. "The German news is probably at least nine-tenths bogus. Certainly the Germans are not beating up Jews as such. It simply happens that a good many Communists are Jews." When Goodman, staggered by the pogroms, denounced the Germans as fiends in human form and began going back into their history to find evidence of it, Mencken took sharp issue with him, and the upshot of this difference was an end to their long friendship. Angoff, exasperated by his pooh-poohing of the Nazi terror, asked, in desperation, "Does Mencken's interest in honor and decency stop at the Rhine?" Apparently it did.

Actually it did not, but his sentimental allegiance to the old Germany was such that he could not bring himself to public chastisement of the Fatherland. Privately he was as opposed to the Nazis as were Goodman and Angoff. "I give up the Germans as substantially hopeless," he wrote a friend when Hitler became Chancellor. "All sorts of authorities report that they are in an exalted and happy mood. If so, it is the kind of euphoria that goes with acute infections." In one of his first letters to Dreiser after their long silence, he said, "God knows what the Nazis are up to. They seem to be a gang of lunatics to me. I hear I am on their blacklist. . . . I don't know a single man among them, and all my friends in Germany seem to be in opposition—that is, all save a few damned fools who I'd hesitate to approach." On May 25,

1933, he outlined his position more fully to Colonel Edwin Emerson, with whom he had corresponded since 1914, when Emerson notified him of his selection to honorary membership in a society called Friends of Germany, one of the first of such societies to spring up in the Thirties among German-Americans sympathetic to the Nazis. Mencken declined to accept on the ground that the "extraordinary imbecility" of German politicians had

> destroyed at one stroke a work of rehabilitation that has been going on since the war, and they have made it quite impossible to set up any rational defense of their course. I can imagine no more stupendous folly. For ten years, thanks to the hard and intelligent work of both Germans and Americans, the American attitude toward Germany has improved steadily, and there was a growing disposition to take the German view of the "reparation" obscenity, and of the whole treaty of Versailles. But now, by talking and acting in a completely lunatic manner, Hitler and his associates have thrown away the German case and given the enemies of their country enough ammunition to last for ten years.

Any defense of Germany was impossible, he concluded, "so long as the chief officer of the German state continues to make speeches worthy of an Imperial Wizard of the Ku Klux Klan, and his followers imitate, plainly with his connivance, the monkey-shines of the American Legion at its worst."

His position was misunderstood, however, and it was widely assumed that he condoned the new regime in Berlin. His arguments for free speech "up to the last limits of endurance" were unacceptable to those who preferred to interpret his opposition, say, to the closing down of the Amos and Andy radio show as merely indicative of deep-seated racial prejudice. When he argued that even those against democratic procedure—i.e., the American Nazis—should be heard, it was generally believed that he, too, was an anti-Semite. Yet he was not, not by the standards by which his generation is to be judged. "For a German, I am quite free of anti-semitism," he had said, and his actions certainly support this. When a correspondent, thinking to strike a responsive chord, railed against the unseemly behavior of rich Jews on an ocean liner, his knuckles were rapped sharply.

It seems to me that you are generalizing from very small evidence. Certainly it would be absurd to say that the kind of Jews you met aboard ship were the only kind in existence. Some of the most intelligent people in America are Jewish, and not only some of the most intelligent, but also some of the most charming.

It was for respite from this sort of thing, as much as for convalescence, that Henry and Sara left for Sea Island, Georgia, in the late winter of 1933. For some months both had been recovering from sinus infections, with slight temperatures and great uncomfortableness, and a week of sunlight and rest was most welcome. Mencken had a tip on the coming moratorium beforehand, and so he brought plenty of cash with him, most of it in the form of gold notes. The law requiring such notes be turned in was already in effect ("I have been caught hoarding gold and must give up two hundred dollars of it. I shriek, as the mandrake root"), but the law said nothing about time and place, and so he turned them in only when he had occasion to spend them. They lolled on the beach at Sea Island, burning in the sun by day and listening to a group of spiritual singers by night, and were splendidly equipped when the banks were shut up. Sea Island was and is a swank resort, and among Mencken's neighbors in their apartment colony were several men of tremendous means—millionaires who lacked a nickle for a cup of coffee. He, with his sheaf of notes, enjoyed a magnificent reputation in this peculiar situation. They returned via Montgomery, for Mencken's first and only visit with the Haardts. He enjoyed Montgomery enormously, though not because of any intrinsic merit in the town itself. The local newspaper editor sent him a bundle of *Evening Sun's,* and he wallowed in them throughout his stay, getting caught up on local news. "The first page looked almost miraculous, and every editorial was a masterpiece."

He returned for a gleeful occasion: the end of prohibition. The club had struggled along somehow on "one lung, one kidney and half a liver" through the last years of the drought, and Mencken had become exasperated with the cruelties of The Horror. "In such freezing weather as this," he complained to Hergesheimer just before his departure for Sea Island, "alcohol is absolutely necessary. Even automobiles need it." In preparation for the great blowout, he devised an elaborate licensing act for Baltimore city—which was, of course, never adopted—and practiced opening his throat for the night of April 6, when the lid was slated to fly up. At Schellhase's he heard wild rumors of enormous shipments of first-rate beer from Germany, and was literally panting with expectation by 11:25 P.M. of the Great Evening, when Patterson picked him up. They strode—or half ran—to the Rennert, where Hamilton Owens and Harry Black joined them. Mencken stood up to the old semicircular bar, accepted the first stein, and, with a cheery "Here it goes," tossed it down. Harry Roth, the Rennert's veteran bartender, and two-score connoisseurs waited breathlessly for the verdict. His blue, Nordic eyes danced; he put down the stein; he smiled. "Pretty good," he announced. "Not bad at all."

Owens pronounced it awful, and they argued their way across town, stopping in all the old haunts, sampling each keg, debating its merits. That Saturday the club emerged from the underground and cast around for a public meeting place. The Rennert had the pull of tradition, but somehow the chairs there seemed harder on the pelvis than they had once been, and jazz dancers, for some inexplicable reason, had taken over the ballroom. So they set up in Schellhase's new establishment on Howard Street. Mencken was inexpressibly relieved over legalization; the home meetings had been a great strain on the host, and when they were held in the country, at Hamilton Owens' place, he had often been forced to stay away, to his chagrin, because of the ragweed menace. Now the club was back to normality. The Thirties, at least, had brought *something*.

But even here, in a sense, he lost. The end of prohibition took away his last whipping boy and one of the few remaining appeals of the *Mercury*. The magazine was now in a dreadful state. It had been sinking steadily since the beginning of the depression, and the time was approaching when something overt had to be done. The circulation had dipped from sixty-seven thousand in 1929 to forty-two thousand in 1932, and was dribbling down to a 1933 average of slightly over thirty-three thousand. If policy had not been shifted after 1924 this would not have been serious, but when sales had zoomed during the late Twenties, Knopf had sunk in a considerable investment, and the magazine had become, by early 1933, a liability. "For the first time in my life," Mencken wrote, "I began to give serious attention to money: it is a new experience for me." His public, each month, was leaving the *Mercury* on the newsstands more often and picking instead such imbecilities as *Ballyhoo,* the opiate of the unemployed. His first reaction was, "If the boobs don't read it, to hell with 'em." Then, under prodding from Knopf, he tried half-heartedly to change the magazine's tone—as if that were possible. Editorials were brought to the front, a letters-to-the-editor department was introduced, and Mencken, despite his pronounced antipathy for Veblen, began printing his pieces on the theory that the public wanted economics jammed down its starved throat. He and Angoff conducted a survey to decide which was the worst state in the union—they picked Mississippi—and introduced various other fillips to "lighten the magazine," though neither was quite certain what the phrase meant.

Late in 1932 they signed a whopping advertising contract with the American Tobacco Company, enabling them to show a five thousand dollar profit for the year. By May, however, circulation had fallen off 40 per cent and advertising revenues were down 25 per cent of what they had been three years before. That June the estate of Knopf's father, who had died the previous year, was made public, and the increasing losses sustained by the *Mercury* were spread before a curious industry. An affidavit filed by Joseph C. Lesser, comptroller at Knopf's, pretty well summed up the predicament of the magazine when it contended that the depression had struck it especially hard because it was dependent entirely on "the activity, ingenuity, and popularity" of Mencken. Class magazines, Lesser pointed out, must be revamped and reorganized if they were to survive, but that could not be expected of the *Mercury* since it was "a one-man magazine catering to a very selective class of readers who are followers of its editor." Deeper and deeper sank the magazine, and that summer Mencken made his decision. A man will always find reason to continue what he enjoys doing, but when his public lost faith in Mencken, Mencken lost interest in his public. His trips to New York had lost much of their savor since his marriage and had become merely annoying. To a certain degree the apathy, the dreadful feeling of inadequacy that gripped everyone that year had laid hold of him, and it seemed less tiring and more pleasant to lie on his bed at Cathedral Street with the file of *Godey's Lady's Book* before him, oblivious to the desolate world outside. So he decided to get out.

The announcement was made October 5. Mencken received reporters in New York, explaining that he was, basically, an author, not an editor, and therefore thought it best he return to his trade before it was too late. The magazine would continue under Knopf's ownership, with Henry Hazlitt as editor. He himself would be more "mobile" and would turn to the rewriting of *The American Language*, a project long overdue. He painted an elaborate picture of the vast philological material waiting to be sorted out; editing the *Mercury*, he said, had been a lot of fun, but ten years was long enough for any job, and now that was over, he felt as elated "as the boy who killed his father." Sara joined him in explaining his position to old friends for whom the magazine had become the last symbol of the dead harlequinade. "I was sorry, in a way, for Henry to give up the MERCURY but glad in a number of other ways," she wrote Jim Tully later in the month. "The work was becoming pure routine and it was very bad for him: he had no time to put on his own books." Significantly, perhaps, his last review that December considered a number of books about Nazi Germany. He got out the last issue and spent that evening quietly drinking beer with August. The public reaction was apathetic. Ed Howe, retiring in Kansas at eighty on December 28, summed up the reaction of the old guard when he paid tribute to Mencken as the greatest writer in the country, adding "the public don't like him any more, so he's quitting, too." The *American Spectator* sounded a different, and perhaps more popular, note when it stated editorially, "It was most fitting that his last pieces were contributed to an ideologically bankrupt American Mercury and that intellectual hara-kiri found him there." Mencken, all agreed, was through.

The book before him was not, as advertised, *The American Language.* That was still in the future. In late 1933 he was still working on *Treatise on Right and Wrong,* begun after his return from the West Indies two and a half years before. Not since the days of "The Free Lance" had he been so unproductive of books. Worry over the *Mercury* had sapped his energy to a point where his stature as a practicing author, during those two and a half years, was very questionable indeed. Despite its secondary nature, his protest that editorial work had drawn him from his rightful occupation was not without merit. For a time he had averaged less than a page a night, and for long stretches he had not written a word. Now, with the magazine off his hands, he plunged into it, and by the end of January it was done. Then he decided to take another rest. Both he and Sara had gone on a reducing diet that October—he weighed 195 stripped, "surely too much for an esthete"—and its rigors had taken quite as much out of them, as the morality book.

Late in February, 1934, they sailed on the *Columbus,* Mediterranean bound. As always, life aboard ship ("that of a *canned* vegetable") set him purring. The *Columbus* was thickly peopled with Christians that trip, en route to the Holy Land for succor. One of them, a Catholic bishop from Oklahoma, turned out to be an old *Mercury* customer with whom Mencken had corresponded, and the two mixed beer and theology pleasantly in the smoking room, debating whether Mencken's heaving of a Y.M.C.A. delegate overboard would qualify him for absolution. In Algiers he and Sara toured the more colorful sections and jabbered with the natives. Mencken left with the decided conviction that the world would be far better off if all the Arabs were put to death, but his opinion was probably colored by an unhappy adventure in an Arab taxi. The driver, hanging desperately to the wheel, whooshed him through the town at terrific speed, and his terrified croaking was ended, suddenly and violently, when the car skidded on a hairpin turn, tossing him out on the cobblestones. Fortunately, he landed on his ample buttocks and suffered only a small—but very painful—bruise.

Algiers proved difficult to shake. They had, they thought, put it behind them when, two hundred miles out to sea, a dust storm pursued them, coating the ship and giving Sara a severe cold. Egypt was no better; there were "too many ruins" and the air, again, was quite dusty. But the Holy Land was admirable. The roads were good, the scenery splendid, and the sacred spots magnificent. Mencken stocked up on souvenirs for his friends—a supply of Jordan water and "a gallstone passed by Abraham in 1700 B.C."—and gathered a formidable stack of notes on the adjournment of religion in Palestine. On April 5 they returned to New York, refreshed and supplied with a treasure of anecdotes on the odd behavior of foreigners. It was, however, to be the last such jaunt. Mencken had "promised the local coroner to remain within easy reach of his eye."

The reviews of *Treatise on Right and Wrong* were tepid. Most of the more competent critics appreciated its soundness, but the country still lacked leisure and inclination to enjoy in large numbers an informal essay on the development of moral ideas, and the book did not stir up the storm of protest so necessary for a Menckenian ten-strike. The *Catholic World* reviewer took him over the tortuous Jesuit rack, describing him as "temperamentally unsuited for philosophy, or theology, or ethics, or—I add by way of good measure—logic," but most of the Christers simply passed it by. And the more mature critics did not give the boosting for which book buyers, wary of their pennies, were looking. This was disappointing, for it ended his great trilogy on a sour note. *Notes on Democracy* had already passed into merciful obscurity, and of the three, only *Treatise on the Gods* seemed likely to survive, and that only by virtue of the dollar reprint Mencken refused for *Treatise on Right and Wrong*.

After the end of his magazine career, the *Sun* had offered him a job, but he found the prospect of regular working hours, after nearly twenty years of freedom, distasteful. He preferred to work out his destiny in his own way. The peculiarity of his position had only increased since his retirement; with the easing of the depression an entirely new set had moved on the American stage, and if Mencken elected to continue his role as common scold, new devices were necessary. The absence of a regular national forum was a tremendous handicap. He could not bring himself to contribute to the *Mercury*, which, after four months under Hazlitt, had passed into Angoff's hands, was sympathetic to the regime in Washington, and thus had become, in Mencken's opinion, "somewhat Red." Lacking such a mouthpiece, he appeared less frequently in the public view and sank, as a consequence, more deeply into the shadows. Occasionally he appeared in print, as when Elizabeth Dilling listed him in her *The Red Network*[5] or when he invited Commonwealth College, investigated by the Arkansas legislature for Communist leanings, to come to the Maryland Free State. But his public statements, and nearly all his writing, save for the incipient *American Language* revision, were largely confined to a growing polemic against the New Deal.

Mencken had voted for Franklin Roosevelt and had even predicted that within ten days after his election America would be back in the high tide of the Coolidge prosperity. But that was when Hoover was President and anything was cricket that would reduce his chances of succeeding himself. Mencken had, it must be remembered, a perfect record in national politics. He had never supported a President in office. Roosevelt was ill-suited to break that tradition. He was a poseur, and Mencken loved to needle poseurs. He spent large sums of money, alarming to a conservative middle-class German. Further, he spent the money on unfortunates who, under the Nietzschean scheme of things, should yield to the law of survival. Finally, he committed the unforgivable sin. He brought college professors to the White House.

It was the Brain Trust which got Mencken. He had first

[5] "I was in hopes this wouldn't get out," he told a reporter. "But now that Mrs. Dilling's researches have exposed me, I might as well confess. I have been receiving $100,000 a year from Moscow since 1920, and for the past several years have been printing inflammatory propaganda in the papers. . . . WOOF! WOOF!"

cracked out against it on his return from the Mediterranean, when he announced that planned economics were fine, but that they were possible only in fascistic or communistic countries and were inconceivable in a democracy. "Give the people time to watch the tax bills roll and pile up," he said. "They'll throw out the quacks." In his *Evening Sun* articles and in contributions to *Liberty* and the Hearst papers he blasted the "slimy false pretences and idiotic contradictions of the Brain Trust . . . the blind, envious fury of Upton Sinclair, the cow-state Utopians, and the kept idealists of the *New Republic*." The "cony-catchers," he said were "crowding the public trough in Washington"; the Brain Trusters were "embracing the public teat." Once Angoff had been succeeded by Paul Palmer, a young conservative more hospitable to vilifications of the Roosevelt regime, he carried his war to the *Mercury's* pages, labeling F.D.R. as "the boldest and most preposterous practitioner" of political quackery in modern times. Roosevelt, he said, was "solely responsible" for the New Deal's "dreadful burlesque of civilized government"; he had saddled the country with a "camorra of quarreling crackpots, each bent upon only prospering his own brand of quackery and augmenting his own power. The greatest president since Hoover has carried on his job with an ingratiating grin upon his face, like that of a snake pill vender at a village carnival, and he has exhibited precisely the same sense of responsibility."

To those who protested his appearance in *Liberty* and the Hearst press he replied that Roosevelt was the enemy, and that anything which would help oust him was a patriotic act. He got a grim amusement out of appearing in the "Hearst seraglio," and his *Liberty* pieces he frankly admitted were done, not only out of patriotism, but out of a need to boil the pot. At four hundred fifty dollars a whack, he could ill afford to question the reputation of the paymaster. That such forums were damaging to a critic of his stature apparently never occurred to him. He continued to cram his breech and fire away, oblivious to the irony manifest in the fact that he who was once castigated regularly on the floor of Congress was now quoted glowingly by such as Senator Hastings of Delaware and Ham Fish, Jr., of New York. When the Gridiron Club invited him to appear as chief lampooner of the President, he accepted eagerly, and the character of his periodical articles, together with his radio appearances, led some of his friends to suspect he was really in need of money. James M. Cain, Baltimore's literary gynecologist, became convinced of it, and went so far as to cook up a deal with Warner Brothers to bring him to Hollywood as a script writer. When a studio agent approached with an offer, he received a polite No. Mencken was still Mencken. He simply did not like Roosevelt.

The new *American Language* edition proved the most exhausting yet. Late in 1933 he had begun to burrow through the vast material which had flowed to him in a thick and never-ending stream since the publication of the third edition, now hopelessly out of date but still selling. Much of it had been filed away in the mahogany cases in his office, but it had somehow gotten out of hand, and one Victorian sofa was littered with five hundred contributions from volunteers, some running as long as ten thousand words. There were more than one thousand newspaper clippings—Durrant, the English bureau, had been supplying him with everything in the field for twenty years—and an extensive accumulation of books, not to mention the files of *American Speech*, which had been set up ten years before. All told, his notes weighed about fifty pounds. Throughout the summer and fall he sweated to make sense out of all this, and the more he struggled the more hopeless the task seemed. He would escape it if he could, he told himself, but the job had to be done, and there was no one else to do it. Sometimes he would work all evening over a single page and that, in the end, would be torn up. Between adventures in the sofa notes, he scoured the country, via mail, to find authorities on local dialects or the authors of unsigned pieces in philological journals. By the end of November, after five months of terrific labor, he had made small progress. He swore a solemn oath never again to write a book containing a single reference and plunged ahead. "I am still plugging away at that infernal book," he wrote Edgar Lee Masters. "There is very little straight writing in it. Most of the work consists of pasting together a multitude of small notes. After a couple of hours of this labor I begin to be tortured by an overpowering thirst and so I rush out to the nearest kaif. In the long run, I suspect, Schellhase will get far more out of the book than I do."

The plain fact was that he was terribly worried about Sara, and what little he did on the *Language* was the result of her great encouragement and enthusiasm for it. Ever since her nephrectomy he had known her chances were poor, and her pleurisy in the first year of their marriage had alarmed him far more than he would admit, even to himself. After the West Indian cruise she had flourished, and the trip to the Mediterranean had been made in the great hope that shipboard life would once again set her squarely on her feet. It had not. That May she had gone to the hospital with a small fever of mysterious origin—probably picked up in Algiers—and throughout the summer she fared poorly. In September she had ventured down to Montgomery to visit her ailing mother. Mencken went down to North Carolina to bring her back, and the following month she was in the hospital again with pleurisy. She recovered slowly; the house was lonely and gloomy; work was virtually impossible. Dr. Benjamin Baker, her physician, feared for the worst; he told Mencken so, and this contributed little to household cheer or the incentive to write. By mid-December she was ill again, and on Christmas Eve her mother died in Alabama, pitching her spirits downward. "Let us give the Holy Ghost credit," Mencken wrote Masters in desperation. "He has got off some masterpieces in 1934."

Sara had been ill too many years to share his dejection for long. She continued to write in bed on a wheeled table that slid over the blankets and to chat with Anne Duffy, who came to see her daily. She now had two large enterprises under way: *The Plantation,* a novel, and *Southern Album,* a miscellany. Her short stories had sold readily all through the depression, and she had every reason to believe that her career would continue to flower. To a small degree her optimism was contagious. Each sojourn to the hospital brought expressed hope from Mencken that she would be home in a few days, by the next week, by the week after next; that soon his neckties and shirts would match again and the haunting loneliness at Cathedral Street would be over. But by March, 1935, his energy had spiraled to a new low. Sara was back in the hospital, he himself was down with bronchitis, and the future looked pitch black. He had been writing a few language pieces for *The New Yorker* in an attempt to prime the pump, and one he submitted was so confused the editors were forced to return it. He turned to the reading of *True Detective* stories and was so upset by March he canceled a speech he was to deliver for Noyes of the Associated Press in New York—an unprecedented move.

Late the following month transpired an incident that shed some light on his state of mind and the estate to which the once mighty *American Mercury* had arrived. The previous November Mencken had joined the *Sun* board of directors, and in that role he was planning work on a centennial history of the paper, to be published in 1937. In March he had consulted Walter Abell, still living, and armed with an outline of the book had gone up to New York several times to see Alfred Knopf about an estimate of publishing costs. The *Mercury*, meanwhile, had run into labor troubles. A pitifully small shop committee, consisting of three clerks, two stenographers, one switchboard operator, and a bookkeeper had asked Lawrence E. Spivak, then publisher, and Paul Palmer for a twenty-one-dollar-a-week minimum and two weeks' vacation a year. Mencken was in the office at the time, and after he, Palmer, and Spivak had put their heads together, he sat down and typed out a company manifesto. As Menckenese it was very good—though, astonishingly enough, few recognized the style—but as a document for labor relations it was preposterous. It described the "world revolution" which had struck at the *Mercury* office, declared that the editor and publisher had decided a shop committee was inadequately equipped to run their organization for them, took some vigorous swipes at "Moscow and Fourteenth Street," and wound up with the declaration that all manuscripts entering the office were being carefully searched for bombs.

The employees struck. Mencken, passing the building one raw afternoon, ran full tilt into the pickets—headed by Edith Lustgarten, his old editorial secretary, who had been discharged after eleven years for "inefficiency"—and a mob of reporters. The reporters asked him what he thought of the strike. "I'm friendly to both sides in this controversy," he replied, "and I reserve the right to picket for the side that asks me first, but neither side has asked me yet." Edith approached and asked him if he had ever found her inefficient. "Did I ever fire you?" he asked. Then, as she returned to the reporters with this voucher for her record, he added hastily that he had always thought her political opinions odd. "You know damned well you never did," she snapped back. "Now look here," said Mencken, "did I ever curse or swear in talking with you in all those years?" "No," said Edith. "But you used a lot of funny words." Mencken replied that he thought the strikers were fools and Edith said "Damn!" again. He pretended to cry at the sight of a lady swearing and told her she might catch cold out in the wind. She replied she was wearing a heavy coat and extra underwear and would survive. Mencken blushed at this, told the reporters the strike was futile, reminisced vaguely of strikes in his reportorial days, and passed on. Later, when the strike was over and the magazine running full blast once more, he sent the National Labor Relations Board a lengthy wire, testifying to the satisfactory nature of Edith's service with him, and, when her husband was in the hospital, moved heaven and earth to get him proper medical attention. But though no one present appreciated it, the strikers, Mencken, and the reporters had held a full-scale autopsy of the Paris-green *Mercury* of the Twenties on that windy corner.

Sara returned from the hospital in mid-April and seemed to be making excellent progress. Mencken planned to take her to the Adirondacks for two months beginning June 1. She was full of plans for this when, in late May, she was stricken suddenly and for the last time. To Johns Hopkins Hospital she came, nursing a dreadful headache, to the white cot of which she had written so movingly in "Dear Life."

Here it was again, in a hospital in the heart of Maryland—that curious air of the South; birth and death, promise and annihilation, in a single breath. . . . Well, death, a full tropical death at the moment of greater promise, was the peculiar heritage of the South, and of all Southerners. I was merely coming into my own.

At first there was no clear diagnosis; Mencken knew only that her trouble was "something on the order of influenza." Through Saturday and Sunday—Sunday she was placed on the critical list—and Monday he continued to hope, despite all the signs discouraging hope. On Tuesday, for the first time, he doubted her chances, and on Wednesday he knew she was doomed. She had meningitis, with tuberculosis bacilli in the spinal fluid. Rather curiously, tuberculosis of the lungs, which she had always believed would take her in the end, did not trouble her. The headache passed, and she slept comfortably. Mencken stayed by her side in a terribly low state of mind, clutching the letters that arrived for her in the morning post, knowing she could never read them. She fought magnificently, if hopelessly, in the shadows, with a strong heart and steady pulse, but the morphine made it difficult to rouse her. She might wake for half a minute, but hardly for more.

Sara died on Friday, May 31, 1935. She was thirty-seven years old. He was with her until the end.

Funeral services were held the following Monday. Gerald Johnson stopped by at Cathedral Street for a few minutes that morning. The servants had been sent away and the house was very quiet. Mencken talked slowly and dispassionately of everything but that which was on his mind. At the funeral parlor her immediate family and a few friends—the Knopfs, the Hergesheimers, the Pattersons—were present. It seemed intolerable to part from her without a word, so he asked an Episcopalian minister to read the brief service. She was to be cremated. It was her wish.

On the street afterwards, he was in a state of near collapse; the week of waiting had left him utterly exhausted. That afternoon Doctor Baker took him for a long ride in Green Spring Valley, north of Baltimore. They passed the old house on Belvedere Avenue where, half a century before, August Mencken had taken his family each year to escape the heat at Hollins Street. Mencken had been quiet through the drive but now, as they passed the old haunt, he turned to Baker. "I used to spend my summers in that house as a boy," he said slowly. "I haven't seen it for twenty-five years. I've been in the bowels of the city that long."

That night he walked slowly up the two flights of stairs under the skylight, to the deserted apartment of gold, rust, and green brocade, to the archaic pinboxes, the Valentines, the mechanical farmyard picture—slowly he walked, a broken and pathetic figure in a neat blue suit, alone in his terrible tragedy.

"It was a beautiful adventure while it lasted. Now I feel completely dashed and dismayed. . . . What a cruel and idiotic universe we live in!"

Chapter 10

Alas and Goddam

(1935–1949)

MENCKEN WAS in his fifty-fifth year when Sara died, and that is not an age at which a man readjusts quickly. The day had passed when he could turn to new projects and hatch fresh schemes; only the store of blueprints designed in his youth remained, and of these, many had been exhausted. His amazing vitality still flourished, as we shall presently see, but the shock of his wife's passing left him temporarily an emotional cripple. He had been only too aware of her slender chances from the very first; but, understandably, he had not prepared himself for the brutal event itself, and now that she was gone the pain was almost unendurable. August, but recently acquitted of a sinus operation himself, had moved into Sara's old room to be with him; Gertrude was out of town, and the house at Hollins Street was, therefore, closed. After a few days Mencken began to get hold of himself. He wrote his thanks, in a barely recognizable scrawl, to those in attendance at the funeral, "for the lovely flowers . . . ," "for all your kindness . . . ," and made what plans were necessary to cope with a desolate future. He decided to continue at the apartment. "It is very comfortable and convenient, and I suppose I'll have to learn to endure the fact that my wife is no longer in it."

Both he and August, who was still wobbly, felt a compelling need to get away from Baltimore for a few weeks. Once the stack of correspondence accumulated during Sara's last days was out of the way, they packed and sailed for London, thinking to escape the depressing sympathy of old friends, who, however well-meaning, fenced Mencken in and made a resurgence of his congenital good humor impossible. But even in England, it seemed, escape was impossible. His attempt at joviality on the dock—"Fine! They have chromium-plated the whole damned thing! But where is the monument to Crippen?"[1]—went unnoticed, and the London *Daily Express*, as if to demonstrate that American tabloids had no corner on bad taste, headed its story, in greasy black type:

FAMOUS U.S. SATIRIST ARRIVES IN ENGLAND

Trying To Forget
The Past

STILL SUFFERING FROM SHOCK OF WIFE'S DEATH

They stayed, as always, at the Savoy. Patterson was in London when they arrived, and by the time he sailed on the *Normandie* the Mencken brothers had renewed older contacts and paved the way for a more satisfactory visit than the *Daily Express'* reception had augured. Newton Aiken of the *Sun's* London bureau wangled them tickets for a session in the House of Commons, and they sat, much impressed, during a histrionic speech by dashing young Anthony Eden. In London they ran into James Bone of the *Guardian* and his wife, and with Bone and Patterson's son Maclean, then studying in Paris, spent a delightful day on the sunny Thames, picnicking and punt-racing. The race did him a tremendous amount of good, and for all the amusement it may have afforded Londoners on holiday, the spectacle of Mencken coxwaining enthusiastically under his flat straw boater while Bone punted frantically against young Patterson was an excellent omen. Numbed by tragedy though he might be, the zest for life that was part of his fabric would not stay long suppressed.

On July 12 they returned to America. In New York he glibly advocated a king for America (Huey Long would make an excellent Prince of Wales, he said) and rode back to Cathedral Street in infernal heat. Internally he was still floundering, and the duties attendant on his position as executor of Sara's will were little help. Her friends were invited to lunch; afterward, he took them through the apartment, ask-

---

[1] H. H. Crippen, a North London physician who murdered his wife in 1910 and was subsequently hanged. His arrest marked the first time wireless telegraphy was used in criminal detection.

ing them to choose whichever of her curios they most admired, to be taken in remembrance of her. Her personal library of four hundred volumes—largely histories of the Civil War and of Victorian life, but including autographed first editions from Hergesheimer, Cabell, and Robert Frost—she had bequeathed to Goucher. These Mencken presented in a little ceremony at the college. Joe came down from West Chester to stand with him, for it promised to be a trying occasion. Ellen Glasgow sent up a book published that summer, inscribed "To Goucher College Library, in memory of my beloved friend, Sara Haardt Mencken, a loyal, lovely, and gallant spirit." Somehow he weathered the function, but it was hardly the sort of thing calculated to bring him out of the haunting past.

The surest way for Mencken to draw himself together was to dive into work. Fortunately, a challenging undertaking lay before him: the uncompleted fourth edition of *The American Language*. Once the summer heat had rolled away he submerged himself in this, working fourteen or fifteen hours a day, turning from it only to dictate his daily mail to Rosalind Lohrfinck or to dine, alone, at the table prepared by Hester, Sara's old cook. He slaved at fever pitch, finishing a draft of the text in early September. The word list of twelve thousand entries—by far the most valuable and time-consuming section of the book—came next. In this incessant toiling Mencken found contentment again, giving himself to the vast design with an ardor unmatched since *Treatise on the Gods*. For the first time in over a year, the old note of gaiety crept into his correspondence. "Word by word, line by line, my manuscript fills itself up," he wrote Masters.

I now have 82,750,000 words and I am adding to the stock at the rate of 32,100 words a day. This leaves me very little time for my devotions, but I yet manage to get to mass every morning, to read 30 chapters of the Holy Writ and to sing a couple of hymns. The Holy Ghost stands beside me, guiding me to the truth. When the wind shifts I can actually get a whiff of him. The aroma is more Mongolian than Caucasian, but there is also a touch of sulphur.

The word list proved particularly vexatious, holding him, in its editing, through the early months of 1936, but he romped in the mysteries of philology, captivated by the task. When the pedagogical wheels slowed down temporarily, he turned desperately to other work, dreading the inactivity which meant depression. In early October, stalemated briefly in the *Language,* he wrote a detailed outline of the *Sun* papers book, forwarding it to Gerald Johnson, who was to write the opening chapters. In February, when a faulty heating system brought on an attack of bronchitis and left him too ill to deal with the massive lexicon, he turned to the editing of two Leipzig lectures of Johann Burchard Mencken which had been translated for him in 1929 by a Latin professor at the Johns Hopkins University. The *Language* proofs finally left his hands as winter ended. They represented three hundred twenty-five thousand words, a colossal achievement ("When Alfred sees it, his eyes will roll and his breath will come fast"), but his great energy roared on unabated. He gathered Sara's short stories together, wrote a long preface to them, and sent *Southern Album* to the publisher; he dug through the business files of the *Sun,* dredging up material for his section of the paper's history; he toured Johns Hopkins Hospital ward by ward and wrote a series of twenty articles on it for the paper. When, in mid-May, he suddenly ran out of projects, he frantically launched the most elaborate prank of his career: the Maryland madstones.

The madstones were certainly from Maryland, but if they possessed any genuine supernatural powers, none of those favored with their attentions could find them. Yet it is doubtful if grosser claims have been proposed for any property in the history of wizardry than were advanced for these shapeless boulders, said to have been quarried from "the famous madstone mine in Kitzmiller, Maryland, in the foothills of the Alleghenies," a locale once given to producing loose girls "conspicuous in the public stews of Baltimore" but since become devoted to scientific and theological concerns. In letters and in little cards wired to the crates or the rocks themselves, he told Masters, Sinclair, Hamilton Owens, Dreiser, and DeCasseres that the stones were efficacious, not only against hydrophobia, but against 10,000 other diseases, most of them fatal. The chairman of the board tells me that clapping it on the head behind either ear for two minutes will cure the most frightful headache ever heard of. It is also said to be helpful in cases of impotence, but on this point I offer no opinion.

One stern warning accompanied each gift, "Dr. Mencken, Maryland State Madstone Inspector," pointed out that in the presence of this cosmic energy, the bearer must treat his stone as if it were radium. A lead receptacle was preferable, but whatever he did, he must not carry it in his pants pocket. Several predecessors, unfamiliar with the powerful properties of the boulders, had been severely burned for their carelessness. The talismen were worth all sorts of trouble, however, for they were the greatest discovery since the contraceptive. They had one defect. "Unfortunately, these madstones are ineffective against the clergy. You will have to use an ax."

The wonder of all these achievements—of which the madstones certainly were not the least—is that they were accomplished in the midst of moving. The Cathedral Street apartment, full of reminders, had become more and more depressing each week, and by late February it was "so horribly lonely" that he couldn't stand it. Gertrude, meanwhile, had been agitating for an end to housekeeping, and so it was decided that Mencken should move in with his brother, bringing his servants with him, leaving his sister free to settle in an apartment north of the city. Thus would his yearning for constant companionship be satisfied; there would be "meat on the table, with a drink beside it and someone to talk to whenever I get home." Moving was a stupendous problem, however; an immense store of accumulations had to be got rid of, for the little house simply would not hold them all. Mencken decided to let this problem take care of itself. He had everything shipped to Hollins Street—and found, when he got there, that the floor was completely invisible. He had enough furniture to outfit the block, and there was virtually no place where he could stand. To complicate matters, August, in the midst of this furor, was attacked by a throat infection and had to be packed off to Johns Hopkins Hospital. Somehow Mencken bulled his way through the mess, tearing down the old sleeping porch and setting up his study in his mother's old second-floor bedroom while he was about it. He was to sleep in the third-floor workroom, which had seen all his writing before 1930. It took him literally six months to get things straightened out, but once it was over, the home was as comfortable as it had ever been, and far less crowded. His new office particularly pleased him. The three wide windows behind his desk looked out on Union Square,

> and in the next block there are the gardens of a nunnery. It is pleasant to look over the wall and watch the nuns practicing golf strokes and playing badminton. Their brewery is in the corner nearest my house, and when the wind is from the west the odors emanating from it are highly conducive to literary composition.

It was the summer of 1936, the hottest summer in the memory of political hatchetmen. Now, with the great Hate Roosevelt movement at its height, the small but very articulate minority which demanded a new President scoured the country for enlistments. Mencken sprinted to the colors. He had been among the first to cry out against the New Deal, and as the election year approached, his long and continuing philippic reached a crescendo. Shortly after his return from London he had told Patterson he actually believed the President could be beaten, and the following spring, through the *Mercury* and the Hearst press, he called for an end to "jitney messiahs." In December he wrote that anybody, save only Hoover, could beat Roosevelt, but by March he began to doubt this. Publicly he kept up a brave front, laying himself open to misquotation by declaring that "If Roosevelt can be beaten, he can be beaten by a Chinaman."[2] Yet to DeCasseres he wrote, "Give your mind seriously to the question of the

---

[2] This was widely circulated as, "Even a Chinaman could beat Roosevelt," and Mencken lost considerable prestige after the election.

Second Coming. I really begin to suspect that the signs and portents are upon us. Read the Book of Revelation and you will find a truly magnificent description of Jim Farley." For the first time in his life Mencken was preparing to come out in support of a Presidential candidate. His political spoutings, anathema to the Republicans ten years before, became an integral part of the litany of hate sounded in thousands of editorial pages, and so right-wing a mouthpiece as the Chicago *Journal of Commerce* wished wistfully he had not said so many unpleasant things in the past because "He really can be convincing." E. B. White, paraphrasing him, neatly summed up the reactions of the literati in the *Saturday Review of Literature:*

> Poetry, religion, and Franklin D.
> The three abominations be.
> Why mince words? I do not feel
> Kindly toward the Nouveau Deal.
> Hopkins peddles quack elixir,
> Tugwell is a phony fixer.
>   Another lapse
>   For Homo saps.
> Yahweh!

He went to the Republican convention hopeful someone would pop up capable of unsitting the sitter. "As you probably know," he wrote Pearl, "the Holy Ghost has been a member of the Republican National Committee since 1861. He is not visible to the carnal eye, but he is always there and he always votes." Unhappily, for all this ethereal ballot and the prodigious sweating of Henry Mencken in smoky corridors and the labors of the boozy delegates, the Republicans brought forth Alfred M. Landon, or, as he was henceforth known to Mencken, "Poor Alf." He was, he broadcasted, firing his chaplain and hiring a colored wizard in the hope of electing Alf, but he had little faith in the chances of a Republican victory. Nor were his spirits improved by the Democratic fiasco in Franklin Field, where he set up to cover Roosevelt's speech and succeeded only in getting sopping wet. He began to suspect, indeed, that the end of the republic was really at hand. Fortunately, August proved a far happier month. It was in August he traveled to Cleveland to cover the convention of Father Coughlin's National Union for Social Justice. Here, at least, were men who still knew how to politic in the grand manner—glorious idiots like Townsend, Gomer Smith, and Lemke—candidates unafraid to give the peasants what they wanted. "This Townsend show is really colossal," he wrote Hergesheimer. "Imagine 20,000 morons penned in one hall, and belabored for eight hours a day by the most magnificent rabble rousers on earth . . . a small sacrifice to lay on the altar of God and country."

Patterson was all for sending him to cover the Harvard tercentenary, but Mencken would have none of it. "I like politicoes much better than I like professors. They sweat more freely, and are much more amusing." The *Sun,* a Democratic journal since its founding, held a council of war on the contest and decided, over Gerald Johnson's protests, to support no one at all. Mencken cast the deciding vote and then stepped aside from his Monday space for Johnson's reply to the Sunday editorial attacking Roosevelt. That afternoon he and Johnson left Baltimore to join the Landon entourage. Mencken resurrected the old Corona, worked at breakneck speed throughout the trip, and astonished the junior reporters with his knowledge of nearly every local politician greeting the candidate. He was, as always, the confidant of every correspondent in a jam, spelling out names, spotting personages, and even filing copy for those behind in the edition scrambles. When the campaign ended at last in Portland and the starving press crew piled out of the train, he led them to the waterfront and an enormous platter of fried lobster. By then he was convinced of Landon's hopelessness, however, and for all his promise to nourish poor Alf in Baltimore with a terrapin and puddle duck dinner after the election—a promise fulfilled the following December—he was quite unamazed at the November verdict. "Our ignominious defeat is unquestionably due to our neglect of God's word," he wrote DeCasseres. "If we had prayed instead of boozing, Alf might be in the White House today, and you and I might be training for ambassadorships. As it is, we'll be lucky if we escape Alcatraz."

His great interest in the 1936 campaign was significant, and not only because of the preoccupation with politics it evinced. That trend had been in progress for fifteen years now and had nearly run its course, excluding all interests save those philological. Of more immediate interest was his relationship with the *Sun*. He had resolved, on his resignation from the *Mercury*, never again to enter the magazine field, except as an occasional contributor, and the newspaper provided him with his one regular forum. He seized upon it, giving himself increasingly to the consideration of what would benefit the papers, both in the daily news and in the somewhat more ethereal matters of policy. To his duties as board member were now added the functions of consulting editor in both the news and editorial departments. He kept himself informed on developments in the local scene, sent the paper tips on story possibilities, and maintained a genuine interest in the quality of writing in its columns. His advice in editorial matters was seldom followed, but when a topic particularly interested him, he was urged to write of it for the editorial page. The week of Landon's defeat he finished editing *The Sunpapers of Baltimore*, written in collaboration with Johnson, Kent, and Hamilton Owens, and, once the manuscript was on its way to Knopf, set about the drafting of a new constitution for Maryland. Every ten years the state has, under law, the opportunity to call a constitutional convention, and while the politicians always snub any attempt to change the existing document, the approaching end of each decade invariably brings a flurry of proposals from the politically conscious. Mencken's instrument, while hardly calculated to break that precedent, was nevertheless a sober, cogent draft, vastly superior to that on the books. There were a few Menckenian touches—the exclusion from the legislature of ministers, bankrupts past and present, anyone who had ever been a lunatic, and persons serving as lobbyists for five years preceding their candidacy—but the reforms, in the main, were logical. He would have abolished the bicameral legislature, set up in its stead a legislative council of fifteen members elected from the state at large, and wiped out the counties, substituting four districts. The voting age would have been raised to twenty-five, and a more drastic bill of rights, constitutional authority to social security schemes, and rational marriage and divorce laws were included. The Baltimore City Council would have been cut to nine members. Naturally, the constitution never got beyond the talking stage.

As a newspaper executive he entered into the powwows such mystics hold from time to time, addressing the bigwigs of the Associated Press and the American Society of Newspaper Editors and describing, invariably, the iniquities of editorial pages. He enthused about big news stories—Edward's abdication for a Baltimore girl was "the best story since the resurrection"—and sounded off to Patterson about this or that menace which needed exposing. Patterson's invariable reply was, "Expose it yourself." The trouble with this arrangement was that Mencken, when he set out with pencil and paper, was quite apt to succumb to the charm of him he attacked, and to end up praising the menace. Such was the fate of his ambitious series against Dr. H. C. "Curley" Byrd, president of the University of Maryland, the slickest and most active politician in the state for all his cloistered position. Mencken set out to track down Byrd in his lair. He wound up liking him enormously.

It was at about this time that American Newspaper Guild activity began to fever the city rooms of the two papers. The Guild won an election among the reporters handily, and Mencken, perhaps because of his outspoken opinions on the subject, inherited the role of company negotiator. His position, for all the vehemence with which it was expressed, was rather vague. The aims of the Guild he thought excellent; reporters, he had long believed, needed some sort of machinery to raise wages, secure tenure, and protect "their individual impudence." He went so far as to declare that had he been working on a newspaper when the union was organized, he would have been among the first to join. But—the Guild had fallen into the wrong hands, notably those of Heywood Broun, who lusted to be a mighty man and was probably a Bolshevik anyhow. It had become a conspiracy of the incompetent men against the management and the able reporters. Office boys, telephone operators, and girls who take want ads had joined its membership, and this was intolerable.

Mencken's basic argument against the Guild seems to have

been the forty-hour week. To him it was inconceivable that reporters should want to work eight hours a day and then quit. He had enjoyed his own reportorial days too much to understand men who preferred to leave a story at its height and go home. That, and a sense of shock that such a man as Broun should lead the union, conspired against the Guild's appeal to Mencken. Present-day reporters, he concluded, didn't want to be reporters at all. They would far rather be druggists. Wasn't it rumored that newspapermen had taken to wearing plus-fours and playing golf? Well, that was just obscene. "You can no more have a forty hour week for a reporter than you can have a forty hour week for an arch-bishop!" he cried. The negotiations, as a result, slowed down and ground to a halt. The Guild got no acceptable contract.

The peak of his *Sun* activity came in early 1938, when he assumed, for three months, the post of editor of the *Evening Sun*. John Owens had been elevated to editor-in-chief, executives were moving up all along the line, and the new *Evening Sun* editor was not ready to assume his duties. Mencken agreed to take over for February, March, and April. On May 8 the arrangement was to end. It was well that it was, for those three months were probably the most hectic the staid old editorial chambers had ever seen. He had long held pronounced views of what an editorial page should be, and into his temporary job he poured his tremendous energies, stored up during a West Indian cruise with August in early January. The trouble with editorials, he reasoned, was that they read like editorials. *Ergo:* to hell with them.

The first alarming product of this decision came on February 10, when a pressman picked the first edition off the press, started, and bounded upstairs, shouting, "Hey! What's the matter with the editorial page?" The bulk of the page, it seemed, was given over to a mass of tiny dots—1,000,075 dots to be exact, the number of Federal jobholders as of that morning. They had been produced, thirty-five hundred to a square inch, with what is known to commercial art as a Ben-Day screen. In column one appeared an explanatory editorial, written, of course, by Mencken. It was headed "Object Lesson." The page, he said, was too large for pasting in the hat; he advised his readers, as an alternative, to hang it between "The American's Creed" and the portrait of Mr. Roosevelt.

Next came the longest editorial in history—"Five Years of the New Deal"—sprawling across the entire page, written by Philip M. Wagner and Gerald Johnson, with a sour introduction and a conclusion by Mencken. It was impossible, his staff found, to get anything in the paper as written. Before an article was sent to the composing room, it first went under the editor's pencil, where enough Menckenese was injected to change the flavor of the entire argument. Any suggestion from his subordinates precipitated a terrific brawl. "Life with Mencken continues to be full of zowie," Robert Harriss, one of his assistants, wrote in his diary.

> Phil Wagner and I have frequent loud but good-natured arguments with him over the make-up of the editorial page. We had a really violent row today. He began waving his arms and bellowed: "No, *no* NO! You two are ganging up on me and by God I won't *let* you put that katzenjammer over on me!"

The chief sufferer, however, seems to have been Gerald Johnson, whose reputation as a scholar was by then clearly established. Two days after he had taken over, Mencken called Johnson in. "Look here," he said. "The prohibitionists are mobilizing for a big fight. I'm going to ask you to do an editorial every day. Not yet—read up on it first. Watch all these publications—" he named a list as long as his arm, including the *Congressional Record*—"and get ready. Don't do anything else. Just read." Johnson buried himself in prohibitionist and anti-prohibitionist literature and was ready to begin writing when, a week later, Mencken called him in again. "Look here," he began. "The conservationists are getting ready for a big show. I want you to do an editorial every day. Not right away. Start reading these periodicals—" "How about the prohibitionists?" asked Johnson. "Never mind that," Mencken replied. "Read about conservation. Don't do anything else." Another week passed, and another project for Johnson popped into Mencken's head. As it worked out, Johnson did no writing at all. He simply read, furiously, every obscure publication in the state of Maryland, waiting, grimly, for his next assignment.

At the end of three months, during which Nice Old Ladies bombarded the paper, protesting Mencken's reproduction of Max Broedel's gruesome drawing of a kidney-stone operation, and the City Council shrieked over Harriss' biting depiction of its huddles, Mencken doffed the Princeton beer jacket he had worn to the composing room each morning and the regime ended. He immediately adjourned to Johns Hopkins Hospital for a rest; his staff, unable to afford this luxury, sprawled weakly among the carnage of paste and copy paper, staring numbly at the walls.

On June 11 he sailed aboard the *Columbus* for Germany, his first trip there since the eve of his wedding. August expected to go along, but at the last moment, for some reason or other, he couldn't make it, and Mencken, as a result, was rather lonely during the six-week tour. He motored through East Prussia, visited Hindenburg's enormous tomb on the Tannenburg battlefield, and talked to German staff officers, who told him they could dispose of Russia's entire air force in a month. The political situation seemed to confuse him. From the Unter den Linden he wrote Patterson:

A good deal of the news emanating from Berlin seems to be bogus. The London Times has twice announced that its issues have been confiscated here, and yet I have bought it on the streets every day. The Moscow Pravda is openly for sale, and so are all the French papers. . . . I have kept away from newspaper men and official persons, and listened to actual Germans. The situation of the Jews is dreadful. They are no longer roughed, but the pressure on them is terrific. All decent Germans seem ashamed of the business. But they insist they must get out. Where they are to go is not mentioned. The American consulate is jammed every day.

He returned via the Rhine, convinced the unpleasantness would "never go beyond the making of faces."

The coming of war fascinated him, as it fascinated all Americans that year, and like everyone else, he had it all figured out—wrong. In article after article for the *Sun*, in statements to the Associated Press, and in public addresses he pooh-poohed an outbreak of hostilities. Germany had been peaceful as a church; the Russians were ill prepared for conflict; Hitler was a Ku Kluxer, but "the German army is still only half-organized, and will not reach anything like effective strength for at least three years." As for the English and French, the idea of war between them and the Nazis was simply insane. No one wanted it; who would start it? And this constant mauling of Hitler as a fee-faw-fum and the Germans as a race of wolves: it wasn't true, and what purpose did it serve? The plain fact was that they were all fee-faw-fums, all wolves, and the sooner that was admitted, the sooner some sort of solution could be reached. "The one gang, led by Hitler and Mussolini, is trying to chase England and France out of the Mediterranean and all the territory east of the Rhine and run both areas for themselves. The other gang, led by England and France, is trying to build a doghouse around them to keep them in it." It was as simple as that. Why the uproar?

At home he found the festivities of Martin Dies "and his goons" and Fritz Kuhn "and his Halloween Nazis" amusing, but he rather doubted that either had anything valuable to contribute to the country's culture. Roosevelt, it was true, was lobbying for a war to keep himself in power, but even Roosevelt should know that he would be re-elected anyway; that, indeed, it would take "the whole twelve apostles, working in eight-hour shifts like coal miners, to beat him." As for the debates between the America Firsters and the Anglophiles, he never listened to them. "The plain fact," he wrote Tully, "is that I am not a fair man and don't want to hear both sides. On all known subjects, from aviation to xylophone-playing, I have fixed and invariable ideas. They have not changed since I was four or five years old."

When news of the Berlin-Moscow pact broke he was "seized with a fit of mirth and could not be restored by the faculty for twenty-four hours. No better story has been loosed on the world since Apostolic times." And when the war actually began, he decided it was 1914 all over again, with Adolf

Hitler substituted for the Kaiser as chief villain. Hitler, he was convinced, had no designs on the United States, and an American citizen could therefore sit back and enjoy the hoop-la with impunity. As for the Poles, they were "a gang of brutal ignoramuses," fit only to "produce piano players." When France fell and the Nazis poised on the brink of the English Channel, he decided that perhaps England would be knocked off after all and that then there would be "a circus in the grand manner." America, he concluded, should seize Canada immediately. The entire British Empire was breaking up, it seemed, as surely as Rome had broken up. Once the English incubus had been got rid of, the world would go on peacefully. Then, just as the drama was reaching respectable proportions, Roosevelt horned in. Were there no limits to the efforts of this tin-pot messiah to save England from the law of selection?

The morning's news is that Roosevelt is openly shipping planes to the Allies. This, of course, is an act of war, and I assume that Hitler will be heard from. Thus the constitution is evaded once more, and the country is thrown into enormous hazard and expense by the act of one jackass.

In this frame of mind he packed himself off to the 1940 conventions. Willkie's nomination he found thrilling; it could have been accomplished, he decided, only with the aid of his old friend, the Holy Ghost. ("The event was shot through with evidences of a miracle. At one time I actually saw an angel in the gallery reserved for Philadelphia street railway curve-greasers. To be sure, the angel had on a palm beach suit, but nevertheless it was clearly an angel.") Roosevelt's triumph in Chicago was, of course, "obscene to the last degree," but that after all, was to be expected and even relished. Mencken spat on his hands, picked up his portable, and headed out to Louisville to join Willkie's campaign train, leaving instructions with Hergesheimer to stuff his carcass and place it in the national museum should he perish in the public service. Unfortunately, his patriotism was in vain. Willkie conducted "an almost incredibly ineffective campaign" and went the way of Landon in November. The stage was thus set for more paying of England's bills, more toting of the British slops.

For a time it looked as though the English, on the ropes, might leave Roosevelt holding the bag, and Mencken prepared to laugh himself to death. But just as the picture was beginning to brighten, the Japanese—a preposterous gang of whose existence, one feels, Mencken was never quite convinced—bombed Pearl Harbor. Barring intervention by the Ghost, he would probably be in the trenches in two weeks. Well, he would not repeat past mistakes. This time he would enlist in the Y.M.C.A.

The brothers Mencken lived quietly together in their old home, growing, their friends swore, to look more and more like one another. Once the house had been shaken down and the superfluous furniture disposed of, it became a functional, comfortable home ideally suited to the tastes of two serene and distinguished gentlemen, one widowed, one a bachelor. They saw eye to eye on everything of any importance, from the massive idiocies of the world to the cultivation of the crocuses in the back yard, and such social functions as they attended generally found them side by side: gracious, genial, and supremely temperate, as befitting their station. Their adventures were simple and of a pattern. Discovering, perhaps, a new and delectable rum punch, they would put up a jug, hail a hack, and ride out to Guilford to try it on Paul Patterson. Or they might attend the less demanding functions of August's tiny club on Hamilton Street, a pleasant little downtown byway which had somehow escaped the now sprawling business section and flourished quietly near Mount Vernon Place. Both loathed Christmas; they assured one another that the first man to think of bringing out a calendar leaving it unmarked would make a fortune, and in 1936, after spending the holidays together in the hospital, they decided it was the best Christmas within the recent memory of either. Both were hospitalized with increasing frequency, partly because of the advancing years, but largely because they had agreed that since neither was capable of nursing the other, the first alarming symptoms should send the victim to Johns Hopkins until he had recovered.

They vacationed together, on ocean cruises or, more frequently, in winter trips to Daytona Beach, Florida. There they lay on the sand, letting the sun bake the bacteria out of them, or wandered in the jungle behind the town, investigating the indescribable filth in which the crackers lived. August, more withdrawn than his older brother, always seemed on the point of retiring from society, and for several months late in 1937 he actually did, while working on a history of hangings. Mencken was then completing work on *The Charlatanry of the Learned*—the Leipzig lectures of Johann Mencken—and the brothers, each night after supper, rode down to the Peabody Library, August to dig after lurid details, Henry to read old German encyclopedias. After an evening of work they would retire to Schellhase's for a few peaceful beers. "It was a pleasant life, and my tracheitis gradually disappeared."

Mencken seemed to relax more in his personal habits; his tastes were passing from Brahms and Beethoven to Schubert and Strauss. Late in 1937 he joined the Maryland Club, the hangout of Baltimore's prosperous and retiring citizens, because, he said, he wanted a place to fête visiting friends. This astonished many who knew him well; it was unthinkable, they argued, that the old "Free Lance" should even be seen in the neighborhood of the club, and if he needed a place for entertainment, he surely need not have chosen *that* club. But he had reached an age where a man tires quickly, and it seemed less exhausting to dine where, at least, one need not be troubled by rebels. Besides, there were no women permitted in the club, and this tickled him. "It even refuses to employ charwomen. When one of the older members falls ill and a trained nurse is necessary he is thrown into the street."

His hair began to turn shortly after Sara's death and thinned on top, giving him, he advertised, the appearance of a man prepared for the electric chair. "Every now and then," he wrote, "I realize with a shiver that my own days on this earth are not likely to be greatly prolonged. I need not add that I look forward to the delights of Heaven without any doubts or fears. There are no pianos there. I shall probably take up one of the wind instruments, say, for example, the bassoon." One by one, his old friends were passing on—Max Broedel, Raymond Pearl, Phil Goodman, DeCasseres, Boyd —and each death was a terrific blow to one who valued his friendships so highly. "I am writing just after coming home from a funeral, which seems to be one of my principal occupations these days," he told Tully. "During the past six months I have actually lost nearly a dozen old acquaintances."

The central interests of his life—medicine and the farcical aspects of the American scene—continued undiminished. He read the *Journal* of the American Medical Association as assiduously as he had twenty-five years before, and in the fall of 1938 he actually traveled to Duke University in North Carolina, to argue before a medical symposium that failure to sterilize the unfit was brutally anti-social. The following month Orson Welles gave him one of the greatest thrills of his life with the Martian broadcast. The demonstration reinforced Mencken's belief that the American people were rapidly returning to the family of apes, and he spread it about that patients jumped out of windows at Johns Hopkins Hospital, that the Maryland Club was emptied in twenty-two seconds, that three members of the cabinet fainted in Washington, and that at Yale the broadcast broke up a Sunday-evening session of the Oxford Movement.

Week ends were spent with Dr. and Mrs. Hanes in North Carolina, with the Knopfs, and with the Hergesheimers. In Joe's guest house, he and Dr. Baker would rise, of a sunny spring morning, to discuss the glory of the day—and how it meant a decrease in immorality and an increase in automobile accidents—before breakfasting with the hosts and Marcella and Alfred Dupont, who were often present. He took to wearing loud striped pajamas whose clashing colors offended Knopf's sartorial sensibilities; these pajamas, and a predilection for sleeping later in the morning, were the only change in Mencken his out-of-town friends noted. But in Baltimore it was observed that he talked more often of the old days, when he was a boy and the city was free of industrialism.

He sought out Hamilton Owen's wife, who had lived opposite Union Square as a girl, to talk of bygone days in the now gently decaying neighborhod. He spun yarns of the old days in his father's tobacco business and reminisced. The *Herald* days took on overtones of old rose; "We were passing through Utopia, and didn't know it," he wrote Masters. With cronies of long standing, he attended the Rennert's last night, joining lustily in a chorus of "Auld Lang Syne." And when the hotel was being torn down, he stopped by the site daily to reflect bitterly that Baltimore's most charming hostel would soon be reduced to a parking lot. With a lesser man this deepening nostalgia would have merely signified the onset of senility. With Mencken it heralded a resurgence of his popularity.

His reputation had struck bottom in the two years which followed Roosevelt's re-election. It was in 1937 that he lectured before college students at Columbia and Yale who had never heard his name; that young intellectuals, reading Malcolm Cowley's *After the Genteel Tradition,* asked one another curiously, "Who's Mencken?" It was in that year he and Patterson, traveling through the West in a second Grand Tour, received scant notice in the press,[3] and it was in the year following that Angoff wrote his cruel "Mencken Twilight" for the *North American Review,* which the editors subtitled, with equal cruelty, "Another Forgotten Man—that enfant terrible of our Era of Nonsense." He was rarely heard from, save as the advocate of a Republican administration or the proposer of sterilization for the unfit, and only the fourth edition of *The American Language* received anything properly describable as a splash from literary editors. Even in Mississippi and Arkansas, it seemed, he was assumed to have died or become a convert.

---

[3] The Chicago *Tribune* did send a photographer to the railroad station, but the photographer had never heard of Mencken. Once the necessary business was over, he explained that in newspapers, pictures had what were known to the trade as "captions." If the gentleman would please tell him his home and occupation . . . Two hours later a glossy print was posted on the *Tribune's* art board. The legend read: "H. L. Mencken, Baltimore. A retired six-day bike rider."

So late as 1936, a writer first encouraged by Mencken won a Pulitzer Prize,[4] but this passed unnoticed by the literary chroniclers, who now knew him only as an "authority on the American language," never as a critic. As a critic, indeed, he appeared but once in these years, to castigate John Steinbeck in the *Sun* for ruining *The Grapes of Wrath*, "by inserting those *New Republic* editorials between the chapters." None of the authors popular with the intelligentsia appealed to him. Thomas Mann he could not read; Sandburg had made a mess of his Lincoln biography; Gertrude Stein had no ideas and could not express them; Henry Miller had a fantastic political credo. The New Deal had wobbled all such fellows, and they were no longer worth taking seriously. The literary business, indeed, was "wholly in the hands of radicals." Even James T. Farrell, whose craftsmanship Mencken admired enormously, and with whom he exchanged confidences about carbuncles and head infections, mystified him with his "political mission-arying." The basic trouble with the Thirties, he argued, was that its authors believed in the blah of their times, and no art could come from such a lamentable situation. Grant him this, and he was right. American literature had turned to economic, sociological analysis, to Lewis Mumford's *Culture of Cities*, to Hortense Powdermaker's *After Freedom*. These had re-placed the great writers of the Twenties as surely as Mencken, as a critic, had been replaced by such frumps as Oscar Cargill. More and Babbitt had died, and with them had passed the last glimmerings of the controversy which had stimulated the national letters. Sinclair Lewis was in a dreadful decline, Hergesheimer had given up writing, and Cabell was utterly unknown to a new generation. It was in 1938 that a Holly-wood producer, talking with a visitor from the East, mentioned Scott Fitzgerald. "Why, I thought he was dead," remarked the guest. "If that is so," replied the producer, "I've been paying $1,500 a week to his ghost."

Mencken read the current magazines carefully and indig-nantly. He grumbled over *Time's* inaccuracies, fretted over *The Reader's Digest's* incompetence, and pronounced it out-rageous that any periodical should keep a manuscript from

---

[4] H. L. Davis, for his novel *Honey in the Horn*.

four to six weeks before reading it. A few articles written by friends, especially doctors, were still edited privately. He was amazed to learn of the discourtesy shown authors. Even on the *Mercury*, it seemed, the old gallantry was gone. Only *The New Yorker* appealed to him. For Harold Ross and St. Clair McKelway he suggested profiles, cartoons, and articles, criticizing this department, praising that story. Significantly, it was *The New Yorker* which printed the first of the nostalgic sketches which were to resurrect the ghost of H. L. Mencken.

Shortly after his return to Hollins Street he had taken to watching schoolboys passing his wide front windows each morning, and contemplating his own boyhood days he had written two tales of long-gone Negro characters of his youth. These Ross printed. Mencken was no less pleased than were his readers, and early in 1939 he undertook to expand his reminiscences to book length. The spring and summer were not uneventful—in May he was temporarily disabled by lumbago; in June he covered the Indianapolis Townsend convention; in July he attended the American Youth Congress for the *Sun* and spent ten days in Johns Hopkins immediately thereafter—but the work was engaging, and it advanced steadily through this series of crises and adventures. *Happy Days* was rattled off at last in August, at Dr. Hanes' North Carolina mountain home, and published the following January. It did not, as Mencken wrote Dreiser, describe "my arrival in America from Poland, my early schooling in a Hebrew school in New York, and my gradual conversion to Christianity." Instead, as nearly all its reviewers noted, it was an effective picture of universal boyhood, the balanced chronicle of childhood for which a world infected by an overdose of sociology had long been clamoring. It sold very well, and Knopf began agitating for a series of decade-by-decade reminiscences. Mencken balked at this—his teens, he pointed out, were serious years, and could not be treated lightly—but he did agree to write up his days on the *Herald*.

Unfortunately, there were other fagots in his rolling mill. In November, he had begun the sorting of some thirty thousand quotations gathered through the years, with the view of rendering Bartlett obsolete. He had a schedule of speaking engagements at Columbia and Harvard, Virginia Mencken's marriage was coming up, and Roosevelt was on his mind. The second volume of his memoirs, together with the quotation book, was thus put off indefinitely. It might, indeed, have remained in the foetal stage permanently, so absorbed was he in the kaleidoscopic political scene, had not history, repeating itself monotonously that eventful year, intervened. The *Sun*, Mencken's outlook notwithstanding, was growing more and more excited about developments in Europe and was, indeed, advocating American intervention in the war. His vilifications of England, printed beside Duffy's cartoons and the feverish editorials, were as absurd as "The Free Lance" had been twenty-five years before, and it became rapidly evident, even to Mencken, that he would soon have to shut down. Appreciating the *Sun's* position, he went to Patterson and resigned, not only from his literary chore, but from his role as advisor to the news and editorial departments as well. Patterson refused to accept a complete withdrawal. Mencken protested that to remain would be an affectation. He could not, he argued, accept any responsibility for the editorial page. Finally they agreed he should remain as news consultant, and Mencken, over Patterson's protest, insisted on drawing only half his previous salary.

These very civilized negotiations were completed in early January, and Mencken, for the umptieth time in his life, was out of a job. His affections were evenly split between his reminiscences and quotations, and he therefore decided "heroically but idiotically" to do them both at once. Through February and March he struggled along, expanding the fragmentary *Newspaper Days* and sorting and classifying the biblical quotations, proverbs, and retranslations of old saws that were to go into the dictionary. By late May he was in a terrific lather. Knopf and *The New Yorker* were calling for the *Herald* sketches, long delayed; he was making the final arrangements for Virginia's wedding—Charlie was in Ohio, and his duties thus fell on his older brother—and he pushed himself too hard. On April 19 he wound up, flat on his back, in Johns Hopkins Hospital, the victim of sheer exhaustion. His doctors advised him to rest, and so he embarked for Havana on a United Fruit steamer at the end of the month. August, unfortunately, was laid up with a severe case of laryngitis and could not go. In Cuba Mencken recuperated rapidly. He powwowed with a bartender of enlightened ideas, attended the Havana Philharmonic, and sat fascinated through a rollicking performance of *Carmen*, watching the girls "throwing their ramparts all over the stage." He even attended a bullfight. At the last minute a municipal edict forbade the killing of the bulls, but he went along anyhow and enjoyed himself enormously. ("Inasmuch as the bulls will still be free to kill the fighters, I shall be in attendance.") After a week of this, he was in the best of spirits. He returned via Miami—"I have seen Jerusalem, and may as well see Miami"—and arrived in Baltimore looking like a fried tomato. For a week he peeled painfully, and his shredded skin, for some curious reason, delighted him no end. "My sunburn is wearing off," he wrote Hergesheimer, "though several hard patches of skin are still hanging loose. I hope to have them glued back with Duco, and in a week or two I should be restored to my usual loveliness."

Once back, he made short work of the reminiscences. By late July the galley proofs were in the mail to Knopf and the first sheets for the quotation book were arriving at Hollins Street. Until November these kept him at his desk, bitterly complaining that he should have stayed in his father's tobacco business, and declaring, frequently and emphatically, that all authors were, by definition, lunatics. That fall the book reviewers fell on *Newspaper Days* with a sentimental sob, writing ecstatically of its charm and dragging in, whenever possible, stories from their own golden reportorial days from which, the reader was frequently reminded, modern journalism had strayed so far. Young reporters in the *Sun* city rooms read it feverishly, dreaming of the days when the city was colorful and journalism had oomph. But one critic protested. Frank Kent, completing the chapter on "A Girl from Red Lion, P.A.," buttonholed the author in a corridor. "Henry," he demanded, "why do you tell lies like that?" "Well," Mencken said defensively, "it made a good story, didn't it?"

The heavier quotation book came out the following April and was similarly acclaimed, though most reviewers regretted the lack of an index. It was his autobiographical books which really radiated appeal, however, and they cried for more. "If

Mr. Mencken doesn't continue with vols. III., IV., V. and so on, of his memoirs he will be guilty of a major crime," declared the New York *Times*. The book sold very well, though not quite as well as *Happy Days*, and Knopf promoted a third in the series. Mencken was certainly nostalgic enough. Shortly after completion of his childhood memoirs, he and August explored the Union Square neighborhood and Ellicott City, photographing hundreds of well-remembered spots, and these pictures were bound in a scrapbook as a companion to the original typescript. Goodman's daughter, failing to find a publisher for her father's posthumous memoirs, sent them to Mencken, and he, delighted, shaped them into *Franklin Street*, which Knopf brought out in 1942. The completion of *Newspaper Days* had by no means slaked his thirst for this sort of thing; he began to dictate more reminiscences, and by October Rosalind Lohrfinck had taken down one hundred fifty thousand words of these. *Heathen Days*, the third and last of the trilogy, was therefore spun out easily. The end of the trilogy brought him a tremendous sense of relief: "I feel like the mother of the Dionne quintuplets—that is to say, I am happy but hollow."

It also brought his reborn popularity to a new crest. Joseph Wood Krutch compared him to Swift—the comparison was twenty years old, but no one seemed to remember that—and added: "Time has served only to perfect a style which was always robust and exuberant, but which has grown with the years better balanced and better integrated until it has achieved now an almost classical perfection without losing its individuality." Gray-haired insurance salesmen recalled their faraway college days, when hip flasks, flaring trousers, and H. L. Mencken were the marks of an educated man. They remembered him now without bitterness, with only affection, and he prospered quite as much on their nostalgia as on his own. From the foxholes of New Guinea came franked postcards: young GI's, meeting for the first time the Lorelei who had lured their fathers, wrote him: they wanted more Mencken. And Mencken, who had almost forgotten what it was to be hymned by a younger generation, promised beer to his admirers on their return, observing that this enterprise would probably put him in debt, but that he did not care:

debt was the only commodity on which a man did not have
to pay taxes. The customers were settling down once again.
The graph was swinging up from its long dip.

The war years were spent quietly at Hollins Street, dictat-
ing philological notes to Mrs. Lohrfinck, polishing up his
obituary of Paul Patterson, or simply sitting by the front
window, watching the children at play in Union Square.
When the rush of domestics to war industry began, he was
certain the house would be without servants and that he and
August would be reduced to eating in Greek restaurants and
sleeping in dirty beds. But Hester and Emma stayed on
loyally, and save for the mitigation of his *Sun* duties, life
went on much as before. He still rose at 8, breakfasted lightly,
read his voluminous mail, and lunched at home. Afternoons
he dropped by the *Sun* to chat with Patterson, disclaiming,
always, any knowledge of the war's progress. The late afternoon and early evening were taken up with writing; two or
three nights a week he drank beer with the small corps of
friends who had survived to his age. Saturday nights still
found him with the Club over Hildebrand's violin shop, with
adjournment, as always, at Schellhase's. Hildebrand himself
was long dead, Mencken was the last charter member alive,
and the newer members were somewhat awed by the tangle
of legends which had grown up around him. But the relaxa-
tion of music was still priceless. He never missed a meeting,
was always the first to arrive, and threatened, indeed, to get
out writs against those who were tardy. When a member's
birthday rolled around, it was Mencken who remembered and
struck up "Happy Birthday to You"; when the old piano became dilapidated, he it was who arranged for a new one—
after solemnly proposing that the money be raised through a
series of bingo games.

Save for an occasional trip to Pittsburgh or to Gertrude's
farm in western Maryland, where he chopped wood and
battled furiously with summer chiggers, his routine had
solidified beyond hope of change. Special occasions were
spent in the same manner, year after year: Christmas evening always found him tottering up the front steps of Gerald
Johnson's home, clutching a bottle of rare liquor in his chubby

fist and insulting his host cheerfully at the door. ("Where'd you get that jacket? You look like the Whore of Babylon!") New Year's Eve he arrived at Maclean Patterson's annual party to welcome what would be, he promised, the worst year the world had yet seen. Time had not diminished his courtesy with women nor age the brightness of his eye. He remained the gallant, the cultured gentleman whose distinctive little notes followed each invitation promptly and whose bouncey personality assured the success of any occasion. "If I'm still alive and not in jail, I'll certainly be delighted to stop in on you," he would write in the return mail, or "Unless the Heavenly Father plays one of his frequent jokes on me, I'll certainly present myself at your house on December 31." Only sometimes the parties wearied him, and on one New Year's Eve the host, searching everywhere for his prize guest, found him in an upstairs room with little Tina Patterson, gravely teaching her to play the piano, oblivious to the orgies below.

Three times a year he rode up to Stone Harbor, New Jersey, to the pleasant little seaside house where Hergesheimer, feeling the pinch of nonproductivity, had moved, there to palaver with Joe and Dorothy of the great days that had passed for all of them. On the steps he would embrace Dorothy, present her with a fifth of Maryland rye, and vigorously denounce her husband as unworthy of her. Then he would wander out on the shore, alone, perhaps, to collect seashells for his little great-nephew, or with Huntington Cairns, another frequent guest, to discuss life among the crustaceans. After a nap and an evening of conversation, he would retire to his room, appearing, fleetingly, in his outrageous pajamas of electric red, violet blue, or absolute purple, only to be ordered back sharply by Dorothy: "You're a bad boy! Go to bed!" And back to his room he would paddle heavily, a stocky little figure in a rainbow suit, chuckling softly to himself. In the morning he was at his best, raving about the glory of the day and of Dorothy's cooking: "What a wonderful egg! Dorothy, where did you get that egg? Huntington, look at that! Great God! Joe, look at that!" And this enthusiasm, this wonder at the universe, would continue, undiminished, all the way back to Baltimore, along the depressing ride from Philadelphia: "Look at that cow! Look at that barn! My God, what a tree!"—the irrepressible outcry of a spirit to whom all of life remained a magnificent mystery, a colossal performance whose flavor had grown only the more tasty with the years.

The last and, to his old admirers, most satisfying product in Mencken's nostalgia was his reunion with Nathan. It was the only time in his life he ever took up the broken threads of a friendship, and it can be simply explained: there was too much to talk over. They drifted together gradually—a letter here, a chance meeting there, and finally planned week ends, as in the old days. Nathan still lived in his quaint apartment in West Forty-fourth Street; he had, indeed, refused to let the management of the Royalton paint it, and its tapestried, mask-bedecked walls leered as weirdly at Mencken now as they had thirty-five years before, when two callow young critics met to dissect their elders and enthuse about Shaw, Ibsen, and Conrad. Nathan had changed little, Mencken found; his hair was gray and his face slightly lined, but he still looked far younger than he was, and his sartorial correctness had not lessened one whit. As in the First World War, as it was now called, he vaguely admitted there was some unpleasantness abroad, but he did not permit it to interfere with his beloved theater. The *rapprochement* between the two was relatively simple, since Nathan had never admitted that any real difference existed between them. To Luchow's, then, they went, as before; customers at their old haunts blinked and looked again sharply, unwilling, at first, to acknowledge that these ghosts from a bygone day could be real. Yet real they were, and functioning, as Henry Seidel Canby found when he thought to drop by for a whimsical chat. "My God!" they chorused. "Are *you* still around?" Canby admitted that he was. "You look terrible," said Mencken. "So do you," replied Canby, defensively. "We always look terrible," Nathan put in, philosophically. Mencken pulled at his Uncle Willie. "What jackass theories," he croaked, "are you behind now?" Canby excused himself.

Their conversation now was marked by a curious avoidance of any major subject; as Nathan had observed in his *Notebooks,* "the four-handed scherzo that we used to play vivacissimo together on the barroom piano of life has become for him—as, I suspect, for me as well—rather more suggestive of a Ländler waltz." There were no editorial decisions to ponder; Harry Kemp was not pestering them for money; Dreiser was not around to plague them with his one-act dramas of the supernatural; the comstocks were not pounding at the door. This saddened Nathan, whose heart was in the old *Smart Set* and who keenly felt the lack of a decent magazine in the Forties. But not Mencken. The past, he acknowledged, had been extremely edifying, but he would not revive it if he could. It was pleasant to dream of the old days only so long as one did not believe that by dreaming one could bring them back or even make their return desirable. His views on literature were steadfast: no authors and no criticism were allowed. Dining one evening with Nathan, he received, via a waiter, a note from Charles Jackson, sitting across the room. Jackson wanted to join them. Mencken vetoed the request. "He just wants me to tell him how much I liked his book," he told Nathan, "and I haven't even read it."

He was as drawn by the medicine of his fabulous body as he had been when Nathan first met him, and to the routine descriptions of a bloodstream so full of vaccines that he gurgled as he walked were now added an anticipation of the coroner's professional interest. He proceeded, he assured everyone, into senility with unbroken steadiness and would be, before long, a cherub, singing by the throne. "On gloomy days I can hear the rustle of angels' wings, and sometimes I can smell the angels. They smell a good deal like ordinary barnyard fowl, but rather somewhat more pungent. Their pungency, I suspect, is due to overtones of incense." In his declining years, he announced, he was devoting himself to theology, and it is certainly true that the fascination religion had always held for him increased. The Holy Ghost was constantly inspiring him, advising him, punishing him, or simply getting in his way, and the Father and the Son were present also. Borrowers of books were reminded that the penalty for failing to return them was set forth in the book of Leviticus; when Maclean Patterson married, he was presented an enormous copy of the Bible, on the ground that a home without the Book was hardly more than a den of infidels. Even a punch recipe could not go without a suggestion to help it along with a reading from the Scriptures. "The second chapter of I Chronicles, verses 10-41 seems to have a good effect upon the coagulation of the colloids. I have also got good results from Revelation XIII, verses 1-13, inclusive. It does no harm to add a hymn, say, 'Throw Out the Lifeline.' " When he became godfather to Maclean's little girl, he took his duties with great seriousness, announcing that he was, in preparation for the task, increasing his daily reading of the Good Book from ten chapters to twenty-five. When she was six, little Tina received a prayer book for Christmas, and he was forever apologizing for his laxity in instructing her in Christian principles. His very evenings with August, to believe him, were spent in solemn prayer.

His attitude toward the war was perhaps the most unrealistic in the country. Nathan ignored the war: Mencken played with it, but found himself unable to take even the gravest development seriously. "I had a dream last night in which I saw an army of 100,000 angels descending upon England to save it," he wrote Tully. ". . . Some of the angels were colored, but the majority were white." It was the war in the Pacific, however, which engaged him most. He could not bring himself to fear or even respect the Yellow Peril. He was constantly sending out bulletins announcing that the streets of Baltimore were swarming with Japanese spies, that he was afraid to go out into the streets, that only yesterday a couple of them had tried to burn down a brewery, and that their troops had reached Garrett County in western Maryland and were marching eastward at the rate of one hundred miles a day. On the backs of his envelopes were pasted stamps depicting servicemen marching against a star-studded field of red, white, and blue, advising the correspondent to "Read the Bible: the Sword of the Spirit," or to "Stand by the Bible, the Christian—the American Way." Occasionally he grumbled about the pantywaist vocabulary of the GI's, but his chief objection to the war, it seemed, was its influence on Baltimore, now teeming with transient war workers. The old Baltimore, he observed, was falling to pieces, and in its place had come a society overrun with sharecroppers from the Carolinas and hillbillies from the Appalachian chain. "They are really almost incredibly barbaric. In the slums where I live they are increasing steadily, and in a little while life will become almost impossible." The effects of these peasants on the town morality were especially deplored: "The police report that 1765 girls under 16 were put to the torture [venery] between January 1 and January 15. Of these, fully eighty per cent liked it so well that they are now leading lives of shame." Periodically he pined for the draft or hoped these numskulls would be eliminated by fire engines, ambulances, and beer trucks during one of the city's blackouts, but no relief arrived. In the end he became despondent and planned to retire to a monastery in southern Maryland, there to devote what was left of his life to engraving the Lord's Prayer on the heads of pins.

As in 1917–18, he declined to write for the magazines, convinced that the official and unofficial censorship would conspire to keep his most cherished opinions out of print, as they doubtless would have. "I'll simply wait, as I did the last time," he wrote. "As the fever wore out my chance came." He appeared but rarely in public; save for one brief speech on the retirement of Baltimore's Judge Eugene O'Dunne and an adventure at the theater when Dorothy Gish was in town —he wore a boiled shirt and looked precisely like a bouncer —he was absent from all civic functions. It seemed more pleasant, while hostilities lasted, to sweat over his language notes, stuffing an envelope with odds and ends for the Pratt Library, or to entertain his relatives—Virginia Mencken, perhaps, with her two-and-a-half-year-old son. He still paid his respects to the *Sun* and the Maryland Club, of course, but he took scant chance of recognition in strolling down Charles Street at even its busiest hour. While most literate Baltimoreans knew his name, few had seen him in the flesh, and it was highly unlikely that the crowds swarming along the narrow sidewalks would recognize the florid little man who dodged furiously among them, consulting the timepieces in each jewelry window, digging out his watch on the run as he neared the dingy Sun Building, as the most famous of the town's citizens.

Just as he had begun to give up hope of ever escaping a world in which the English were worshiped as "great moral engines," just as he had reconciled himself to retiring on the dole, the war ended. V-J Day came at an auspicious time: *Supplement I, The American Language* was in Knopf's offices, ready for publication, and if there were, as he believed, elaborate parallels between the two World Wars, he was well equipped to meet and ride with the stupendous reaction which was bound to come. He had begun work on the supplement the day after the quotation dictionary was published and had poured into it the same channeled energy which had produced its predecessor in 1918. As always, he belittled his work in American speechways, commenting that it was inspired by the *Congressional Record* and that if anyone else wanted the job, he would be delighted to turn it over to him. A few crusty professors still held out against the series, and he docilely agreed with them. "Experts like Kemp Malone at Hopkins wouldn't be interested in my stuff, and they're right," he told Cairns. "It's just journalism." The reviewers, as always, disagreed with him. Edmund Wilson heralded the supplement as the most readable *Language* installment yet; the New York *Times* gave it an enormous spread, and tank town papers which had forgotten him in the Thirties dredged up old memories and boomed him mightily. Inaugurated by the success of the *Days* books, a genuine Mencken revival, it seemed, might be in the making. Roosevelt was dead, all politicians were unpopular once more, and the returning veterans were, if anything, more disillusioned than their fathers had been.

In its fashion, the revival prospered, abetted by the publishing, in 1946, of his whimsical little sketch *Christmas Story*. The intelligentsia was more aware of him than it had been since the crash, and certainly he was again news. When he filed suit against a neighbor for harboring a dog whose barking was "abnormally and extraordinarily harsh, penetrating, violent, unpleasant and distracting," thereby interfering with the pursuit of his professional livelihood, the press displayed it happily. And when a Canadian film company, in return for rights to the Bathtub hoax, agreed to send him a case of ale a week for life, the contract made front pages everywhere. For the first time since the depression, Mencken was sympathetic with the tastes of a respectable number of people.

Toynbee, from the beginning of his remarkable vogue, had Mencken's enthusiastic support, and veterans of the Pacific war found it refreshing to discover someone who would denounce MacArthur for the impostor he was and is. MacArthur, to Mencken, was what Attorney-General Mitchell Palmer had been twenty-five years before—an enemy of civil liberties, a coward wreaking vengeance on an opponent who had beaten him in a fair fight at Bataan.[5] The Congressional Library became interested in a long recording of his voice for posterity; a swarm of graduate students wrote theses on his contributions to literature and philosophy and found him hospitable to overtures; *Life* published a profile of him, and even *Life's* incestuous sister *Time* recognized Mencken as news once again and informed its Baltimore correspondent that any items about him were eminently acceptable. Knopf brought out a new edition of *Treatise on the Gods;* his Canadian publishers moved to withdraw *Christmas Story* on the ground that it was sacrilege; *The New Yorker,* in on the ground floor, signed a contract with him for more articles. And Mencken, alternating between benadryl and penicillin cures for hay fever, began to get interested. Business was perking up.

It perked up even more in the spring of 1948, when *Supplement II* was published, and he began to work seriously on his own variations of a project Knopf had long proposed. It was to be an anthology, though not, as Alfred had conceived it, a gathering of others' writings which had appealed to its editor. This arrangement of an old theme had little attraction. Instead, Mencken proposed to go through his own out-of-print books and periodical articles to dig out the juiciest passages. Starting with his first *Smart Set* criticism, he culled the millions of words he had written on every conceivable subject, setting them up in the greatest scissors-and-paste job of them all. Interestingly enough, he ignored the

[5] When MacArthur ruled that only religious works could be sent to Japan, Mencken succeeded, through the press, in getting the ban lifted. "Bombarding the poor Japs with Christian propaganda is really too much," he remarked. "The enterprise has probably convinced them, and on sound ground, that the United States is not and never will be a really civilized country."

vast and impressive accumulation of prophecies in his magazine work before 1914, when, warring on the mewling, sterile
authors of "glad" books, he had fashioned the ark which
carried him so far and so high a decade later. From this
period he chose but one paragraph, an eulogy of *Huckleberry
Finn,* and a few epigrams. With this lonesome but Himalayan
exception, the book was representative of the mass of contributions forgotten by all save his greatest admirers. The
title proved something of a problem. Knopf objected to *A
Mencken Chrestomathy* on the ground that no one would
understand it, and Mencken could not stomach omnibus,
reader, treasury, miscellany, panorama, or portable. Finally
Nathan suggested a solution. "Ask him," he told Mencken
"about my *Autobiography of an Attitude.*" Mencken did, and
Knopf, remembering his objection to the title of that memorable book and its success despite his protests, acceded. *A
Mencken Chrestomathy* it was to be. The cover picture was
to be of Mencken holding *Language* proofs, standing by one
of Sara's old glass bells.

Late in 1947 the Pattersons, father and son, began a campaign to get him to cover the 1948 political conventions for
the *Sun.* He rejected the idea violently. The paper had, over
his strenuous protests, set up a television station, and it stuck
in his craw. "I quit writing for the *Sun* in January, 1941,
and it is highly improbable that I'll resume for the two
conventions," he wrote Maclean. "Thus you had better chalk
me off. I am beginning to yearn for television. In a little
while you'll hear and see me crooning." Privately he grumbled
that he had been driven from the paper twice by world savers
and he would not, no he *would not* go back again. Actually,
he pined for the convention press stalls, as everyone on the
paper well knew. Shortly after Taft announced his candidacy,
he showed up in the office wearing an enormous button bearing the legend "Taft for President," which, under close inspection, turned out to be a souvenir of the convention of
1908. Paul Patterson was particularly anxious he should cover
the Progressive convention, which was certain to match the
imbecilities of the Townsend slapstick, and so he pressed
the point vigorously. Mencken continued to refuse, though

his defenses were obviously weakening. "Alas and goddam, but I fear that one all-night session—and the Democrats always have them—would deliver me to the Pathology Department. Better not count on me." Then, while he was in New York, a *Herald Tribune* columnist brought up the conventions. Mencken insisted he did not want to go, but he added: "I'll probably end up by going and blowing up and coming home on a shutter. Oh, well. It's a heroic death." The Pattersons redoubled their efforts, and finally, after long coaxing, he agreed to tag along if Paul would go. Dr. Baker was called in for advice, and he prescribed that since the conventions were to be in Philadelphia, two hours away, he might attend with impunity. Once this drawn-out but very necessary business had been gone through, Mencken looked forward to the coming summer eagerly. "Either they'll restore me, or they will kill me," he wrote Hergesheimer gleefully.

He arrived early, according to his custom, and moved through the great hall, watching the workmen haul in the trappings for the circus, buttonholing policemen and doormen as Max Ways had taught him nearly fifty years before. In the past he had always devoted most of his time before the opening to gabbing with the band, but this time there was a new and even more absurd wrinkle on the convention face: television. He sat fried in the lights, fascinated, his horn-rimmed glasses on his nose, his mouth open in amazement, while a featured comedian tried to teach a pugilist to say "How now, brown cow?" punching him all the while. It was Harding all over again—too good to be true. And as the Dewey glad-handers rushed from corridor to corridor, sewing up the nomination, Mencken happily set his typewriter up on his bureau, slipped in a sheet of copy paper, and rapped off his first dispatch:

Philadelphia, June 19—The traditional weather of a national convention began to clamp down upon Philadelphia last night. It started with a thunderstorm so vociferous that the sound seemed to be coming through the loudspeaker of the convention hall, and it continued today with a rising temperature, very high humidity, and lazy puffs of gummy wind from the mangrove swamps surrounding the city.

The heat really was outrageous. The *Sun* crew had just finished congratulating itself on its air-conditioned quarters, however, when Mencken began to feel the approach of a summer cold. Turn the damned thing off, he demanded. And turned off it was, to the horror of everyone but him. Unfortunately, this did not solve the problem. The cold arrived, in force, and he was obliged to retire to Baltimore halfway through the convention. He was back for Truman's show, however, sweating lustily in his tightly buttoned seersucker suit and pecking away rapidly, "end lead, Mencken pick up, 1st add beginning: The walkout of the Alabamans," and so on. The Democratic split delighted him, but an even better performance was waiting in the wings: the Wallace convention. Together with Westbrook Pegler he ganged up on friendly Henry in a press conference until Henry, no longer friendly, left the interview in a frightful tizzy. Mencken's reporting of the Wallaceites, as Patterson had anticipated, was his best of the season, and was, indeed, among the best he had ever done.

The Progressive Party of Maryland thought otherwise. Its leaders drew up a resolution declaring that he had made "Hitlerite references to the people of this convention. Mr. Mencken Red-baits, Jew-baits, and Negro-baits." After a number of whereases pronouncing that his articles had demonstrated that "the fighting spirit of brotherhood and equality" was entirely lost to him, that he had resorted to "un-American slander of the people of this convention," and that his "obscenities against the American people mark him as unfit to report the proceedings of a people's convention," this illustrious document reached the splendid climax: "Therefore be it resolved by the delegates here assembled, That this convention severely censures H. L. Mencken and his contemptible rantings which pass for newspaper reporting." Mencken danced about happily, following the resolution's progress, and none of its authors was more disappointed than he when the convention chairman refused the motion on the ground that it would start a flood of such denunciations. He had so hoped it would get through.

He assuaged his grief the last night of the convention,

when Patterson, who kept him away from the hurly-burly of all three performances, let him go. It was like the old days, with Landon, Roosevelt, Smith, Cox, Wilson, Taft, and Bryan. They phoned for beer and sandwiches, sang the catchy Wallace songs, and gassed until 4 in the morning. At about that time Patterson heard some Wallaceites singing across the street and sent someone out to ask them to join the *Sun* men. Everyone promptly forgot about this, and when, a half hour later, the door opened and a pleasant, buxom woman followed by several teen-agers and a dour-faced man strolled in, everyone was naturally surprised. "Someone you wanted to see?" asked Patterson. "Who," demanded the dour-faced man, "are you?" "We are representatives of the capitalist press," answered Patterson. A long and unpleasant silence followed, and the meeting was about to break up on this unhappy note when someone, catching sight of the *Sun's* envoy, suddenly broke into "Hen-ry Wallace, Friend-ly Hen-ry Wallace," and the ice was broken. In the singing that followed, Mencken was utterly in his element. He gathered all present into one group, posed as an orchestra leader, and exhorted them through chorus after chorus, winding up at last with a final beery rendition of "Maryland, My Maryland." He arrived home next day exhausted but supremely content. He could not remember when he had had so much fun.

He had passed the barnstorming age and thus had to leave the campaign coverage to younger men. But whenever a candidate was in town, he was certain to be on hand to cover the speech. The more preposterous the politician, the more eager he was to have at him. Barkley, whom he considered the most feeble-minded man to run for national office in modern history, was tracked across Baltimore, and J. Strom Thurmond was superb. ("It was the first time in many years that any force of Confederates had invaded the Baltimore area. In fact, it hadn't happened since July, 1864, when Col. Harry Gilmore and his cavalry swooped down on the Glenn L. Martin plant, and scared a great many Baltimoreans out of year's growth.") When Thurmond rattled off at last, and the knot of elderly ladies who had turned out to hear him filtered out of the Lyric Theater, Mencken was as disappointed as the policemen who had turned out in force in hopes that the Wallace boys might show up to pay back a certain debt of eggs and tomatoes, and who had departed earlier, "to resume their weary hunt of murderers." He also wrote several short treatises on Truman's remarkable campaign, setting everyone gasping by proposing that the atom bomb be dropped on the Russians and defending the extraordinary summer performance of the Un-American Activities Committee.[6]

Truman's election he thought the funniest thing that had ever happened. As was his practice, he listened to election returns in the *Sun* office, which was equipped with a great bulletin board on which results were chalked. Hamilton Owens' editorials analyzing the Republican victory were in type and of the decision, of course, there was no doubt. Then the incredible began to happen, and Mencken, sitting among his colleagues, began to feel and share "the same tremors and tickles that ran up and down their vertebrae." When, next day, the astounding show was over, he was overcome by paroxysms of mirth—a mirth which the other elders at the paper could scarcely share. That week he rode up to Philadelphia to address the American Philosophical Society. Truman's election, he declared, was mathematically and humanly impossible, yet it had happened. He hoped to participate in the coroner's inquest to determine why. Then he let go in the old Mencken manner—the manner of one delighted with, and entranced by, the absurdities he loved to hate:

> You may gather from what I have said that I have certain doubts about the democratic process—that I believe it adds to the immemorial curse of government by loading it with too many dubious and nefarious men. This, I regret to have to say, is a fact. But don't expect me to do any-

[6] It is difficult to take this seriously. Even when Landon's campaign and Mencken's interest in it were at their height, he had scoffed at the Red menace. His position, with the above exception, was always that there were no communists in the country, save in New York, where at least half the population, including the children, was infected.

thing about it. When it comes to matters of state, I am a pathologist, not a chiropractor.

On November 24 he was to have lunch at the Maryland Club with Evelyn Waugh. Waugh had never met him, but he was anxious to, and had made overtures while visiting the president of a Jesuit College in Baltimore. This ecclesiastic was to serve as Waugh's second; Mencken's was to be an *Evening Sun* reporter. The evening before, Mencken brought a manuscript to Rosalind Lohrfinck. As they sat, chatting idly over a cocktail in her apartment, she noticed he was behaving a trifle oddly. Suddenly, in the midst of a perfectly lucid sentence, he began to babble incoherently. She, alarmed, called Dr. Baker immediately. When Baker arrived, fifteen minutes later, Mencken was greatly agitated; he referred to the doctor as Stalin and talked wildly of Roosevelt. Baker decided not to call an ambulance, since he would have objected to that. After a time they quieted him down and helped him down the elevator to the doctor's car. Lingerers in the lobby of the building thought they were merely taking a liquefied old gentleman home. They wished it were that simple.

He had been stricken by a cerebral thrombosis, affecting his speech center and paralyzing his entire right side. His condition was critical. Baker doubted he would live.

At Johns Hopkins Hospital, the paralysis spread rapidly. He hovered in great pain at the threshold of death for a week; then, slowly, he began to improve. The improvement was slow and limited in scope. The disability in his right side eased gradually, and, after a month and a half of extensive treatment, left his arm and leg completely. But his speech center remained affected, and he could neither write nor read. For several sentences he might talk quite coherently; then the rest of his message would be senseless. The remembrance of names, dates, and specific events in their entirety was completely beyond him. Nevertheless, by Christmas he had so convalesced he was taken home. August had fashioned a little gate across the third-floor stair, against the possibility he might awake at night, walk to the landing, and topple down the flight. This proved unnecessary; he slept soundly

Physically he was depleted, but he could handle himself adequately about the house and in the garden, and with sufficient rest it seemed likely he would soon recapture his old vigor. That was not the problem.

The great tragedy of his situation was that everything which had given life meaning for him was gone. Since his boyhood days the pattern of his life had built around the reading of the written word and the expression of his reflections. For sixty years, since his discovery of "The Moose Hunters," the cultivation of that expression had been the moving purpose of his life, and he had developed it to an art unmatched in his time. Now that was impossible, and he was left to vegetate back to a robust physical health with the purposes of his very being withdrawn. It was a terrible blow, and he was the first to recognize its magnitude. Dumbly he sat by his books, with the faithful August hovering near, assaying his difficulty and searching for a solution which remained elusive. Mrs. Lohrfinck dealt with the flood of correspondence which still came to Hollins Street, explaining that he could not, for the present, answer letters, and discouraging further mail. Visitors were rare. He saw only his oldest friends, and when Waugh, returning to Baltimore in March, again asked for a meeting, he was politely told that Mencken's health simply would not permit it. For the first time within the memory of anyone at the *Sun* he did not drop by each afternoon to dance his little jig by the editorial offices and plague Patterson with barbed comments on the day's paper. Since he could not hold his own in repartee, it seemed, he did not want to see people. He tried to tell Patterson, during an evening at home, of the great services Mrs. Lohrfinck had done for him. He threw up his hands in despair. "She's been my secretary for twenty years," he cried, "and I can't remember her name." "I've known her as long as you have," Patterson replied, "and I can't remember it either."

It was the very thing he had worked all his years to prevent, and now it had happened he was lost. Shadows had been cast before. On April 12, 1938, though he was unaware of it at the time, he had suffered a slight coronary thrombosis. This omen, far darker than it was thought to be, was swift, fleeting, scarcely discernible; it was gone before it could be properly assessed. But in December, 1940, Baker had discovered definite evidence there was something wrong with his cerebral circulation, and on August 6, 1947, Mencken himself had warning of impending disaster. He awoke that morning feeling dull and confused; he had a headache; his speech was thick, his right hand numb; he could not use his typewriter. The medical knowledge which had been accumulating all his life told him he had had a minor stroke. He accepted it gracefully. That day he rested at home, seeing no one and attempting no work. The following day he felt better, and on the third day he was back at his desk, working as hard as ever. The next week he told Baker what had happened. An examination showed him to be in perfect condition. That he would hear again from this trouble seemed likely, but there was little he could do about it beyond effecting a complete change in his personal life, and that was impossible. So he worked and waited, privately anticipating his death, publicly remaining unchanged. All references to his advancing age he treated as a vast joke. When someone suggested his *Sun* obituary be brought up to date, he dismissed it briefly. "Leave it as it is," he ordered. "Just add one line—'As he grew older, he grew worse.' "

In his present state he rested and hoped for a clearing up of his difficulty—enough to permit him to write. But nothing happened. So he bided his time. In February he and August vacationed at Daytona Beach, and the following month he spent a few days at Gertrude's farm. At home he worked in the back yard and searched for amusement to take up the enormous slack in his life. He tried to listen to the radio— tried earnestly, for the first time in his life—and was astounded at the tripe which gushed forth. Recorded books from the Congressional Library were tried, and they too failed. Then Dr. Alan C. Woods, the celebrated Johns Hopkins ophthalmologist, prepared a special set of spectacles which brought distant objects to the proximity of twenty feet. He still could not read, but he could go to the theater, and this proved somewhat more satisfactory. Evenings August and Mrs. Lohrfinck took him to the motion pictures, sometimes going from one to another. The more preposterous the movie, the better he liked it. The inanities of Betty Grable and Mickey Rooney, for example, were preferable to Laurence Olivier's *Hamlet*. Once, when the costume committee of the Gridiron Club arrived from Washington to be fêted by the *Sun,* he came along, and another time he dropped into Siegfried Weisburger's book shop for a few minutes. But mostly he stayed at home, attempting, with scant success, to pore over the mass of accumulated correspondence he had begun to sort out before his stroke. In New York Nathan handled his affairs, editing the proofs of the last numbers in a series of "Postscripts to the American Language" which had been prepared for *The New Yorker* the previous summer. *A Mencken Chrestomathy* was published in June and acclaimed almost universally in the latest manifestation of the great appeal he had for postwar America —an appeal which, despite Louis Kronenberger's ill-tempered piece in the anniversary issue of the *Saturday Review of Literature,* was increasing. That he had to sit idly by, unable to write for this new and expectant audience—this merely added to his personal tragedy.

On a raw, windy day in the seventh month of his illness, a friend stopped in for a chat. They sat in the second-floor study overlooking Union Square as Mencken talked of his rich life and of the book about that life his visitor was writing. And as he talked of the long ago and the far away, of Sara's promise and her untimely death, of the books on politics, American slang, and American philosophy which he had planned to write, and which must now remain unwritten, as he thumbed through the bulky folders of correspondence before him—letters from Huneker, DeCasseres, Fitzgerald, Dreiser—as he talked thus, his eyes bulged and sparkled and his florid face took on the old, radiant glow, the translucent light which had always given his expression so much animation and which bespoke an inner kindling, an inner flame which could never perish so long as the man still lived.

The afternoon waned; sunlight, breaking suddenly over the leafy park below, cast long shadows by the little square-keeper's house; the guest arose and made his farewells. Mencken saw him to the banister.

"Remember," he said cheerily, "write what you damn well

please. But be sure and tell 'em I've always been a Christian. And a patriot."

Dulce et decorum est pro patria mori: it is sweet and seemly to die for one's country. But death stalked him slowly. He lived until the early hours of January 29, 1956, when he died in his sleep; his ashes were placed beside those of Sara. After the stroke his condition had been hopeless, and he had known it. Treatment at the Johns Hopkins speech and hearing center had improved his speech, and he had been able to supervise the assembly of correspondence and *American Language* notes for future scholars. Yet he had remained unable either to read or write.

Toward the end his biographer would visit Hollins Street each morning to read aloud from the works of Twain and Conrad. Frequently this writer would also drop in after dinner to drink beer with Mencken and his brother. One day the three of them found an old Victorian commode in the alley behind the house. That evening Mencken burned it while playing a Liberace record some ill-advised admirer had sent him. Afterward he threw the record in the fire, too. "When I get to Heaven, I'm going to speak to God sharply," he said. "He has treated me very shabbily. I've been waiting for him for seven years. Where is he?"

Thin and wasted, he celebrated one of his last birthdays with a few old *Sun* friends. He looked quite spent, but the spark was still in him. When the candles on the little cake were lit he leaned over, hesitated, and looked up. He chuckled softly.

"Well," he said, "I'm ready for the angels."

Then he blew them out.

Bibliographical Note

Bibliographical Note

Despite the abundance of material by and about Henry Louis Mencken, little has been done to reduce the field to order, and the result, to a pedant's way of thinking, is pretty much of a mess. In 1924 was published Carroll Frey's *A Bibliography of The Writings of H. L. Mencken* (Philadelphia: Centaur Book Shop); the study was incomplete even then, and since 1924, as readers of the foregoing are well aware, much has happened. Three years ago Herbert F. West of Dartmouth updated Frey in a chapter of his *The Mind on the Wing* (New York: Coward-McCann, 1947). Within self-imposed limitations, he did an excellent job, but whole fascicles of Menckeniana—periodical literature, contemporary criticism—await investigation, and the first man to the tape will be venerated by future scholars. This garland I leave to others; my purpose here is simply to account for the preceding data and to guide those with unslaked thirst. It seems only right, however, to mention previous books wholly or largely concerned with Mencken. They are Ernest Boyd's *H. L. Mencken* (New York: R. M. McBride, 1925); Isaac Goldberg's *The Man Mencken* (New York: Simon and Schuster, 1925); Joseph B. Harrison's *A Short View of Menckinism in Menckenese* (Seattle: University of Washington chapbooks, 1927); and Benjamin DeCasseres' *Mencken and Shaw* (New York: S. Newton, 1930). Of the four, Boyd's is far the most penetrating, but it is a critical appraisal, running to but eighty-six pages, and is in no sense biographical. DeCasseres, who loathes Shaw and adores Mencken, is quite without discrimination. Harrison's book is a curiosity. The author apparently thought to castigate Mencken in his own style, but since he did not understand that style, he worked under a crushing handicap. Goldberg's book is the longest and most ambitious of the quartet. It is mainly given over to the biographer's gassy comments on art and life. Those sections dealing with Mencken's antecedents were contributed by the critic himself, however, and are stenographically, if not stylistically correct. I used them freely in reconstructing the early years of the Menckens in America. In a related, if more cloistered, field there are five theses on file among Mencken's papers. They are "The Creative Destructiveness of Pío Baroja and H. L. Mencken," by Esther Frances Barnett (M.A., University of Illinois, 1929); "The Principles of Literary Criticism of H. L. Mencken," by Ivan J. Kramoris (M.A., Marquette University, 1938); "H. L. Mencken,

Humorist and Reformer," by Wheeler Sammons, Jr. (honors paper, Harvard University, 1937); "Henry Louis Mencken's Debt to Friedrich Wilhelm Nietzsche," by Edward Stone (M.A., University of Texas, 1937), and "A Critical Study of the Work of H. L. Mencken as Literary Critic of *The Smart Set Magazine,* 1908-1914," by William Manchester (M.A., University of Missouri, 1947). All were valuable in gaining degrees for their compilers.

In preparing this work I became enormously indebted to the Mencken collection in Baltimore's Enoch Pratt Free Library. This mine is available to scholars who have permission and can manipulate the complicated locks without—as Mencken himself once did —padlocking themselves to the wall. There, handsomely bound in blue morocco, are the typescripts and/or proofs of the Ibsen translations (done with Holger A. Koppel); *A Little Book in C Major; In Defense of Women* (first and revised editions); *Heliogabalus* (with George Jean Nathan); *The Antichrist* translation; the first, third, fifth and sixth of the *Prejudices* series; *Notes on Democracy; Treatise on the Gods* (first and revised editions); *Making a President; Treatise on Right and Wrong; Happy Days; Newspaper Days; Heathen Days; A New Dictionary of Quotations,* and *The American Language* (original typescript; typescript of the first edition; fair copy and manuscript of the second edition; original typescript, fair copy with corrections, and galley and page proofs of *Supplement I;* carbon of the first draft, original typescript, fair copy corrected, and galley proofs of *Supplement II*). Near these are the eighty-eight clipping scrapbooks compiled by the critic himself, beginning with the first reviews of *Ventures into Verse* and including virtually every newspaper story ever written about him. Other volumes from the collections which I used include: The Stock Book (1883-92), Letter Book (1894-95), Ledger (1878-80), and Salesmen's Commission Books (1887-1902) of Aug. Mencken and Bro.; the eight volumes of "Hatrack" case clippings, compiled and prefaced by Mencken in 1937; scrapbooks of his Early News Stories (1899-1901), Early Fiction (1899-1903), Editorials, Dramatic Reviews, and Other Pieces (1904-1906), Editorials and Dramatic Reviews (1906-1910), The Free Lance (1911-15), Editorials and Other Articles (1910-12), Miscellaneous Articles Baltimore Sun papers (1912-31), Editorial-Page Articles (1915-16), Miscellaneous Newspaper Articles (1904-1936), Syndicate Articles Chicago Tribune (1924-28), Contributions to Books (1920-36), Miscellaneous Statements and Interviews (1924-36), Miscellaneous Book Reviews (1909-1936), Miscellaneous Magazine Articles (1913-36), Translations (1920-36), Foreign Reprints in English (1920-36), and assorted speeches, pamphlets, and souvenirs, including music, which defy cataloguing.

Apart from these invaluable papers, I am indebted to the Pratt Library for the use of its files of the Baltimore *Morning Herald*, the *Sun*, the *Evening Sun*, and *The American Mercury;* its general periodical files; and the always prompt and painstaking service of its literature and reference departments. Other bibliothecae which proved helpful are the Kansas City Public Library, which shelves the only complete file of *The Smart Set* during those years when Mencken was serving his apprenticeship to fame; the Library of Congress; the Princeton Archives of American Letters, and the library of the Baltimore *Sun*. In the Congressional Library's Recording Laboratory, Division of Music, is a set of long-playing records cut on June 30, 1948. Under the interrogation of Donald Kirkley, dramatic critic of the *Sun*, Mencken reviews his entire life for the edification of the listener.

The archives of the *Sun* and Princeton University deserve special mention. Since 1920, when its functionaries shifted into high gear, the newspaper's morgue has filed and classified every article and dispatch signed by Mencken, and before the neatness and thoroughness of the job I salaam. Further, the clippings of Sara Haardt, Frank R. Kent, Gerald Johnson, and scores of unnamed reporters writing on pertinent subjects were read and digested there with interest and gratitude. The Dayton dispatches of Henry M. Hyde, to cite but one example, provided me with most of the supporting detail for the Scopes trial account. To Julian P. Boyd, Princeton's librarian, I am indebted for the loan of ten thousand-odd microfilmed Mencken letters—a priceless treasure, contributions from which may be found on virtually every page of this book. Letters from the collection quoted or used in other ways represent correspondence between the critic and Thurman Arnold, Harry Elmer Barnes, Bertram M. Bernheim, Ernest Boyd, Gamaliel Bradford, Max Broedel, James M. Cain, Louis Cheslock, Marquis Childs, Barrett H. Clark, Joshua W. Combs, Major Vincent Cunningham, Dr. H. K. Croessmann, H. C. Davis, Clarence Darrow, Benjamin DeCasseres, Theodore Dreiser, James T. Farrell, William Feather, Philip Goodman, Mrs. Julian LaR. Harris, A. H. MacDannald, Edgar Lee Masters, St. Clair McKelway, Samuel A. Nock, Fulton Oursler, Herbert Parrish, H. M. Parshley, Roscoe Peacock, Raymond Pearl, Harry Rickel, Harold Ross, Porter Sargent, George S. Schuyler, Ellery Sedgwick, Charles G. Shaw, Upton Sinclair, Dent Smith, Victor Thaddeus, Jim Tully, Louis Untermeyer, Carl Van Doren, Irita Van Doren, Herbert F.

West, A. G. Wheeler, Owen P. White, Edmund Wilson, and Miss Lou Wylie (Mrs. L. W. Van Sicklen). For the loan of letters to Joseph and Mrs. Hergesheimer, Paul Patterson, Maclean Patterson and his family, and Burton Rascoe, I thank these correspondents.

The Kansas City Public Library's early *Smart Set* file I have mentioned. Toward the end of 1914 the trustees there apparently discovered what they had got hold of, and there both *Smart Set* and biographer stopped dead. Again, Mencken stepped into the breach, loaning volumes from his personal file until I had reached the more abundant years of *The American Mercury,* and even there providing pedagogical manna in his carbons and corrected proof sheets of *Mercury editorials.* Periodical articles about the critic are legion; *The Reader's Guide to Periodical Literature,* at last glance, listed 164 entries, and the *Guide,* which apparently never heard of *The Smart Set,* is choosey about whom it lists. Mencken articles which I found especially significant are "Newspaper Morals," *The Atlantic Monthly* (March, 1914); "Ludendorff," *The Atlantic Monthly* (June, 1917); "In Tennessee," *The Nation* (June 1, 1925); and "Utopia by Sterilization," *The American Mercury* (August, 1937). Those who wish to recapture the flavor of current opinion and criticism may enjoy Edmund Wilson's "Appreciation," *The New Republic* (June 1, 1921); F. Scott Fitzgerald's "Baltimore Anti-Christ," *Bookman* (March, 1921); Carl Van Doren's "Smartness and Light; H. L. Mencken, Gadfly for Democracy," *Century* (March, 1923); L. M. Hussey's "A Note upon an Artist," *Saturday Review of Literature* (November 22, 1924); E. B. White's "H. L. Mencken Meets a Poet in the West Side Y.M.C.A.," *Saturday Review of Literature* (May 9, 1936); and Charles Angoff's "Mencken Twilight," *North American Review* (December, 1938). Editorial opinion on Mencken's retirement from *The American Mercury* is offered in *Christian Century* (October 18, 1933) and *Catholic World* (April, 1934). A Roman bull is presented in I. J. Semper's "H. L. Mencken and Catholicism," *Catholic World* (October, 1929).

Those looking for a dispassionate account of the Mencken-New-Humanist controversy will find none. The best I uncovered was in Robert E. Spiller's "The Battle of the Books" section in *Literary History of the United States* (New York: Macmillan Co., 1948). Mr. Spiller headed the syndicate of authors and editors preparing this monumental study; it is probably the most useful text produced to date for this sort of work. Other chronicles of the critical war appear in Ludwig Lewisohn's *Expression in America* (New York: Harper and Brothers, 1932); Irene and Allen Cleaton's popular *Books and Battles* (Boston: Houghton Mifflin Co., 1937); Oscar Cargill's *Intellectual America* (New York: Macmillan Co., 1941); and Alfred Kazin's *On Native Grounds* (New York: Reynal and Hitchcock, 1942). For the spark that set off the blaze in the academic world, see J. E. Spingarn's *The New Criticism* (New York: Harcourt, Brace, 1911). Candid statements of the New Humanist position are found in Paul Elmer More's *The Drift of Romanticism* (Boston: Houghton Mifflin Co., 1913); *Aristocracy and Justice* (Boston: Houghton Mifflin Co., 1915); and *The Demon of the Absolute* (Princeton: Princeton University Press, 1928); in Irving Babbitt's *The New Laokoön* (Boston: Houghton Mifflin Co., 1910); *Rousseau and Romanticism* (Boston: Houghton Mifflin Co., 1919); *Democracy and Leadership* (Boston: Houghton Mifflin Co., 1924); and "The Critic and American Life," *Forum* (February, 1928); and in Stuart P. Sherman's *On Contemporary Literature* (New York: Henry Holt, 1917) and *Americans* (New York: Charles Scribner's Sons, 1922). Chrestomathized presentations of the two sides appeared in 1930, in *Humanism in America,* edited by Norman Foerster (New York: Farrar and Rinehart), and *The Critique of Humanism* (New York: Brewer and Warren), edited by C. Hartley Grattan.

The flavor of early Baltimore was tapped from Hamilton Owens' *Baltimore on the Chesapeake* (New York: Doubleday and Co., 1941), and much of the history of the *Sun* and the *Evening Sun* was taken from *The Sunpapers of Baltimore,* by Mencken, Hamilton Owens, Gerald W. Johnson, and Frank R. Kent (New York: Alfred A. Knopf, 1937). From *The Intimate Notebooks of George Jean Nathan* (New York: Alfred A. Knopf, 1932) were taken the Mencken-Nathan letters here quoted. Isaac Goldberg's *The Theater of George Jean Nathan* (New York: Simon and Schuster, 1926), though privy to the same defects that plagued *The Man Mencken,* also had the cooperation of its subject and provided me with the account of Nathan's early life. Much of *The Smart Set* history first appeared in Burton Rascoe's preface to *The Smart Set Anthology* (New York: Reynal and Hitchcock, 1934). A more detailed account of the adventures of *The "Genius"* may be found in Robert H. Elias' *Theodore Dreiser: Apostle of Nature* (New York: Alfred A. Knopf, 1949); the "Hatrack" and Scopes adventures are recounted in Arthur Garfield Hays' *Let Freedom Ring* (New York: Liveright, 1937). Darrow's part in the Dayton trial and background for the case appeared in Irving Stone's definitive *Clarence Darrow for the Defense* (New York: Doubleday and Co., 1941). General information about the Twenties came from Frederick Lewis Allen's *Only Yesterday* (New York: Harper and Brothers, 1931); Virginius Dabney tells of Mencken's friendship with Bishop James Cannon, Jr., in his *Dry Messiah* (New York: Alfred A. Knopf, 1949). The story of Emily Clark's magazine and Mencken's contributions to it appears in her *Innocence Abroad* (New York: Alfred A. Knopf, 1931). Sara Haardt's life and work are enshrined in Mencken's poignant preface to her *Southern Album* (New York: Doubleday and Co., 1936), which he edited and from which the "Dear Life" quotations toward the end of chapters 8 and 9 were taken. Sketches and appraisals of the critic are manifold; notable are those in Walter Lippmann's *Men of Destiny* (New York: Macmillan Co., 1927); Nathan's *Intimate Notebooks;* Burton Rascoe's *Before I Forget* (New York: Doubleday and Co., 1937); Jim Tully's *A Dozen and One* (Murray and Gee, 1943); and Edmund Wilson's *The Shock of Recognition* (New York: Doubleday and Co., 1943).

I am grateful to the subject of this work for the loan and presentation of assorted pamphlets. Especially helpful were *Pistols for Two* (1917), by the immortal Owen Hatteras; Burton Rascoe's *Fanfare*, Vincent O'Sullivan's *The American Critic;* and F. C. Henderson's *Bibliography*, gathered together by Knopf in 1920; and *Suggestions to Our Visitors* (1923); *A Personal Word* (1922); *Spiritual Autopsies* (Boston: Houghton Mifflin, 1922); and *James Branch Cabell* (New York: McBride, 1927)—all from Mencken's pen.

H. L. Mencken: Disturber of the Peace

Index